MW00397583

Coca's Gone

Coca's Gone

OF MIGHT AND RIGHT IN THE HUALLAGA POST-BOOM

Richard Kernaghan

Stanford University Press
Stanford, California

Stanford University Press
Stanford, California

©2009 by the Board of Trustees of the Leland Stanford Junior University.
All rights reserved.

No part of this book may be reproduced or transmitted in any form or by any means, electronic or mechanical, including photocopying and recording, or in any information storage or retrieval system without the prior written permission of Stanford University Press.

Printed in the United States of America on acid-free, archival-quality paper

Library of Congress Cataloging-in-Publication Data

Kernaghan, Richard.
 Coca's gone : of might and right in the Huallaga post-boom / Richard Kernaghan.
    p. cm.
 Includes bibliographical references and index.
 ISBN 978-0-8047-5957-1 (cloth : alk. paper) -- ISBN 978-0-8047-5958-8 (pbk. : alk. paper)
 1. Coca industry--Social aspects--Peru--Huallaga River Valley. 2. Insurgency--Peru--
Huallaga River Valley. 3. Political violence--Peru--Huallaga River Valley. 4. Huallaga
River Valley (Peru)--Economic conditions. 5. Cocaine industry--Peru--History. I. Title.
HD9019.C632K47 2009
985'.440643--dc22
                        2009006807

Typeset by Bruce Lundquist in 10/14 Minion

for Angela

Contents

Coca's Gone

Introduction

Image: a hard crease in time. So many things concealed in an abrupt fold. Money flows and the people who followed behind. Imported Japanese motorcycles and four-door sedans, speeding up and down muddy streets of nameless towns. Semiclandestine airstrips and Cessnas packed with kilos—now off to Colombia, now back to the Huallaga, stuffed with dollars. And with the arrival of every plane, how the festivities would begin. Topline acts brought in from Lima. An ever-expanding wave of parties in the bars and brothels that popped up all over the place. A decadence of lavish expenditure. Crowded dance floors. Sex behind plywood partitions. And beer. So much beer kicked back or tossed to form pools at people's feet. But touch the coke, *never*. All "serious" *narcos* knew better than to hit the stuff. The point was to send it on.

In the years following the Huallaga cocaine boom, narrated images such as these populated the stories people told about what had been a vertiginous, accelerated, and lethal time. Such images were called upon to mark the crease between the boom event and the event of its wake, which for those who remained became a more subdued, less extreme, if depressed present.

Scattered among scenes of dizzying consumption were other images, too. Competing political flags and disfigured corpses, used as signs to trace the advancing lines of new law. These images stemming from civil unrest were distinct from those associated with the drug trade, and yet the two sets commingled to become the driving force behind narratives of radical rectitude—of bloody attempts to set "straight" the unruly lifeways of the boom. Who was crooked, and how, would change according to the perspectives of those doing the killing. Which perspective would dominate in any one place varied according to the historical moment. Looking back, however, it was possible to speak of two broad epochal shifts within the cocaine boom itself, in which corpses and flags had played a formative role in asserting new law: the first belonged to a Maoist insurgency; the second, to the Peruvian army.

What I explore in this book is how hard folds in time—separating historical eras but also denoting the rise of legal regimes—could be read from the stories people shared in their attempts to make sense of the historical experience of social conflict. Specifically, I consider what happened in the eastern foothills of the central Peruvian Andes in an area known as the Upper Huallaga Valley, when the trade in unrefined cocaine fueled an economic surge from the mid-1970s to the mid-1990s that overlapped with an insurgent-counterinsurgent war.

In these pages I do not write a history of those years but rather an ethnography of their immediate aftermath: a phase of residual political emergency in which historical memory was formed collaboratively between incidents of violence and the ethical valuations people made as they sought to lend the boom a retroactive coherence. In so doing, I sift through narrative modes that told about, conjured up, and re-created the past: forms of memory that were at once multivocal and fragmentary. I also point to how violent acts were implicated in the creation of laws and drawn upon to craft a sense of time, whether to differentiate between current and past conditions or to trace out horizons of anticipation.

What distinguished the period Huallaga residents called the *apogeo de la coca* (coca's peak) from other cycles of boom and bust in the Peruvian Amazon (most notably rubber but to a lesser extent timber and gold) was the decidedly illicit character of the commodity at its center. This robust illegality, together with the tremendous economic force of the emergent drug trade, effectively pushed the Upper Huallaga as a region—and, more important, the settlers who lived there—beyond the formal guarantees of state justice. The sheer magnitude of the boom quickly turned cocaine production into the dominant activity of the valley and converted the local population, above all in the eyes of the police, into de facto criminal subjects. This situation set the conditions for what would become a major front in the internal wars that dominated Peru in the 1980s and early 1990s. The Maoist Shining Path (Sendero Luminoso),[1] in particular, moved in to provide generic state functions of protection and administration of justice to Huallaga communities while simultaneously selecting out and refunctioning subjects for its armed insurrection.

The episodes related here I learned about or experienced during three years of field research conducted between 1995 and 2000. In the Upper Huallaga Valley this was a time of acute malaise, sandwiched between the collapse of the cocaine economy and the later emergence of a regional coca farmers movement. The lived reality of the scarred and not yet peaceful social landscape of the late 1990s is what this ethnography seeks to convey: the *post-boom*, when memories of the heady and destructive energies of the past weighed heavily upon everyday experience. It was a period when anyone who lived or traveled in the Upper Huallaga had to navigate conflicting regimes of law left behind in the boom's wake. Concretely, those legal regimes belonged to the Peruvian state (which controlled the towns and, through a network of checkpoints, the valley's main road) and to the Shining Path (which maintained a diminished though palpable presence in the countryside).

During my fieldwork much of what I "saw" of the earlier boom years came to me in the form of other people's stories. These stories, and the events of which they spoke, ramified within a history of uneven state efforts to impose ambiguous legal and moral codes upon highly mobile groups of settlers who had once attached their hopes to the precipitous rise of cocaine. They told of how the authority of Peruvian law eroded as the police mistreated workers at the lowest rungs of the cocaine economy while entering into business relationships with those at the top. They recounted the brutal attempts of the Shining Path to install a total and puritanical rule over the Huallaga countryside, and what the Peruvian army was later willing to do under the pretense of restoring order.

In this book I look at the boom's narration as it circulated through and around such disparate forms as newspapers, local radio, school parades, political calendars, building materials, and road signs. However, I privilege storytelling practices because this was the principal means through which the historicity of the boom was rendered legible, though never transparent. In the late 1990s there was no direct access to the occurrences of the preceding era, only narrative forms in which the past was expressed and continually reworked. These narratives bore the stress of current conditions as well as the sedimented force of former times. As such, they revealed only in a roundabout and highly refracted sense how events had actually transpired. This mediated quality did not make the narratives, for all that, any less compelling.

Pervading stories in particular were the stunning images that condensed crucial facets of the boom event as they served to enumerate the many reasons why the sluggish and impoverished days of the present held no resemblance to the violent prosperity of the preceding era. Contrasting with these vivid image-motifs, nonetheless, were the disparate material vestiges found throughout the valley during the years of immediate post-boom: cement walls, slabs, and structures; fading Sendero graffiti; hills stripped of foliage. These remains were historical indexes that materially bore witness to earlier trajectories and their points of impact. Recognizing the events to which such vestiges corresponded required knowing how to move beyond their mute character in ways that brought them into dialogue with the stories about the past. Reestablishing their connection to the boom was only possible through those who had been there.

Sometimes people related their own personal exploits. More often they insisted they had been but passive spectators to the events they recounted. Their stories were one of the few places where the history and the continued life of the boom persisted and occasionally could be inferred. As oral renderings of boom time, both fragmentary and spoken in confidence, the stories frequently contracted moral lessons from defeated aspirations and sobering contacts with extreme violence. In so doing, they threw into relief quotidian dimensions of political emergency and the ways people warded off, but sometimes had to traverse, the time-space of a no man's land where signification and the force that animated it became all but indistinguishable.

historical sense

The relationship of signification and force plays a crucial role in this ethnography. One of my primary concerns is how violent events left their mark on the form and content of stories and storytelling practices. Indeed, a central presupposition of this work is that the multiple valences of historical sense that amassed around coca/cocaine—both in the moment and retrospectively—were inseparable from the acts of violence for which the boom time became known. What I mean by "historical sense" should become increasingly evident over the course of these pages. The phrase is redundant by design. Sense is always historical because it is produced by real events. What's more, it is indelibly linked to those events in at least two ways: as acts of "sensing" that seek to discern what is happening *within* a state of affairs, and as practices of "sense making" that articulate what has come to pass from a distance in time and space. Grasped under this dual aspect, sense rises from events but undergoes transformation when seized upon through interpretative acts. Sense shifts with the times, all the more so across perceived breaks in history. Here those breaks appear as turning points in the clash of political forces.

To borrow two analytical concepts from Reinhardt Koselleck, the boom created a unique "space of experience" and generated hopes and fears that traced out "horizons of expectation" of what was to come.[2] That experiential milieu and the anticipatory horizons it contained drastically changed in the movement to post-boom. Retrospective accounts were thus fashioned from a place in time and within future orientations that contrasted strikingly from those of the boom itself. Above all, those accounts emerged from a political and social environment that was far less turbulent than the ones about which they spoke.

Violence not only saturated most major events during the period that cocaine thrived; it was responsible for lending the Upper Huallaga Valley a distinctive atmospherics of threat, as different armed groups attempted to appropriate the drug trade in order to steer it in directions favorable to their respective interests. "Atmospherics of threat" refers to the plural forms of sense that the violence produced, which in turn shaped expectations of coca/cocaine and its potential. Shaping expectations was tantamount to orienting the history of coca/cocaine as it later came to be narrated.

The act of recounting history is foremost an exercise in sense making, because it involves crafting some kind of coherence that can be attributed to the past. That exercise happens from a place no longer experientially contiguous to the events narrated. Sense making continually moves farther and farther from what happened, that is, from the space of experience of events themselves and from the historically unique ambience they precipitate. Sense would appear, nevertheless, to travel *between* events and how they come to be apprehended. In other words, the work of sense is more intricate than would be implied by the dual division sketched so far. Sense, rather, encompasses many things at once: a sensorial *atmosphere* felt by some(one's) body and a *sensibility* or affective disposition, but also a direction or *good sense* that foresees as well as a faculty of judgment or *common sense*.

I take the idea that sense is plural and transformed through force from Nietzsche. However, the idea that sense extends across a broad spectrum comes from the work of Gilles Deleuze.[3] Though I follow his framework only loosely, I am indebted to it. I am especially indebted to his insight that sense, while actively participating in the production of signification or meaning, also moves outside discourse as *affects* that register the impact of events upon those whom they touch. With respect to the Upper Huallaga Valley, the events in question often entailed circumstances in which human life was directly harmed or threatened. So, while this book is about history and its narration, more specifically it considers how acts of violence engendered divergent *modes of sense* that at once accrued to those acts and flowed from them: as atmosphere, as disposition, as good and common sense.

How do the atmosphere or visceral tone and ambience precipitated by violent acts become an "orientation"—a good and a common sense understood as abstract modes of reasonable expectation and judgment? And how do those orientational senses then guide and direct how people inhabit a place and experience time as lived dimensions of present, past, and future? These two questions make up my general field of inquiry into the aftermath of the Huallaga boom. As a conceptual field, this inquiry has a range of problems that I propose less to solve than to explore in hopes of drawing out their complications. Drawing out complications without flattening the terrain in which they subsist is, as I grasp it, the challenge of ethnography.

In the Huallaga of the mid- to late 1990s, recollections of what had transpired during the boom tended to follow a narrative itinerary that carried the traces of the violence of the previous era, together with the threats that still primed and burdened social relations. Such memories, however, reflected foremost the historical perspective of the present in which they were related, where the lines between winners and losers of cocaine's demise appeared to be clearly established. The semblance of unambiguous boundaries, in the matter of who was up and who was down, paralleled the division of time that seemed to separate boom from post-boom. But this impression was also intimately linked to the overwhelming advantage that the armed institutions of the Peruvian state had gained in the work of dispensing violence during the latter half of the 1990s. This new state of affairs radically altered the political and legal topography of the Upper Huallaga Valley and had profound effects on what could be said about the past. Put succinctly, the knowledge of outcomes, coupled with the sustained assertion of state power, exerted an intense retroactive force on interpretations of recent history.

Thus it is important to stress that boom recollections did not deliver the past by re-presenting it as it had been. They did, nonetheless, convey the strength of the past's hold on the present through the vividness and repetition of stories and storied motifs. These oral accounts were not independent of the events of which they provided narrative form, precisely because the accounts spread across the very ground produced through the violence of that former era. That ground was not in itself representational but more akin to a deep temporal structure or synthesis: a dimension of the present orienting notions of what had been, what was happening, and what was still to come.[4] Boom memories, then, were more than just a record of what had preceded the current moment or an archive that could be weighed against other sources and checked for accuracy. Rather, they were recollections that manifested and reproduced a temporal structure of a present, which was itself the product of its own violent political history and the kinds of sense that history precipitated and made possible.

directions

Everything conveyed about the cocaine boom happened around the river from which the valley took its name, but also on and off the jungle road that launched the Upper Huallaga into its modern era. Locals would tell you that the Upper Huallaga is *selva alta*, or tropical highland forest, flanked to the west by the Andean highlands and flowing northeast toward the *selva baja*, or tropical plains. They would also tell you that the area straddles the political "departments"[5] of Huánuco and San Martín. Up close, however, the valley resembles a patchwork of rolling hills crisscrossed by streams that pour down into the Huallaga River to make it strong. All but one of the valley's main towns, Uchiza, sit on the banks of this river and along the road that hugs it. Such are the basic features of the physical landscape from which boom-time stories borrowed their coordinates.

It could be said that the modern history of the Huallaga began with a road, because the construction of the Marginal Highway[6] in the mid-1960s incorporated the valley into the country's transportation infrastructure and opened it to large-scale migration. Following a model of earlier state efforts to promote the settlement of Peru's eastern territories,[7] thick swathes of tropical forest were plowed down on either side of the new highway to create farming plots for migrants lured by the promise of free soil. Unlike previous jungle road projects, the Marginal Highway was not built out of concern for protecting national territory from the expansionist designs of neighboring countries, but as a response to domestic political pressures and perceived internal enemies. Land reform had become a pressing and intractable political issue since the mid-1950s when peasants and farm workers began to stage mass occupations of highland haciendas and coastal plantations to protest the country's grossly inequitable system of land tenure. For the liberal elected governments[8] that held power until the 1968 leftist military coup of General Juan Velasco Alvarado, eastward expansion promised a path to social peace that would spare the political power and wealth of Peru's minority and mainly mestizo landholding class. The road project, which the United States supported under the umbrella of its anticommunist Alliance for Progress, became for many years the Upper Huallaga's most concrete symbol of the Peruvian state.

The settlement program brought new life to the valley's towns and oversaw the rise of homesteader villages along, as well as off, the road. This impulse to create a new agricultural zone found justification in the idea that—unlike the sierra where land ownership was overtly contested—the Upper Huallaga was an unoccupied region with no indigenous population. The question of what had happened to the valley's original inhabitants was never really asked. For if it was true that in the seventeenth century Franciscan priests had encountered numerous Amazonian groups, speaking a variety of languages and dialects,[9] by the latter half of the twentieth century no explicit traces remained of these indigenous groups nor apparently anyone who could remember them.[10] Huallaga townspeople I met in the 1990s would speculate that the original inhabitants had disappeared into the forest or died out long before the new, mostly Andean and mestizo, settlers arrived. Precise local memories of their plight did not exist, and this amnesia as to their fate only served to underscore the devastation of a historically deeper and geographically broader pattern of violence against Amazonian peoples. However, those now calling the Huallaga home spoke of their communities as being a mix of immigrants from all parts of Peru who had come together—before and during the coca glory days—to form a kind of frontier "cosmopolitanism."[11]

remains

In the immediate aftermath of the cocaine boom, a precise sense of the dimension and magnitude of past events remained elusive to me. To travel through the valley in the mid- to late 1990s was to be struck by how everything on the surface looked less significant or dramatic than I had come to expect from the rumors, anecdotes, and renown that preceded the place. Along the Marginal Highway, pockets of tall grasses obstructed a clear view of the countryside, but in the places where they receded, a largely empty rural expanse was revealed. This vacant air extended into the small towns, which appeared to have more buildings and houses than people to fill them. Tingo María, the Upper Huallaga's lone city, was an exception to this shrunken panorama. Situated at the southernmost edge of the valley and prior to the turnoff onto the Marginal Highway, it maintained a stable population of about fifty thousand inhabitants and was in those days the only urban area with a steady if sluggish commercial activity. For the rest of the valley, however, visual impressions didn't begin to square with the Huallaga's notoriety or even with the kinds of sober census figures found at that time in government reports and in locally produced monographs about the region. Tocache was often said to have a population of about twenty thousand, followed by Aucayacu and Uchiza with ten thousand each and Nuevo Progreso with around four thousand. Meanwhile, the number of rural inhabitants, clustered in villages and farms outside each of these population centers, was claimed to mirror or surpass that of town dwellers.[12] Such modest numbers, however, corresponded poorly with what was available to the eye, begging the question of where everyone had gone or was now hiding. This at times vexing dissonance—between lingering fame, official statistics, and a visual backdrop of bleak and diminutive farming communities—was overpowered, nevertheless, by the force of secrecy that imbued the place with a presence larger than life.

Tingo María distinguished itself from the rest of the valley in ways other than size and the relative prosperity that it had managed to hold onto even in the face of the drug trade's steep fall. In part this was because Tingo María's era as a frontier town had come a generation earlier than the settlements to the north. In the 1930s it became a major stop on the new Central Highway, which was built to establish the first overland link between Lima and a navigable tributary of the Amazon (the Ucayali River). Though Tingo María started as little more than a trading post with a government settlement office and a U.S.-funded agricultural station, it became in the coming decades a launching-off point: for pioneers intent on carving small farms out of the jungle thicket; for gold prospectors; and for venture capitalists looking either to deal in tropical commodities of rubber and cube or to set up large coffee, tea, and coca plantations. This role of frontier gateway only intensified during and immediately following the construction of the Marginal Highway, when the state began to actively promote the Upper Huallaga Valley as a future agricultural heartland for the country.[13]

Because of this historical trend, the valley's population north of the city tended to be more recent and fluid, and there were few who lived there who could trace their family lines in the Upper Huallaga back more than a generation. People arrived and moved on with the rise and decline of the valley's fortunes. The first major exodus came in the early 1970s when the new homesteaders began to endure increasing hardships in their efforts to make good on the agricultural promise of the jungle frontier.[14] Small-scale farmers, whether independent or associated through agrarian cooperatives, struggled to locate dependable markets for the crops of yellow maize, rice, coffee, and cacao endorsed by settlement officials. Their precarious situation only got worse when the successive military governments of Velasco and Morales Bermúdez gradually phased out state subsidies, causing debts to mount and become unpayable. It was amid this general downturn that many settlers left the Huallaga. It was also then that coca began to insinuate itself as the solution to the valley's woes.

Coca was hardly new to the Huallaga. The stocky evergreen shrub of small, elongated oval leaves had long grown wild in the rugged, humid forest fringe of eastern Huánuco. The plant was domesticated at a very early date, and throughout the Andes migrations from the highlands to the tropical *yungas* or *selva alta* for the purpose of harvesting or trading coca went back thousands of years.[15] The plant's leaves, highly prized for their ability to provide endurance during strenuous work and to alleviate thirst and hunger on long journeys by foot, occupied then, as they still do today, a fundamental and multifaceted place in the economic, social, and religious practices of Andean agrarian communities.[16] But it was not until the twentieth century that the deflection of coca into the production and trade of its "industrial" derivative cocaine—at first legally, but increasingly criminalized over time—emerged as a perennial feature of the area economy.[17] Thus what changed in the 1970s was not the introduction of coca nor even of cocaine but the degree to which coca leaf cultivation, now destined overwhelmingly for illicit markets, came to dominate the new agricultural lands opened along the Marginal Highway.

Farmers say the shift to coca came on suddenly and that by the end of the decade it had pushed all other cash crops aside. This across-the-board transformation coincided with an upsurge in world demand for recreational cocaine and was part of a much wider regional phenomenon from Bolivia to Peru to Colombia that, under ever-changing configurations, continues to the present day.[18] Then, as now, coca was grown in all three countries, where it was converted into cocaine paste—either as cocaine sulfates (known in the Huallaga as *la bruta*) or as a purer cocaine base (*pasta básica de cocaína*). From the 1970s until the early 1990s, however, the final processing phase of Huallaga cocaine—from sulfates and base into hydrochloride—happened not in Peru but in Colombia.[19] The so-called "cartels" based in Medellín and Cali dominated the trade: they purchased Huallaga cocaine paste, airlifted it to Colombia, and then oversaw its refinement into hydrochloride before shipping it to illegal markets in Europe and the United States. It was during this period of Colombian control that the Upper Huallaga developed into one of the region's leading producers of coca and cocaine paste. The valley even outpaced most other areas of the Andes where the leaf was grown, that is, if Peruvian and U.S. government statistics can be read at face value.[20] Yet in the Huallaga what gave the boom its extraordinary social force was not the extent of coca cultivation as much as the valley's emergence as both the principal national market for raw cocaine and a near-liberated zone for its production and trade. Cultivation also increased elsewhere in Peru as demand swelled, especially in the valleys of Monzón, Rio Apurímac–Rio Ene, and La Convención (Cusco). Throughout the 1980s, however, the Upper Huallaga enjoyed a virtual territorial monopoly over the national cocaine economy. Nowhere else did it seem to happen so massively and so out in the open.

atmosphere

The concentration of the Peruvian illicit drug economy in a single, relatively bounded geographic area helped secure a lasting place for the Huallaga in the Peruvian national imaginary. In the 1980s the valley's name, but also those of Tocache and Uchiza, came to be intimately associated with the dark prosperity of the cocaine boom and with the reckless abandon of lifeways rumored to accompany it. For a new chance at life, for "easy money," for good times, the Huallaga became *the place* to go. Whether to work directly in the production and distribution of raw cocaine or in the myriad support activities that clustered around the blossoming drug economy—from retail sales of food and agricultural supplies to musical entertainment and sexual services—people set out for the Huallaga in hopes of getting rich, of finding adventure, or of just taking in some of the then-wild ebullience of the place.

The valley's settler population referred to this latest round of newcomers as the *buscavidas* (literally, "life seekers"). The vast majority of these were young: sons and daughters of peasant families from the central Andean cordillera and working-class teenagers from highland and coastal cities. Many shared some initial disappointment or failure in their hometowns: aspirations to study denied or the inability to find work that promised a better future. They also shared the conviction that nothing could be much worse than what they were leaving behind. And so they left. At times they did so without ever telling their families or friends that they were going away, much less where they intended to go. Sometimes they themselves didn't know their exact destination but made the journey on no more than a vague tip that there was good money to be made in *la selva*. Once beyond Tingo María, chance frequently determined where they ended up and what they became. At least that was how several people would later describe their initial journeys to me.

In those days, they said, everything in the Huallaga happened because of who you ran into and how things unfolded from there. They spoke of the boom as enabling chance encounters as much as it fostered anonymity. Few went by their real names: everyone had their own *chapa*, or nickname, and most people knew better than to inquire further. Besides, people came and went in wave after wave after wave. It was easy to get lost in the place.

The boom's powers of attraction were such that the insurgent-counter-insurgent wars that engulfed Peru in the 1980s quickly converged upon the valley. Shining Path militants began clandestine operations in the southern end of the Huallaga around the area of Aucayacu as early as 1980. Over the next several years the Party would consolidate control over the countryside as it gradually pushed northeast, organizing rural villages and defending its turf from the MRTA, a rival insurgent group that would also attempt to gain a foothold in the area.[21] As elsewhere, Sendero targeted local officials and policemen for assassination, and when the police proved unable to repel the Party's advances, the army was called in to "reinstate order."

Unlike in other regions of the country, in the Upper Huallaga Sendero had little trouble building an initial base of support. Since the late 1970s paramilitary and anti-narcotics units of the Civil Guard had been launching raids into the valley to confiscate coca, burn fields, and detain small-time *narcos* (drug traders).[22] Coca farmers, sensing that their very livelihood was under attack, welcomed outside help in fending off the police. Shining Path offered the farmers protection from police raids and government efforts to eradicate coca, as well as from the economic exploitation of the town-based cocaine *firmas* (firms). In exchange, farmers had to submit to the dictates of Sendero's Maoist state project and ongoing armed struggle. In the communities it organized, the Party established rules of play for the drug trade: setting pricing standards, arbitrating disputes, and charging taxes for its services. In this way, Sendero generated an alternate form of legality around the market of raw cocaine.

The confluence of Maoist Shining Path, flourishing drug trade, and wavering state attempts to counter them cast a uniquely lethal air upon the valley's patchwork of hills, farms, and towns. Journalists early on found it difficult to work there, and a few who tried ended up floating face down in area streams. Little news came out of the valley during those years, and as the overlap of boom and war persisted, the notion that the Huallaga was very hazardous territory became common sense. Dangerous living seemed to come with the place; if someone went there and suffered misfortune, well, that was just the gamble she or he had made.

This aura of danger, however, was as ambiguous as it was diffuse. It related imprecisely to the actual political topography of the valley and the conditions that prevailed there. From outside the Huallaga, the signs and stigmas of extreme peril could accrue to places that in actuality were shielded from the brunt or full force of political emergency. Such was the case of Tingo María. Geographically it was part of the Upper Huallaga and as such shared nationally in the valley's distinction as an extremely lethal place. Yet throughout the years of the boom, state authority and control over the city was never challenged. To the contrary, as conditions grew inhospitable for government officials and employees in the boomtowns and farmlands to the north, the small city was transformed into a fortified position of the Peruvian state, serving as the logistical headquarters as well as the main staging grounds for all major police and military operations into the Huallaga.[23] Tingo María became the last secure outpost of the state's political, legal, and military bureaucracy. Beyond it lay a major, if undeclared, fault line in the political geography of the valley, a no man's land where distinct orders of law and violence frequently faced off, only to become enmeshed.

threshold

In the next chapter I will tell how I became involved with the Huallaga. For now, let me say, my first exposure to the place was fortuitous. In the summer of 1995 I was in Lima doing research. I had no plans to travel anywhere else, when a priest I will call Orlando extended an unlikely invitation. To Orlando I owe my initial acquaintance with the Huallaga Valley and, more crucially, with the extreme touch-and-go situation prevailing in Aucayacu at the historical juncture of the boom's demise. The singularly intense atmosphere I sensed in that Huallaga town made a profound impression and convinced me to return later for a much longer stint.

In contrast to Aucayacu, not merely on that first trip but during all of my subsequent visits, an air of peaceful normality reigned in the city of Tingo María. Except for the occasional movement of troops and the arrivals and departures of police and army helicopters, there was little sign of a guerrilla war simmering in the countryside. News of such things circulated in the city, but they seldom upset its daily rhythms.

The region to the north of Tingo was another matter. While the boom was already over or quickly receding by the mid-1990s, the implicit political boundary between that city and the rest of the valley was still in force. Several things expressed this undeclared division and, as one traveled deeper into the Huallaga, created the sensation of crossing over into another realm. Most compelling were the constant interruptions imposed on the flow of traffic as it persevered up the Marginal Highway. These interruptions were caused in part by an impressive intensification in the number of army and police checkpoints.

Though roadblocks had been a common feature of Peruvian highways since the 1980s, in 1995 more army and police checkpoints figured along the fifty-kilometer trip between Tingo María and Aucayacu, the next Huallaga town, than on the five hundred–kilometer stretch of road that separated Tingo María from Lima. Also on the Marginal Highway were groups of shallow trenches, cutting across the paved surface, which jolted vehicles as they plied the road. These, I was told, were vestiges of the Shining Path's attempts to destroy the highway in the late 1980s, done in part to impair the movement of police and army patrols from Tingo María. Until they were repaired a decade later, those trenches registered the history of political violence as it physically merged into the lived present with every jolt on every trip up and down the road. Also marking the spatial transition from Tingo María was the sudden proliferation of Shining Path graffiti on the paved surface of the road as well as on almost every scattered building that lined the way to Aucayacu and beyond. Much of this graffiti was faded or had been blotted out slapdash as if by a hurried hand.

I came away from my first trips to the Huallaga convinced that the territories up the road from Tingo María—where illicit economy and political conflict had for many years intermingled—would have much to teach about the interrelationship of social phenomena commonly grouped under abstract notions of state, violence, and law. On the strength of that hunch I would later attempt to follow firsthand the historical process of the Peruvian state's reassertion of authority over the valley. The reaffirmation of political control was then being figured through narratives of homecoming and restoration, most notably in the form of insurgent "repentance" as well as through patriotic parades of area schoolchildren.

My initial research impressed upon me the dense social complexities of the Upper Huallaga as a topography crosscut by competing political-legal regimes: one in ascension, the other in steady decline. While in the years of immediate post-boom the "return" of the Peruvian state was undeniable, the territorial coverage of its law was still partial and thin. The outer contours of that law fluctuated and were chiefly defined—once the drug trade was gone—by those places where the Shining Path continued to maneuver at will. The intricate lay of this political and legal topography manifested most pressingly through the difficulties and unanticipated obstacles that inhibited movement. Sometimes these took material form as official or informal checkpoints. At other times, as sudden acts of armed robbery and homicide. Often, however, the obstacles were less seen than felt—by those who lived and traveled in the Huallaga—as a deep tension that came to be projected onto the physical landscape. Depending on the situation, that tension found expression in many forms, among them rumor, awkward silences, and the avoidance of all but the most necessary of eye contact. While the degrees of tension tended to vary from locale to locale, it attained peak force along the boundary that everywhere separated town from country.

Between 1997 and 2000 I spent extended periods of time—some as brief as two weeks, some as long as eight months—in the towns north of Tingo María. I also traveled to many points along the Marginal Highway. Getting off the road and into the countryside during the latter half of the 1990s was complicated because it involved entering what was still an active war zone. I did so only on rare instances when a momentary relaxing in political tensions and a serendipitous invitation from rural farmers happened to coincide. This was one of the unwritten rules of my early time there: "Stay in the towns or on the road, and there will be no problems." To the extent that the villages along the Marginal Highway and the main towns were the only places in the Huallaga where the army—through an ever-expanding network of bases— had reestablished the dominion of the state, this rule of thumb was a concrete manifestation of how a particular political time marked and organized a geographic space.

The Huallaga of the late 1990s was one of the few places where Sendero continued to be an aspect of everyday experience. In contrast, for the rest of Peru then still governed by the authoritarian regime of Alberto Fujimori, political violence had become an expression of a disturbing past that had no place in the country's present or future.[24] Following the capture of the Sendero national leadership and the dismantling of urban cells and most of the guerrilla army structures outside Lima in the early part of the decade, the Party's armed actions had lost ferocity and frequency. Sendero's territorial reach had also been reduced to what, from Lima at least, seemed to be remote, outlying areas: the unpopulated heights of the Andes and the coca-growing regions along the Huallaga, Monzón, and Ene rivers.[25] From Lima—Peru's seat of bureaucratic power and for all purposes its representational center—the country could be imagined as putting distance on the political violence of the past. The Huallaga Valley and similar areas still struggling with a problem that most in the country would have preferred to simply leave behind, meanwhile, seemed to be out of temporal synch with the national present.

law as event

Throughout this book I conceive of law solely as it relates to state formations and then in three specific capacities or levels: (1) as legal code and process: a body of written rules, edicts, directives, and statutes, including the traditions of jurisprudence from which they emerge; (2) as legal regime: embodied through state institutions and representatives of justice, police, and military; and (3) as unwritten prohibitions whose visceral presence is inferred experientially in historically particular social contexts. According to the latter two conceptions, I examine the relation of violence to law. This is because in the areas of the Huallaga where I did research, courts of law were only beginning to be introduced. Prior to the late 1990s, Peruvian procedural law had been at best a distant specter, one that at times appeared to be approaching and gathering strength and that locally had at best a weak, objective presence. Consequently, during the boom, much of what happened in people's encounters with agents of Peruvian law (as legal regime) took place figuratively "before" or "outside" what the legal code ordained. Those who depended on the cocaine trade considered the police to be a foreign power, while the agents of Peruvian law themselves tended to regard the Upper Huallaga as a zone and time of legal exception. Sometimes the actuality of that exception would be formalized by presidential decree when the Huallaga was declared an emergency zone at the disposition of the police or military. More often, the exception was a de facto condition on the ground: a situation in place and time in which the precise dictates of legal code and procedure did not hold sway or else were applied only arbitrarily.

This threshold of exception was where acts of violence turned most palpable and direct. As the cocaine trade began to dominate life in the valley, the Huallaga became an outlaw realm where people could go to escape the jurisdiction of Peruvian law and where both the police and military implicitly had license to do as they pleased. These two facets of the exception— flight from Peruvian law and the excesses of state agents—created auspicious conditions for the Maoist Shining Path to install a legal regime of its own in the countryside. Sendero did so less through outright military conquest than through specialized techniques of capture and subjection. These techniques combined a horrific, carefully targeted violence with a "softer" semiotics of control.[26] But whether at the margins of the Peruvian legal code or at the genesis of Sendero's legal regime, the interplay of violence, threat, and law became pronounced.

In these pages I call "violence" those human acts that destroy life, whereas "threat" designates the ambient effects that the possibility of destruction can generate. Threat and violence are in this way inseparable, though properly the former is lethal force in a virtual state, waiting for the moment of actualization. Violence haunts through threat, which is its implicit presence. Threat draws strength from a connection to prior acts of destruction. The reference to those acts may be perceived, but it need not be overt or even legible.

How violence relates to law is less transparent.[27] The clarity of their relation is impeded in part because the term "law" is used to designate social phenomena of radically disparate orders, whose differences are rarely delineated. Without distinguishing between the distinct registers of code and process, legal regime, and unwritten prohibitions, commonsense notions often present an either-or choice between two abstract propositions: "Violence makes law" or "law excludes violence."[28] In the first case, law is understood from a perspective of origins: as domination founded by means of a brute or destructive force, which is imagined to exist in itself as pure manifestation. In the second, violence is understood from the perspective of a preexisting legal framework that classes it as an illegitimate application of force: violence is that which transgresses the categorical limits of "the lawful" and provokes the activation of countermeasures that respond in a rightful defense of the legal order.[29] That such countermeasures, irrespective of their lethal quality, are seldom described as violent per se indicates that what is important from the perspective of law is the judgment as to what constitutes the terms of legitimate use.

The mere resilience of these commonsense articulations is sufficient testimony to their rhetorical currency. I take them less as statements to be proven true or false than as analytical propositions that lend themselves for expressing particular positions, approaches, or claims. In the first proposition, "violence makes law," violence is primary and creative precisely through its potential for destruction; little consideration is given to what that violence "says," how it says it, or exactly what it inaugurates beyond the fact/statement of sheer domination. In the second proposition, "law excludes violence," the act of assigning significations predominates, though without shedding any clarity on how violence may inhabit, infuse, or even reinforce the framework of law. Regardless of their differences, these propositions need not be conceived as mutually exclusive. They are sometimes attributed to distinct temporal moments in a "civilizing" arc of law: the first, to describe the law's "primitive beginnings," as in its relation to violence when a legal regime is being constituted; the second, to describe the relation once the regime is fully formed.[30] This logical resolution of formerly opposed propositions could then be summed up by a third: "Before law was protective, it was predatory." Yet this would seem to bring us full circle. For what remains of law once deprived of any claim to protect? If predatory, what would law be but violent?

For these reasons, I treat "violence" and "law" not as opposed but as intertwined. What binds them is not of a conceptual order alone but involves the ways in which force meets and overflows significations across a spectrum of sense. This is to suggest that anchoring their semantic terms cannot in itself clarify their connection. For if all lethal force has a lawmaking potential,[31] within a threshold of exception the precise circumstances to which the terms "violence" and "law" refer would not only be unstable, they would also affect the very words used to describe them.[32] As such, none of the aforementioned propositions can provide the ultimate solution, because the essential relation of violence to law is not logical. What's more, that relation becomes paradoxical if divorced from the situations to which they are applied. The value of ethnography for exploring this question lies in its reticence to adopt a transcendent approach that attempts to impress a logical diagram upon actual circumstances and real relations. Instead, ethnography proceeds by way of a dogged embrace of the detail in the cluttered movements and inertias of everyday life where events happen that force thought.

the political

If I draw on the recent history of the Huallaga as an apt scenario for studying the relation of violence and law in the founding of state-type regimes, I do so in specific ways. Borrowing the terminology and insights of legal philosopher Carl Schmitt, I call the process whereby such systems of rule are established "the political." By this I refer to two conceptually discrete but related domains: (1) a repertoire of practices that direct a spectacular violence toward the ends of creating law-bound community and (2) a concrete historical situation in which the friend/enemy grouping emerges as the underlying principle of social classification.[33] As an analytical concept, "the political" lends itself especially well to grasping the local dynamics of insurgent-counterinsurgent warfare in the Huallaga of the 1980s and 1990s. Furthermore, I lean on this notion for understanding how spectacular violence could seem to inaugurate new blocks of time.

It is precisely the illegal nature of the commodity at the center of the boom, however, that presents an opportunity for examining how types of regime-founding (and defending) force butt up against and overlap with the contractual violence intrinsic to illicit economies. It was there, in the intersection of the distinct but coinciding realms of Sendero rule, Peruvian states of emergency, and cocaine trade, that "law" in the third capacity—as unwritten, visceral prohibition—imposed itself as a predominant and often confusing feature of life in the Huallaga.

One of my aspirations in this ethnography is to relate how, in light of recent local history, the taking or damaging of life and the threat of doing so affected, saturated, and overdetermined social fields and interactions during the post-boom. In the course of my fieldwork, the intermingling of threat and violence was most palpably conveyed through the preponderate weight of rules, which were rarely spoken but made known through oblique reference. Such inferred rules are a privileged site for exploring how lethal force seemed to fuse with significations and animate protocols of daily life. I attempt to understand this process by considering the ways in which violence served as an instrument for establishing vectors of causality—as so many arrows in space and time—against which people made decisions about how to live their lives. At the basis of those decisions was an intuition about the direction of the violence and, thus, of shifting political and legal conditions.

In thinking about the relationship between violence and its causal vectors, I have found inspiration in the writings of David Hume, who argued that the necessity of causation is not registered in thought as much as it is felt.[34] According to Hume, causation is not a product of the understanding. Instead it is a relation that happens in the mind, and one might say *to* the mind, through the observation of a perceived repetition. Causation happens when a recurrence of dissimilar elements comes to be intuited by their beholder as fused together into a constant and rigorous union.

In the Huallaga, visceral prohibitions emerged through repetitive acts of violence; such acts worked to confirm the necessity of connections between certain kinds of behavior, proscribed categories of persons, and perceived rates of survival. To the extent that these causal inferences came to be felt as compelling, they could be described as minor "events of law." Such events, to invoke the language of Deleuze, were *ideal* or *ideational* to the extent that they involved apprehending intangible but potentially life-threatening transformations in ongoing states of affairs.

During moments of extreme violence, the affective hold of causal relations can be profound, even while the vectors themselves may remain unstable. Armed groups, for example, can and will use violence to interrupt those relations in order to impose cause-effect orientations of their own. In times of political emergency, causal lines are a primary means through which people infer law in their lived presents: as implicit rules of thumb indicating how best to move through risk-laden social worlds.

Paradoxically, while law can be viscerally inferred through a concrete proximity to lethal acts, violence also plays a role in the constitution of places and times imagined to subsist as if *without* law—what Huallaga residents frequently called a *tierra de nadie,* or land of no one. In this case, the experiential relation has changed. The unruly appearance is assayed from afar or at least requires distance. It is violence as contemplated and "appreciated" from the safety of spatiotemporal separation. Places and times without law are surely fictions. Yet as fictions they become attributed to real situations where they acquire social vitality.

locale

Most of the events I recount occurred around the town of Aucayacu, which serves as a central location of this book. In a region and time where secrecy, distrust, and paranoia made getting even a basic sense of what was going on elusive, Aucayacu was where I felt I had my surest foothold. Over time, I was able to build an extensive network of friends and acquaintances there, and these efforts were greatly furthered when I taught classes at a local teachers college in 1998. Working at the college afforded me a role and an identity in the community. This made my interest in local history as well as my research activities less threatening to townspeople.

In the Huallaga, news between town and country tended to travel through an intricate maze of hearsay that seemed to cover its tracks as it spread forward. Though locals readily passed on rumors, few dared to elaborate on, much less inquire about, their origins. The play between what was secret and what was unknown often made for an environment of weighty and charged silences. In moments of sudden tension, nervous glances and oblique remarks would gesture toward the larger situations and unseen collectives. These loomed as obstacles people preferred not to name even as they steered their lives around them. The intensity of prevailing conditions reflected the severe scrutiny to which the valley's residents had been subjected (and to which they had in turn subjected each other) since the start of the boom. The sedimented layers of this history of surveillance contributed to the fragmentary quality of what I experienced in the Huallaga. In truth, it shaped most everything I learned there, as I gradually came to appreciate the town's place within the larger history of the valley.

Aucayacu, I would learn, had been an important boomtown until antinarcotics operations launched from Tingo María in the late 1970s succeeded in pushing the epicenter of the trade to the north. During the 1980s the cocaine trade would remain strongest around the towns of Uchiza and Tocache, where it operated largely out in the open. During this same period raw cocaine continued to dominate the local economy of Aucayacu; but, because of the town's proximity to Tingo María, traders were forced to operate more discreetly and to transport smaller volumes than in other areas of the valley. Unlike Tocache and Uchiza, Aucayacu did not have a municipal airport from which flights could be dispatched to Colombia, and the makeshift landing strips that were opened on both sides of the river were subject to raids by the police. Aucayacu would later reemerge in the early 1990s as a major hub of the trade. This happened thanks to agreements hashed out with local army commanders, which permitted the drug trader *firmas* to use the paved surface of the Marginal Highway for clandestine drug flights in and out of town.[35] The army's protection, however, was short lived. When it was withdrawn in 1994, the local trade entered a crisis from which ultimately it would not recover.

As for the Shining Path, the rural expanses surrounding Aucayacu are where it first appeared in the valley, intent on organizing rural communities for its revolution. The left bank of the Huallaga River, from the village of Venenillo to that of Magdalena, became the Maoist party's bastion throughout the boom years. Today the Shining Path maintains an important clandestine military and political presence around Aucayacu, though with little capacity to challenge—even locally—the state's hold on power.

ethnography

The question of how to write about situations of political emergency and illegality is not straightforward. Perhaps the vexing uncertainty over the written form is true for all ethnography. Yet in realms of life and study where authoritarian discourses already shape the terms by which whole worlds may be received and experienced—as they did in Peru in the form of anti-narcotics interdiction and agrarian "development," counterterrorism, and Maoist revolution—this question acquires greater urgency.

Throughout the crafting of this text, my priority has been to render a composite picture of the Upper Huallaga Valley as I came to know it in the mid- to late 1990s. My encounters with the region—as a place, as a series of lived moments, and as a set of engagements and relations with people I met there—were always partial and discontinuous. This was due in no small measure to the mercurial conditions of the valley in those years and to the social and political legacy of the boom. Thus I have tried to avoid forcing the text into a fluid or seamless account and, where possible, have let the patchiness of those encounters mark the writing. I hope to have done so without unduly impairing overall cohesion.

The chapters of this book are autonomous strands. Each one elaborates upon one or more fragments of boom history as they inhered in the ethnographic present of post-boom. My approach has been to create a collage of multiplying and overlapping voices, a gradual accretion of elements and stories to form an open-ended mosaic. It is a method that I picked up as the writing unfolded and as I sought to present a plurality of perspectives. To do so, I have relied on a variety of narrative frames as well as degrees of proximity and distance to events.

While I have gathered together the voices of many characters in hopes of achieving that plurality, I have struggled most with what to do with *information*—those disembodied facts that linger around established topics of study and become obligatory to know and then repeat. I have tried to keep those to a minimum and, where necessary—whenever they threatened to upset flow—have pushed them from the body of the text and into notes at the end of the book. There, more than offering evidence, their purpose is to provide additional coordinates for the reader.

In the process of writing I imagined my ethnographic task to be less the production of knowledge than finding ways of telling that would adequately express the tricky situations and harsh circumstances that people in the Huallaga Valley had to contend with over the course of the boom and its aftermath. This practical concern was what first attracted me to stories and storytelling in that they provided glimpses of contemporary conditions and recent history not found in other sources such as newspaper accounts, scholarly literatures, and institutional archives. However, in relying on oral sources, I immediately became aware of several qualities that the stories I was told seemed to possess. They tended to favor flow over the stolid density of fact. They had an intimate relation to ordinary spoken language. They also demonstrated an ability to portray an event without sacrificing altogether the intensive dimensions of how that event was actually experienced. In other words, the stories I heard had the potential to get close to that which they conveyed and, in so doing, articulate something of the historical sense of moments already past. They did not always live up to that promise. Stories sometimes fell well short, especially if the storyteller sought a moral interpretation of events instead of allowing the stories to reach toward those same events in their own time.

As a result, stories play a prominent role in this book as raw material and finished product. They do so out of considerations that are not only pragmatic but ethical. In the Huallaga, people shied away—and for good reason—from relaying the particulars: above all, the names of who did what, when, where. I have followed their lead and made extensive use of pseudonyms and occasionally altered specific details to protect the identities and privacy of those who appear in these pages.

People skillfully avoided divulging anything that might harm themselves or others. Yet once you earned their trust, they enjoyed telling stories about the exceptional character of times past and the many curious and cruel turns of the boom years. It was the exquisite care with which they related those experiences that would eventually lead me to observe more carefully the unique ability of stories to skirt along the frontiers of fact and fiction.

Stories in the manner I encountered them depended on narrative devices but did not simply make things up. They hovered close to empirical details but without a rigid devotion to them. More content with following than with unmasking, stories grew involved in what happened instead of pinning things down in any permanent way. While often shunning the stasis, precision, and clarity of firm dates and identities, they would nonetheless draw on such ostensibly solid referents as passageways toward ever-greater complication and convolution. Rather than going after "the facts," stories appeared to seek out and thrive on the power of what was most unconfirmed. In brief, they offered a piece of concrete advice on how to go about writing of illicit communities and times of political emergency. They said: *Focus attention on the affective winds that reverberate through lived events while ever weighing the remarkable resistance of all that fears being revealed.*

Ethnography of course strives to do more than tell stories. Even so, the treatment of language, by which I mean the modality of speech that ethnography creates, is a crucial part of its practice. Ethnography attempts to echo tones and voices that are frequently drowned out or suppressed by authoritarian modes of address. Unlike the latter, ethnography does not proceed by unmasking with little regard for the subtle atmosphere of historical events, much less for the intricate lives and vulnerabilities of those affected. Rather, the ethnographer is acutely aware that persistent unveiling deprives words of their image-making power and makes them ill suited for the task at hand. That is why it is better, perhaps, not to equate ethnographic inquiry with the pursuit of knowledge, and all the more reason why ethnographers of the political might learn from stories, above all, how they continually bring forces of animation into play.

condensations

During the years immediately following the boom, an intense air of surveillance pervaded public spaces. Recent history had taught Huallaga residents to have a profound fear of informers and of the potential of being so accused. As a result, the spaces that fostered storytelling and other modes of historical narration were almost always enclosed. Often these were domestic interiors; the minimum requirement was to be out of sight and earshot of passersby. In Chapter One I describe the intimacy of one such place: the kitchen of the family home of my friend Marusha, where I lived during many of my stays in the Huallaga.

Judgments about the boom as it was talked about in this and other similarly secluded settings regularly took the form of curt, deceptively dense phrases.

These bore the burden of imparting prevailing wisdoms about what had come to pass. *Ya no hay coca ya* (coca's gone) was one refrain I heard many times. It was the reply people frequently gave when asked if the rash and opulent times of cocaine could ever return. While the phrase served to express a widespread sentiment that the boom would not come back, it also narratively marked the temporal shift to a lethargic present, beset by economic scarcity and uncertainty over what the future would bring.

Those whom I met in the Huallaga had no trouble putting a date on when times began to slow: 1995. More complicated for them was relating a precise measure of the magnitude and proportion of the distinct moments of the boom itself, which in their accounts unfolded as a series of disparate and yet interlocking pasts. Their struggles to make sense of the boom years brought to the fore the tension between narrative and historical time: one could not be accessed without the other, and their mutual dependence made the force that events exerted on practices of narration difficult to grasp. For boom events extended in a temporal milieu that diverged from that of their post-boom recitation. What separated these two time-spaces were drastically different orientations toward the future.

The post-boom was widely perceived to be a moment of radically transformed, if not shrunken prospects, and the social consensus about that fact gave the experience of the present a tendency and disposition as a time at once new and critically distant from the preceding era. Pithy, evaluative refrains the likes of *ya no hay coca ya* expressed the abrupt shift in how the future could be framed. At the same time, such refrains were spoken with a verve that pointed beyond the linguistic significance and function of the words themselves and seemed to indicate another, perhaps less overt plane on which the past wove itself into the present. Such slogans could not do justice to the boom in any representational sense. Nevertheless, they served as vehicles for registering the relentless force of the past, which propelled the words along and instilled them with an ineffable charm.

Chapter Two explores the limits of certainty in the post-boom Huallaga by examining the disjuncture between an event as it unfolded in its own time and subsequent attempts made to verbally convey what transpired. I relate a violent incident that occurred in 1998 at dusk on the Marginal Highway north of Tingo María. I then assess remarks later made by the district attorney of Aucayacu, to the effect that the victims "should have known better." Explicitly, I discuss how the purported "obligation to know" invoked a quasi-juridical (and yet everyday) concept of a no man's land. This concept suggested a compulsory type of awareness about emergency conditions in ways that not only marked off a territory of suspended rights but also gave commands to life.

At stake were the temporal horizons of Peruvian state justice: their relation to violence, figured indiscriminately as criminal or political, and how those same horizons could drift unevenly across local and national landscapes. Some places appeared covered by Peruvian law; others, beyond its reach and thus imbued with the fateful air of an altogether other legal order, the law of Sendero. In the late 1990s, on that stretch of road between the city of Tingo María and the town of Aucayacu, the village of Pacae was one such fateful site: a place where misfortunes were believed to reign and where people went only to get what was coming to them.

Fate was a halo effect of historical sedimentation that seemed to hover over locations deemed threatening. It was a commonsense orientation based on the outcomes of previous events but interpreted in ways that staked ominous claims upon the future. Chapter Three turns toward that broader history of violent outcomes, which had preceded the incident in Pacae and which provided an interpretive context for how certain locales in the Huallaga landscape could be perceived as intensely forbidding.

Specifically, I contrast the Huallaga River and the Marginal Highway as two sites where dead bodies appeared with a consistency that became a defining attribute of the boom. Regular and often normalized encounters with human corpses would later populate stories in which arresting images of rotting flesh were called upon to express a steep depreciation in the value of human life.

Throughout the boom, the river was a place of "out of sight, out of mind" disposal for drug traders, police, or whoever sought a convenient means of discarding their kill. There—along the Huallaga River—when people came across human remains they often did not feel personally addressed by them. The Shining Path changed that, however, when in the mid-1980s it began laying corpses on the valley's main road. Cardboard signs planted on top of each one explained the offense allegedly committed by the deceased. The deadly messages were intended for those most dependent on the highway: the populaces of the towns, among them government officials. The use of the road for this purpose would taper off in time; precisely, by the early 1990s. That was when black sacks stuffed with body parts began turning up on the shores of the Huallaga. Coinciding with major counterinsurgency operations, the sacks were rumored to be of the army's doing and directed at those with ties to the rural expanses where Sendero held sway.

Thus, between river and road, human corpses operated as temporal signs on several levels and in different ways at different times. At historically specific moments, insurgents and counterinsurgents strategically placed dead bodies as a means of imposing local rules, which in their stead shaped perceptions of political time and space. Images of those same bodies would later play a major role in the work of post-boom historical memory, where they served as touchstones for drawing out categorical differences between present and former times and, through their very recurrence, suggested that some events could never be told whole.

While an overt and sustained violence accompanied the boom, many of the valley's residents felt that the eventual downfall of the cocaine economy clouded their present and future prospects. For others, it created possibilities hitherto nonexistent. Chapter Four reflects on the upward fortunes of my friend Marusha in the post-boom era—from private lawyer to town council member to human rights activist—through the lens of her family's move from a mud-brick dwelling into a large cement house just off the main plaza of Aucayacu. Marusha's new residence drew attention to her up-and-coming status among the townspeople, who otherwise ignored her ever-precarious economic situation. Essentially, the house had been abandoned, and not even Marusha herself knew the story of the true owner. He had been a coca farmer and leader of a Sendero-controlled village who was forced to flee and make a new life selling hardware in an outlying district of Lima.

Here I portray the biting life of rumor as it swirled through this house, where I too stayed. Rumors were an important anonymous and sometimes ruthless expression of political speech, and in that house they regularly took aim at Marusha on account of her work. And yet, if one strayed from the concerns of the present and simply looked around the house, many layered histories could be read, if only as fragments, from the interiors of the place.

In the Huallaga few visible traces remained of the wealth generated by cocaine, and that was one grievance of people who lived there. They complained that the boom left little of use behind: no running water, no electricity, no paved streets. One of the few lingering remnants of those ebullient and more lethal times was, however, cement. Vacant-looking buildings made of the stuff abounded, giving the towns of the valley an underpopulated or partially abandoned feel. With the boom's passing, many people still moved through the valley. Some lived for a time in hollow structures whose material substance quietly pointed to the utopian yearnings of others, now unknown and nowhere to be seen.

One of those no longer in Aucayacu continued very much on the minds of those who remained. He was an army officer sent in 1991 to break the hold of the Shining Path on the town. People only knew him by his nom de guerre: Capitán Carlos Esparza. Chapter Five tells a version of his story composed from what I heard about him and which I use to probe the tension between event, narration, and political time. In and around town the name Esparza was inseparable from the black sacks filled with chopped-up human remains, such as those found dumped along the shores of the Huallaga River in the early 1990s. But to think of Esparza as a mere butcher, a sadistic torturer-executioner, would underestimate his complexity as a historical figure and the "work" that he did. The difficulty Esparza presented could be inferred from the strange fact that many in Aucayacu remembered him as an upright captain and good neighbor who revived civic parades and respect for the Peruvian flag. Even more telling was the local, strictly towncentric esteem Esparza acquired for his service to the nation as the implacable dismemberer of terrorists.

My concern is with how the memory of brute force secretly inheres in civic sentiment and the patriotic rituals called upon to express it. Examining the captain's arrival through an implicit conversation with the second essay of Nietzsche's *On the Genealogy of Morality*, I describe how Esparza worked up "order" and "civilization" to the nocturnal sounds of a chainsaw and how some townspeople softly applauded, even long after the fact. Their enduring regard spoke to the inscrutable relation that sometimes holds between acts of extreme violence and the prestige of authority—a connection that is enigmatic precisely because it does not lend itself to straightforward exposition.

In the final chapter, day breaks in town to nervous words about the appearance of a red Maoist flag in "the port," Aucayacu's main canoe landing on the Huallaga River. Six years have passed since Esparza was last seen. It is Sunday, and schoolchildren, soldiers, and local authorities assemble in the main plaza for the weekly patriotic flag raising. Immediately after the ceremony, the army base commander calls to order a special meeting with villagers from the other side of the river. The subject of the gathering is the creation of *rondas* (civil defense patrols) in what the townspeople and the army know to be Sendero territory. The army commander, new and yet to make an impression on anyone, insists the villagers form patrols to help out with the "pacification effort," implying that compliance will be read as evidence of their allegiance.

The year is 1998. Almost anywhere else in Peru, talk of red flags and *rondas* would seem a throwback from an earlier era. Conflicting political calendars, conflicting heroic dates, and how time and place grow intense through them raises some questions:

How much force still lingers in a Sendero flag?

Why couldn't the army simply impose its will?

But also:

What would the answers tell about the political moment and under whose flag those living in the Huallaga must now stand?

Such uncertainty, where question is followed not by answer but by another question—which only complicates the terms of those before it—speaks to an immanent perspective of what everyday life was like in the post-boom. Expectation could crowd the air, first intruding, then backing off when "nothing" happened, ever ready to tense up again.

Certainty comes where distances can be drawn and when, through the artistry of force, a direction can be given to "the times." Uncertainty speaks to the provisional character of all interpretative frames and the cushions they provide against the brutal jolt of the unanticipated—which is, after all, the substance of the event.

1 *ya no hay coca ya*

The knocks would start every morning by eight-thirty, if not before, and Sunday was no exception. On the steel plate doors out front, the rattle of knuckles, the rap of keys in sudden metallic bursts: sometimes timid, sometimes impatient, always insistent. It was Carito who would go to answer, whether she was helping Abuela in the kitchen, drawing water for Marusha's bath, or sweeping and picking up around the sitting room and office.

¿Se encuentra la doctora[1]? was what they asked almost without fail.

Marusha would either just be getting up or be already dressed and at the breakfast table, downing a cup of instant coffee with yesterday's rice reheated, or whatever else there might be—boiled yuca or plantains, even some fish if Magno was around and between jobs. *Maaaru, te buscan,* Carito would call out as she pushed open the swinging door and ambled down the hall toward the kitchen. "It's the señor from Cotomonillo. He wants to know if his papers are ready." Or "It's the señora who showed up last night just as you were closing. She doesn't want to give me her name." Marusha would reply with an "Ask them to come back in an hour," or an "Open the doors to the office, I'll be out in a bit." Unless, of course, she was about to head out of town, in which case she would have them come back the next day or the following week. Marusha was always just arriving or just about to leave again, and so when she stuck around for a stretch people dropped by all day long. When the office doors were open, they would pop their heads in or take a seat on one of the benches inside—especially if it were early and a clear day, because the morning sun landed something fierce on the front side of the house and would push you in toward the shade. But if the office doors were closed, which they were at lunchtime, at the end of every day, and whenever Marusha was away, then the metallic knocks to which we were so accustomed would return to interrupt whatever was going on inside the house.

So many came looking for Marusha that it was just expected that the visits were for her. If not a client, then someone from city hall or a local journalist on his daily rounds aiming to tease out a quote. Sometimes one of the local news talk shows would phone her early in the morning to do an interview, and while Marusha sat at her desk taking the call, the rest of us would crowd around at the kitchen table to listen to her on the radio.

The kitchen table was squat and rectangular with wiggle enough to slop your coffee. Its surface stayed bare most of the time, exposing long strips of wood discolored with age, though occasionally Abuela would drape a soft yellow cloth over it and then lay a transparent plastic sheet on top. A long bench ran one length of the table, pressed up against the wall, while chairs tucked in around the other sides. Abuela always sat at the far end with her back to the patio doorway so as to be close to the stove top and her blackened aluminum pots and kettle. Marusha took her place on the bench to Abuela's right so as to make sure her grandmother didn't eat anything she wasn't supposed to or attempt to drink her soup or tea before it had cooled. Others in the household would fill in where they could: Carito, Magno, and me, sometimes Nico and rarely if ever Bianca.

The kitchen was the innermost space of the house where Marusha had moved the family following the death of her mother Herminia in 1996. It was where they took meals, and no one who was not living there was ever invited in. That went for close friends, too, with exception made, at most, for a relative or Marusha's secretary. I suspect the reason was more modesty than anything else, there being no way to receive people in the kitchen without having them promenade past the open bedrooms and their visible disorder, then through the patio past the plastic tubs of soaking laundry and the buckets of food scraps that crowded just outside the kitchen doorway. A meal of any holiday or ceremonial importance spared guests those unkempt sights and was served instead on the long dining table out front.

Such formal dinners were rare events and had none of the intimacy of the kitchen, where the family regularly met to engage in the conversations of the day. The kitchen was where the latest rumors and news would be spread out and picked through or apart, and where the old stories would come round again and show their power—especially when Marusha was home and had a moment to spare. On account of her work on the municipal council and the legal cases she attended to every day, Marusha forever had her finger to the wind of news that blew through town. And while everyone in the house would have his or her turn to bring something to the table, Marusha was the generative source of much of what was discussed.

That's not to say the atmosphere that dominated our meals was all serious. No. We could get pretty worked up, get on a roll—the good-humored air suddenly taking on a mocking tone. In those moments, jokes barbed and needling got the best of anyone perceived in the least as lowering his or her guard. True, it was pretty clean fare with none of the cutting double entendres that were staple fare on the street. Some of the jokes were bad, others stupid, and most of the time we got off on just being silly.

Magno, except where Abuela was concerned, was a quiet, never-make-the-first-move kind of guy, but once he got started he enjoyed the fight and just wouldn't let it go, sometimes not for days at a time. Nico, meanwhile, didn't open his mouth if not to make some playful gibe, and he had this way of joking that made him endearing even when he took it too far. Whereas Carito, poor Carito, she liked to tease but took more than her share of punishment. This had to do in part with her being the youngest of the family, which allowed the others to tell ridiculing stories about her that she was in no position to challenge. There was the one about the time some neighbors who were in deep with the *terrucada*[2] gave her a grenade to slip past the army checkpoint at the port. She was only six or seven years old at the time, and she did their bidding—so the story went—without realizing what the object was or what she was doing. The humor turned on family knowledge that Carito sometimes did imprudent things when she should have known better, and the story pretended to prove it was a pattern that started even before she was conscious of the significance of her own acts. Carito never protested and would look up with a sheepish grin that only served to seal the truth of the tale and perpetuate a situation in which all the cards were stacked against her.

I was pretty slow and flat-footed when it came to joining in on the teasing and joking, even to my defense, and like Carito suffered the brunt of it from time to time. But there wasn't one of us who didn't manage to toss in a devilish line now and again, which did earn each one some respect. Marusha, ever the matriarch, was never the target and was good at staying out of the fray.

But no meal ever passed without someone coming to the front door and leaving one of us midsentence. Many interesting stories got put off in this way until the next time we were all together, if not completely lost in the meantime. Invariably it was Carito who went to see who was calling, just as it was her job to get up for anything that was missing from the table: to rummage through the cupboard drawers, to re-serve the plates, or to run across the street to buy last-minute items.

Once Nico was in town when Marusha was away, and we were all talking about something when the pounding started at the door. Mildly annoyed, Nico spat back as loudly as he could in good Huallaga colloquial, *¡No hay nadies!* (No ones are home!), and that just threw us all into fits of laughter, though no one more than Magno, who from that day on made it his. Anyone who knocked too much and too long would get a resounding *¡No hay nadies! ¡No hay nadies!*—even as Magno himself went for the door and swung it open with a grumpy "Who is it?" that only seemed to mock, while acknowledging, the general sentiment that when Marusha was gone no one who was anyone was at home.

When she was there, the news Marusha would bring home often had the taste of a tabloid police beat. Like the time she returned from a council meeting to announce that the police were finally being forced to move out of the "Proyecto" (Project), a government administrative and housing compound, and into a new headquarters behind town hall. The station house had been completed for several months, and having the police force deployed to its own building in the center of town was supposed to be one more sign that things in Aucayacu were getting back to normal. Yet the police could never manage to put a date on when they would abandon the Project compound, and as they procrastinated the empty building—freshly painted in the pea and moss green colors of the PNP—had become a sanctuary for thugs and a favorite spot for derelicts and vagrants to go and relieve themselves. The municipal council was already annoyed by such unseemly activity happening right out its back-door steps, as it were, when one morning a fourteen-year-old schoolgirl was found dead inside the new headquarters, the victim of gang rape from the night before.

The municipal council generally took a "live and let live" attitude where the National Police was concerned; after all, it was outside the council's jurisdiction. But the enormity of this scandal was too much to let slide. Following much fretting over the problem, the council sent a petition to the departmental authorities in Huánuco, complaining that the empty station house had become a menace to public peace and demanding that the police be ordered to move into their new headquarters. Apparently the petition had been well received, because Marusha appeared certain that the transfer would now be imminent. At least, that was her good news. As for why the police were reticent to leave the Project compound in the first place, Marusha said that the new station house was no more than an office, whereas in the Project they had living space as well. If they moved, the police would have to find accommodations elsewhere and pay rent from their already meager paychecks. The police also grumbled that the new headquarters had not been built with the proper materials and that the clay-brick walls would provide unreliable cover in the event of an attack by Sendero or a drug gang.

Marusha had few details about the rape itself, which had happened several days before she brought it up at the kitchen table. As was her style, Marusha's news was less about the crime than about the action taken by the town council. But when a friend of Magno's dropped by later that evening, we learned that people were saying the girl had been coaxed out of one of Aucayacu's two discothèques and led across the plaza into the empty headquarters—after someone had slipped a common cow tranquilizer into her soft drink. She had still been alive, so we heard, when the men—all eight of them—abandoned her, bleeding, on the station house floor. In the impossible-to-know details of the recounting, the girl tried to get help but was too dizzy to stand, and she died several hours later. What could be proved was that in the following months the police staged several late-night raids on the discothèques to enforce a local ordinance banning the admission of minors. Yet they never moved into their headquarters, not while I was in Aucayacu. Nor was the rape case, as far as we knew, ever solved.

The *tombos,* as police are called in Peruvian lingo, were always taking a hit in the stories told around town, and those told in Marusha's kitchen were no exception. Their exploits, both of actions and inactions, were the cause of indignation and derision. Even the dominant versions of the region's recent past of violence and lawlessness were plumbed for origins in a prehistory of corrupt and treacherous cops. And it was hard to miss that in the telling of so many stories much dark enjoyment came at their expense.

Take the time Puricho, the number two of the Champa drug gang, escaped from jail in Huánuco. It was Father's Day, and big mafioso that he was,

Puricho had invited all of the prison staff to celebrate the day with a big feast of chicken and wine, the whole works. They must have been hungry because not only did they accept his hospitality, they left only one guard posted outside to keep watch over the prison while the rest joined the festivities. Puricho and two others waited until the party was in full swing to make their break. But the policemen never moved; they were either too busy eating or too drowsy to even get up from the table. It seems the chicken had been laced with a powerful sedative, or that was the word we got in Aucayacu. Puricho was a native son and the town was all abuzz with how he had tricked the police or paid them into going along with the charade, which was effectively the same thing. The head of the prison was promptly arrested, Marusha told us, adding that it was no surprise that Puricho had given the police the slip when he did. His twenty-year sentence for drug trafficking had just been upheld by a court in Lima, and he was about to be transferred into one of the maximum security penitentiaries from which there would be no buying his way out.

But it was more than just the *tombo* stories. So many things, a whole world beyond the house, passed through that kitchen. From the *chacra:* that Sendero came through over the weekend, calling people to overnight meetings, handing out tasks again. From Avenida Lima: that the soldiers passed by escorting two prisoners captured on patrol near the village of Chimbote. From the *cruce:* to take extra care in traveling on the Marginal Highway, that armed bandits have been stopping traffic near the one-kilometer mark. And many times the knocks at the door were merely to let Marusha know about some situation in the making.

Word of something heard in the late afternoon might make its appearance at the evening meal and then build throughout the next day or even week—details and updates gathering round and nourishing it every time we came together. Outside of this stream of local news and rumors, whatever was happening in the rest of the country or carried in the national press was generally far from our discussions. No one in Marusha's house tuned in regularly to what was piped in from Lima on television or picked up by local radio stations. Nor did the family buy any of the newspapers that showed up on the late bus from Lima each afternoon. Getting the paper was a habit they considered beyond their means. Money was too tight to go blowing a couple of sols[3] like that every day. Much of the town must have felt the same, judging from how few newspapers were actually sold. Never more than a handful arrived at the only two kiosks where you could buy them: in the *cruce,* or crossroads, where the Marginal Highway entered Aucayacu proper at the head of Avenida Lima; and on the main plaza across from the public telephones. But the papers never arrived before six in the evening, by which time the news was already beginning to make for a stale read. Whether speaking of the tabloids, with their fleshy, front-page vedettes clothespinned at eye level, or the "serious" news dailies, inevitably a copy or two were left over to send back the following afternoon.

People were most curious about what was happening elsewhere in the country when it somehow affected them. No one would think of missing the president's annual Independence Day address, for example, and townsfolk would stay pressed to their TV sets for the duration of the speech on the chance of gleaning some real intention of government aid from what were mostly only vague words of promise. But matters of importance to the day-in, day-out life of the town hardly ever found their echo in the national media, and whatever was reported—all too often catering to the taste of the wealthier store owners, radio announcers, and other self-proclaimed defenders of local pride—often took the form of unwarranted smears on the town's name. Thus all coverage was bad coverage in their eyes, and nothing could anger the townspeople more than when a journalist or television announcer got the geography wrong and reported something that had happened in an outlying hamlet as having taken place in Aucayacu. The problem was less one of geographical imprecision than the result of Aucayacu, as the district capital, appearing as the dateline for everything that occurred within its jurisdiction. And the national press was unaware of and just as likely insensitive to the gulf that the more affluent townspeople believed separated town from country.

In many ways, the gap was a real one. Indeed, the local news that carried nationally was the cause of much hand-wringing, because it was feared that the lingering curse of an ignominious past—"maliciously" sustained by the Lima press establishment—would forever prevent Aucayacu from shrugging off its celebrity as drug haven and ultimate lair of Sendero terrorism and moving on to a more promising future. As if bad press alone were damming up a swell of international development dollars just waiting to be unleashed on this region brimming with jungle potential. In the Huallaga, rumors of such schemes were never in short supply: fruit-packing plants to be installed by Dutch investors, beetles to be exported to the Japanese, toads and butterflies for that German scientist who came around a few years back, or the ever-

promising tourist trade locked up in area waterfalls and deep natural caverns
. . . if only the tourists would arrive.

Marusha had no truck with that sort of dreaming and was not one to white-
wash the score for the sake of misplaced pride. And that was in part why
the kitchen table was where I would bring whatever I had learned about the
area's history from my interviews or conversations—for confirmation, for
different versions, or just for suggestions about how to pursue the ideas further. The kitchen was where I could float any question that was too hard
or impossible to ask anywhere else—the table, and by extension the house,
being for me one of the few pockets of confidence I had in town initially,
only equaled perhaps by the back room of the store of my two close friends,
Mariela and Alex. In the Huallaga such spaces, where I felt freed of the need
to measure every word or skip around what was really going on, were as valuable as they were rare.

Our meals in the kitchen were also times when I would try to probe the
local common sense about the things I'd hear repeated again and again until
they took on the impenetrable air of truth. Like all the talk I encountered in
1997, during my first return to the Huallaga, about how the coca money had
dried up. Everyone would tell you as much, saying *Ya no hay coca ya* (coca's
gone) in voices that oscillated between resigned lament and self-assured anticipation, depending on who was speaking. No denying it, there had been
a qualitative shift, though no one knew what it meant or what to expect,
and that alone kept people on edge. Because when the bottom dropped out
from coca in 1995, nothing rushed in to take its place. Sure, those with an
"agricultural calling" eventually would plant bananas and papayas and rice,
lots of rice, and get stiffed plenty by the complications associated with legal
crops—the high cost of transportation, fickle markets, and gouging interme-
diaries—that are just part of business as usual. That's what was special about
coca, you didn't have to have a flair for the farm life to make it grow and in
time improve your lot. At least that was the hook.

Ya no hay coca ya, people would say, but still it was hard to fathom. True,
you wouldn't see any inside Aucayacu town. Try to buy it in the market, and
you'd come back empty-handed. You'd have to go as far as Tingo María, where
the dry leaf was sold on the curbs adjacent to the Mercado Central by peasant women tending bulky plastic bags. This legal leaf was technically grown by
farmers registered with the government for sale as personal chew and medicinal

tea, though I never found the clean separation of licit and illicit cultivation all that convincing. Once it left the farm, who was to say what was what?

Ya no hay coca ya . . . but sometimes, outside city limits small quantities of leaves could be seen laid out to dry on the asphalt of the Marginal Highway, an arroba (11.5 kilos), maybe more, pushed to the edge of the road and surrounded by bread loaf–sized stones to make sure the traffic left them well enough alone. But if asked about this rare appearance of coca, people would scoff as if to say it was nothing compared with what things were like before. They would then point to the horizon as proof and say, "See those hills, all dry and bare of vegetation? *Those hills* used to undulate a bushy green, back then." *Ya no hay coca ya*. And that's what had everyone waiting, waiting for a new president, because "that Fujimori, he just doesn't let us get any work done."[4]

When raw cocaine prices went tumbling in early 1995, nothing filled coca's place beyond an extended lull, a phlegmatic life in which it was boredom and not bullets that would put an end to your days. Yet the townspeople did not dislike the president. No! Sentiment about Alberto Fujimori started with begrudging admiration and tilted toward complete awe. Deserved or not, the president won much of the credit for getting guns off the streets and restoring a little peace and quiet to Aucayacu. In those days, it was hard to find anyone who would bad-mouth "el Chino." And even as people complained about having their wings clipped by Fujimori's restrictive measures, most were quick to admit that things had truly spun out of control, that dire solutions were called for. *A buena hora, el Chino* (Not a moment too soon, Chinaman), they would say. The question was what to do now.

Ya no hay coca ya, and in such matters Magno was the house expert, the definitive voice. Maybe because he once had his own coca farm, maybe because he paid his dues back in Monzón, stomping leaves in the maceration pits. And maybe more because he had friends who stayed on in the business as best they could. They were always tipping him off about what was going on. Basic shoptalk, nothing more: where the price per arroba was hovering; who was working the leaf and whereabouts. Magno was reticent to speak more than in vague terms. News about coca still being cultivated was hush-hush, something tucked from view but always present. Magno himself would repeat the common wisdom that coca was gone and in the next breath counter with, "yet there'll always be coca." He supposed that the mafia might even come back to town if the price kept going up, but for coca to ever return to what it was like before . . . *eso, ya no ya* (never again), he'd insist. Because for all the talk that coca had disappeared, it was not because there was none *at all*. Rather it was the sudden absence of the life that coca had once provided—when coca was everywhere and when anything and everything seemed possible. And that was what Magno appeared to be saying: there would always be coca but never again the heady boom to which it had given rise, sustained in fits and starts for nearly two decades and whose abrupt departure left everyone talking about past times as if they were that much more important than the present.

picture this

Where stories were concerned, little could compete with the past, whether at the kitchen table or anywhere else. Marusha especially liked to marvel at those times "when this place was *tierra de nadie*" (no man's land). She had been raised in Aucayacu but came to know those "most difficult years," as she called them, only in fleeting glimpses on visits from the university in Huánuco where she went to study in 1983. In the years that followed, every trip she made back home was a wealth of experience and news, her mother being her most intimate and reliable source. Marusha would later tell and retell what she learned and witnessed on those trips in a broken sequence of snapshots. The gaps were many, and Marusha was spared so much because she hadn't had to live through coca's "peak" day in, day out. That gave her, I often thought, some means to step back and grasp the magnitude of the transformation of her hometown. Above all, she was cognizant of how different life was in the Upper Huallaga, especially when compared with the world immediately beyond it—places such as Tingo María and Huánuco, both cities that coped under the general fear and uncertainty of those violent years but that, in Marusha's view, suffered far less:

> No comparison. This town was no man's land. There was no one who could watch over the physical integrity of anyone else. Somebody gets murdered . . . Did the army do it? The police? Sendero? The mafia? Used to be, you'd never find out. Police investigations stopped at the removal and burial of the corpse. You could be killed by anyone. There was no safe haven. Death could come at you from any side.

But that was hardly all of it. Marusha would frequently point out how screwed up, how really out of hand things got. And though I never quite understood where to draw the line between those earlier times when conditions were "really bad" and later—the moment we were sharing—when they were only timidly so, Marusha had a way of conveying the past in succinct and potent images, enveloped in the tremor of her own amazement. Those images served to trace the divide between then and now.

Marusha liked to tell about the *traqueteros* (drug couriers) and how they would line up on their motorcycles in front of the Colegio Inca Huiracocha when classes let out, waiting to carry off the teenage girls as they walked past the schoolyard gate. About the families of humble means and how they went along, and even quietly approved of these matter-of-fact unions, maybe just crossing their fingers that it would mean advancement for their daughters and perhaps even indirectly for themselves. The parents' innocence (or was it guile?) startled Marusha a little, while the schoolgirls' own desires were absent from the telling. Still, it is hard to imagine what clean choice parents or their children actually had before the heady swirl that a few guns and a wad of dollars could pack. Because the *narcos*, they did what they wanted with Aucayacu. At least that's what everyone would have you believe, and one ready means of making that point was conjuring depictions of adolescent female sexuality spinning prematurely out of control.

Marusha recalled the late 1980s. She came home once to find all of the girls of thirteen, fourteen years of age with their stomachs swollen. No matter where she looked, she could not find a young woman "without her belly," as she put it. It was a sad thing to behold, she said—so young, and in that condition on a previously unimaginable scale. But what really surprised her when she returned the following year was to find not a single schoolgirl visibly with child. That things could go from one extreme to the other, and so fast, was yet more proof of the wacky and mercurial humors of those times.

At first Marusha could not imagine how schoolgirl fertility had been brought swiftly and totally under control until a friend at the health post let her in on the secret. Faced with what health workers understood to be a full-blown public health emergency, the medical staff embarked upon a massive antitetanus campaign for the local high school, four times in one year, and only for the girls. "Tetanus?" Marusha had asked, puzzled. "What does tetanus have to do with anything?" Her friend, a little surprised Marusha didn't know, informed her that the tetanus vaccine worked as a birth control if administered frequently. Thus to stave off the negative repercussions of a spate of precocious pregnancies, the health post quietly took this "service" upon itself, clearly without much regard for informed consent. Marusha seemed satisfied with the medical explanation but wondered why no one had caught on to the ruse, why no one asked why boys were not just as much at risk of contracting tetanus, or why the inoculations, which are usually good for several years, had been given so many times.

Amid such scenes of social disorder emerged pictures of calm. Marusha would tell of how it had been *before*, when thanks to Sendero you could leave your doors unlocked or lean your bikes against the wall outside your house. "Like they do in places like Japan," she'd say, "without fear of someone walking in uninvited or running off with your stuff." I can only imagine it must have been a wholly unreal experience for some people, since in Peru the anxiety over loss of personal property can preoccupy daily life. But those were the mid-1980s. The boom was well underway, and Sendero was making itself felt in town with a stern message of justice that stirred up a general expectation. It was a hope to which even Marusha was receptive. "Sure," she insisted, "we welcomed them . . . at first. Who wasn't happy to see the thieves go into hiding or the legal authorities acting with a little more discretion?" Sendero's threat of death had a chilling effect on petty crime and everyday corruption.

Whereas now, in these new, presumably less violent times, theft was once again a constant worry. People never stopped talking about break-ins at some neighbor's place down the way; about the television set, the stereo, or the small appliance that disappeared through the window, over the fence out back, or through a hole pried open in the wood planks on the blind side of the house. The blame for these crimes fell to a familiar group of bad seeds, young men reared on the so-called easy money of the cocaine boom and educated in the ways of firearms. Poorly adjusted to the new times of "hard, honest work," they preferred theft and armed robbery as the best way to get by. Or so went the claim.

The loss of a new mountain bike or, worse, a motorcycle, caused special concern, as it was known that once these items were slipped out of town and onto the *chacra* there would be no seeing them again. The term *chacra*, in precise terms, referred to cultivated or fallow farmland, and *monte* referred to the jungle thicket—though people often used *chacra* as a catchall phrase for the two. This outback region was alternately a lawless realm and a realm with its own laws; it sat beyond the two rivers and the stream that bordered the town of Aucayacu and straddled both sides of the Marginal Highway to the north and south. The distant hills, with peaks that sloped back onto hidden valleys and heights beyond, were where Sendero was said to still call the shots and where from time to time the big *narcos* were rumored to be hanging out and biding their time until "the situation" once again allowed them to bring their operations back to town.

Something was always going on outside the city limits during the times I lived with Marusha's family, first for several weeks in 1997 and then off and on for longer stints of ethnographic research between 1998 and 2000. Somebody shot, killed, bloodied up by machete blows? If it didn't happen on the main road, nine times out of ten it happened in the *chacra*. Accessed only by way of small roads or trails, one went there only when invited or in the company of someone well known to the area. Although the trip was surely not as dangerous as some eagerly implied, if this precaution were neglected it could turn into an uncomfortable time for all involved. The prevailing logic was: if you went into the *chacra*, you went for something in particular. And if that purpose was not obvious and obviously innocent, then your presence was not only unwelcome, it gave cause for worry.

In their topography of dangerous places, the townspeople could speak with equal mystery of the *banda*, which partook of the forbidden character of the *chacra* but referred specifically to lands west of the Huallaga River and where, now and again, the guerrilla was imagined to be amassed, looking for any opportunity to stage a raid on the town. There was a strange way in which the past glory of Sendero and the *narco* bosses got displaced onto the countryside, and the perceptions of Sendero's different threats kindled fears that the situation could deteriorate into its previous state. This helped to explain the dread with which people could still speak of the areas beyond Aucayacu, which was one common way of expressing the deep tensions between town and country that ran throughout the Huallaga.

All the same, Marusha's image of a previous time free from the fear of petty theft in the midst of so much personal vulnerability—the *tierra de nadie* that coincided with the boom—was a peculiar idea. It also underscored the unevenness that inhered in the notion of a more peaceful present. For a relative calm had come to prevail over the town. And despite being occasionally punctuated by violent acts, that calm seemed to stand in for peace and made the hope for a definitive break with the past more tangible.

There was something illusory in the way Marusha spoke of that earlier time when the fear of Sendero's justice had kept thieves at bay. It was well known that during the cocaine boom the threat of armed robbery weighed heavily on those who used the Marginal Highway to transport drugs or drug money, and not only on the road. *The concern* and *the problem* was how to hold on to what you made. So, if the homes in town suffered fewer burglaries during the heyday of the drug trade, Sendero may not have been the sole reason. The thieves may well have had their sights fixed on more lucrative prospects.

Still, there was no question that Sendero's prohibitions had left their charge in the air and their mark on the townspeople. They remembered well what Sendero said they could and could not do, although I never heard reports that the more preposterous steps Sendero had taken to shore up local morals in area villages had ever happened in Aucayacu. Forced marriages were one such measure: a local delegate, seeing a young man inviting a girl for a soft drink, orders the two brought over and in that very moment decrees, "You are now husband and wife." Nor was Aucayacu subjected to the horrific public executions or "people's trials" for which Sendero was so famous, in which spectators were obliged to take part in the bloodletting of the condemned. For that more ceremonial form of doing justice, Sendero generally favored the *chacra,* which it considered its rear guard, and then only when the main guerrilla column happened to be passing through the area. Because even at the height of its strength, the urban zones of the Upper Huallaga were never more than forward positions for the guerrilla. Aucayacu was unique in that it was one of the few towns that had a well-developed Sendero militia—La Urbana[5]— with Party delegates on every block ready to receive complaints about local quarrels to which they would promise speedy resolution. People would tell you though that during its short life the Urbana was at best a scrappy band of post–high school–age males in love with their own guns and more notorious for charming girls or gunning down drifters—on the offhand chance they might be informers—than for the strict enforcement of Sendero law. That was the general complaint with the Urbana: too quick to kill without as much as a question asked.[6]

In Marusha's telling, and not in hers alone, there seemed to be very different and yet interlocked pasts, distinct thens and nows that played out on separate registers and came together in mysterious ways: the *narcos* with their licentious free rein, preying on family honor and, on the other extreme, the radical rectitude of Sendero's law with which people agreed in principle though perhaps not in practice. Both of these were somehow brought on by the withering of the legal authority of the Peruvian state, which took years to return, and then only through a most violent intervention of the army. What eluded me was how these distinct forces in the boom days past hung together, meshed, or layered on top of one another. Even what marked the disparity between past and present and seemed at first blush to be no more than a difference in magnitude, was not at all clear, especially when things could swing so dramatically from one year to the next.

The boom, as an era, was no more. Yet, for being recent history, people spoke as if an insurmountable gulf separated it from the present and the possible futures that the same present appeared to contain. And this distancing suggested important ethnographic questions. How was I to square what I recognized in the late 1990s to be an ongoing sequence of unsettling and often violent occurrences with what others described as a more peaceful era of postboom? Moreover, and even more basic, how was I to differentiate between the historical time of real events and the stories told to make it intelligible?

a time in between

In the precipitous movement from coca abundance to coca drought, the present increasingly distanced itself from the boom even as those former times seemed to never go away. For if the postcocaine era manifested somewhere toward the latter half of 1995, it spread forward, ever tentative, under the dark and weighty shadow of a more intense and spectacular block of history. In this new time, the boom continued to make itself felt through the enormity of its absence. Yet it was the apparent decisiveness of the temporal rift that lent itself to storytelling and fanned the desire in the late 1990s to speak about what had happened on the other side of the chasm. In such retrospective accounts, the past blurred; and it was precisely in the stories that the blur of time itself became most evident—evident in the episode-motifs repeated again and again and that stood in for events that had come to shape the world as people in the Huallaga knew and lived it, blurred through so many events.

In the Upper Huallaga new states of affairs seemed to arrive swiftly only to pass on through. The critical situation of a week, a month, or a year ago often faded away quickly to be replaced by others of equal intensity. So much history accumulated in this place. Luckily, my conversations with Marusha and many others provided me with a basic outline of the last twenty years.

First to be imposed was the influx and dominion of coca over Huallaga agriculture. Then came the large-scale anti-narcotics operatives and operations, which milked the trade as they worked to displace it. Next up: the waves of Shining Path incursions and the destruction of the valley's main road. Those expressions of Maoist force eventually gave way to the Peruvian army's imposition of state rule in the towns, which in turn—another fold—led to major counterinsurgency assaults on the countryside where Sendero had its strongholds. In Aucayacu proper, thanks in part to the army's work in clearing out the Urbanas, there emerged the ruthless competition of the Cristal and Champa drug *firmas*. Their bloody conflict would locally become the boom's final reprise. Elsewhere in the Huallaga the end of cocaine's rush would take other forms.

Major events like these served as significant points in narrative accounts of the boom. They often overshadowed the multiple, more minor occurrences that gathered together to radiate a loosely cohesive atmosphere. Events emanated their own plural sense that in retrospect came to be selectively ordered as thin strata of a history people referred to as the *apogeo de la coca* (coca's peak). In the accounts of these events, each stratum would unfold on top of another as it itself became enfolded in what preceded, only to make up what was still to come. Those narrated layers of historical sense could be mapped as a linear chronology, but only at the cost of tempering or flattening out the intensity of the events themselves, both as they materialized and as they fell back upon each other in overlapping and entangled flows.

Rather than linear, stories of the boom time tended to be episodic. They shunned strict chronology and began in the middle of things. As such, they seemed to require a convoluted treatment of time, as if convolution allowed for a more attuned and intuitive presentation of how people and the things that happened to them hung together in ways jagged and complex.

Layers of historical sense were secreted through the stories told in the boom's wake. Sometimes they arrived by way of dates of vague specificity: "one May seventeenth . . ."; "June twenty-fourth of that year . . ." Sometimes they were intimated in the names of places—Pacae, Consuelo, Culebra, and many others—that traced out vectors toward a present-day topography where it was still dangerous to tread. These myriad temporal strata were most arrestingly conveyed, however, through startling images of what had been, and which for all who had not directly experienced those years could only be believed with a leap of faith. In the stories of the boom, all of these (dates, place names, images with no actual or visible referents) served as markers of temporal intensities and conferred upon the post-boom, the period in which they were told, the mood of a time in between, not yet free of its onerous ties to the past and still unsure of what the future would bring.

Images of disorienting abundance and caprice animated stories that compressed critical aspects of the boom experience. People seized upon those images to separate the dearth of the present from the wild affluence of previous times. I was told the boom did not start off violently. But in time guns so flooded the Upper Huallaga that their regular discharge became the sonorous background of everyday life. Human corpses proliferated, too, as death was tucked into the already hearty consumption of food, drink, and sex that workers and traders alike bought at inflated prices.

Everything in those days cost much more than anywhere else in the country. Surprisingly enough, cocaine *use* was never said to be an important part of the festive mix. Raw cocaine was good for running, not for smoking. People drew a strong distinction: there was prestige to be gained in becoming a *narco,* but only bad things could come from consuming one's own merchandise. Recreational cocaine use was something people tended to hold in low regard—a sign of serious moral depravity—and it was said that *narcos* who did so risked losing the respect of all.

Another important marker of the passage away from the boom was the social status of coca itself and the radical permutations it underwent with the decline of the cocaine economy. This shift in status overlapped chronologically with my initial visits to the Upper Huallaga and continued as I returned. Over the course of those years, I caught glimpses of transformations in coca's prestige—that is, to the degree that such alterations could be discerned from nuances in the ways locals talked.

Coca, whether through its glorious past, current tribulations, or long-term prospects, never ceased to insinuate itself into conversations. Townspeople in the Huallaga—whether in Aucayacu, Uchiza, or Tocache—fretted over what they called the "coca problem," though the conclusions they drew from the sudden turn of fortunes were not all the same. Some spoke as if coca were down and out but ever waiting for a chance to come back. Some spoke as if coca had lost its future altogether. Others claimed *coca no tiene buen fin,* that farming it or getting involved with the trade never ended well. They insisted coca had been a bad road from the start, and yet they were at a loss to say what would come to take its place. For them, all ills of the previous twenty years had their genesis in coca. Everything it had been and made possible became in retrospect fraudulent and chimerical. In their version, the promises of coca had proved illusory because they had been based in what became popular to describe as a "fictitious economy": fictitious because it was unstable and because whatever prosperity coca had ever produced had ultimately neither lasted nor served to create any enduring social good. Or so went the refrain, in which "coca" was shorthand for a long list of catastrophes.[7]

This was the predominant view from the principal towns of the Upper Huallaga to which I would be largely constrained on account of political conditions in the late 1990s. During the immediate post-boom, intermittent warfare between Sendero and the army continued in the countryside, and because of this, travel to villages not located directly on the Marginal Highway was discouraged. That is not to say that town was cut off from country. Farmers and their families regularly came to town to buy supplies and to sell crops, and in this way town residents, especially the merchants and shopkeepers, learned something of what was going on in the *chacra*. The townspeople also included many who had once had farms of their own but had fled the general violence of the war or Sendero's direct threats. Among them were those who at some earlier point had been on the "losing end" of coca and who, from the space of the town, could afford to dream of other possibilities.

ideal events

Regardless of their specific perspectives and interpretations, the way townspeople spoke of coca revealed it to be a synthetic notion that stood in for a manifold of relations, strategic calculations, and random histories, both as realized outcomes and as twists of fate. "Coca" enveloped so many things beyond the green bushy plant to which it literally referred. An ever-tense relationship among town, country, nation. A trade and a series of lifeways that formed as people plugged themselves into them. A time of promise and aspiration for the many who took the risks of riding coca's potential. But also, the many directions in which that potential had later panned out, when it was revealed to be the sheer delusion that in hindsight, and only in hindsight, "it always was."

"Coca" was notionally metonymic for the boom itself, which—as a movement that came, hovered over, and then pushed on—generated a constellation of sense that people drew upon as they made their way. "Sense" as I use it here denotes an ever-plural atmosphere of incorporeal effects that arises at the point where material things meet propositions. In this case, right where "coca"—not as a word but as vegetational matter entangled in historically specific social, political, and economic relations—met an "if . . . , then what?" calculation.

Coca? What can be done with it? What happens then?

Answers to such questions would shift as the boom gave way to its aftermath. They would shift with the historical sense of coca itself.

As mentioned in the Introduction, I derive my understanding of the "mechanics" of sense from Gilles Deleuze.[8] Investigations into "sense-production" spanned his published work and emerged from early studies of Hume, Kant, and Nietzsche. The insistence of those explorations and the multiple forms they took suggest that *sense*, at the very least, resists reduction to simple definition.

In his most extended treatment, titled *The Logic of Sense*, Deleuze developed a line of inquiry based on Stoic theories of language, which employed paradox to underscore the difference between things and what can be said about them. Schematically speaking, sense in this Stoic-inspired formulation has two principal aspects: it is an ideational attribute of real circumstances, but it is also what propositions "express" in regards to those same states of affairs. What propositions express, however, is not what they explicitly say but is rather an intangible *something* they convey and that plays "like a mist over the prairie" at the surface of words and things.[9] Deleuze called that *something* "ideal events" or "sense-events," which are not to be mistaken for material realizations in space and time; that is, the definition of "event" in ordinary language. Ideal events are instead the incorporeal effects produced by the actions and passions of bodies, both by what those bodies actualize in an ongoing state of affairs and what they will to happen for a future still to come.

Deleuze's conception of sense thus contains a theory of the event. That theory distinguishes between material or realized outcomes and the life they acquire through what is or can be stated about them. More critically, it forces a sustained engagement with their difference, which unfolds as an opaque and extremely intricate relation. Events for Deleuze cannot be grasped in the present, because they have either already happened or have yet to occur. As such, they only appear to gather consistency and coherence in a time other than the current moment and only through language, which Deleuze considered the proper domain of sense.

Sense insists through language, but it does not perform any representational functions. Sense does not indicate, manifest, or signify; it does not name qualities or bodies nor occupy the position of a subject or predicate.[10] Rather, it is a "paradoxical element" that animates language as it forms a border between things and propositions, between real circumstances and what can be said of them. Because of this, sense is never directly stated, only obliquely inferred,[11] for it resides neither on the side of states of affairs (where it "crops up") nor on the side of language (where it subsists). Instead, it traverses the two—here turning toward acts, bodies, and passions; there toward names, words, and propositions.[12]

Along that border, sense articulates bodies and things with language, allowing them to communicate but never mix. This articulation makes representation possible and in turn potentiates other operations of sense making— what Deleuze called a whole "tertiary organization" of good and common sense. Across this broad spectrum there is no original stratum of sense. All of its orders must be produced.

The sense that real events precipitate is in itself neutral and sterile, yet it affects those who infer it and who give it perspective, both as sensation and as disposition. Assimilated in this way, sense can also be rendered "meaningful," but only through a radical transfiguration that makes it uniform and removed from the messy complications of actual circumstances. If apprehended as an *orienting vector*, from which empirical selves pick up bearings or establish headings in space and time, it becomes a good sense that foresees and predicts. If apprehended as a *general consensus* about prevailing conditions, it becomes a common sense that makes upright judgments.

In relation to the Huallaga boom, Deleuze's formulation offers a path for tracing between the intensity of experiential encounters and the narratives later told about them. Specifically, it lends itself for conceiving how the incorporeal effects engendered by historical events in their own time may be apprehended by immanent acts of inference (or "sensing"), and how those same effects can subsequently be conjugated through interpretative practices that "make sense"—good sense, common sense, and even moral sense—of what has and will still come to pass. It does so, however, without analytically subordinating experiential modes of inference to those of verbal interpretation nor by proposing a one-dimensional empiricism. Rather than knowledge deriving directly from "experience," words and states of affairs collide at a frontier of sense where they engage but never resolve their difference.

Again: *Coca? What can be done with it? What happens then?*

Again: in the Huallaga, responses to these questions changed with the circumstances that marked the boom's departure and with the atmospheric sense that gave the times their singular sheen or patina. While that shift could not be conveyed in itself, it affected those who perceived it and impelled the stories they told as well as the judgments they made. Most concisely, the displacement from boom to post-boom came to be expressed in verbal refrains such as *ya no hay coca ya* or *coca no tiene buen fin*. These refrains pointed to permutations suffered by coca's social prestige in the wake of the boom, where townspeople spoke as if the cocaine trade had gone from making sense to losing it altogether. All of a sudden, it was clear as day that coca was gone. Just as it was obvious that a dismal end must come to those who insisted on sticking with it.

Townspeople spoke as if sense itself were a possession that could be obtained or wrenched away. The sense that coca/cocaine might "gain" or "lose," nevertheless, belonged to the tertiary modes of good and common sense that could be directly stated but that remained at varying degrees of distance from the immanent, sensorial landscapes of lived time. Orientating vectors and upright judgments had a relation to those landscapes. In fact, they could not exist without them, but only as compound figures that emerged by way of a resonance created at the crossroads of multiple layers of atmospheric sense, as these were cast by events actualized in space and time.

If coca/cocaine had once made (good and common) sense, that was because circumstances in the Huallaga had unfolded in a way so as to imbue the trade in raw cocaine with an auspicious coherence. Such coherence entailed a collective recognition, one that was not "lost" but that suffered a change of valence in the transition from boom to its aftermath.

Yet there was another, more subterranean frame in which coca literally made or rather produced sense, that is, through the very manifold or aggregate of relations, calculations, and often violent histories that "coca" as a notion covered. This manifold was what ultimately engendered sense in all its plural manifestations: the atmospheric modes that activated sensations and dispositions, the orientational modes that conveyed direction and foresight, the modes of general consensus that rendered judgment, but also—as a kind of copresence—the modes of "non-sense" expressed through paradox and the absurd. Because for all the ways coca once seemed to *have* and *make* sense, the boom itself created impossible and unforeseeable situations as well as multiple expressions of *locura*, or "goings mad."

The stories of boom time were full of paradoxical encounters: of being pulled simultaneously in opposite directions and of losing all balance and measure. They might tell of the abrupt appearance and then departure of widespread early teen pregnancies, or of the beloved relative from distant lands who visited unannounced and was killed on the spot, mistaken for a government spy. There was also that oft-repeated theme of how the boom had promised—and sometimes granted—formerly inconceivable wealth, only to deny those who attained it any means of keeping it or putting it to good use. And then there was the matter of sheer visibility. Everything was so blatantly there for all to see, *a vista y paciencia de todos*, people would say—the production, the trading, the transportation of illicit raw cocaine—and that nonchalant openness was perhaps the most far-fetched of all.

Whether as a visceral ambience, a social prestige, or an all-encompassing synthetic notion, the modes of sense that accrued to coca did so relative to the ease or difficulties of getting and staying involved in the cocaine business. During the boom this flux in access translated into an increase or reduction in the severity of prohibitions surrounding the economy. Those prohibitions affected not only those who were direct participants but all who lived in the valley or had cause to travel there. Their reach and relentlessness moved with the political conditions of the moment. In their stead, those conditions continually shaped what might be called the "value" of coca, by which I refer to something other than its ever-variable market worth, abstracted from social relations and rendered as numeric indicators. Rather I mean an ever-fluid evaluation, or *evaluative-value*, immanent to a social field of interaction. The evaluative-value of coca drew upon the sense coca made for singular lives in that collective field but as it came to be expressed in short-term assessments through which one appraised his or her own place within a prevailing hierarchy of competing forces. In that specific context, coca acquired its "worth" from that relation of forces to the degree that its evaluative-value bore directly upon lived, interpretive acts. Such acts sought to intuit risk from one's surroundings as a veritable direction of "the times," understood as the course of prevailing conditions.

Temporal directions in the boom changed often, because the trade in raw cocaine was neither monolithic nor steady. It was an iffy, transaction-to-transaction game of chance, which from the late 1970s to the mid-1990s had suffered chronic ups and downs. Moments of severe crises followed upon others of extreme prosperity, and through it all drug traders operated under a constant, if erratic, threat of violent intervention: whether by the police, the army, Sendero, or even (and especially) their own competitors. When those threats actualized as violent events, the effects could often be seen in the displacement of the trade across the valley in search of new, less exposed areas and in the regrouping of operations in the very places where they had been disrupted, if only under more prudent, less vulnerable terms. In each of those swings of displacements and reconfigurations, new people arrived while others were forced to leave or else to adapt to emerging circumstances. *Just staying* in the Huallaga was never easy, if only on account of the disruptions. For what constituted the boom was less a consistency in the cocaine trade itself than the magnitude of activity and extension that the drug economy achieved in those years. Only in their absence would those times later appear—and come to be narrated as—more stable than they ever were.

Thus, considered as a changing state of affairs, the temporal shift from boom to post-boom involved far more than a severe depreciation in the economic value of coca and raw cocaine. Multiple circumstances coincided to make the bust of the mid-1990s appear as not merely one more storm to be weathered in the ongoing, ever-tumultuous life of the boom. Their convergence signaled that coca as a way of life was gone. Suddenly, attaching one's fate to coca by putting one's hope and faith in the trade seemed to make less and less sense. Huallaga townspeople would speak as if the disenchantment with coca had become collective, and they frequently pointed to the fact that coca/cocaine had lost its economic value as the sole reason. Implicitly, however, they were saying that the plural sense that accrued to coca had suffered a thorough transformation. Real events had overlapped to produce an ideal event: that of the boom's definitive demise. This transformation became narratively figured as a new era in the making, an era when the commonsense idea that coca no longer made any sense had gotten the upper hand.

many forces

Perhaps I would never have become sensitive to the crucial distinction between narrative and historical time, much less to how the two could splice together, had I not first visited the Huallaga—and the town of Aucayacu specifically—in June of 1995 on the invitation of Orlando, a Catholic priest of the Oblate order. As I returned in subsequent years, memories of that initial trip would impress upon me just how much could significantly change over the span of a couple of years and how, within much shorter stretches of time, "the situation" could suddenly turn. When it did, simply sorting through the competing versions of what had happened and what was still to come became the essential if perplexing task. On my first visit it was the sheer eventfulness of the place that resonated most deeply for me, even as I was completely unaware of the dimensions and true implications of the cocaine boom's collapse. I knew only that *something* much more immediate had happened in the previous few days, and because of it many were dead. The number I heard was fifteen.

Shocked by the sudden rush of killings, townspeople were doing their best to stay indoors, whereas the Oblate priests I was staying with tried to keep *me* indoors, that is, inside their residence, because the feeling was that the danger had not all passed. Things were just heating up, they said, and victims, well . . . there would be more.

Several of the dead were teenage boys who had belonged to one of the church's youth fellowship groups. Orlando, with whom I had traveled to Aucayacu, said he would not want a rumor to start that he had brought in a "journalist"—that would be me, a pale-skinned American, no less—which could result in the loss of any more of "his people."

Orlando's rumor threat struck me as possibly more imagined than real. All the same, it was effective in keeping me off the streets. It also underscored the peril of appearances: how they might be misinterpreted and how that fear gripped everyone's thoughts. Orlando knew I was not a reporter and that if not for his invitation to get to know the town where he worked I might never have gone to the Huallaga at all. Certainly I had no intention of going there when I arrived in Peru in late May of 1995. My plan was to stay in Lima and do research on a "repentance law" *(ley de arrepentimiento)* that the government of Alberto Fujimori had employed in its war against the country's two leftist guerrilla organizations. As I would learn, the law was more counterinsurgency strategy than pure legal statute. It combined elements of mass propaganda and police and military reconnaissance with prison-sentence reductions and a witness-protection program. The strategy borrowed directly from anti-terrorist laws Italy had used against the Red Brigades in the late 1970s and early 1980s,[13] but it also had roots in other armed conflicts, such as the "hearts and minds" campaigns waged by the British in post–World War II Malaysia and later by the United States in Vietnam.

Like Italy, Peru is a country of largely Christian faith, majority Catholic, though as elsewhere in Latin America Evangelical denominations have acquired increasing influence, most notably since the 1980s. In the context of the internal conflict, "repentance" became an avenue for the Peruvian government to wage battle against the moral, though not overtly religious, dimensions of insurgent political speech by applying ideological pressure on MRTA and Shining Path members, supporters, and their families. Of the program's diverse facets I was most interested in the conversion rituals the military and police had staged with captured insurgents to publicly demonstrate the insurgents' supposed change of heart as well as to provide tangible evidence of government gains.

In Lima I camped out at the offices of a human rights organization that had generously given me access to its extensive press archives. I spent hours sifting through newspaper clippings, taking notes, and arranging interviews with people who were familiar with the law and its effects: mostly lawyers and journalists but also government officials, retired military, and a nun who helped me meet former Party militants released from prison under the leniency provisions of the law. Though "repentance" had been a nationwide strategy, the government claimed its biggest impact had been felt in Upper Huallaga Valley.[14] There, the program been used to recruit Shining Path members into acting as scouts for raids against secret refuges of the Party. In the spring of 1994, the army had held mass repentance ceremonies at the Los Laureles base in Tingo María, where scores of men and women described as "terrorists" had burned red hammer and sickle "rags" and embraced the "true" Peruvian red and white flag.[15] A journalist invited to the events surmised that many of the participants were not members of the Shining Path at all, but poor farmers the army had coerced into showing up for the cameras.[16] This detail didn't stop images of the ceremonies from being presented at face value when broadcast nationally and then retransmitted later during Fujimori's 1995 reelection campaign for the presidency.

Though the Huallaga's connection to the repentance law was clear, I never imagined I would have a chance to visit the region that year. Between what I had heard about the region over the years, what I picked up from recent news reports, and what people at the human rights office told me, I knew that going there without the proper contacts was a reckless idea. Besides, there was enough to do in Lima. Every day I went to the office, where I had a desk and the use of a phone and could arrange for the many interviews I scheduled in the city. Those who worked there soon got used to having me around and began to give me names of people and other leads they thought I might pursue. One morning, one of the lawyers in the group told me about a Catholic priest who had a congregation north of Tingo María. He was visiting Lima that week, and she gave me a number to call. That afternoon, hoping for little more than informative conversation, I went to see Orlando at his order's residence.

As I explained my project to him, Orlando listened carefully. He said that at his church they were familiar with the repentance program and the many abuses that had been committed in its name. He did not elaborate but instead suggested I get to know his community firsthand. There was a lawyer who belonged to his parish who could fill me in on everything I wanted to know. If I liked, I could accompany him when he returned there later that week. Orlando's invitation came with no words of warning or provisos about traveling to the Huallaga. And when I asked him about the precautions I should take, he smiled and said that if I went *with him* there was nothing to worry about.

Two days later we met up, early in the morning, at a bus station off Manco Capac Plaza in the La Victoria district of Lima. Orlando arrived a few minutes after me and asked with a smirk if I was still up for the trip. Passengers were already being called to begin boarding, but Orlando said that before leaving he needed to check with his parish. So he set his bags beside mine and headed for a nearby pay phone.

Moments later Orlando returned, but his expression, cheery just minutes before, was taut and severe. "Something ugly has happened," he said, speaking now barely above a whisper. "There's twelve lights out" *(hay doce focos apagados)*. Aware that I had no context for understanding what he was telling me, Orlando savored my look of confusion for a second and then explained. The church had a radio phone, and his conversations with the parish could easily be intercepted, so they always spoke in code. "'Twelve lights out' means twelve victims," he stated. Who was responsible, Orlando couldn't say. He had been told that "the neighbors" had done it, and he suspected that meant the army, but he would not find out for sure until we arrived in Aucayacu. Apparently the code could confuse even those who supposedly knew it.

"What now?" I asked, fearing he would want me to postpone my visit, almost sure of it. Yet Orlando said in a tone both terse and unpromising that we needed to be "prudent" *(Hay que ser muy prudente)*. I didn't know what he meant, but without saying more he grabbed his bags and with a nod motioned to the bus.

About an hour later, as we departed Corcona, the first police checkpoint east of Lima, and embarked on the steep climb to Ticlio, Orlando handed me a magazine. It was opened to an article about the murder of an American journalist almost six years before who had gone to Uchiza to inquire into the

Peruvian military's involvement with the narcotics trade. The case was old and, because of the victim's nationality, well known. The article told of eyewitnesses who had recently come forward with additional details. According to this latest version, several days before the reporter's body was found dumped on the streets of the town, soldiers had detained him and, claiming he was a DEA agent, handed him over to the Shining Path. The case brought attention to the strange alliances and mixtures made possible by cocaine and insinuated how the dictates of the trade could trump the expected rules of war.

As I glanced over the pages, Orlando remarked: "That's what I mean . . . *hay que ser prudente.*" I bristled a bit at his readiness to draw a direct equivalence between situations: mine now and that of the journalist several years back. The bluntness of Orlando's implied "this could be you" only added to what was beginning to feel like empty advice. I wondered: What good was "prudence," whether as discretion or foresight, when faced with circumstances and places of which I had no familiarity or direct knowledge?

Orlando was either having second thoughts about bringing me along or having some enjoyment at my expense. Maybe a little of both.

Late the following afternoon we were dropped off by a car service in front of the parish grounds in Aucayacu. We had traveled by bus only as far as the city of Huánuco, where we stayed the night, before taking *colectivos* (car services) the rest of the way. Orlando's assistant Saúl met us at the front door of the priests' house and almost immediately began to fill us in on what he knew. He told us about one of the killings he had partially witnessed. A man and a woman, both strangers, had come to town and taken a room at a cheap hotel on Avenida Lima. Saúl said they must have been inside only a moment or two when the man walked back out to the street, this time alone. Seconds later: the sound of gunfire. Saúl heard two shots. Half a block away at the time, he ran to see what had happened. He found the man collapsed at the edge of the road in front of the hotel, blood pouring from a wound to his head and a large hole ripped open on the left side of his chest. As Saúl knelt down beside him and began to perform final rites over the body, he could see the heart exposed through the hole in the chest, beating still.

"In this town, just showing up is the best way to get yourself killed!" Saúl announced while throwing me a knowing look, as if to say I was lucky to be learning the lesson secondhand. The tragic end that often awaited naïve outsiders was a motif I would hear time and again. This potentially lethal state of affairs could be sidestepped, you just had to have someone to cover you—an important social tie. This much I was made to understand: you needed to have a *garantía* (literally, "guarantee"), someone to vouch for you before the townspeople and the groups that operated there. Here began my education in the ways of the Huallaga.

On that first trip, my *garantía* was the church. From what people told me it was a good one, because the parish was the only unarmed institution in town that commanded any respect. Sendero had never attacked it directly, and the army begrudgingly left it alone. This is not to say that the priests and the nuns who worked there took their situation to be anything but precarious, and— except for Saúl, who fancied himself the intrepid one of the bunch—they were fastidious in watching over each other's every move.

Consider the dead man's female companion. She went to the nuns to see if they would receive the body for a wake. But the ranking sister declined, later justifying her refusal to Orlando, saying, "He didn't have any family here in town!" Harsh words, I thought, and yet this was but another sign that, here, any and every action had to be weighed according to how it would play with the "other forces." A lot of energy went into second-guessing the interpretations that different armed groups might attribute to one's own acts and intentions.

secluded places

It was hard to weigh with any degree of precision what was happening in town during my initial visit that year. I didn't know enough about the place or what it was like on a "normal" day. There was nothing that felt ordinary about the atmosphere I sensed or what I heard during the two weeks I spent there. I wanted to see what was happening with my own eyes, but at first I was too confined by the priests—who insisted I stay inside—and by my own wish to respect their good judgment while benefiting from their hospitality. What I can say is that once the critical danger appeared to have passed—three days after I had arrived—and the priests told me it was now safer to come and go, I felt an air of foreboding and intensity in the town unlike anything I had ever experienced. Almost everyone I met during the remainder of that trip spoke with guarded and roundabout words, signaling time and again there was good reason not to be overheard.

Still, there were two places where people expressed themselves openly in my presence: inside the priests' residence—which seemed to enjoy a secure remove from the events outside—and in the storefront of Marusha's old home.

Marusha turned out to be not only the lawyer Orlando had told me about but someone the human rights group in Lima had suggested I contact. Her mother's store was the first place the priests said it was safe for me to go alone. However, even there, where Marusha and I sat inside at one of several wooden tables, the street was close and we talked together in hushed voices.

The threat, it seemed, was in the street, and all the more so for me because I had arrived on no business other than wanting to find out something. The repentance law, people told me, was sensitive—*un tema muy delicado*—which was not at all surprising since the law touched, albeit in opposing directions, both the Shining Path and the state intelligence services. What I came to appreciate more fully through my conversations were the complicated ways the repentance law and strategy directly affected Aucayacu, many details of which had never circulated beyond the strict confines of the local area.[17]

Yet what had most townspeople on edge in late June of 1995 was not the army, and it was not Sendero, at least not in the days I was there. Something else altogether was on everyone's minds, something that made the repentance question seem like old news. A turf war had just erupted between the town's two main drug bosses, Champa and Cristal, for control over the flow of raw cocaine out of the area. Faced with a dwindling local market no longer large enough to support the both of them, the leader of each drug *firma* sent his *sicarios* (hired gunmen) to prowl the streets.

That was the word we got at the priests' residence, which I came to realize was not the worst place to be if you wanted to learn what was going on in town. People were constantly coming by to consult with "Padre Orlando" and to pass on the latest developments.

On account of the most recent violence, many were said to be leaving town, above all the young men, because anyone with the slimmest of ties to either gang was in danger of being killed by the other side. There was talk of a high school girl being hunted down by a group of *sicarios* because she delivered a message scrawled on a piece of notebook paper at the request of her boyfriend. There was also talk of a clandestine airstrip recently repaired and days later blown up. And then there were the police, nowhere to be seen when the killing started, who hit the streets the following day in mad pursuit. In a painstaking house-by-house search they made sure to check underneath the mattresses.

Amid the struggle between the Champa and Cristal gangs were reminders of "that other war," beyond the limits and immediate concerns of the town. One morning a man showed up at the residence to let the padres know

Sendero had killed his sister and three others in a village several kilometers north on the Marginal Highway. The four victims had recently formed a communal council, most likely at the direction of the army, and Sendero, as Orlando later explained, frowned on organizing of any kind. Those who lived in the villages along the highway had over the last fifteen years done their best to cope with the rules and ways of the Party. Now they were being forced to adapt to the demands of the army and its decrees.

Such adjustments were complicated by the fact that Sendero would show up from time to time late at night before disappearing again into the forest. The army's constant patrolling kept the Shining Path from regaining the uncompromising political control it once held over the rural communities on either side of the highway. The Maoists, though greatly weakened, were still formidable enough to make sure no one else moved in to take their place. Villagers were caught in the middle. Each side demanded their allegiances and tried to turn them against the other through threats and explicit violence.

Across the river a different situation reigned. The army entered the west banks of the Huallaga less frequently but with more overt violence, because it still considered the villages of the *banda* as forming part of a de facto Sendero territory. Ample evidence of this point of view had come during massive counterinsurgency operations mounted there in 1992 and then again in 1994. On those occasions the army had made little attempt to distinguish between civilians and "senderistas," or Sendero combatants, treating both as the same enemy slated for elimination.[18]

Meanwhile, in my discussions with Orlando, Saúl, and the nuns I became acutely aware of just how fractured space had become under the political emergency that persisted in the Huallaga. They all impressed upon me the very basic and everyday political obstacles that hindered people's ability to get around. To move along the highway, to move in and out of town, meant answering uncomfortable questions of some kind. With the army and the police, everything depended on showing the right papers at the many checkpoints that lined the route to Tingo María. Many people, they said, had no identification nor any means of obtaining it. Sendero had destroyed municipal civil records whenever it had the chance, and there still was no place north of Tingo María to request new birth certificates or other civil documents to substantiate one's identity.

Of course, reaching Tingo María meant navigating the checkpoints, and without papers one risked arrest and possibly a long and unpleasant detention. Having a valid identification card wasn't enough. At the controls the army and the police compared one's documents against requisition lists of criminal suspects. Many people, I was told, had papers but could not use them because their names appeared on one of the lists. Sendero kept records of its own, and while it had no permanent checkpoints on the highway, sudden encounters with a guerrilla column were not uncommon and could in the short run be far more deadly than encounters with anyone else. Those who still worked actively if surreptitiously in the drug trade had far less to fear from the army or Sendero as long as they didn't leave town, but they always had to be on the lookout for raids by the anti-narcotics police who could roll in unannounced from Tingo María. In the eyes of the police, few who lived in town could claim to be above suspicion altogether. Cocaine had been the only economic force in the Huallaga for the last twenty years. Anyone not directly in the business was involved in one of the supporting trades. Those who had made a good living during the boom in an unrelated trade had been able to do so thanks solely to cocaine. That is what made the ongoing disintegration of the drug economy so devastating.

the project

Such was the tenor of the moment I grasped while staying with the priests, whereas what Marusha shared with me was a preliminary view of the past. In between giving me leads about the repentance law and who else I might talk with, she told me about the local political history and its connection to the drug economy. She also spoke of the area's long and trying relationship with state power imposed from afar: emanating from Lima but channeled most frequently by way of Tingo María. While Saúl, Orlando, and the nuns were outsiders on extended if ultimately temporary assignment to Aucayacu, Marusha's perspective was that of someone identified as native to the town, strongly influenced by a background in legal studies and a discreet but committed advocacy on behalf of human rights causes.

Marusha explained to me that the town's political and legal authorities fell into utter disarray in the late 1970s when the drug trade came to dominate the local economy. Several years before the Shining Path began to organize the valley's rural communities, the pressures of the lucrative commerce in raw cocaine severely eroded the administration of justice and undercut even a minimal trust in municipal and state officials. She said that in those days no problem was too serious for money to resolve. There was no crime that could not be overlooked for a price. Marusha was the first person to tell me this, but over the next several years I would listen as many others expressed what was a constant motif of local historical memory: rampant corruption accompanied the boom and fanned the flames of political violence.

Townspeople who had been present back then tended to talk scornfully about the former state of "the authorities." Anything to do with government in those years had a bad name, they would say, though many reserved their most vitriolic comments for the police, who in the name of "enforcing the law" had spent their time feeding upon the hard-earned dollars of good, working people who were just trying to get ahead. The police's flaunting of Peruvian law, they insisted, had been a major factor in encouraging others to do the same. No wonder the *tombos* were often the brunt of jokes. Moreover, the widespread perception of official corruption pointed to a deeper epistemological quandary that had once plagued everyday life in the Huallaga. For where custodians of the law were on the take, the meanings of words themselves could get confused. A confiscation could look like robbery; an arrest, like a kidnapping—especially when a negotiated payment sufficed to overcome the problem. Just listening to people talk about such things was enough to make one dizzy. So I could only imagine the kinds of disorientation people might have felt, and how difficult it might have been for them to gather their bearings, when words about matters of vital concern could slip so easily away from their expected referents. At the very least it made it easier to grasp why so many people implicitly voiced a desire for clear, straight lines, and why some saw in violence the only remedy for what had become an increasingly confusing state of affairs.

Unchecked corruption figured in every narrative account of the boom, but not everyone agreed about when its worst moment had been. Some said it was before Sendero showed up. Others said it was before the army had decided to put the senderistas in their place—particularly members of the Urbana, who in this alternative interpretation were cast as the most crooked of all. Yet to judge from the claims of official abuse that abounded during the latter half of the 1990s, it was hard to ascertain to what degree there had been a drastic change of character on the part of local officials, much less a good lesson learned by the police. Perhaps money had not lost its power to melt legal barriers at all: there were simply fewer people now who had enough left over to continue doing exactly as they pleased.

In Marusha's account, corruption reached such extremes in the early 1980s that few complained when Aucayacu's elected and appointed officials fled in droves after Sendero began armed incursions on the town. "Everyone resigned," Marusha told me. "Even the school principals left town. At the Ministry of Agriculture, too." Meanwhile, the Civil Guard—the only state institution, she said, that never pulled out—replaced the personnel who had been killed during Sendero's attacks.

Because it was a district capital, Aucayacu had a wide array of representatives of both local and national government. Besides the Civil Guard,[19] there was a municipal council, an office of civil records, a local post of the Ministry of the Interior, a Justice of the Peace, and a public health clinic. The Ministry of Agriculture, Marusha noted, had kept a local office in town since the construction of the Marginal Highway in the mid-1960s. That was during the first government of President Belaúnde Terry (1963–68), when Aucayacu served as one of the administrative centers for the state-run frontier settlement program.[20] Belaúnde returned to the presidency in 1980 following a twelve-year period of military rule. As part of the farm policy of his second government, the Ministry of Agriculture began to share responsibilities for rural settlement support with the newly formed Special Project for the Upper Huallaga (Proyecto Especial del Alto Huallaga, or PEAH).

As one of eight Special Projects funded by the United States for rural development east of the Peruvian Andes, the PEAH's mission was ostensibly to build feeder roads and to encourage the diversification of agriculture and the growth of agribusinesses. The Project's underlying and implicit objective was to steer the Upper Huallaga away from the emergent cocaine trade. Nevertheless, reversing the course of the boom required much more than new infrastructure and fresh promises of government farm aid. This was why "development" not only became code for crop substitution, it was given a repressive arm. A special branch of the Civil Guard—the Mobile Rural Patrol Unit (Unidad Móvil de Patrullaje Rural, or UMOPAR)—was formed in 1981 to carry out anti-narcotics raids in the countryside. Work crews of manual coca leaf eradicators were assembled two years later by a new government office known as CORAH—Control y Reducción de los Cultivos de Coca en el Alto Huallaga (Control and Reduction of Coca Cultivation in the Upper Huallaga). Taken together, crop substitution, mobile police units, and coca eradication teams would serve as the signature pieces of a new regional anti-narcotics strategy designed, financed, and directed from Washington.

Aucayacu was chosen to be one of the PEAH's centers of operations. The agency took up residence in a large rectangular grassy field enclosed by tall cinderblock walls on the northeast side of town. Multiple-bedroom wood houses were built inside for its employees. The matching façades of those and of other interior buildings gave the place the air of a company-run outfit, and years later locals would still refer to the compound as the "Proyecto" even though the agency had long since ceased to direct its programs from there.

Marusha told me the Project had initially been one of the most prestigious places in town to hold a job. The agency retained a large staff of engineers, agronomists, and economists as well as mechanics and other support personnel. However, in June of 1984, after Sendero launched its second and most brazen attack on the Civil Guard station in Aucayacu, martial law was declared in the Huallaga and most of the Project's staff were pulled back to Tingo María—together with the other legal authorities and state employees who abandoned town. A small local annex was left to manage its affairs. In their place, the Civil Guard relocated its headquarters behind the Project's protective walls as the military arrived in town to organize the state's response to Sendero. Although the army set up its first base on the second floor of the municipal hall on the main plaza of town, eventually it, too, took up permanent residence in the compound, not far from the Civil Guard. Until the mid-1990s the Project served at one time or another as the physical home for all state institutions in Aucayacu. Whereas Tingo María was the nearest point of safe retreat for all agencies and government officials, for the ones who in Aucayacu stayed or later returned, the compound became the place of refuge. As such, the Project would become for many years the most condensed expression of the Peruvian state: for the functionaries it protected but also for the unspeakable acts committed there by its armed agents in the purported "defense of the nation."

During the ten years following the flight of civil authorities there was no state-run administration of justice in town. Under the terms of martial law, the settling of legal disputes within Peruvian law fell to the armed forces: in this case, to the army. Nevertheless, few townspeople sought its services, because the eyes of a thinly veiled Shining Path presence were ever upon them. "No one went to file a complaint," Marusha said, "because they would have been taken for a snitch." Instead, many quietly went to Sendero, though Marusha could not elaborate on the Maoists' role in resolving local disputes. Having spent much of that time away at the university, there were gaps in her knowledge. She did say that the army, despite its permanent presence, did little for several years to inhibit the actions of the Shining Path. As a result, no justice of the peace dared to reside in town on a permanent basis. "Not that the government ever failed to fill the post," she explained, "simply that the appointees refused to come. At most they would keep an office in Tingo María and visit from time to time." This did not change until the army began to destroy the Urbana in the late 1980s.

Marusha would have a chance to become intimately familiar with the legal situation that had prevailed in Aucayacu only much later, in 1994—already the twilight of the boom—when she returned to live in town and took a job as a law clerk for the justice of the peace as she saved the money she needed for the bar exam. Working for the prosecution of narcotics-related cases, she got to know hands-on the ins and outs of her new profession while gaining an enhanced perspective on the social problems facing the Huallaga. This is what Marusha was doing when I met her in 1995, when she gave me the first narrative frame I would have for understanding the recent history of the town and of the lands that lay beyond—a frame that traced the decay, flight, and return of Peruvian procedural law.

In the months following my first visit to the Huallaga, a district court opened just outside the walls of the Project. Shortly thereafter, Marusha, attorney's license finally in hand, would quit her law clerk job and rent a space across the street next to a cockfighting ring. There she would share offices with a handful of other lawyers—all of them out-of-towners from Lima, Huánuco, and Tingo María—who had been attracted perhaps by dreams of reaping windfalls from the narcotics cases that might well dominate the docket of the new court.

Her competition would not stick around for long. Maybe, as Marusha's brother Nico later boasted, it was just no good going head to head with "a local girl." Or maybe it was because the pool of lucrative clients dried up as *narcos* skipped town to avoid prosecution or even to escape the severe crisis of the trade—the hostilities between Champa and Cristal being only its most explosive symptom.

Whatever the reason, their departure left Marusha the only practicing attorney in town. And for the next few years she would embody—on this very local level—a new figure of law for those who sought her services: above all the most desperate, destitute, and politically squeezed of rural families. In Marusha they would find an inviting face, one that seemed to say "yes, in these new times, there is a real possibility of justice through law"—that is, through the legal system of the Peruvian state.

horizons

Alongside considerable changes in political and legal conditions, several broad phenomena exemplified the "time in between" of immediate post-boom. Coca and raw cocaine ceased to be the dominant productive and commercial activity of the Upper Huallaga as their market value fell well below minimum levels required for a capital return. It became increasingly difficult to move cocaine paste out of the region. The problems stemmed in large part from the successful disruption of clandestine aerial trade routes to and from Colombia by the Peruvian Air Force. With the help of U.S. anti-narcotics and intelligence agencies, the elimination of air transport turned out to be perhaps the most successful of all state strategies for killing the boom. It completely altered the economic rhythm of the trade. Suddenly, there was no quick way to get the product out, and the ripples were felt at all levels.

When transactions stopped revolving at the rate allowed by the flights, the social life of the boom, in all its staggering speed, came to a no less breathtaking stop. In Aucayacu, local drug traders such as Cristal and Champa had no means for staying solvent or even for ensuring the complacence of the Civil Guard through payoffs. They were forced to flee, go into hiding, or suffer imprisonment. Furthermore, the Peruvian state's (re)constitution of its political and legal bureaucracy in the towns created the expectation of a progressive expansion of state law over the entire valley, even as the foundation of its rule was, for the time being, geographically limited to a network of army bases along the Marginal Highway. From those points of secured territory and in step with classic counterinsurgency tactics, government agencies would offer to build rural schools and roads, promoted as dividends of "peace," while the army applied pressure on villages to appoint communal presidents and lieutenant governors as the only way to get their share of development assistance. During this period, levels of violence dropped severalfold from what had been common during the times of boom, though without disappearing altogether. The Shining Path would try to call the Peruvian state's emerging political hegemony into question by raiding villages along the highway, by executing communal officials or anyone they suspected of spying, by ambushing the police and army patrols, and by making pleas to the local population for support. Yet their actions were too sporadic and too locally focused to reverse the basic equation of power in the valley as a whole.

This was the scenario that prevailed in the immediate aftermath of the boom, when people still claimed coca was all but finished. As the decade of the 1990s came to a close, however, signs appeared that suggested coca's status was undergoing another transformation. In the economic order of things, switching to legal crops had brought far more headaches than prosperity, and in the towns there were murmurings that the price of coca was on the rebound. Rumor had it that many farmers, dissatisfied with the weak or negligible returns they were getting out of crops of bananas, papaya, and rice, were looking to make a serious go at coca once again.

A transition seemed to be underfoot toward another era in which coca would have a renewed economic, political, and social-historical potential, albeit under new terms and conditions. This time coca would not form a single-crop economy but would be cultivated alongside, and under the cover of, a more diversified, legal agriculture. For its part, the cocaine trade would operate out of sight and with little of the reckless abandon that had epitomized the boom at its heights. Wholesale cocaine markets would no longer be located in the main towns but dispersed, and harder to pinpoint, in select and ever-shifting areas of the countryside. Nor would the Upper Huallaga be the epicenter of a revamped cocaine economy, as it had been throughout the 1980s, but merely one of several coca-growing and cocaine regions—where the production would no longer be restricted to an inferior *pasta básica* (cocaine base) but would churn out full-grade hydrochloride instead.

As coca cultivation increased, the United States renewed pressures on the Peruvian government to step up eradication operations. With much less to fear from a now militarily depleted Shining Path, it was easier for the government to comply aggressively with U.S. requests. When it did, Huallaga-area farmers became infuriated and began a series of organized protests in late 2000 against the government and its anticoca agrarian policies. Those protests evolved over the next couple of years into a vocal though not always united grassroots movement.

For the first time in nearly two decades, coca farmers in the Upper Huallaga Valley, above all those north of Tingo María, could organize themselves politically into associations free of the influence or control of the Shining Path.[21] At times their new associations joined forces with coca-grower organizations from other areas of the country—the valleys of Monzón, Apurímac-Ene, Aguaytía, and Pichis-Palcazu—and staged regional strikes and long marches on Lima to oppose government eradication efforts and crop substitution programs.[22] The imminently rural character of the Huallaga *cocalero* (coca farmer) struggle left the towns to play an ever-ambiguous role in the face-off between the interdiction pressures of the government and the political-economic demands of coca growers. The appearance of the *cocaleros* as a new political force strongly suggested that the valley had entered a new era: that the in-between time of immediate post-boom had come to a close.

The factors involved in this historical transformation were various and complex. In the Andes as a whole, the impact of interdiction efforts against major Colombian cartels and the eventual breakdown of the Peruvian coca economy had resulted in a rearrangement of the regional map of the trade. By the late 1990s, a majority share of coca cultivation had shifted to Colombia into areas controlled, and fought over, by the leftist FARC and right-wing paramilitaries. Bolivian coca would also garner a larger share of the international market, as growers from the Chapare emerged as a national political force over their opposition to U.S.-backed eradication policies. In Peru, meanwhile, the cocaine economy slowly recovered as new trade routes were forged. With airspace under continual surveillance, cocaine traveled by land and river as it had before the boom. Now those routes would lead less toward Colombia and more toward Peruvian coastal ports as well as to Ecuador, Chile, and Brazil.

In the Huallaga, the gradual recuperation of the drug trade did not stay the Shining Path's overall decline. The Party was no longer powerful enough to dictate the terms of political activity in the countryside as it had done for many years. It could not impose itself on the rural population as the only option of political representation, nor enforce its wish that Party activities be the sole form of engaging in politics. Going forward, who would exercise state power was not in question. For the foreseeable future, politics would happen on a different footing, one in which the recourse to spectacular violence—and thus the power over life and death—was far less in play. This was because the Peruvian state had largely prevailed in the battle for political sovereignty.

In the years prior to the rise of the *cocaleros*, however, the horizons of the state's law were still fragile and inconsistently distributed across the valley. What's more, the past continued to overshadow the present. People's efforts to make sense of the boom years registered the weight of that past, when cocaine had intersected with political violence, only—in the end—for the Peruvian state to acquire the upper hand. Nonetheless, the brutal reassertion of state sovereignty strongly influenced the temporal structure of the political present. There, within expanding topographical boundaries, the state's dominance conferred a perceptible direction to the times of post-boom. That direction would impart interpretative pressure upon what had come to pass and what now could be. Attempts to account for recent history thus had to contend, consciously or not, with orientations toward past and future, which had been forged through violent struggles for power affecting what could be thought and said.

The post-boom emerged amid this gradual but fierce affirmation of Peruvian state rule. Its law was still tenuous in the countryside, but once townspeople felt assured it was in the valley to stay, a chasm seemed to open between eras of time. The chasm was a fold separating boom from its aftermath, which grew into a hard crease in the ways people spoke about the past. The fold was also a temporal frontier separating boom events from their narration. Along it traveled a historically produced sense that animated how local understandings of that earlier era would be expressed.

Here that frontier becomes a special concern of ethnography. This is because ethnography's methodological focus on the lived present creates possibilities for appreciating the intensive modes of ambience that inhabit moments in time and may give them a singular presence. To do so, ethnographic practice strives to get ever closer to events and to find a manner to make that proximity come alive on the page.

2 shooting in pacae

may 27, 1998

"Alex is gonna kill me," Mariela said, as soon as we turned the corner and saw the brown sedan pulling away from the curb and driving off. We slowed our hurried pace to a stroll, weighted down with bags of supplies, and walked the remaining two blocks in silence.

The problem wasn't transportation. There would be other cars for a while yet. In fact we could already see a maroon and surprisingly new Toyota pulling up in front of the office of the local Comité de Autos and a passenger's belongings on the curb waiting to be loaded. Mariela's concern was simply the time. Dusk was setting in, and she knew she would get an earful from her husband, Alex, for not returning before dark.

When we got to the stop the *embalador*, or "car packer," assured Mariela with a grin that as soon as three more riders showed up, we'd be off. So we found a place to sit inside the office on a long wooden bench. The *embalador* followed behind us, grabbed our things, and started working them into the trunk of the Toyota.

Sitting not far from us was the only other passenger who had shown up so far—a man dressed in the professional attire of a government employee, with a small brown portfolio of documents clutched to his side. "He works at the Ministry of Agriculture," Mariela whispered to me, as if sensing my question, though I knew she was asking herself something else: How long would it be before we could take off? We were already pushing on five o'clock, and with her wristwatch Mariela nervously began to keep close track of our progress.

Midafternoon was the peak time to travel. Though after five, and as night-fall approached, demand for cars to Aucayacu would fall off. This was silent recognition that "things" happened on the highway after dark. By five-thirty it became increasingly hard to catch a way out of Tingo María; and after six, passengers might just have to wait until morning. It all depended on riders; if there weren't enough, the *colectivo* stayed put. Which was why Alex had urged us to get back while it was still light and why Mariela was now fretting.

A good twenty minutes passed before two more passengers appeared. They were a middle-aged couple who ran a filling station down the street from Mariela's store. The man—looking quite relaxed in a blue sports shirt and tan windbreaker, and with hands tucked deep into trouser pockets—lingered at the curb to make sure several packages were stowed to satisfaction. The woman, meanwhile, walked into the office and acknowledged Mariela with a simple "Señora . . ." before finding a place to stand at the far end of the wooden bench against a white plaster wall; from there, in between sorting the interior of a black handbag and pressing the wrinkles out of her matching skirt, she gazed distractedly at her partner, who didn't come to join her but stayed out-side to talk with a group of Comité employees.

Mariela responded to the woman's greeting with a slight nod of the head, only to go back to glancing at her watch and to wondering if the sixth and final passenger we needed would ever arrive. That was when the *embalador* unexpectedly motioned us to take our seats. The car was about to leave, even without the final fare-paying passenger. As we were ushered in, the driver was already behind the wheel, and when the last door slammed shut he turned the key and raced the engine a few times. Reaching to adjust the rearview mirror, he quickly studied who was riding in the backseat and then, as he inched the car forward, told a pair of drivers standing nearby that he wanted to get home early and call it day.

I had known Mariela since my first visit to the Upper Huallaga Valley in 1995. She and her husband Alex ran a general store in Aucayacu. A friendship grew up between us, and on my subsequent visits I was always welcomed into their home. Now, three years after our acquaintance and a month since I had re-turned to begin extended fieldwork, Mariela asked me to go with her for the day to Tingo María so she could introduce me to several people at the agrarian university where her son Nestor studied. Tingo María was the nearest city and thus the cheapest place to buy supplies. It was also the location of the provincial government and of the only commercial banks within a few hours by car. So if you were a merchant, a local politician, or a civil servant, regular trips to Tingo María were a part of living and working in Aucayacu. In my case, during that first year of what became my doctoral research, I worked as a volunteer instructor at the local teachers college and at one of the town's high schools as I learned the ropes of being an ethnographer. As such, I was nominally identified as a teacher but more so as an unusual stranger to the area. Local inhabitants were unaccustomed to having U.S. nationals in their midst, whom they couldn't help but associate with the foreign government that since the late 1970s had designed and financed intrusive and highly destructive strategies of anti-narcotics enforcement in the Upper Huallaga Valley.

The Comité office sat a half block from Tingo María's central market and directly across the street from the two other means of public transport that went to Aucayacu. There was La Marginal, a small, green and white bus or "micro" whose boxlike hull was so full of dents and fractures and rust—gnawing away at every broken edge—that it looked as if it had been around almost as long as the road for which it was named. Unlike the *colectivo* sedans that provided express, nonstop service to Aucayacu and departed only when there were enough passengers to fill them, the micro left on a regular timetable, regardless of the number of seats it had filled, and stopped at any and all points in between, picking up and dropping off people and cargo along the way. The fare was cheap at two sols (roughly sixty U.S. cents), a third of what the sedans charged, and like all micros in Peru, La Marginal was roomy and slow. It required an hour and a half, or double the time of the Comité sedans, to run the distance between Tingo María and Aucayacu.

Parked in front and behind the micro were a couple of younger Toyota vans. The *combis*, as they were called, were far more cramped than the micro or even the *colectivo*. For half a sol more than La Marginal, they did the trip in a just over an hour. Like the *colectivo*, they left only once the seats filled up, but passengers could get on and off anywhere along the way. When there was no place to sit, people stood stooped over in the aisle, their heads banging against the low aluminum roof with every bump in the road. While preparing to depart, the *combi* driver's assistant would scan the street and sidewalks for potential recruits. *Au-ca-YA-cu! Aucayacu!* he would yell, ready to descend upon anyone who so much as looked the part of the traveler, pulling at their bags, promising that the van was about to leave, or whatever it took to coax them over and into a seat. The *embaladores* of the Comité could be just as combative, whenever they had just one seat to fill, but as a rule they never fought with the *combis* for passengers. They had different clientele and most of the time they ignored each other, such was the breach between their respective worlds.

Beyond such functional details of price, speed, and space, the distinct modes of mass transit reflected a hierarchy of not so subtle distinctions in class and station, which in the Huallaga Valley were not always apparent at first glance. People who took the micro tended to be peasants from the highlands, landless agricultural workers, and the urban poor whose lack of access to currency made considerations of price win out over those of time or comfort. People who preferred the *combis*, meanwhile, were generally those who could afford to have no spare time. They were a rural middle class with tight schedules to meet—village teachers, small shopkeepers, itinerate salespeople, and landowning farmers, many of whom kept residences or had family they stayed with whenever necessary in Aucayacu or Tingo María. For them, the small increase in fare over the microbus was all but inconsequential as they moved with far greater ease between city and country. Less so the peasants and poorest of farmers who had difficulty staying for any length of time in urban areas, where "everything was money."

The Comité's cars, meanwhile, served the professional and merchant classes of Aucayacu: doctors and nurses, engineers and affluent shopkeepers, teachers and civil servants. They were town folk of relative means with few immediate or lasting ties to the countryside. In large part detached from the war that continued in the expanses between the towns of the Huallaga, they lived less exposed but also less versed in the arts of survival. It was only when they traveled along the Marginal Highway that they ever ran the risk of having to confront the violence face on. And for them, everything on either side of the thin line of the road was danger and foreboding.

The *colectivo* sedans had seats for four not counting the driver, one in front, three in back, but as a rule the *embalador* packed in—hence his name— an extra two bodies. This not only meant one more in the back than there was space for, but that someone had to sit next to the driver on a cushion lodged between the two front bucket seats, which, when running over holes or going around sharp curves, could make for a pretty uncomfortable ride. No fewer than six passengers made for a full car, and it was rare for a *colectivo* to depart with less. Even so, a Comité driver struggled to break even. At six sols a head, the best he could collect each way was ten dollars. From this he had to subtract his dues to the Comité, pay for gas, and make repairs. It was a wonder he had anything left over.

The sun had dipped below the horizon of the valley by the time our car wended its way through the paved streets of Tingo María and began to head northeast on the Central Highway. The city lights were only then coming on, and they continued with us for several minutes—filling station signs aglow and scattered incandescent bulbs dangling from the ceilings of roadside shops and farmhouses on the outskirts—before falling back. Soon the traffic of cars and three-wheeled taxis became lighter and lighter until we had the road and its enveloping darkness to ourselves.

Mariela and I had been given the back seat. She sat behind the driver, I next to her with the Agriculture employee on my right, while the couple shared the front.

There wasn't much talking on the trip between Tingo María and Aucayacu. People faced forward and kept to themselves. Occasionally, if the driver knew one of the passengers, he might strike up conversation to ease the monotony of a run he made several times a day, though it was far more common for there to be complete silence from the ride's beginning to end.

Ever since my first trip to Aucayacu, there was an unmistakable tension that permeated this journey, brief as it was—only forty-five minutes, at most an hour. This time, deprived of the light of day, the stress seemed greater. I suspected it had everything to do with knowingly going against the "word," against that common sense rooted in the local knowledge of the Huallaga of what one should and shouldn't do. Anyone who had lived there, even for a short while, knew there were basic rules of how to avoid unnecessary problems or trouble—rules that changed depending on the fluidity of "the situation"; all the more so now that we were well into "the season": twenty-seven days since May Day; nine since the anniversary of Shining Path's armed struggle; eleven more to go until Peruvian Flag Day.[1] Not traveling after dark was one of those rules. While Mariela was not looking forward to how Alex would react to our indiscretion of leaving Tingo María so late, I presumed part of her concern stemmed from the potential hazards of trip itself.

As for what was going on in the minds of the others, I could only wonder.

Whatever they were thinking and feeling, fifteen minutes out of Tingo María the air in the car grew heavy as we neared La Garganta del Diablo (Devil's

Throat), a long, slender passage hemmed in by jagged walls of rock and earth that extended for fifty meters or more of road. This stretch of road lay in the remnant of a large hill that had been cut through years earlier to clear a path for the highway. Once a vehicle entered the narrow passage, it was impossible to pull off the road quickly and turn about. Because of this, the pass had become a notorious place for bandits to hold up traffic. La Garganta, as a physical feature of the landscape, was nature pressed into the service of crime . . . late in the day or in the very early hours of the morning.

As we entered the open-air tunnel, the silence in the car intensified as everyone held back not just words but breathing itself. Yet when we sped through without a hitch and barreled into a long arc that veered to the east, a momentary relaxing followed, as the driver braked and then made a sharp left onto the Marginal Highway. It was roughly here that the outer reaches of Tingo María gave way to another threshold, one that pushed northwest toward the town of Aucayacu and the rest of the Huallaga Valley.

We traveled a kilometer up the gray, patchy asphalt of the Marginal until we came to the first checkpoint. Here the army had a small garrison on top of a steep bluff from which it kept watch over a trestle bridge crossing the Tulumayo River. The garrison was not visible from this direction of the road; the only thing indicating the army's presence was a rustic bamboo-and-palm leaf sentry box that sat at the foot of the bluff to the left of the highway. This evening the sentry post looked empty. Even so, our driver eased the car slowly over the gravel floor—ready in case someone bolted out and ordered him to stop—before accelerating across the bridge.

The road meandered through the hills for a couple of kilometers until we reached another bridge and just on the other side of it another army checkpoint. This one was known as Pendencia for the tributary that flowed under the bridge. Though we found it as vacant and silent as the one at Tulumayo, this time our driver barely slowed before gunning the engine and hurling us into the next curve. It appeared that with the onset of night all the soldiers had retreated to the safety of their bases. Not that any of us in the car complained. An unmanned checkpoint was one less obstacle on the road and only meant we'd be getting home that much sooner.

As we put some distance on Pendencia, the hills that now hugged the Marginal Highway on the right gradually dropped away before a wide, grassy plain, which spread out underneath a cloud-splotched night sky. Here the road bent slowly to the left before locking into a long straightaway. Halfway down this stretch was the third checkpoint on the way to Aucayacu, a place called Santa Lucía, named for a tiny village that overlooked the highway from a distance. Few who traveled the Marginal knew Santa Lucía, the community; for most, this was merely the place where the anti-narcotics unit of the Civil Guard got its chance to bring traffic to a halt.

As we approached, a thin fog hovered barely above the tarmac and rose up into the night. From a hundred meters out we could see three thin, luminous beams flickering about playfully in the middle of the road. Below them several dark, humanlike forms wandered about. Unlike the army, the Civil Guard kept watch round the clock, and as we closed in on them the thin beams turned toward the car and became flashlights flagging us to stop.

Everyone knew the routine: "Get out of the car and line up!"—outside the lime green cement shack on the left side of the road—"Identification papers in hand!" While agents sifted through the car looking for weapons, drugs, or contraband, one by one the passengers would be called inside to stand before a metal desk where an officer would review their documents and cross-reference them against their register of fugitives and outstanding warrants.

The Civil Guard claimed its presence in Santa Lucía was necessary in order to stay the flow of criminals and illegal goods, yet most Huallaga locals viewed the *controles* (police checkpoints) as little more than a scheme for the cops to drum up extra income. Along Peru's main highways, minor though sometimes major infractions of the law were treated as opportunities to require a bribe in exchange for letting people continue on their way. The police were famous for finding pretexts for asking for money or inventing them when none could be found. Deliberately misreading travelers' papers, asserting they were expired or even counterfeit, was a regular ploy at checkpoints all over Peru— a sort of first line of deception to test the intelligence or attentiveness of the person being "controlled." However, the Upper Huallaga Valley's reputation for generalized illegality only exacerbated the police's willingness to aim way beyond the limits of its own legal authority. During the most heady years of the cocaine boom the Peruvian police had not been content with bribes alone but had practiced, wherever possible, a rampant confiscation of anything of value, as if entitled by some strange right to spoils snatched in the fight against narcotics. Some of that sense of prerogative still seeped into the present situation of post-boom through the police's insinuation that many if not most people from the region were either *narcos* or lived off one. Even several years

after the trade in raw cocaine had gone completely underground, this impli-
cation translated into unusual and at times exacting demands on the lives of
everyday people, that is, whenever they needed to travel.

Carrying even moderate amounts of cash was a bad idea without some
very convincing way of demonstrating the money had been legally obtained.
People even avoided traveling with such personal items as radios or Walk-
mans unless they had the original sales receipt, out of fear of losing them at
the *controles*. Days were long and lonely at Santa Lucía, and it was best not to
give the police cause for temptation. For nothing, not even having the right
paperwork in hand, could completely shield travelers from the charge that
their personal effects had been purchased with drug money.

Over the next few years I would see checkpoint encounters between locals and police become less tense and more automatic, but in 1998 there was
nothing certain about passage through Santa Lucía. At times it seemed that
everything boiled down to the mood of the officers that chance put in one's
path, and what they thought they could get away with. Even when nothing
improper happened, there was always the potential that it could.

On that score, people doled out plenty of advice: be wary, don't leave yourself open to surprise, and never look scared, unsure, or weak. Because it was
in the push and pull of that face-to-face encounter with the police that the line
of their law, and your fate within it, would be drawn.

Luckily tonight the Civil Guards didn't seem very concerned with the passengers and contented themselves with shining their torches at us through the
windows. Only the driver had to get out, hand over his license and vehicle
registration, and open the trunk. This seemed to be the signal for three or four
women and children who had been waiting in the wings—a shallow, dirt-bare
ditch on the right side of the road next to several food stands. They rushed
over to the car and held up small bags of yuca rings, peanuts, and fried plantains against the windows. "Buy from me! Buy from me!" they insisted for the
half minute it took a Civil Guardsman to poke around back, hand the driver
his documents, and wave us on.

From here the road continued straight for a good five kilometers before
reaching Pueblo Nuevo and, not far after, its sister community, Anda—both
small villages that lined either side of the Marginal. People from Aucayacu say
that it was here that the cocaine boom first got its start back in the mid-1970s
before constant raids by the police forced it across the river as well as farther

up the road to the larger towns that lay to the north. Those were the early days when making and running drugs was not only something new and exciting but also a discreet and well-guarded activity. In those days, they say, the white balls of *la bruta* never circulated out in the open, the drug labs stayed tucked away in the hills, and transactions were done in Peruvian sols. Dollars were still unknown. But in Anda and Pueblo Nuevo, the signs of boom were hard to miss. Hard to miss in the newcomers who arrived from all over to turn the twin farming villages overnight into thriving one-street towns, if only for a year or maybe two. Hard to miss in the motorcycles that became the rage together with the small cars, the same Toyota sedans later prized by the *colectivo* drivers, some of which—twenty years later—looked like they'd been around ever since. Hard to miss, too, in the parties that happened every night and lasted until the beer ran dry or the sun came up. Guns were rare in those days. Few possessed them and even then nothing bigger than a revolver. The trade had yet to turn violent.

But as we drove by now under the cover of night, there was little that pointed to those earlier, more ebullient times. The *narcos* of Anda and Pueblo Nuevo had long since moved on and the villages themselves had returned to a slower, more rural cycle. Here, late in the day as the air blew coolly off the Huallaga River, the highway became a place of casual congregation for children and adults alike. They would sit at the edge of the road or on top on the asphalt itself in the dark and talk. It was as if they took the road for themselves, oblivious to the scattered flow of traffic, such that it was not uncommon for drivers to have to honk or even swerve suddenly to avoid running someone over. More often, drivers just pressed down on the pedal, forcing villagers to scurry off as best they could. The army had maintained bases in both villages ever since it occupied them in the early 1990s, but tonight—just as at Tulumayo and Pendencia—we found their highway checkpoints empty and drove straight through.

Leaving Anda, the Marginal held north for a short distance before shifting to the east. From Santa Lucía to Anda, the highway had marked a course parallel and in close proximity to the swift currents of the Huallaga River. Here, however, it pulled away, moving eastward for several kilometers until coming to a small tributary known as Pacae, where the road made a kinklike turn back to the west before reestablishing its path farther out and again parallel to the river. Experienced from the car, the kink was a hook shape that moved first to the right, then to the left, and then back to the right. Halfway into the first turn, there was a short, squat cement bridge that lifted the road across the stream, but we didn't get that far. Our driver braked hard when a lanky figure stepped out into the middle of the road and marched toward us, one hand extended, the other clutching a rifle.

"Bandits?" murmured hopefully the señora in front. But the rest of us well knew, at Pacae, that couldn't be right. "No," the driver said as he brought us to a stop. "It's *THEM*."

The man with the gun yelled at us to turn off the headlights, and out they went. Then he shouted in the direction of a pair of rustic sheds below the left shoulder of the road where a group of people appeared to be gathered in the shadows. His voice was coarse, aggressive, more bark than word. *¡Prisa! ¡Prisa!* (Hurry up! Hurry up!)

I could feel the Ministry bureaucrat next to me, slowly stiffen up in his seat while both hands pressed down on the brown bundle of paper perched on his lap. I could see our driver shaking his head. I could hear him mutter, *Piña . . . piña ¿Por qué tuvimos que ser los primeros?*[2]

Because that's what we were: the first ones to fall, *los primeros en caer*, as people would say—like when you fell into a trap, were duped, or otherwise got taken. In the Huallaga it was believed to be a hugely infelicitous stroke to be at the head of the random flow of traffic when it happened; that is, right at that instant when you, and no one else but you, sped haplessly around the bend of a road only to have robbers or the guerrilla—these days it was not so easy to tell them apart—appear out of nowhere and catch you in their snare. Especially when five, three, even two minutes before a car or truck or motorcycle had gone through that same pass or turn without any problem. It was doubly bad luck, because if you weren't the first you had at least a fighting chance of throwing the car into reverse and hightailing it out of there before the assailants could get off a shot. But being first in line, there wasn't a whole lot you could do, short of making a foolhardy move that was sure to get you killed. And so you were screwed, even jinxed, or as our driver grumbled, you were *piña*, which was somewhere in between.

The guy with the gun walked up to the car. He seemed young—late teens, early twenties. Clad entirely in black, he had a long cloth wrapped around his head, covering all but his eyes and mouth. When he got to the driver's window, I looked down, hoping he wouldn't see me. No longer yelling, he gave instructions with cool, practiced words. "Bring the car around," he motioned to the right. "Cut the engine. Sit tight."

As our driver moved to comply, another Toyota appeared behind us. It was not one of the Comité's assortment of *colectivos*, more likely a car bound for Tocache, and the kid who now commanded us ran over to them, waving his gun, telling them to turn off the lights.

A minute later both cars were parked across the highway, leaving the pass completely blocked. Inside our car no one said a thing, expectant for what was about to happen and what the armed guy's plans, and those of his still unseen cohort, would be.

I had thought about this moment so often I had lost track of the times. Running into the guerrilla was always a possibility in the Huallaga. In fact, continually thinking about the likelihood of such an encounter was one condition of frequenting the region—a contingency that haunted the experience, mine and others', of being there. Such was the brutal mystique of Sendero Luminoso. Shining Path—so extreme, so ready to render justice even for a revolution already run into the ground.

There was nothing predictable about such run-ins except that they were inextricably permeated by the threat of death. And to judge from the stories people told, in the moment of encounter it was a toss-up as to whether "reason" would prevail, which is not to say the historically mandated Reason on which the Party claimed a privileged hold, but rather a purely discursive reason predicated upon that minimal space of time required to talk things out. Dialogue with the guerrilla could quickly degrade into a one-sided frantic pleading to spare one's life . . . or so went the stories. And that was the risk: that the one in charge, like the guy on the road who held us now in check, would be completely unapproachable, utterly beyond the reach of words.

I turned to look at Mariela for a clue as to what she was thinking, and perhaps for a little reassurance as well. She was sitting there motionless and withdrawn. Beneath the shadows her face appeared long and tight. She looked as if transfixed, her eyes so open that the lids had completely disappeared into the recesses of her head. I couldn't tell if she was scared, incredibly concentrated, or caught in some intersection of the two. She didn't return my glance at first, but when she did, she held it for a second without saying a word and then nodded slightly as if to say, "hold on, we can only wait and see."

We had talked about this eventuality before. Mariela had even rehearsed what she would say. I was to be her niece's husband visiting from Lima, and that would make it okay. A family tie created a plausible alibi for my presence, or so she hoped. At the very least, it was a plan. Tonight, if it came to that, she would vouch for me, much like that time in the late 1980s when she had covered for a Cuban doctor who had come to stay with her family for a few weeks. Mariela would vouch for me. While far from a sure bet, it was better than the next to nothing I could do *for her* in this situation.

If ever since the start of the boom the Huallaga had turned plain skittish toward strangers, seeing in every new face a potential spy or police informer, no one was as zealous as the Shining Path in carrying paranoia to the extreme. Over time, others too would learn to imitate its ways, thus it was always necessary to provide explicit cover for one's visitors. And so when the Cuban doctor arrived, for anyone who asked, he became Mariela's *cuñado*, the husband of a sister she didn't have back in Ancash, and on the strength of that claim she and Alex's brothers took him almost anywhere he wanted to go. They took him to friends' farms on the other side of the river and to the hamlets and small villages just north of Aucayacu, even to see family in Tocache. In and through Shining Path territory they went, and wherever they were stopped, they covered for their guest and never had any problems at all.

However, the late 1980s was another time altogether. Then, the Shining Path was still ascendant in the Huallaga and looked as if it might be on its way to rule the country one day—something that in retrospect was as hard to believe as it was easy to forget. In those days Sendero was a shadow law in Aucayacu and openly ruled in the countryside. That fact alone made the Party much closer and far more accessible to people who lived in the Huallaga than it was during the time of my visits. Back then, there were few in town who did not know someone in Sendero and how to suss out where it stood. There were sure means for getting and keeping in touch, and a far greater margin existed for working things out. Not that maneuvering in those times was ever easy, but there were ways, and there were ways because there were channels. Familiarity counted for something and so did one's word when problems or questions arose, especially if you were from one of the more affluent families. Because for as much as the Shining Path championed the interests of the poorest of the rural poor, the landless peasant being the emblematic figure here, it didn't refrain from seeking out ties with the merchant elite of the towns, an elite to which Mariela belonged.

But the days of a closer, more familiar Sendero began to fade in the early 1990s after the Peruvian army decided to retake the valley. When that happened, the senderistas people had come to know fled or died or landed in jail. It was in the large towns that the Shining Path first became scarce because that was where the army began its offensive in earnest. But as counterinsurgency operations moved on to rural villages and farms, Sendero went into hiding there as well. In no time, locating a familiar emissary or militant in the Party became more and more rare, just as the risks for trying to do so increased. The army stayed on the lookout for anyone who collaborated or provided logistical support to the guerrilla, and in the eyes of the military there was no contact with Sendero that wasn't aiding the foe.

"The problem with Sendero now," Mariela had told me more than once, "is that it's all new people. You don't know them, and they don't know you." Because of this, she would say, not only were they harder to gauge, there wasn't any way to know exactly who you were talking to. It might be some-one willing to hear you out, it might be someone only looking to extort money or to kill you . . . or it might not be the Shining Path at all, but an informer for the police or army intelligence. After nearly a decade of unrelenting counterinsurgency, the guerrilla was a pared down, financially strapped and ever more fractured group. The Sendero across the river from Aucayacu did not necessarily know or communicate with the Sendero that gathered around villages on the road to Tingo María, or with the Sendero in communities on the way to Tocache. Having good relations with someone who appeared to speak for the Party in one place didn't help much if you went anywhere else.

Surely these complications were not far from Mariela's thoughts, and surely the difficulty of the task she might now be called on to perform was not lost to her. Here was the predicament: Mariela's plans for vouching for me in any run-in with Sendero were tailored to it happening someplace around Aucayacu, where she knew how to make her way. And while this little twist in the road known as Pacae was only twelve kilometers south of town, because it was beyond the threshold of Mariela's contacts with people who kept ties with the guerrilla, it might as well have been another world. Speaking up for me here, a person so unequivocally a foreigner—and worse, an American—in front of senderistas who didn't know her and with whom she might have real trouble dropping a name in hopes of pulling influence, was not a prospect that could have settled well with her.

I knew that, but there was nothing either of us could do.

So we sat there and waited. And as we waited our eyes gradually adjusted to the night. It wasn't so dark after all. The clouds had broken up and a moon had appeared, close to full, to spread a soft luminescence over the road top as it wended its way above the stream and around to the left. The short bridge was visible just ahead, as was the hazy outline of a wooden billboard on the other side. Though the sign's message faced away from us, no one in the car was unaware that its letters were bold black and set on a sea of yellow, just as no one had failed to ignore—countless times on the way to Tingo María and back—the seemingly innocuous and yet ambiguous admonition that the sign delivered: "This is your bridge. Take care of it."

Past the billboard there were no other cars to be seen. Either there was no incoming traffic or else, around the bend, another senderista was holding back the flow at gunpoint. It was impossible to know which. It was also impossible to see what was going on to the left of the road. The ground dropped off so sharply that at best we could make out the lean-to rooftops of twin mud shacks and the dim and partial outline of restless bodies below. Nothing else appeared in our limited field of vision, nothing except for an exceptionally large sow that loitered about near the road, three piglets tucked at her side.

With the highway obstructed, the man with the gun gave the word and a column of people began to pour out from between the sheds. They scuttled over the road in clumps of threes and fours, burdened by overstuffed duffel bags that made their crossing lumbering and prolonged. Intermingled with the thud of their feet we could hear the muffled rattle of metal as the sacks they carried pounded up and down. The male passenger in front whispered that the bags they hauled on their backs were without doubt filled with guns. That the clanking noises were the same that military firearms made when knocked together. I realized then I did not know the sound of which he spoke. What I heard seemed higher pitched, more like tin cans and pans and assorted kitchen things.

The train of people was in midprocession, filing before our car, when a large cargo truck drew up from behind us. Its driver, oblivious to what was going on, slowed to a stop, headlights glaring away. The sack carriers hesitated in their tracks, turning toward the twin glow of reflectors. Alarmed by the truck's sudden appearance, the guy with the mask raced down the road, past us and past the second car, shouting as he went, "Shut off your lights! Shut off your lights already!" until he was right in front of the truck and flailing his arms, "Turn to block the road! Now keep quiet!"

He then rushed back to his team of mules, hollering, ¡Agarren!... ¡Apúrense! (Move it! Get a move on!) Upon which they jumped to redouble their choppy pace and, gaining speed, became a fluid current of skeletal bodies, streaming over the road and up a steep hill to the right.

In the car we remained at a loss as to what was going to happen to us; and while we waited for our answer, time itself seemed to stretch and become unbearably long. That was when Mariela noticed that, pushed along with the flow of sack carriers, two men were being carted away, hands bound behind their backs, and led up the hill along a footpath that disappeared into the brush and night.

When the convoy of people cleared the road and had withdrawn from view, the leader of the operation calmly walked over to our car and doled out new instructions.

"Stay put, headlights off, thirty minutes. After that you can go."

Our driver nodded, Ya-ya, and the masked guy, not once looking at the rest of us, moved on to the other vehicles. Moments later he trotted back up the road, past us and vanished up the footpath. The whole thing seemed to be over. We hadn't been the target at all, and for the first time, as that realization spread and as each one of us simultaneously traced out its full implications, the dense, intolerably taut atmosphere of the car—with us since being forced to stop—began to dissipate.

For a minute all was silent, and as a cool breeze blew in through the window on the driver's side, we stared at the empty road and said nothing.

Then, all of a sudden, we heard shouts from the hill, followed by the crack of a gun, a shuffling of feet moving back down the trail, and then, behind that, the spray of machinegun fire. "Must have broken away!" blurted out the woman in front. "One of the men tried to escape!"

And there we were, overtaken by an image we could not see of one of the prisoners—stumbling down the hill, struggling to tear hands free and reach the road—with a flurry of bullets behind him . . . and both moving in *our* direction.

Unnerved by the quick turn of events, our driver opened his door, stepped out onto the asphalt and crouched down next to the car, peering over the edge of the window, as if ready to hurl himself over the side of the road. The rest of us tensed up too and ducked down in our seats as best we could. Everyone except for the man next to me, the man from the Ministry. He stayed where he was, sitting up straight as if unconcerned or maybe just more attuned to what was going on.

"They're not firing at us," he chided the driver. "Get back in, get back in the car!"

And then the señora, "Get in! What are you trying to pull?" which was enough to goad him back behind the wheel.

Through all this neither Mariela nor I uttered a word. And until then, I had been incredibly calm. In fact, I was surprised by how calm and composed I felt, coming so close to Sendero and knowing full well that at any moment I could be taken prisoner or killed as a spy or a DEA agent. But when a couple of shots then came our way, so much for poise. I ducked with the others. Being accidentally maimed seemed so much worse than death at that instant. Hospital beds raced through my head and then images of myself immobile, nursing an unserviceable limb. Now *that*, I thought, was something worth getting scared about.

But as quickly as it had started—the shooting, the shouts, the scrambling about—it all stopped, and we returned to the most appalling quiet, broken only by the rustle of questions murmured in the dark: What of the men they were taking away? Did they manage to escape? Did they make it to the road?

Because of the night and because we were too afraid or prudent to leave the car, we could see little beyond what was directly in front of us. And save for the huge sow that had been startled by the gunshots into abandoning her young and now wandered aimlessly about, the road was empty. Inside the car we were left not knowing what had happened, not knowing how the captive men had fared, and yet with every passing second of quiet, sensing that the danger was gradually moving on, leaving us behind.

We were in suspense like that, obediently waiting out the thirty minutes, when someone came bolting down the hill and headed straight for the front passenger-side window. It was a teenage boy, his chest bare, wearing nylon soccer shorts and the tall black rubber boots used by farmers or anyone else who worked the jungle thicket. He appeared so fast, there wasn't time to feel scared.

"They're gone," he said in a loud whisper. "They're already gone! Let's get out of here," he said, grasping at the back-door handle but finding it locked. "Let me in!"

But our driver called back insistently, yet without raising his voice: "No, no, you can't. There's no room," he lied.

"Then put me in the back," the kid said and ran behind the car. "Come on, let's go," he pleaded until the driver, reluctant, hit the switch for the trunk. The kid hopped in, pulling the hood over his head. Only later did he explain.

The driver, now unsure of what to do, careened his head to the right trying to get a glimpse of whether anyone else was coming down the hill, but the passengers in front urged him to get us out of there. So he started up the engine, and we crept forward, over the bridge, accelerating bit by bit, around the bend, to the left and then back to the right, forward and ever faster . . . leaving behind the other car and truck, which we never saw again.

The highway continued straight from there on, and we barreled down it in the dark for half a kilometer, moonlit pampa to the left, steep and craggy hillsides to the right, before the driver flipped on the headlights.

At first no one spoke, but as we got farther and farther from Sendero, from Pacae, and from the incident we had all somehow taken part in, people started to talk in a normal tone for the first time.

"And what of the army in Pendencia?" asked the woman in the front seat. "All that shooting, and the soldiers . . . nothing!"

Ay, said the driver knowingly, "they never leave their base at night!"

Ay pues, she said, nodding, "that's the army."

And then the driver said for all to hear, "The gringo was scared . . . weren't you Gringo?" shooting me a glance. I chose to forgo the bait and kept quiet, but the señora, she turned it back on him, scoffing at how he had jumped out of the car when the shots started to fly.

"What were you going to do, run off and leave us there?" she reproached. No one said anything and her words hung in the air. The driver didn't come to his own defense. He just drove on.

Soon the lights of Aucayacu appeared in front of us and we coasted into town. Past the roadside kiosks, past the mechanic shops and tire repairmen, past the Hermanos Rober gas station, over the Sangapilla bridge until we pulled up alongside the *colectivo* office. Out front I was surprised to see another Toyota filled with passengers, looking as if it were about to depart for Tingo María. It must have been seven, going on seven-fifteen in the evening. We had been stopped at Pacae for what seemed like forever, but thinking about it now, altogether we couldn't have been there more than twenty-five minutes. During that whole time not a single car had approached Pacae from the opposite direction. How desolate the Marginal became after dusk.

I fully expected our driver to say something to the people outside the office about what we had just been through. At the very least, dispense soft words of warning to the car that was about to take off: that maybe it wasn't such a good idea to travel tonight. But no, he just yelled over to the *embalador*, "Mark me down," as if he were coming in from a routine commute.

The couple got out here, retrieved their things from the trunk, and paid their fare to the driver, who told the rest of us that he needed to sign in, but that he'd be right back to take us into town. As he walked off, the kid who had stowed away in back slid into the front passenger seat and, turning toward us, started to tell his story.

He was coming down the trail, he said, from his *chacra* when he saw *los tucos*[3] on the highway below. Frightened, he jumped off the path, hid in the bushes, and waited as they began their ascent up the trail. Then the commotion started, gunshots and shouts. He didn't know what to do, but since they were still below him, he stayed put. A few minutes later they resumed their march and filed by, not more than a few meters from where he lay. They didn't see him, and as soon as they had gone past a ways, he jumped up and sprinted downhill as fast as he could. He was almost at the road when he nearly tripped over the body of a man. The body was still and silent, and the kid just kept moving, overwhelmed by fear.

By this time our driver had walked back over to the car, and as he got behind the wheel, the kid, cutting his version off in midstream, hopped out and walked away in the direction of town. Nothing more was said about the incident. The man from the Ministry merely stated he wanted to be let out at the plaza, and Mariela instructed the driver to drop us off on the way.

A minute later we pulled up in front of Mariela's store, and the driver got out to help us unload our things from the trunk. Once everything was out on the curb and Mariela had grabbed a load to carry inside, where I could now see Alex behind the counter, I handed the driver a bill.

He took it, rubbed it to make sure it was good, smiled broadly and then said: "Well, Gringo. How about that? Just like in the movies, no?"

the law . . . by day

That something had happened at Pacae was confirmed the next morning when the *fiscal*, or district attorney, of Aucayacu went under tight police escort to the spot where we had been stopped the night before.[4] There he officiated over the recovery of the bodies, for as it turned out, not one, but two men had been killed. The victims were brothers and had died not far from their homes. How word of their deaths first reached the public prosecutor, I did not know. Had our driver gone to the police station after dropping us off? Had the bureaucrat of the Ministry of Agriculture quietly passed along the information? Had Mariela said something? Or had the family of the victims or even a neighbor come to Aucayacu at first light to report the incident?

The *levantamiento*,[5] or removal of the corpses, took place around mid-morning, but it was midday before news of the incident became public in town. I remember I was in my room with the radio on when the story headlined the noon broadcast of a local station. "Two men perish during overnight incursion by terrorist elements on the Marginal Highway," the radio announcer said, before playing a clip of a journalist interviewing the district attorney, a man of sixty-some-odd years and of frugal words.

"What was the cause of death?" asked the journalist, with a tinge of excitement in his voice.

"Gunshot wounds," the prosecutor replied.

"Well," the journalist insisted, "what was the motive? I mean, why were they killed?"

This was the question that had lingered with me through the night. Who were these men? And why them? I turned up the volume, so as not to miss his response.

La vida, the prosecutor said, *hay que saberla vivir.* Life, you must know how to live it.

The journalist hesitated for a second as if caught between expecting more and not knowing exactly where he was being led; but when the prosecutor didn't continue, he abruptly brought the report to a close: "There you have it, dear listeners, the words of the honorable *fiscal* on last night's incident at the village of Pacae, kilometer twelve of the Marginal. Back to you, studio."

The news program proceeded on to the next story, but I was stuck with the prosecutor's choice of words. There was something familiar, cryptic, and even scandalous about them.

La vida, hay que saberla vivir.

The saying itself was not obscure but a variation of the commonplace Spanish-language maxim, *Hay que saber vivir la vida* (You must know how to live life), that was in no way peculiar to Peruvian Spanish, much less to the Huallaga vernacular.[6] It was ordinarily invoked in the face of a sudden, accidental, or otherwise unanticipated death, as an everyday contemplation on the value of life. However, the phrase was rarely left on its own but qualified by some positive injunction or precept—such as enjoining one to live life to the fullest, within measure, decisively. In fact, the possible renderings were endless, depending on how life and its worth were reckoned, because this seemed to be the point of the maxim: to give direction or sense to the value that should be accorded to life.[6]

By leaving the phrase without further elaboration, to float, as it were, the *fiscal*'s commentary not only was ambiguous but required that his audience, invisibly linked through the ether of radio, fill in the missing pieces. That the men had died at the hands of Sendero Luminoso did not seem to be in question. Yet by invoking this saying the prosecutor appeared to place blame on the victims themselves, suggesting that they would still be alive if they had made better life choices.

What the *fiscal* intended was not at all evident. This was not a statement of law, or at least not the kind of legal enunciation a prosecutor might be expected to make about a crime. How, then, were his words to be understood? A purely personal reflection spoken in the face of death? The prosecutor speaking not from his vested office but as a private citizen before the irreducible finitude of the two corpses now in his charge? As an individual he certainly could identify with the predicament of the men whose dead bodies he tended to that morning. He concretely shared something of their vulnerability. As a state functionary, he was an enemy in the eyes of Sendero, and a death sentence weighed over him, just as it apparently had over the two men. What separated him, nonetheless, besides the privileges and protections that came with his position, was that so far he had managed to stay out of harm's way.

La vida, hay que saberla vivir. It sounded so commonsensical and yet seemed to communicate a certain quotient of wisdom that the prosecutor, by merely uttering the phrase, claimed to possess. Through it, he seemed to point to a secret that rested upon a hidden or implicit chain of presupposition: an a priori reason called upon to inform actions before the fact; an arcane knowledge guiding one through dangerous straits; a unique local understanding familiar to anyone who had spent much time in the Huallaga Valley about what *to* and what *not to* do.

La vida, hay que saberla vivir. Life, you must know how to live it.

As a sober message of survival the phrase was perhaps less incomplete than unraveled. For the prosecutor had spoken conclusively as if imparting the moral to a story. It appeared as though he were gesturing toward an unwritten rule or an invisible law that his local audience was supposed to somehow appreciate.

I imagined they did appreciate it, because it was hard not to hear in the prosecutor's words a veiled or implied reference to the recent past; to a time when human life in the Huallaga Valley had had such little value, a rapacious time that—if only by mere chronological proximity—could still crowd the present and echo forth every time another person came to a violent end. What was curious about this nervous contention between recent past and living present was how the very same actions could have entirely different significance depending on the "era" in which they occurred. Ten, even five years before, the point of emphasis in the report about the event at Pacae would not have been the brutal murder of two men but rather the surprise that someone from the district attorney's office dared go out on the highway at all. Between the 1980s and early 1990s so many deaths occurred along the road. Most just went unregistered because back then the Marginal was far too dangerous for the representatives of state justice to fulfill their duties. Thus there was arguably a measure of "progress" in the fact that the *fiscal* could finally go out to recover the bodies. The short arm of Peruvian legal justice was now extending its reach beyond the towns and into the countryside, even if only sporadically, to take official note of incidents in the region.

Perhaps it was this tacit inflection of recent past into the present that gave the saying some of its peculiar force, making it less empty phrase than winged words. But there was something more. An imperative was clearly contained and communicated through the urgent *hay que saber* (must know), which made the expression more than mere counsel and rather like a command.

La vida, hay que saberla vivir (Life, you *must know* how to live it) prefigured an unspoken "Or else!" upon which logically followed another unspoken, "Or else what?" and finally an understood remainder, "Well, here we have the bodies of two men who didn't."

A bad end awaited those who failed to heed such good advice. The *fiscal*'s remark, while at first glance off-the-cuff, carried a promise or better still a propositional statement, an "if (not) . . . , then . . . ," of death. Backed up with two corpses as compelling examples, his words were thoroughly threatening.

violence through language

Elias Canetti in his sociological treatise *Crowds and Power* observed that all commands contain a threat of death. It is through the execution of death sentences, in particular, that commands gain momentum and rekindle their force.[7] *La vida, hay que saberla vivir* carried within it the frightening force of the dead bodies. The presence of the corpses, reiterated through the prosecutor's statement, pointed to another vital characteristic of the command: how it relays the threat of physical violence itself. Theodor Adorno remarked once to Canetti in a radio discussion that the latter's command theory "expresses in a very original and unconventional way that the threat of direct violence lives on in all mediations."[8]

Here the *fiscal*'s statement was not explicitly a command, though it certainly enveloped one. It was more akin to what Deleuze and Guattari called "order-words" (*mot d'ordre*—literally, "word of order" but also "slogan" or "password"), which by linking explicit statements with implicit or nondiscursive presuppositions open up a field of social obligation and give orders to life. The notion of "order-words" was central to Deleuze and Guattari's reformulation of the illocutionary and built upon Canetti's earlier insights on the command. They were emphatic when they noted:

> Order-words do not concern commands only, but every act that is linked to statements by a "social-obligation" . . . The relation between the statement and the act is internal, immanent, but it is not one of identity. Rather, it is a relation of *redundancy*. The order-word itself is the redundancy of the act and the statement. Newspapers, news, proceed by redundancy, in that they tell us what we "must" think, retain, expect, etc.[9]

The *fiscal* suggested not only what one should know but with whom one should make alliance. But what was the ultimate source of the threat? It could hardly be said to emanate from Peruvian law. The dead men had not transgressed anything in the state criminal code; there was no positive offense for which they could be blamed. Yet the prosecutor's phrase intimated that the men had brought ruin upon themselves through their own negligence, and in so doing had exercised a choice for which they had been condemned. I could imagine only one such decision: the men had chosen to live where they lived. By residing in or near the village of Pacae, and by extension anywhere Sendero Luminoso could still operate unfettered, they had willingly gone outside the state and subjected themselves to this terrible eventuality.

This was something of an inversion of the Lockean doctrine of tacit consent, whereby residence directly signaled one's submission to sovereign authority.[10] Here though, in the rural expanses of the Upper Huallaga Valley, where the central state's control was tenuous at best, the principle could be turned inside out to demonstrate one's decision to opt out of the state's protections and to accept the costs of living dangerously. One did not need to reach to liberal political philosophy to interpret the prosecutor's statement. It resonated with events that had set a far more local and compelling precedent for a doctrine of consent implied in residency. Throughout the 1990s, the Peruvian army had often operated on the assumption that anyone living in rural areas where Sendero was active was obedient to Sendero rule and thus openly rejected the Peruvian state. Obliterating distinctions between the civilian population and the guerrilla, seeing all who coincided in the same area as hostile, facilitated the operational aspects of military planning and found acute expression in the indiscriminate bombing of villages, most notably during the Peruvian armed forces' Aries offensive in 1994.[11]

Of course, choice was not something everyone could exercise under an equality of conditions. The choice to live in Pacae, or in other rural and thus existentially precarious areas of the Upper Huallaga Valley, would have to be weighed against what options the two victims had for living elsewhere: whether there were kinship relations that could be drawn upon, a parcel of land to work someplace far from Sendero, or enough money or the right trade to make a go of it in the nearest town. It was also worth keeping in mind that in the history of the republic, despite the often inclusive language of its laws, the Peruvian state had seldom if ever managed to extend and ensure the protections and rights of citizenship to all those residing within its territorial boundaries—least of all in what concerned the administration of justice.

La vida, hay que saberla vivir.

The threat came, so it seemed, from outside Peruvian law but, because uttered by the state's prosecutor, nestled up alongside it. It came not in the law as codified but as an understood residual order.[12] Through the act of conveying the threat the *fiscal* had expressed a territorial taboo or prohibition, which was nothing less than an evocation of a no man's land. Not a suspension of certain rights—sign of a legislated state of exception—but the withdrawal of law in its entirety. This image of "no law," which the prosecutor seemed to conjure without ever explicitly naming it as such, was impossible to confirm. That is to say there was no solid evidence to point to that could clarify the matter once and for all. Yet above all it was the uncertainty of intent that seemed to heighten the performative impact of his statement.

an excess of law

If the notion of no man's land imposed itself here it was not only because its Spanish rendition, *tierra de nadie,* was how many people in the Huallaga described the years when the cocaine boom merged with the insurgent-counter-insurgent war: a time when the ubiquity of violence and the proliferation of corpses became one of the defining facets of everyday life. Nor was it only because Huallaga townspeople in the late 1990s talked about areas of the countryside, villages with names like Pacae, where it was still just "better" not to go.

While very much an everyday concept, no man's land was also intimately related though not identical to "states of nature"[13] in Enlightenment political philosophy and "states of legal exception" of Western constitutional law. Carl Schmitt, in his *Nomos of the Earth*, referred to the Hobbesian "state of nature" and "no man's land" almost interchangeably, though he employed the latter term for its spatial character as a topological realm beyond the line of the law, where bad things were known to happen. No man's land for Schmitt was a delimited though uncharted space imagined as free of all "legal barriers."[14] That freedom referred to the free reign of violence, prefigured in the dialectic of the concept itself: a land of no one already suggested a land of everyone, everyone free to take violence into their own hands. Less a "camp" than where one went at one's own volition and risk, no man's land was not properly a legal concept but an implied notion.

Even while not explicitly acknowledged by Peruvian constitutional law, the concept of no man's land can nonetheless be inferred if only from its absence. In the modern history of Peru, national governments have taken regular recourse to regimes of legal exception, alleging threats to the state's institutional survival.[15] Throughout the counterinsurgency wars of the 1980s and 1990s, the executive branch declared the suspension of rights (assembly, inviolability of domicile, and so forth) in delimited portions of the national territory and handed local rule over to the Peruvian armed forces with a charge to take whatever actions were necessary to "restore order."[16] While declarations of such "emergency zones," which regularly included provinces of the Huallaga Valley, outlined specific exemptions to legal guarantees, they were expressly worded to avoid contemplating the absence of legality itself or even the possibility of the law's own dissolution. In this sense, it can be said that the figure of no man's land, as that which is deliberately *not* recognized by the letter of the law but invoked in everyday speech as the point of law's limit, is quasi-juridical.

Though more could be said here, I wish only to suggest that the condition of a withdrawal or dissolution of law (to which the no-man's-land concept ostensibly refers) describes instead places and times where distinct expressions of sovereignty meet and overlap. The denotative paradox of no man's land is that its concept points to a lack of law, whereas the conditions it designates reveal an excess: the coincidence in one place and time of two or more groups, each aspiring through violence to impose its own rule. In this way the no man's land/*tierra de nadie* notion involves a distancing from concrete situations. As a generalizing figure or an image of thought, it conjures its object only to appreciate it at a remove. In common usage it seldom conveys the experience of an actual here and now, much less captures the temporality of the event. Instead, no man's land *appears* to be always "over there" or "back then"; wherever it is claimed, a collectivity bound by law is not. It *appears* from a distance to designate the place where violence has become second nature. As such, no man's land takes on a timeless and inevitable character. Timeless not because nothing happens but because the things that do, happen so much that they lose their singularity as distinct events. Inevitable because what happens comes with the territory. When projected onto a real topography and onto someone else's lived time, *tierra de nadie* reveals itself as a natural historical construct. There and then violent events become taken for granted. As a repetition of the same, they are emptied of their historical content and accrue to the place or time in question as a nebulous atmosphere, thick and forbidding.

Which brings us back to Pacae, the district attorney, and the political moment of May 1998.

law's time

Pacae's reputation as a precarious spot on the road to Tingo María was no secret for anyone living in Aucayacu. It had been the site of numerous ambushes on the police and military since the early 1980s and was a site where, townspeople said, Sendero frequently appeared. The prosecutor seemed to have a clear sense of Pacae's local notoriety as well as an inkling of the village's history when he, in effect, acknowledged concrete territorial limits to the guarantees offered by the public power he represented as well as to the state's responsibility—or lack thereof—for what happened beyond those limits. From the

perspective of Peruvian law, again not as written but as enunciated by its functionary (and situated at this moment in time only in the town), the hamlet of
Pacae lay in an extralegal terrain. From this perspective, Pacae could equally
be said to subsist in a prelegal domain to the extent that the Peruvian state
had yet to thoroughly impress its rule upon the place; even though, and here
was the rub, that within the social-historical imaginary of Huallaga towns in
May of 1998 there was little doubt that Peruvian law would eventually prevail.
A decade of brutal counterinsurgency had injected a sense of direction into
time and convincingly traced a historical trajectory for most people in the
Huallaga. The defeat of the Shining Path and its alternative state project was
considered nearly accomplished, even if the guerrilla dragged on, unwilling to
call it quits. Against this horizon of inescapable victory, the rule of Peruvian
law would "someday" surely extend to Pacae and so many other places like it.
Only then would the law take over the management of infractions, mediate
through and separate out who was who and what was what and, above all,
introduce a different order of time, a time of process or procedure that at first
blush would promise to deliver a more seemly form of justice.

In the meantime, all who went to Pacae would take their lives into their
own hands. If something went wrong they would have only themselves to fault,
and from the distance of the town of Aucayacu it would look as if that were
just the "nature" of the place. In Aucayacu the state's prosecutor, by implicitly
assigning the attribute "no man's land" to where people already feared to go,
affirmed local knowledge as juridical fact and injected a fateful causality into
events, events unleashed by two men guilty of not knowing better.

In no man's land, life punishes you if you don't know how to live it, as if of
its own volition; much like Kant once observed of vice, that it punishes itself.
For the German Enlightenment philosopher, such punishments of "nature"
were of no juridical concern.[17] Law either had no time for them, or they simply
did not partake of law's time.

But the matter didn't rest there and was more complicated than I've let
on so far. Because in this not quite settled time between war and peace, in
this provisional here-and-now of the Peruvian state's almost-but-not-yet-
actualized victory, the threat to which the *fiscal* gave voice was, at the very
least, double. On one hand there were the general and unpredictable dis-
orders that swirled about beyond the purview of Peruvian law, the unruly exterior that any juridical system must conjure as its necessary foil and fiction.
Under this rubric the killings by the Shining Path could be subsumed and

generalized as a diffuse criminal or outlaw violence. On the other hand there was the very real if diminished vitality of another juridical regime altogether: Sendero as law in its own right, still capable of asserting itself through the taking of life and to which the prosecutor also gestured.

This ambiguous duality was for me the most compelling thing about the *fiscal's* cryptic appropriation of a most common phrase: the twofold reference to a "state of nature" as the obverse side of the law he represented, and yet resonating with it, to Sendero—not as criminal violence but as competing law. In this sense, the prosecutor stood at the border of one legal regime and looked out onto the uncertain terrain of another. There, faced with the killing of two men, he emitted a crude warning or "public" advisory. In so doing, he lent his voice to separate juridical registers. The prosecutor announced limits in Peruvian law and marked off the line where peaceful coexistence gave way to chaos. But with the same words he also performed a service for Sendero. The *fiscal* passed along the terrible message to the people of the valley—"this could have been you"—that accompanies the execution of every death sentence. Through this, he recognized the lingering currency and force of Sendero law.

Though it could be disputed that the Shining Path ever constituted a legal regime, the answer would depend on how one interpreted the fluid history and territorial character of Sendero's hold on specific regions of the country. It also would depend on how one understood the relationship between violence, law, and land.

In the 1980s and early 1990s the regimelike quality of the Party's presence in the Huallaga manifested itself through the creation of village-level "people's committees." Through them Sendero exercised enormous influence over the most basic facets of rural life: from land tenure to social mores. Sendero's manner of domination combined brute force with "softer" techniques of control by means of which the Party decided who could live on the land and what kinds of conduct and commerce would prevail. In this respect it could be said that the Shining Path generated its own forms of legality in the Huallaga, above all in the rural areas that it held less through the armed defense of fixed positions than by occupying spaces that the Peruvian state had effectively ceded or could not consistently protect. In the Huallaga those legal forms were merely virtual when Sendero's forces could not maintain a consistent presence; they became most fully actualized at historical moments when the Party reached its greatest strength and territorial expansion, specifically from the mid- to late 1980s.[18]

A decade later, however, the situation of Sendero law had qualitatively changed. Relentless army operations had disrupted the rural people's committees and severely weakened the territorial character of Party rule. Though the Shining Path still exercised considerable influence in the Huallaga countryside, it had a far less preponderant presence than before. Nevertheless, the exact nature of its influence was not apparent, and that created all kinds of uncertainty.

In May 1998, at the time of the Pacae shootings, could it be said that Sendero law still had force? If so, for whom? Moreover, if some people still acknowledged and followed that law, what was the actual object of their respect? Was it the law of the diminished entity that Sendero had become by 1998? *Or* was it rather the ghost of the force that Sendero had formerly projected when the Party had a firmer territorial grip on the valley? In other words, in 1998 could it be said that the violence exercised by Sendero's armed groups still had a law-creating power?

Clear-cut answers to such questions were elusive that year and would become all the more so as time passed. Then again, because of how they served to frame the problematic relation of force and law, arriving at definitive conclusions was less important than posing the questions themselves.

crowned by fate

The intense charge that animated the place-name *Pacae* was based on political conditions that were not only ephemeral but in some respects entirely local. For the townspeople of Aucayacu, the village appeared as a formidably dangerous place, yet its foreboding atmosphere was of limited range, extending at most a half hour's distance in either direction along the Marginal. Beyond this zone its name did not resonate at all. In Tingo María, with the exception of those who had regular occasion to travel north, few people had any inkling as to Pacae's special status. Yet this anonymity did little to redeem the village's name because, for the general population of Tingo María, most if not all communities beyond the outskirts of their city partook of the same air of unruliness and insecurity.

This broad indistinction was similar to how the Huallaga Valley continued to be depicted by the national press and to be perceived by the rest of the country: as a lawless region of generalized violence where cocaine and "terrorism" ran hand in hand. As such, there was a curious symmetry between how the Upper Huallaga Valley figured in the national imaginary and the role Pacae played as "no man's land" for Aucayacu. It was a symmetry that in the late 1990s repeated itself between all Huallaga towns north of Tingo María—as firmly established military, police, and legal outposts of the Peruvian state— and the countryside into which Peruvian legal justice rarely extended. Each town was a separate zone, with its own urban center of state law and with its own rural topography of dangerous places. Each had its own Pacaes, for there were always more than one: places on or off the main highway where people knew better than to go or linger for very long. The infamy of such spots did not transcend the immediate local area, which is only to say that precise knowledge of these places scarcely traveled from one town to the next. What did travel was a general impression of acutely inauspicious states of affairs and an impenetrable remoteness that detached itself from specific circumstances and accrued to the entire Huallaga region as a perilous place. Against this screen not only could the rest of the nation appear to be at relative peace, but the particulars of places like Pacae—the singular events that happened there as well as the kinds of special knowledge people required to navigate them— faded away.

Between the former boom days, which had established the Huallaga in the national imaginary as a *narco* haven and the persistence of Sendero as a very present threat—precisely at a moment when the rest of the country seemed to be putting ever more distance on the insurgency wars that had dominated the recent past—the *fiscal* had substantial inertia on his side. From the outside and at a remove it was all too easy to imagine the Huallaga as a place where danger came with the territory and killing was no more than a regular or even natural affair. There was no scarcity of social truths that local law officials could draw upon to excuse not pursuing injustices that fell so squarely within their jurisdiction.

From the inside, however, and close to what was happening, events were never anything but trenchantly historical. Continuous political rule by the state, and the legality that emanated from it, seemed to depend on some kind of permanent concrete control over the earth. In late May 1998, the main towns of the Huallaga were the unquestioned locus of Peruvian authority, and state officials and most townspeople still hesitated to go into the countryside. Between the towns snaked the Marginal Highway from Tingo all the way to Tocache and points beyond. By day it was a secure enough thoroughfare, as surely as if the Peruvian state had spread out across its winding surface of asphalt, gravel, and dirt as the only law of the land. By nightfall, however, that same law would withdraw back into the towns and the road would lose much of its public character, leaving places like Pacae all on their own. All on their own until sunrise the following morning.

and what of "human rights"?

As the day progressed, no further mention was made of Pacae or of Sendero or of the two deaths. Though the *fiscal* did stay at the morgue that afternoon to oversee the medical examiner's work, and though the police collected what additional information they could, the incident dropped from public view. By Thursday evening nothing about the killings circulated through town, nor were they the pressing subject of gossip or rumor. They were at most a distant concern moving on to oblivion. That is, until the next morning when a young journalist, Rino Baluarte, revisited the incident on his radio news show.

I made a habit of tuning in to Rino's program whenever I could. More of an editorialist than a reporter, he had a combative style I liked, a keen analysis, as well as a biting critique of local affairs that most other radio journalists shied away from. Rino considered himself something of a moral conscience for the town—a pretension that had earned him the enmity of some colleagues and not a few local officials.[19] His intentions were earnest and as for his program, there was nothing like it in Aucayacu.

That morning, as he often did, Rino reviewed the news from the previous twenty-four hours, to pick out a few items and spin them against the grain. I was curious to see whether he would have more information about Wednesday night's incident. As it turned out, the Pacae killings were one of the first items on Rino's plate. Though he had nothing new to report, he went right to the *fiscal*'s words and replayed the tape. After that, Rino remarked:

"Ya just gotta know how to live life, huh?" his voice lilting somewhere between bewilderment and subtle derision. "And human rights? What about those, Mr. Prosecutor?"—his tone now turning contemptuous—"They wouldn't be your responsibility, would they, Mr. Prosecutor?"

"Just incredible!" he said with a huff before moving on. "Next up! What do we have here?"

I had begun to suspect I was alone in thinking what the *fiscal* had said was in any way odd. However, the fact that Rino had picked up on it and had found it provocative gave me some company even if I could tell we weren't coming from the same place. Rino seemed to react to what he considered a flippant attitude or callousness on the *fiscal*'s part, as if the prosecutor had decided upon absolving the law of all accountability for the deaths. At stake for Rino was the state's responsibility to fulfill its most generic duties. He invoked human rights not as it often was, to impugn terrible abuses by the military or police forces, but to point out the state's obligation to assure the rule of law upon its territory. His demand was that the state live up to its ideal: to protect citizens from enemies, foreign and internal, within borders that it claimed by fiat.

Yet what Rino's brief editorial intervention did not contemplate was that the problem entailed more than the state according due respect for the victims' security within its domain. It also involved the conditions under which such rights could be said to be guaranteed and, particularly, how those conditions were determined or judged to be obtaining. On that score the *fiscal* and his radio critic each had an implicit point to make and separate claims to assert within it. Each held distinct expectations about what the state could or should do. They had expressed divergent assumptions about law and its registers of time—temporal relationships that hinged on the ef-ficacy of the rule of state law and, correspondingly, on the promise for some form of legal justice.

The *fiscal* seemed to speak to a specific facticity, grounded in a past of absolute insecurity that persisted in places like Pacae well into the present. The village floated in a no man's land where the protections of state law did not extend. Rino, meanwhile, refused to acknowledge that the Peruvian state had such limits and in effect refused to acknowledge the existence of a zone or region within its recognized territory where the rule of law could not or should not prevail. Rino well knew that the army had bases up and down the Marginal, the closest to Pacae being only a few kilometers away in the village of Anda; consequently, there was no convincing case to be made that the state did not have adequate resources at its disposal. What Rino also knew was that, in Peru, getting the central state to provide minimum guarantees for citizens was a necessary and ongoing political fight. At the forefront of this histori-cally protracted struggle was the propensity of Peruvian state functionaries to deny or suspend a victim's right to protection and legal justice when "circum-stances" made it easy to do so.

It was possible that the *fiscal* was responding less to a legal and moral duty of the state than to what he perceived as a concrete social-historical fact. At that moment a wholly different kind of law and legal temporality applied out-side of town, which was to say at the edge of the state. A different *tract of time* also applied, in which each person had to fend for him- or herself when it came to navigating dangers and teasing out conflicts. "Out there" the distinction between victim and victimizer became blurred, if not suppressed, and it became the obligation of the individual, not the state, to know where the line was drawn as well as on which side to stand.

The *fiscal*'s position, straightforwardly or tongue in cheek, echoed a Kantian command or obligation "to quit a state of nature": to abandon the condition of living in a time or place where there is no public law or external justice.

Following this interpretive logic, the *fiscal* would be waiting for some definitive act that would impose state rule—presuming, of course, such a feat could be accomplished once and for all. This implied that the "legal conquest" of the lands beyond the towns could only follow upon an actual and decisive political-military victory. To fully sustain such a proposition begged the question of the historical basis of rights; that is not to say the genealogy of their emergence as legal concept or doctrine, but a more localized notion of history as the concrete shaping of political topography such that rights obtaining to all could be realized. In the *fiscal*'s reasoning, for there to be rights the rule of law of some particular state would need to be in force over a territory and there could be no rights, human or otherwise, guaranteed by the state in a region beyond state control. In places where the state could not claim to exercise sovereign rule, it would no longer bear responsibility for protecting and ensuring the lives of those citizens who knowingly resided there. Granted these logical assumptions, the *fiscal* could easily have argued that Rino's question very much missed the point, for implicitly ignoring the presumption that Pacae lingered in a no man's land and thereby confusing a normal legal situation with a temporal landscape where state law did not hold.

Then again, I could easily imagine Rino countering that, against all the available forms of temptation legal functionaries faced to hold back rather than push forward in the pursuit of justice, a persistent demand that the state enforce protections was required. He might well have argued that it was only through vocal demands by common citizens that proper enforcement was ever going to happen.

I wondered. And I could only wonder, because a direct confrontation between the radio editorialist and the *fiscal* never occurred. For me, at the heart of the matter was the issue of time—or to be more precise, the different kinds of temporal zones that became shaped through law even in places where there appeared to be no law at all. Whether the state acted to prosecute

the killings or refrained from doing so had real implications for the appre-
hension and molding of potentialities as they manifested in the past, present,
and future. If the state refrained, a causal nexus could be drawn between the
victims' "offense/guilt" (of being on the wrong side in the wrong place at
the wrong time) and the moment of their misfortune. Their deaths could be
figured retroactively as inevitable and having somehow consummated their
designation as condemned life struck down by its own vices. Conversely, to
prosecute would trace causality out into the future to a time between the
unlawful taking of life and the moment when the perpetrators would be held
accountable for their acts. This reversal was crucial, as it seemed to structure
differing horizons of expectation. One horizon belonged to state law, which
promised eventual justice through a rigorous adherence to legal procedure.
The other belonged to the "mythical" workings of law outside itself, where
"bad things" happened to those who dared fate.

Yet mythic terror could not be separated so easily from the law of state,
which less suppressed than pushed it outside (spatially to its territorial margins, temporally into a legal prehistory), or else shoved it forward into a future as a kind of spell on those who would challenge its prohibitions. Such an
operation was not external to the rationality of the state. It could either cast
fate into those places where its law was said to have no force or could fling it
forward to that day when the criminal got his due. This is only to say: state law
pitched fate out along different temporal lines, each one fashioning a claim of
"justice."

Beyond the legal implications for dead victims and their killers, however,
the statements of the *fiscal* and his radio critic even more profoundly underscored a dispute over how to characterize the current state of affairs in the
Upper Huallaga. At the center of their competing perspectives was a judgment on whether the present itself belonged more to the past, remembered
as lawless and extremely violent, or to a future imagined as qualitatively less
so. Which way this judgment went entailed separate incorporeal transformations—contained and expressed in statements about the situation at hand—
of the historical moment we were living.

That the Huallaga seemed pulled between war and peace was indisputable.
While spatially the dividing line appeared for the present to be clearly drawn
at the frontier of town and country, nothing sure could be said about where
the time of one began and the other ended. As an event, the shooting on the
road compressed contrary potentialities into itself and projected them out to

resonate along incompatible lines of past and future. In this way the shooting forced a reflection on the state of the present that seemed to ask:

What time is this that "we" are in?

If neither peace nor war, then toward which do "we" lean?

These were, at root, questions of political place and belonging.

where else but pacae?

After its second airing on the radio, no one bothered themselves about the prosecutor's statement, though he was quoted again when the incident appeared two days later in *El Matutino*, the town's then-only newspaper.[20] The shooting failed to make the front cover but was tucked a few pages inside, evidence of its increasing nonevent status. I looked for the story with special interest, not only to see if there were any new details but also because I knew Rino to be one of the newspaper's editors and main contributors. I thought he might have expanded upon his criticism of the prosecutor. Instead what I found was less editorial than testimony to the hold that Pacae, as a place and as a name, had on the local imagination and also to how difficult it was in the countryside for journalists, even those who had grown up in Aucayacu, to come by the most basic details when a violent event transpired.

It Had to Be in Pacae

THEY CHOP UP TWO VILLAGERS

Wednesday May 27 at approximately 6:30 p.m., in the hamlet of Pacae, located twenty minutes from Aucayacu in the direction of Tingo María, a small group of armed criminals forcibly entered the house of the Ayala Pinedo[a] family, ultimately killing[b] Dennis or Benigno, 30 years of age, and Jeremías (25 years old).

The secrecy kept over the incident, above all by the police, hindered the collection of many facts. Nonetheless, *El Matutino* learned that apparently the motive for the crime may have been "to settle a score."[c] Four years earlier the older of the murdered brothers had supposedly swindled[d] some *narco* couriers of that earlier era[e] out of 10 kg of Cocaine Paste.[f]

However, this version would have to be cast aside if we take into account the placard, found on the victims' bodies, with an inscription that literally said: "This is how snitches die."[g]

Meanwhile, it was learned that Jeremías Ayala Pinedo had served his country some six years back, an explanation that was also a topic of speculation among some villagers, who apprehensively provided information.

Nothing more eloquent than a body chopped up with a hatchet (left arm cut off); gunshot wound (a sharp hole piercing the right collarbone and right armpit); acute wounds (1) right pectoral and (2) abdominal region, caused by firearms, which taken together demonstrate an elevated discharge of rage.

The Police (Aucayacu Headquarters) accompanied by the district attorney carried out the official removal of the bodies. The representative of the Public Prosecutor's office gave declarations and revealed that the incident would be yet "one more example of the presence of subversives in the area."[h] He urged the population to know how to live. He admitted that the zone is not yet at peace.[i, 21]

[a] Pseudonyms have been used for all personal names; [b] *victimar finalmente;* [c] *arreglo de cuentas;* [d] *habría cerrado*—literally, "closed out"; [e] *de aquella época;* [f] *pasta básica de cocaína*—raw or unrefined cocaine; [g] *Así mueren los soplones;* [h] *una raya más al tigre de los subversivos;* [i] *aún no está pacificada*

Going no further than the title of the report, two things jumped out. One was how violent events were presumed to have a certain elective affinity for this particular place on the road to Tingo María. Then there was that extraordinary reticence to invoke the name Sendero Luminoso head on. Much like the driver on the night of the shooting, the paper deferred to a personal pronoun. "*They* chop up two villagers," as if all who would read the story knew who *they* must be.

Getting a grasp on what had actually happened, however, was not so easy, and this "resistance" of the material to a final clarification marked the story throughout. The police mysteriously weren't talking, and they weren't alone. The villagers were too scared to say much. Instead of "hard" facts the prosecutor offered only slogans. Pacae was a very charged space, the article left no doubt about that. Yet from the incomplete pieces of information collected, the story traced out a series of possible motives.

First there was the chance the slayings were a drug-related case of private justice: payback for a crooked deal the elder brother had brokered some time back. But the care the story took to hedge that scenario with the words "apparently," "may have been," and "supposedly" suggested this explanation was tenuous at best.

Then there was the placard scrawled with that most classic of all Sendero catchphrases: *Así mueren los soplones,* which anyone in Peru knew to be the Party's calling card. Suddenly the deaths moved from the obscure realm of drugs over to the perhaps more secretive world of Sendero, which, unlike drug traders, frequently took pains to claim public credit for whom it killed.

The discovery, though perhaps provisional, that the younger brother had been in the armed forces six years before, strengthened this second possibility. Sendero could have killed him because he had refused to join the Party. It was commonly said that the Party eagerly accepted former soldiers into its ranks because they could pass their knowledge of military tactics on to new recruits. Of course, if he had rebuffed their appeals, they might have taken that to be a sign of his allegiance to the military and killed him as a potential informer.

In the Huallaga, *soplón* (snitch or informer) was the default explanation for political and drug-related deaths in lieu of anything more specific. It was the one motive and vital point where the violence of the Shining Path and that of drug traders could even be said to converge. Neither group had patience for informers, and being a *soplón* was the one accusation people feared most and would ward off at almost any cost. Though drug traders did not usually make public announcements of their killings, anyone could put a Sendero slogan on a body to sow confusion about the identity of the killer.

What I noticed next was that in the description of possible motives distinct temporal frameworks came into play. If the killings were the result of drug violence, the story positioned them as if they belonged to or were a hold over of the cocaine boom. The boom was "that earlier era" *(aquella época)* to which the story alluded. Yet, if the killings were an instance of Sendero violence, they belonged rather to an ongoing contemporaneous situation, which created time problems of its own. Because for things to be "on track," that is, for the Upper Huallaga region to be in step with national time, such violence should be a thing of the past. This temporal disjuncture or disjointedness was brought to fore by the story just as it had resonated through many of the statements the killings had provoked.

Once these possible motives had been enumerated, the corpses were called upon to explain through their physical state what had gone wrong. A hatchet was taken to one body, gunshots too, but as the description of the wounds proceeded it was hard to distinguish where one corpse began and the other ended. A dead brother blurred into two to become an extended screen of flesh upon which an unmitigated fury had been unleashed. As a reader it was not clear to me which kind of understanding should be garnered from such a description that began on an oddly lyrical note—"nothing more eloquent"—only to turn forensic in tone and content.

Of all the reasons put forth, the *soplón* theory was the only motive that made its way into the national media. I became aware that news of the incident had spread beyond the valley only on Sunday evening, five days after the incident, when I picked up a day-old copy of the Lima daily *La República* in the main square of Aucayacu. I was on my way over to see Mariela at her store. We hadn't had a chance to talk about the shooting since it had happened, and as I walked across the plaza, flipping through pages of the police blotter section, I found it.

In town of Pacae Bridge, Aucayacu

SENDERO MURDERS TWO COMMUNITY LEADERS

TINGO MARÍA (special correspondent for La República). Presumed subversives of the Shining Path cruelly murdered two community leaders during a raid on the town of Pacae Bridge, province of Aucayacu.

The victims are Jeremías Ayala Pinedo (32), who was shot in the head, and his brother Dennis Ayala Pinedo (36),[a] who was hit by two bullets in the chest and the head. Both were accused of being informers by their killers.

Before committing the murders, the seditionists forced sixty families from the area, as well as transportation workers and passengers intercepted on the Marginal Highway, to attend a two-hour proselytizing meeting.

Members of the National Police and the Prosecutor of Aucayacu recovered the bodies and transported them to this town's morgue.

In a similar incident, two women and a man were killed in the village of Cachicoto, district of Monzón, Huamalíes province, after being accused, as in the above case, of being informers.[22]

[a] Pseudonyms have been used.

As was common with the national press, the report contained factual errors about the place that anyone from the area would have picked up on immediately. Pacae, not "Pacae Bridge," was a small village, not a town, though it did have a bridge of the same name; Aucayacu was a district capital, not a province. Such minor imprecisions did not in themselves impugn the paper's version of what had happened. They did however betray an unfamiliarity with the region that was not untypical of the Lima-based press and expressed a real political distance. For Huallaga residents the differences between village/hamlet and town, and between district and province, were not minor. They reflected vital jurisdictional distinctions and indicated sites of political maneuvering for recognition and greater autonomy from Lima, which influenced the distribution of resources and services from the central state.

These were hardly the only details that did not square with what I knew about the incident. Obligating villagers to attend meetings for political indoctrination, which often involved the enactment of gruesome *juicios populares* (people's trials), was a routine part of Sendero "appearances." However, this was the first mention I had heard of any meeting taking place that night. None of us stopped on the road had been forced to participate, and from what we could tell at least one of the victims had been killed as the group of senderistas retreated from the area. Beyond these by no means small discrepancies, it was hard to imagine how Sendero could have gathered so many people in a place as visibly unpopulated as Pacae. Sixty families, even by conservative count, would have been at least a couple hundred people.

To anyone who had actually driven by it, Pacae exuded an air of desolation and abandon: a cement bridge, a large yellow Ministry of the Presidency billboard, three, maybe four, forlorn shacks. Little else. Even so, from the space of the highway, it was impossible to know what went on in the hilly expanses beyond the road. In fact, for anyone who stuck to the road out of convenience and prudence, the geography that expanded out from it was abstract at best. Conceivably Sendero could have assembled families from area farms and settlements and could have ended the gathering before moving to block traffic on the road. Still it was difficult to figure how there had been enough time, considering it was already past dusk when we had been forced to stop. Holding a large meeting, so close to the road and for so long, with an army garrison only minutes away in the village of Anda, seemed a stretch. It was also a stretch to make what I had less seen than dimly (though unmistakably) presenced—a masked guy waving a rifle, a mule train of sack carriers, yells and gunshots, and the agitated story of a teenage boy who nearly stumbled over a corpse—somehow fit with what I read in the paper.

The victims' names and the descriptions of their wounds departed little from earlier information. Yet subtle but significant differences were introduced as news of the incident moved from a local to national frame. These differences amounted to a complete revaluation of what had happened. The prosecutor was no longer quoted but appeared instead as a mute functionary who, along with the police, merely processed the bodies in accordance with Peruvian law. With the prosecutor now silent, the interpretation of events ceased to center on the part the victims might have played in their own deaths.

The emphasis shifted away from the victims' complicity, either "because they didn't know how to live life" or because of where they lived or who they were. The victims were no longer *soplones* but had only been accused of being so, a rather important distinction in that it injected skepticism into the charge and moved the attention over to a perpetrator transparent to all.

By way of a recognizable series of raid, obligatory meeting, accusation, and execution, this was a Sendero very familiar to the Peruvian national audience for whom the note was written. The convenient inclusion of a "similar incident . . . in the village of Cachicoto" merely underscored the reiterative, even routinized image that served here to make this new yet same old manifestation of Sendero legible. This repetition was, and at the same time made, the message that "here is Sendero simply being Sendero"—killing once again not only with absurd cruelty but as always on the basis of accusations whose truth or falsity have no bearing on the nature of the act.

In spite of this latest portrayal of the Pacae incident, so much was still up in the air for me as a reader of events. I had been physically close to what had happened that night, and because of it I thought I should have more of a purchase on what precisely had transpired than I did. And while it was easy enough to point out the discrepancies between what I had grasped that night and the events as later reported, many aspects of the incident had not been clarified at all: who the victims *really* were, what role they had played, how they came to be accused, much less who this Sendero was—beyond what everyone knew or presumed they knew—that had killed them.

Something had happened. There were two bodies. Not much else was clear.

It didn't help clarity's sake that in this last press report no date was given for the Pacae killings. Nor for the attack in Cachicoto either. Nothing indicated they had happened on the same day or even in the same week. This might have been an attempt to draw attention away from the fact that the paper's reporting was less than timely.[23] It served nevertheless to accentuate the imprecision, generality, and even timelessness that pervaded the narration of events. While this was the first news I had received of a Sendero raid in Cachicoto, a small but important town in the valley of Monzón a couple of hours northeast of Tingo María, that in itself was not unusual. Though the Monzón region was geographically adjacent to the Huallaga Valley and connected by myriad layers of kinship and economy—especially through the secret ways the cocaine trade stitched the two regions together—news from there circulated openly in Aucayacu town so infrequently that it could just as well have been located on the other side of the country. The conditions that affected the dissemination of information in the Huallaga Valley largely pertained for Monzón, and both coca-growing regions projected a remoteness that had little to do with geographic accessibility.

As a matter of concrete space, no location in the Huallaga was far away—at least not in Peruvian terms where communities in the Andean *alturas* (highlands) and in the tropical lowlands could be strewn several days' journey from the nearest road and were rendered even more isolated when bad weather hit. In comparison, the Huallaga was not inaccessible, certainly not from Tingo María, and not even from Lima—which was only twelve hours from Tingo María by the paved and easily negotiable Central Highway. Rather, the remoteness of the Huallaga, and of other areas where political violence had coincided with the cocaine trade, was produced through the amalgam of political, legal, and social prohibitions, most of which were less openly stated than felt. Those prohibitions made unfettered movement to many places as well as obtaining clear information about them complicated when not altogether unfeasible.

The difficulties of knowing what was happening in neighboring regions notwithstanding, in the published accounts of the shooting it was unclear in what sense or under what conditions Sendero, recognized there by a coherent series of actions, could simply still be Sendero. What Sendero was this that was merely being itself? Especially at this historical moment: six years after the capture of the movement's leader, Abimael Guzmán, along with a majority of the senior Party leadership, and four years since the Party had ceased to exercise an overt hold on any area of the Huallaga, much less the country. The Shining Path had long since lost the ability to influence on a national level the political future of Peru. Denied a trajectory of inevitable victory, that unyielding telos that had once afforded the Party so much momentum and in some quarters popular appeal, could Sendero possibly still be Sendero? Was this not instead a degenerate Sendero—a Sendero already defeated because robbed of its promise—but as yet unwilling to accept the fact? And if so, who were these armed groups that still roamed about killing? Were they following the lead of a party hierarchy? Or were they private outfits out on their own, and as such nothing more than marauders or brigands? Who was to say, after all, that they were not imposters, acting the part for pecuniary ends or to settle some personal score? Whatever hallmarks existed for what constituted Sendero violence, this recognized pattern or set of signs could always be imitated or manipulated to give the impression of something other that what had really happened. One common expression of civil war, and what perhaps gives it that feeling of a war of all against all, is how the distinct players will appropriate the garb of the "enemy" to test the true allegiances of "the people" and to perpetrate horrendous acts—often for private benefit—in order to discredit the other side. Surely people already have this in mind when they read such news. Or do they?

fragile links

The ambiguities surrounding what had happened in Pacae hardly ended there. *La República*'s report on the shooting did not specify what sort of role the victims, whom the paper identified as "community leaders," had exercised in their village. Nor did it explain that in the context of insurgent and counterinsurgent violence the term "community leader" was not straightforward. Representation at the most grassroots level of communities was bitterly contested, though less by the people purportedly being led than by the larger forces that vied for their allegiance. It was no secret that Sendero had killed many village-level leaders. Less acknowledged was the predicament faced by all who occupied leadership positions in rural communities: that they were called upon to respond to and carry out the divergent wills of both sides in conflict. If designated and thus recognized by the Party, they were subject to pressures from Sendero. If similarly recognized by the Peruvian state, they were subject to pressures from the army and, to a lesser extent, the police. If identified and targeted by the "other side," they were then forced to go into hiding or abandon the community altogether. Therefore, to be a village leader was to be in the sights of somebody. Often picked more by circumstance than personal choice (such as when Sendero's elite guerrilla column or *fuerza principal* charged in, rounded up villagers, and assigned posts), these leaders generally had no other option than to go along or lose everything they had. Villagers were called upon one minute to be in agreement with the Party and the next minute to be in agreement with the army, and those in leadership positions inhabited the most complicated and impossible places of all.

This conflict over communal leadership began in the early 1980s when Sendero made its first appearance in the valley. As it did elsewhere, above all in the most isolated agricultural communities of the Peruvian sierra, Sendero sought to sever any and all concrete linkages between the rural population of the Huallaga and the central state. In villages organized as "people's committees," no political or community group other than those generated by Sendero was allowed to exist. Sendero and only Sendero would speak for the people. Only the Party would represent their interests. Anyone or any organization that attempted to compete for the claim of channeling popular sentiments or aspirations outside the institutional frame of the Party would be driven out or destroyed.

Sendero by and large succeeded in imposing this prohibition, and its political dominion over the countryside went uncontested for nearly fifteen years. Because of this, during the 1980s and early 1990s a resident "community leader" in a Huallaga village would have had to be almost without exception a Party delegate. There were simply no other forms of representation allowed within rural settlements themselves. By the mid-1990s, however, the most open manifestations of local Sendero political presence and organization had been disrupted by the army, first through the physical elimination of village leaders, and later through their capture and in some cases their subsequent release in exchange for active collaboration. Once permanent Sendero leadership at the village level had been uprooted, the central state proceeded to insert a representational structure of its own through the creation of new communal posts. Through these posts rural communities would articulate themselves with state authorities on the district, provincial, department, and national levels and subsequently enter the long and arduous process of turning de jure political recognition into real economic assistance from the state.

In mid-1998, community leadership in villages outside Aucayacu referred essentially to three offices: communal president, municipal agent, and lieutenant governor. All three violated in a fundamental sense Sendero's stricture on popular representation outside the confines of the Party. However, it was the lieutenant governor's office that most directly drew the Maoist movement's attention and wrath because the post was organizationally linked to the Peruvian executive branch through the Ministry of the Interior, which oversaw policing and espionage agencies. The lieutenant governor was the local representative of the president himself and, in a surprisingly obvious fashion, the civilian face of the state intelligence services. On account of this, in rural areas where Sendero still had an active if hidden presence, the lieutenant governor was far less likely than the municipal agent or communal president to reside in the community on a permanent basis. Instead, for reasons of personal safety, he would chose to live in the closest town and visit the community sporadically and then only when he received information that the guerrilla was far away.

Perhaps much of the dynamic of the political violence of the 1990s in the Huallaga could be viewed as a seesawing motion of implanting representatives of rural communities and then displacing them through threats or acts of physical coercion. For as much as a population may demand recognition and services from a central state and organize itself to get them, a state can lay claim to a people only if someone or some group serves as the people's representational face. Perhaps the historical labor of molding masses into "a people" is less about scoring some kind of internal conviction within each and every person—"winning the hearts and minds"—than it is about creating concrete linkages between mobile masses of individuals and territorializing them into institutional structures. Local leaders constitute this concrete linkage, and in the Huallaga the role of community leader played this critical function—of speaking for "the people" *(la gente, el pueblo, la masa)* and of bearing the responsibility of making sure the will of those same institutional structures, once of Sendero, then of the Peruvian state, was carried out. Because so pivotal, the brunt of the violence came down upon these spokespersons less as singular individuals than for the representative function they performed.

mariela's take

When I got to Mariela's store and went inside, there were candles set out about, on shelves and cardboard boxes of supplies. The town's electricity had gone out sometime before dusk, and it was now half past eight, going on nine, with still no word as to the cause. Whether Sendero had downed another pylon or it was just some malfunction at the electrical plant, no one knew.

As I approached the counter Mariela was busy closing a sale, tallying items with a ballpoint pen while a tall man I didn't recognize packed purchases into a knapsack. From the way they were chatting, with a respectful but guarded familiarity, I assumed they knew each other or that at the very least he was a repeat customer.

Since he had his back to the store entrance, he didn't notice me until I came up alongside him and said hi to Mariela. He cut the chitchat short and asked her what he owed. Passing her a crumpled bill, he gathered up his things and walked out. The exit was so abrupt I asked Mariela who he was.

"Oh someone from the *chacra*," she replied blandly.

"From the *chacra*?"

"Yeah," she said, letting loose now a smile of intrigue, "looks like they're up to something."

"They?" I wondered aloud.

"Well," Mariela said, "you see, that man had a long list of things. Food-stuffs mostly, but also flashlights, lots of them. You tell me: you are a farmer, what do you do with twelve flashlights?" She held one up for me to see, a shiny aluminum penlight, of Chinese make.

"Well," I suggested, "maybe he has a big family, or he's buying them for his neighbors."

"No," she said, shaking her head. "They're planning something." An ab-surd image came to mind of guerrillas in full battle gear navigating pitch-black thickets with these miniscule flashlights. "They must have sent him on an assignment," Mariela continued, "and so he's going from store to store until he gets everything he needs."

"You mean he's a senderista?" I asked.

"No, no," she said shaking her head again, somewhat surprised that I wasn't getting it. "He *lives* in the *chacra*. They gave him a list of things to pick up, and if he wants to stay there, if he wants to keep his farm, he knows he must do what they say." This was not the first or last time Mariela would intimate how complicated life was in the countryside. "Much like those men from the other night," she said, beating me to the topic.

"What do you mean?"

"Well, one of them had a small bodega. He refused to collaborate, and they killed him, claiming he was a snitch."

"So it wasn't because he and his brother were village leaders," I con-cluded.

Mariela explained:

> Well, they may have been, but that wasn't the reason. More likely he simply got tired of paying the *cupos* [taxes], or he didn't have anything left to give. Because that's what it's like when you're a shopkeeper in the *campo* [country-side], and that's how it was here, too, when Sendero had a strong presence in town. If you had a store, they'd never leave you alone. Someone would come in and take a look around at your stock and before you knew it the Party was pay-ing you a visit or sending you a letter. You had no choice but to contribute.

Mariela all of a sudden slipped into the present tense.

> To show you are in agreement. You must give them what they want. But they aren't satisfied for long. They come back, again and again, and they go on like that, bleeding you until you don't have anything more to give. I bet you any-

thing that's what happened. The poor man just got fed up and said enough is enough. For that they killed him. Perhaps he didn't want to leave his store or abandon his farm, or maybe he just didn't have anywhere better to go. So you see, that's what happens. You saw how they carried all his stuff away.

I *had* seen something, and I heard it too—those tin can and kitchen pan sounds—through the darkness and shadows. Yet what I didn't mention to Mariela was that I still was not sure *what* I had seen, nor did I relate my suspicion that the very ambiguity around the event itself was somehow crucial to how things worked in the Huallaga.

Instead I asked Mariela how it had gone with Alex after she got dropped off that night.

"Oh, let's just say he wasn't happy. He kept insisting we should have known better. More than anything because of the time of year," Mariela said, trying to spell it out for me once and for all. "They"—she meant Shining Path—"have to show they still have some fight left, and that's what they're doing. They just want to let everyone know they're still around." And with that she smiled as if having found something solid to rest her explanation on.

But how could explanation become a thing reliable and firm where precise accounts were impossible to substantiate, as so often was the case in the Huallaga? Mariela had crafted a viable motive for the shooting from her own experience as a bodega owner, which she shored up by citing the prevailing local wisdom about the seasonal rhythms of Sendero violence. Yet her take was only one of many possible versions, and we by no means came into contact with them all. Most crucially, neither she nor I could be sure what the people who lived in Pacae, those who had been so reticent to speak with journalists, would have said if they revealed all they knew.

Remarkably enough, none of the press reports coincided with what Mariela and I had encountered on the road that night. This did not imply we had a better purchase on what had come to pass. We had been caught up in it, but as spectators we were largely blind, and in more ways than one. From the dark space of the highway there was so much we could not make out. We could not get closer without risking our lives, and the immediacy of that existential threat was a big part of what made the off-road rural areas of the Huallaga, by day or night, a world altogether "other" from the one where townspeople dwelled.

Perhaps the difficulty of confirming what happened was simply that we were close but not nearly close enough. Or perhaps proximity could deliver more objects for reflection but never anything close to a firm interpretative hold on the event, which after all far exceeded the sum of possible perspectives and explanations. Greater proximity did not in itself guarantee being able to speak conclusively. Nonetheless, it did open up the potential for rendering accounts that were vividly attuned to the ambient intensities, messy complications, and contingencies of what had transpired.

I now turn toward the larger history that provided a context for local understandings of violent events, such as the shooting in Pacae. During the post-boom years, that history was often expressed through stories in which the encounter with rotting human remains served as the central motif. Within the boom time itself, however, corpses often did a kind of labor that had far more to do with the present than with the past. In *aquella época*, lifeless human bodies and the images they produced became the material of new law. For when it came to the army, and to the Shining Path too, killing was not only about eliminating one's direct enemies but about communicating a most basic point to those larger and more extensive communities that had emerged during the boom. Both sides, through their signature procedures of violence, sought to found a legal order and therein define the terms of political belonging. It was within those circumstances that the figure of a mutilated corpse—as encountered and remembered—could play a pivotal role wholly different from that which it performed much later in the narrative spaces of post-boom.

Thus the next chapter boils down to this: one class of image, two types of labor, two distinct times.

3 river and road

lucky black sack

Night. It was always night in *those days* when Magno went—just to get a break
from things, not because he needed to. For sport. It must have been for sport.
Not like now when he goes in hopes of putting something on the breakfast
table. Yes, in *those days* it was always night when Magno went to meet up
with friends, an hour maybe two after dark, sometimes at the port but more
often just past the "Las Vegas" *chongo*,[a] ever-glowing red on the road to Cotomonillo. *Those days* were years before they built the bridge that's there now.
That hanging bridge the government laid across the Aucayacu River. The one
they painted glossy orange so you wouldn't forget that it was a gift from el
Chino, President Fujimori himself. Deep dark orange, like so many other
public works that went up all over the country that year, 1998, ever with an eye
on the next round of elections.

And who can forget the day of the ribbon-cutting ceremony? How the local
authorities and other town notables—never shy to celebrate—piled onto the
bridge? How they all stood there—all but Marusha, that is, who stayed back
opportunely on firm ground with the crowd of onlookers? Do you remember
how they stood there over the river, the bridge swaying back and forth, gently
back and forth, and how they listened to the chief engineer give his speech
from the riverbank? Listened to him halfheartedly and then not at all, when in
an ugly snap a steel cable broke free? How they screamed and shrieked when

---

[a] brothel

115

the bridge suddenly gave way beneath their feet and fell to the river below? Arms and legs pinned and twisted in a flailing mass of wire and wood as the water rushed and tore at them? And then how the government, so generous with its bridge, was not half as openhanded when it came time to pay compensation to the injured? To the army commander who lost part of a finger. To the rancher and filling station owner who busted up his shoulder. Much less to others of lesser distinction who, scrapes and bruises healed as best they could, even to this day walk about town with limps. Much less to the family of my friend Lidia Morán. She who didn't look half as bad as some, they say, the day of that terrible accident. Just a broken rib, assured the emergency room doctor in Tingo María. She died a month later at the hospital in Lima, of an infection from internal wounds occasioned by the fall. And why that happened, no one can quite explain, much less say who was ultimately to blame.

No, the times I'm talking about were years before the bridge went up, then down, then back up again—so that to escape the oppressive heat of midafternoon, teenage boys and some of the bravest of girls could line up along the planks, take turns climbing the chain-link railing and then dive down into the cool water below, as if the bridge had never collapsed at all. No, long before *any of that*, Magno would walk at night, maybe with a friend or two, down to the edge of the Aucayacu River, and then along it until finding what seemed a good place to try their luck. They would set out the lines, talking a little, passing around a cigarette now and then, waiting to see who got the first bite. After an hour or so if nothing was happening they might move upstream toward the highway or the other way to the port, where the Aucayacu River empties into the larger and more tempestuous Huallaga. From there they might continue down its shores to a small outcropping of rocks that, in the dry season, clears the water enough to make for a good perch.

The catch was often small. *Boquichicos* if they were lucky, *carachamas* if not, and *toa* were always to be had if nothing better was biting. Still, any one of them could tell you about the time he had hooked a giant *zúngaro*—"a hundred kilos, must have been"—and how he wished he'd had a big rig to haul it in.

Their equipment was rudimentary. Magno worked with an eight-centimeter hook he tied to a thick lime-colored plastic cord, spooled around a small, flat rectangular board, which limited what he might have hoped to drag in. That's why years later he would forever ask me, on my next trip to Lima, to bring back a big rod and reel from one of the fancy sporting goods stores on Avenida Abancay, so he could have a chance of landing the big fish he always talked about but never managed to wrestle to shore. And I remember I was always promising to bring him that rod just as surely as he was always promising to take me fishing with him and his buddies, even if neither one of us ever got around to making good on his word.

But back in *those days*, well before I met Magno, which is to say back in the cocaine heyday, catch or not, it really didn't matter. Immediate necessity was not an issue. There was always plenty to eat, and Magno just liked to spend the night on the river under the stars. Because it was relaxing. Because it was away from the nonstop ruckus of town. Not to say the outings couldn't be eventful. Roving as they did from place to place, finding that perfect spot to cast out the lines, he and his buddies never could predict exactly what they might happen upon. A poisonous *jergona* (fer-de-lance snake) coiled up between sand and rock. A *compañero* keeping nighttime watch over the movements outside of town. Or even the booty from a drug deal gone awry, pushed to the river's edge—which was not wholly out of the realm of the possible, especially with all the traffic that crisscrossed the Huallaga during the day: the *traqueteros,* or drug couriers, to the other side to haggle with the campesinos over a few kilos, and then back to town or downstream to Ramal, always in a rush to get the best price from the *patrón,* the boss. No wonder a boat would keel over now and again. It wasn't unheard of, because the Huallaga, even if it did look tame, had a mean streak that could surprise you all of a sudden. Many a valuable cargo did get lost, and not a few lives—all the more so if the boatman, to make a little extra cash, let himself get talked into loading on more than his dugout could stand.

So coming across something washed ashore was not altogether unusual. To the contrary, who hadn't heard of it happening? Some poor farmer or any person generally down on his or her luck, coming across a sack full of dollars or, what was effectively the same thing, raw cocaine. With so many stories, who didn't dream of coming upon a black bag of treasure? Because those nylon sacks, *costales* they're called, tended to come in black.

For that reason, even if Magno didn't go out there at night with the express intent of scavenging about, he would not deny that the idea was always there in the back of his head, of keeping a look out for what might come his way. All eyes peeled for that lucky black sack.

But Magno was never so blessed. He had never struck gold, you might say. Not out there on the river, and not even working in the drug economy, which was where wealth was more reliably to be had. Magno was no stranger to the trade. He had harvested and stomped leaves many times for the cousins of his in-laws near Monzón. And in the early 1980s he had even owned his own *cocal* (coca farm) not far off in the village of Alto Marona. That is, until the day Sendero moved in, called on everyone to assemble, and gave the ultimatum that if they wanted to stay and work their land, they had to join the Party; if not, they had twenty-four hours to go, taking with them only what they could carry.

Magno, not one to live so rigidly under the orders of another, up and left. He moved to town, to Aucayacu, and turned to bricklaying, a trade he had learned as a boy in Cajamarca. It wasn't a bad choice. The local economy was flush with *narco* dollars. Construction was flourishing. The rage was big, cement houses, since wood no longer seemed good enough if you could afford the *material noble.*[a] That in itself was promising for Magno because it meant work was plentiful and the wages it paid were better than anything he could have hoped to earn in any other part of the country. Still, what he earned paled against what could have been had, even at the lowest rungs, working coca.

Moreover, prices were sharply inflated for even the most everyday goods: a kilo of onions or potatoes might cost ten times more than in Lima; even crops native to the area like yuca or plantains were brought in from as far away as Pucallpa—for the mere reason that people weren't fools enough to break their backs growing legal crops. Not when coca paid twenty- or thirtyfold. The result for Magno was that he never managed to put much aside, not even enough to build a house of his own. His place in town, an adobe four-room dwelling on Jirón Huaraz, belonged to his wife, Marusha's mother. After contributing to her family's expenses, there was never much left over, especially now that he had to help pay for his stepdaughter and stepson who were away at school. Getting by wasn't exactly hard, there just wasn't much hope of doing more than that. So I can only imagine the expectation that swelled up inside him that night he was going about from fishing hole to fishing hole and came upon what looked like a black *costal.*

"It happened as if by chance," he told me, what must have been six, seven years after the fact:

We found it. You know your skin? It starts to bristle, *algo te pasa*, it's like something is happening to you. And since there were two of us, sometimes

---

[a] prime building materials (especially cement, steel reinforced concrete, cinderblocks, and bricks)

three, and because we were curious, we opened the sack. We opened it, right there on the river.

And what did we find?

Bodies. *¡Fresquitos!*[a] You should have been there. Just the limbs . . . or rather, of the men we found extremities, but of the women only the trunk. Without the hands. Without the legs. Just the body without the clothes. Without the feet. And not just that, you could see, you could see they had been chopped up with a chainsaw.

Curious we opened the sack. That happened two, maybe three times, and then we just didn't open them anymore.

Black sacks, those big black nylon sacks.

river

It's not as if finding dead people on the shores of the Huallaga was out of the ordinary. In those days there was something regular, even commonplace about it, if you can draw any conclusions from how it's talked about now. One evening I went to visit Doris, a teacher friend of mine, and her husband Carlos at their home in the compound of the Project. Somewhere in their mid-fifties, they'd been married for years but looked and acted as if they were still riding the wave of young love—especially when you saw them out and about town, Doris sitting sidesaddle on the handle bars of their bike, with Carlos pedaling away, just like high school sweethearts do all over Peru.

That evening they told me about the time, early 1980s it must have been, that Carlos had crossed the river on his way to their farm, and how, right when the boat arrived at the other side, he saw two corpses lying there together on the riverbank:

They were wearing these brand-new jeans, and the buzzards, you can't imagine all the buzzards there were, feasting there. And all the while the people, how they went back and forth, and the boatmen . . . on and on. But you know what? There were so many buzzards there that in two . . . no, in just one day's time they had finished them all off. They finished off the two bodies whole, leaving nothing behind, just the skulls. Those trousers, they had pulled them off. You hear me? Those jeans, they had just tossed them to the side.

"Their beaks—they are *specialized,*" Doris threw in, as if I didn't know, while

---

[a] Superfresh!

Carlos went on without a pause: "because the next day I come back and nothing was left but those skulls. And the buzzards? They were still sitting there on top."

Here Doris pressed: "You couldn't have pushed the bodies into the water?" Carlos shook his head. "I was waiting for the river to rise and take them somewhere else," he replied in a playful voice as if indignant at Doris for doubting he had the situation anything but under control.

"And that," Carlos said to conclude his tale, "is what I admire so much about the buzzard: so daring, so quick to eat someone up."

In those days if you wanted to get rid of someone you'd killed, the Huallaga was the place. Dump it in the river: the body would go downstream a ways, until it washed up on shore or got caught in the reeds somewhere, maybe linger there a bit until the water carried it somewhere else. Most likely, wherever it washed up for good, no one would be able to identify it—even if someone wanted to, which was not always the case, because most people knew good and well to mind their own business. Sure, when they got to where they were going, they would tell family or friends what they'd seen, but if they didn't personally know the poor soul, chances were they would finish off their tale with an *habrá sido por algo* (there must have been some reason) and leave it at that.

Being a settler region, most everyone was from somewhere else, and people tended to know only those who lived close by. Because of that, there was no easy way of attaching name to corpse. And besides . . . with the voracious river animals on your side, well, the Huallaga, it was just a good bet.

The favor of those odds was not lost on the "mafia," which was how local people liked to refer to drug traders in the abstract. Take Tocache, several hours downstream from Aucayacu. It has a big bridge suspended high above the Rio Huallaga, which connects the community with the Marginal Highway. Built by a Peruvian company at the end of the military government of Morales Bermúdez—and, as I was told more than once, according to the rigorous design of an Austrian engineer—you might say that bridge is the pride of the place. Its obligatory image appears on the cover of municipal brochures printed up from time to time in expectant preparation for a tourist economy always on the verge of taking off. Throughout much of the 1980s, however, when the mafia all but controlled Tocache, the bridge was a favorite location for tossing off its victims, especially after dusk when the police would pull back to their headquarters, leaving the checkpoint by the bridge an empty shell.

Today it is impossible to know how many were lost to the Huallaga River after being launched from that bridge, much less along the whole length of the river's winding path, from Tingo María past Aucayacu, Pizana, and places beyond. Impossible to know. And not just at the hands of the mafia. Magno once remarked that whenever the army went on patrol in the countryside, it wouldn't be long before the bodies would start floating past town: "Subversives, they must have been, and downstream they came in the plain light of day."

So many dead ended up in the Huallaga, it is common to hear people say the river became a cemetery. And it was a cemetery—minus the fixed place of rest, minus those who would come to revere and remember, minus everything, that is, that would make of a graveyard something more than a place of disposal. As a movement that never ceases to carry away, rivers are well suited to such tasks, and not only for the runoff of fresh kill. The Huallaga also channeled away untold gallons of chemical waste, of pesticides used to grow coca up in the hills, of kerosene and sulfuric acid needed to break down the harvested leaves into raw paste. This made the Huallaga River less a burial ground than a wash for everything those times of boom could throw off.

For a couple of centuries the Huallaga River had been not only a place for dumping, but the principal thoroughfare for non-Indian travelers in and out of the valley. The ferociousness of its *malos pasos,* or rapids, was well documented. Braving its low waters could be done only by canoe or by raft, and then only under the care of an experienced hand. In modern times—that is, until the early 1970s when the new highway would greatly facilitate commerce with the rest of the country—large cargo had to be shipped by raft. The men who ran them, *los balseros,* were predominantly from the department of San Martín. They were the only ones who knew the river well enough to safely ride its singular currents and maneuver its eddies and shallow curves. However, once the Marginal Highway was built and allowed for safer and more efficient travel, the flow of traffic shifted. The towns and communities of the Huallaga that had once faced the river turned increasingly toward the road. Local businesses and stores concentrated in the ports fell on hard times and had difficulty competing with the new places that opened along the highway. Seeing a *balsa* (raft) on the Huallaga River became a rarer sight with every passing day, just as the demand for a good *balsero* grew weaker and weaker. Eventually, few learned the trade, and those who knew it grew old and passed away. With the

river gradually changing its course as all rivers do, today there is hardly anyone who still knows how to run the Huallaga by raft as the *balseros* once did.

With the onset of the cocaine boom the ports on the waterfront found
new life, but the Huallaga River itself—except along partial stretches and then
only for very brief periods—did not return to being a public thoroughfare up
and down the valley. That role it lost, for all appearances decisively, to "La
Marginal," and from that point forward the river became mostly a thing to
be crossed by the long dugout canoes that connected the towns with the coca
farms on the other side. Except for an intrepid handful of independent operators, who would risk their hides moving cargo in night shifts toward Colombia
and thus allow the Huallaga *balsero* craft to persist under new circumstances,
the river current became less something to ride and more an obstacle to pass
over . . . or a place to dump with the certainty that what needed to be gotten
rid of would be carried away.

Which is only to say that in those days happening upon a corpse along the
waterfront was less a surprise than a likely prospect. Lifeless bodies mingled
into the river setting. What made an impression on Magno, nonetheless, was
not the fact of finding human remains as much as finding them in the form
that he did: packaged in those black sacks that should rightly bear contents
of a wholly different order and economy. Then there was the detail of those
chainsaw cuts, and *that* was enough to make anyone take notice.

Years later, encounters like those Magno had at the river's edge would join a
constellation of images that served in stories to provide a kind of temporal
recognition. Those storied images would be called on to separate a norma-
tive present from the extreme living of the past. Within the times of boom,
however, corpse encounters generated forms of habit and habituation that had
widespread consequences, affecting how people lived and traveled in the valley as well as attitudes toward the dead. Long after the fact, those same forms
might well cause expressions of bewilderment, whenever it was asked how
anyone could have ever gotten used to regular encounters with dead bodies.
Such questions reflected the sort of ethical valuations that could be assessed
at a distance from violent events and in what was altogether another time—
which is to say within a different order of sense making and even where a different sensibility was at stake.

Yet honing in on the actual acts of violence and their very real threats of
death revealed a whole other kind of image work: a labor ongoing within the

boom itself through the complex ways that political violence crosscut the co-caine trade and made the Huallaga often appear to be an impossibly danger-ous place. The image work to which I refer operated on an active experiential plane and was a central facet of that boundary-marking use of violence I have called "the political."

In synthesis, the political denotes a time or a set of circumstance where a palpable existential threat prevails. It comes into play where an armed group takes a population as its concern and applies force toward the objective of "making a people"; that is, forging a new collective and shaping the individual subjectivities that will fall within through the designation, discovery, and elimination of public enemies that fall outside. The political requires violence, but not all violence involves the political. Drug traders in the Huallaga, for example, regularly resorted to coercion in order to enforce particular con-tracts or to protect a market share, but they rarely if ever directed their ac-tions toward a larger social "totality" that they explicitly intended to form and regulate.

During the boom, the violence of the political was channeled through the display of human corpses that proclaimed a new law in the making. En-counters with those bodies produced images that in turn traced out visceral horizons of expectation and animated protocols outlining the basic terms of safe living. Later, when figures of mutilated corpses would become a major motif in ex post facto narratives about the boom, those images no longer did the work of the political. The acutely threatening circumstances had largely passed, if for no reason other than because one of the armed groups had suc-ceeded in asserting its dominance.

In other words, the same images or the same kind of images circulated along two distinct temporal strata: those of boom and post-boom. Each tract of time had its own specific economies of sense and reference that were di-rectly tied to actual political conditions. What the images had in common was strictly their representational content: the human cadaver, corpse parts, and remains. How they differed most strikingly was their relation to processes of lawmaking, border marking, and the orientation of time.

road

Ever since 1983 when she began studying law in Huánuco, Marusha made a point of going home to visit her mother every month. After classes let out for the week, she would take the winding road down the Andes and into the

Huallaga Valley, where she would change cars in Tingo María and continue on to Aucayacu. She had made the trip dozens of times but that made little difference: fifteen minutes out of Tingo María, just before the highway forked and where the car turned left onto the Marginal Highway, Marusha would get attentive, her eyes glued to the road. Ever since she first went off to college, whenever she got to this last leg of her trip, Marusha would count the dead. Yes, count the dead. Because there were always bodies along the highway, two or three at the very least. Hands tied behind the back. Head smashed, more often than not. A piece of cardboard would always be laid on top or next to the body with a message scrawled in red, or black, or whatever other color was available. And when the long weekend with her family was over and she boarded another car to return to school, on the way back it was always the same.

Marusha counted in silence but not out of any immediate fear. No good reason to be afraid, when you're not "anyone," when you're not involved in "anything," when you can easily account for yourself. So ran the logic: that for all unnatural deaths there must be a reason. Marusha counted because it gave her a personal, unspoken sense of how things were going back home. In the Huallaga, "the situation" was almost always the first thing people told you about when you arrived. So before she got there, before family or neighbors could fill her in, Marusha would begin drawing her own conclusions about the state of things. She would read them from the road.

The relation was simple and direct. The more bodies, the more fluid the political moment. A slight increase suggested intensification. A striking shift one way or another, qualitative change. And that was what Marusha was on the lookout for, to see and in so doing measure what, if anything, had changed since her last visit.

The drivers—of trucks, of microbuses or of the *colectivo* sedans Marusha always took—did their own measuring as they plied the road day after day. Theirs, however, was a more intimate and exposed relation to the dead, since they had to wend their way past them several times a day, all the while aware that someone could be observing their every move.

They would later tell how the appearance of corpses started little by little on the heels of rumors that the Shining Path had arrived from Ayacucho to organize coca growers and the "rural proletariat." At first, just one or maybe two. In those years, 1981 or even 1982, to come across a body could still cause surprise and not a little fright. Eventually, though, it was something the drivers got used to. Happened everyday: sun up, more bodies on the road. To

pass even ten or twelve on the way to Tingo María was not unusual: four by
the cemetery leaving Aucayacu town, two in Pacae, another in Pueblo Nuevo,
and four or five where the Marginal Highway joined with the Central Highway from Pucallpa. Tossed in the middle of the road or wherever there were
bridges or curves, each body with its cardboard sign.

And the drivers insisted that on these corpses hung a prohibition. You
couldn't as much as touch them without getting permission. At best the victims' families, if they lived in the area, could by asking around get a message to Sendero through one of its delegates and make a request to withdraw
the body for burial. Sometimes the Party would acquiesce, but only after the
corpse had been there a few days, having fully served its purpose of giving notice of the criminal type whose execution was displayed so all would see. For
not only did Sendero take the life of the body, it held onto its death for a time.
The police or army, when someone was willing to pay for their time, would
sometimes go out and carry the bodies back to town and fill out a report. That
was the only way there would be an official record. Otherwise, the bodies
would be left to rot into complete anonymity.

The victims could be women or men. Judging from their appearance, they
were often peasants, though sometimes their clothes suggested a better living:
brand-name blue jeans, black dress shoes, and all that gold—a necklace, brace-
let, or watch; above all a watch. Together these gave you the snapshot of a *narco.*

"You had to pull to one side to be able to pass," one driver told me. "Any
other way you couldn't get by. Corpses without heads or stabbed all over, mutilated, exploded. You had no choice but to drive on."

No choice because the prohibition was strong. At a deadly auto wreck elsewhere in the country, victims might be stripped of money, clothes, jewelry . . .
before emergency workers arrived. Be it in the city, be it along a desolate mountain pass. The pervasiveness, tenacity, and ingenuity of thieves in Peru is something many complain about while others simply marvel at or secretly admire.
But during the Huallaga boom, supposedly the most illegal of all places and
times, the bodies on the road were "respected." I later heard of gold chains left
undisturbed through weeks of putrefaction. No one dared touch the bodies.
That alone should give some idea of the force of Sendero's law back when it still
offered the unblemished promise of a different world to come.

Drive on, you had no choice, so you learned to count, to take notice. You
learned to see but *without* looking, that is, without making apparent that you
had seen anything at all. You drove on, you had no choice, taking in every

perceptible detail that came your way—that was the important thing—taking it in without a word: see, take in, don't speak. Eventually the silence would cease to be strange.

signage

"In those days you lived between a rock and a hard place. The first times it scared you but after that, no more. And since your conscience was clear . . ."
"You'd move on, or stay at home if it called for that."
"We drivers knew *de ley*[a] what things we couldn't do."

Because measuring "the situation" was about measuring your own way through it, discerning patterns, forming predictions, evaluating your chances without fail. See, take in, drive on. Because if you knew the rules, beside them a reason would emerge to guide you in your calculations.

Or, as another driver put it: "He who has no debts has no fears."

While each driver synthesized the situation as best he or she could, they all concurred that observing those rules seemed to be the only thing that could put distance between yourself and the dismal fate of having your own life truncated, your own person reduced to mere corpse: to an unresponsive remnant where what figured most evident was not the name that identified you in life but the sentence laid on top and which came to take its place.

Así mueren los soplones	Thus die the snitches
Así mueren los ladrones	Thus die the thieves
Así mueren los perros	Thus die the dogs
Así mueren . . .	Thus die . . .

Such was the form Sendero death notices took as they announced the arrival of a new and most drastic legal order. Corpse and a sentence, and through that attribution, a criminal type; but it was the erasure of name that came first. For if it is true that these bodies, as those dumped in the Huallaga River, often went unidentified—strangers from another place with no one to claim them—the conditions surrounding those killed and left on the road imposed a degree of anonymity that was far more structural than circumstantial. Even if they were your own kin, and sometimes all the more so if they were. For those deaths, those bodies that you noticed but could not easily acknowledge conveyed a basic order: "We knew what things we couldn't do." At best, if the

---

[a] Literally, "of law"; in this context *de ley* is a colloquial phrase for "absolutely" or even "by heart."

proper name lingered on in death, that name given at your birth or even the *chapa* (tag, nickname) by which everyone beyond your direct family might have known you in your everyday goings about, it did so only in the murmur that flashed immediately after the words *mataron a fulano de tal* (they killed so-and-so), and then only to get lost in the silence that followed fast behind.

Sendero's law was in its primitive dawn: ruthless because not yet strong enough to be generous. For every accusation, the same verdict. Guilt came with a visceral threat of death. One sentence sufficient to set the example, and therein lay a legal foundation from which would emanate a lexicon of offenses. A series of the wrong and illicit distributed through an open set of crimes, each with its own attendant type. Ghastly characters, damned to come to a horrible end: the *traquetero* caught rigging the scale; that high school girl who hung too close to the army barracks at night or danced a little too willingly in the police captain's arms; whoever didn't pay their *cupo* in time; anyone who informed. Alongside this set of proscribed types an imaginary line lay itself down to separate permissible from forbidden, a line that was reiterated with the appearance of every new corpse tossed on the road, tossed so everyone would see.

For it was not a question of punishment as much as the marking of a new frontier: a line drawn by the display of dead remains; a corpse that issued a threat. A public call to take heed and reflect, to size up one's place within the emerging conditions of new law encroaching on old—here bearing down on the same road that only twenty years before was herald of state promise to civilize jungle and bring land to all. A failure now redoubled in the Peruvian state's own apparent powerlessness to stay the flow of the dead on the public space it once claimed.

As the only overland route into the Upper Huallaga, the Marginal Highway became a privileged site for guerrilla actions. During much of the 1980s, the police had no helicopters and the army had only a few; when either force was called in for reinforcements following an attack by Sendero, La Marginal was the principal means for dispatching troops and supplies. Sendero would lie in wait for them at sharp turns in the road and from the bluffs that overlooked from above. Ambushes were common.

La Marginal became a "theater" as well for Sendero's *paros armados* (armed strikes), for its attacks on road infrastructure, and for Party messages addressed to those who traveled the road and formed a public all of their own. These messages came as *pintas* (graffiti): revolutionary slogans and warnings painted on the fronts of small dwellings that were scattered along both sides of the road, but also on the highway's asphalt surface. They came as human corpses, which were signs in themselves as well as the material support for those other signs: the cardboard pieces with their scribbled reasons for the deaths and which aimed to pin a particular sense to the violence that each lifeless body expressed.

The *paros* (literally, "stoppages") were major events organized by Sendero to demonstrate its strength. Farmers and their families from the adjoining countryside would be told to converge upon the road and form work crews. Rocks and trees and other debris would be strewn across the road from the start of the Marginal Highway at Tulumayo all the way up the valley. For two, sometimes three days at a time no motorized traffic would be allowed to pass. Drivers and passengers who attempted to get through might be required to join in on the work before being allowed to continue their journey, this time on foot. Over time, the *paros* became more extreme. Sendero blew up bridges and ordered villagers to dig deep trenches into the asphalt surface that extended north from Tulumayo to twenty kilometers past Aucayacu.

During every *paro* the number of bodies found on the road swelled. By positioning them along the valley's main thoroughfare, the Shining Path signaled quite literally its progressive advance on the Peruvian state. Throughout the 1980s, the fact that the police and army could not protect the highway infrastructure much less keep it free of dead bodies was a key sign of Sendero's upward ascendancy. And by forcing travelers to see corpse after corpse, Shining Path also made a claim on the collective imagination of the towns north of Tingo María. Residents of these towns formed the public that relied most on the road and which Sendero addressed at the outer edge of its rural-based power. Through their repeated encounters with dead bodies, townspeople would passively infer the rules of the place and grasp something of the direction of the times.

Roads permit controls that rivers do not. What is placed on them does not float away, and those who ply them must ultimately come upon whatever lies across their fixed path. Because of these strictly physical qualities, the Shining Path could use the Marginal Highway as a platform for lodging images in the minds of those who coursed it. The road allowed for an intensification through the successive presentation of bodies and thus the brute repetition of a simple message: "*This* is what happens."

This is what happens: several years later in the early 1990s, black nylon sacks stuffed with body parts began appearing on the shores of the Huallaga River. They were said to be the work of the army and seemed to be directed at a public unlike that which traveled exclusively on the Marginal Highway: farmers, farmhands, and their families, people who regularly crossed the river and were believed to form the base of Shining Path support. Getting about as they did on a combination of foot, bicycle, and canoe, rural folk had far more opportunity to come upon one of those sacks. Hopeful of discovering treasure in the form of money or kilos of raw cocaine, they found something they had not bargained for. The army, it seems, had learned a thing or two on the use of the corpse in the image-work of the political.

But strangely enough today, there is nothing at the edge of river or road to indicate that people once died there. There are no *capillas,* or small altars, as are found along highways throughout Peru to commemorate the sites of fatal accidents. The Huallaga landscape is as if emptied of any clear markers of its violent history. In part, this near-total erasure is a consequence of a tropical clime. In part, it is the result of brutal displacements engendered by the insurgent-counterinsurgent war. And in part, it is a legacy of the boom itself, which brought so many people to the Huallaga who never expected to stay. For some, the idea was to earn as much as they could and return to their hometowns and build that house they had always wanted. For others, the Huallaga was merely a trampoline out of the provinces and into a better life in metropolitan Lima. The boom brought so much movement, mass migrations, and because of the onset of violence, mass departures. Much of the historical memory of those times is now dispersed in those faraway places where it circulates in stories only told now and again.

time of rot

"Human corpses reek worse, worse than dead animals," Tony said as he paused to take a sip from a cola and resettle himself at the edge of the couch. We had been sitting in the living room of his home in the Chorrillos district of Lima for over an hour, with Tony doing most of the talking, when his wife Charo brought us something to drink. Gently she set two full glasses on the coffee table between us and withdrew without saying a thing. On her way out she lingered at the doorway, which was beyond the sofa and out of Tony's sight but well within mine, before turning around to face us and lean in a more permanent stance against the jamb. From there she listened as if intrigued by a story she had not heard in some time.

"Seems like a lie," Tony said throwing me a knowing glance, "but the smell of human death is even stronger than animal."

I nodded in reply, feeling obliged to take him at his word about the evaluation of something of which I had no direct experience. I also nodded to encourage him to keep talking as I looked down to check on the tape recorder I had placed on the table at the start of our conversation. Tony stopped all the same and waited until I had reestablished eye contact before going on.

"It *is* stronger," he said, as if a little surprised himself, "though after a while . . . we got used to it. With all we went through and saw, we simply got used to it."

People often described their experiences of the Huallaga cocaine boom to me like that: by telling how they had grown accustomed to living where exceptional acts of violence had become routine. Some spoke of this process of habituation with amazement, others in a cheerless tone that bordered on resignation. All told of there being an initial shock, when you crossed over into that space and time where horrific, almost unspeakable things happened; or when that same wave of superlatively jarring events swept up the place where you found yourself. Then they would say how soon they came to take the carnage in stride, because of its sheer recurrence but also because they knew what they had to do to stay out of harm's way.

The process of acclimation pulsed through encounters with human corpses. And yet it seemed that the very ease and speed at which people adapted back then later became hard to swallow—much less justify—when they would narrate those earlier events in the present day. In such moments, those scenes from the boom time and their own presence in them might come back and frighten in ways they hadn't the first time around.

Something had happened to the value of a human life. And that something and its mystery rumbled underneath recollections of the boom even when not made explicit in the narrative itself. There was a constant interrogation of the human concept and its limits and this, it seemed to me, was partly what spurred many of the stories I was later told. The interpretive weight often fell on loss: on how a basic respect and concern for the life and pain of another had become impaired—be it for a neighbor, a coworker, a classmate, but more often for someone never seen before. It was common for some (especially those first-generation settlers who could remember what the Huallaga Valley was like prior to the boom) to complain how the sudden influx of coca brought with it all sorts of people perceived as threats to both public morals and public health. They would tell you about the hustlers and prostitutes, about the professional thugs and corrupt police. Others, in a more self-reflective vein, would remark on or even express wonder at the changes the boom time wrought on their own interior dispositions. They might tell you that living in the midst of so much violence was something they not only got used to but even—if only for the eventfulness it could bring to each and every day—secretly followed with a dark fascination. They might admit as well that, at least in the beginning, when the Maoist Shining Path arrived with the promise to clean the place of *malos elementos* (bad seeds), it seemed like a good idea.

The stories told that somewhere along the way public and even personal respect for human life went wildly astray. Less asked, however, was whether the cocaine boom, especially as it blurred with the insurgent-counterinsurgent war, had somehow altered or even transformed altogether the sense and value of what it was to be human. Perhaps it was easier to disregard the possibility that "the human" was not only a concept but a thoroughly malleable one with a plasticity that fed upon the semantic obscuring of social, biological, and historical registers. Perhaps, overlooking the complicated notional terrain that "the human" as concept covered and, more important, the ways that terrain could shift, made it feasible to sustain the idea of there being a fixed standard of measure strong enough to be applicable to all situations and times.

Certainly a reified, ahistorical notion facilitated making sense of the boom event itself, while gaining narrative access to it long after. But it did so only at the cost of eliding one crucial facet of what had actually happened: that the rules and rule-forging practices of armed groups had implicitly redrawn the lines of "the human" as a social category, determining what placed someone "beyond the pale" and thus licit to be killed. In fact, an essential aspect of the boom experience itself was having to confront how those lines multiplied and assumed unique forms. Their situational contours were, however, specific to that place and time and did not translate easily into the years of post-boom, much less into faraway geographic spaces, such as the city of Lima. Historical narratives registered the movement of those boundaries while they struggled to reproduce them as they had been, and instead refracted them into evaluative contexts of another mass and intensity.

Little wonder, then, that Tony's talk of rotting corpses resonated strongly for me. Not only did he continue the interrogation of the human concept I had both heard and intuited in other stories, but in his telling it received a new twist. That dead flesh should smell differently depending on the species sounded plausible, even wholly expected. Yet his claim that human putrefaction and its olfactory repulsiveness could be not simply distinguished but *opposed* to that of all other animal remains struck me as a novel way to carry on the questioning of "the human" that so permeated retrospective accounts of the boom.

Tony insisted that a human body rotted in the worst of all ways, and the verity of this he claimed to have personally confirmed. The actual empirical basis of his finding concerned me less than the fact that he considered his observation to be an unusual bit of knowledge and at the same time somehow counterintuitive to prevailing common sense. What interested me was the mystery that Tony wanted to draw attention to. "Seems like a lie," he said, as if to suggest the actual truth of the matter were secreted away or masked underneath a deceptive guise.

Later that day when I had returned to my apartment and began to reflect on my visit with Tony, I kept asking myself: What was the frame of common sense against which he had arrived at his so-called discovery? For his point was not merely that human remains reeked differently than those of other animal species but that, because they were human, after all, one would think they would smell better. This was, as best I could tell, the turn that animated Tony's story: how the encounter with rotting human flesh upset the order of expectation and trumped an all-too-generalized prejudice of human superiority. More precisely, his "discovery" seemed to defy any fast assumption that human preeminence would be expressed in the materiality of the body itself, which is to say in its very animal life, as naturally more pleasant or refined.

While Tony seemed to offer his empirical revelation as a corrective to aesthetic and moral notions of supremacy, he neither collapsed the human and animal distinctions nor forced them into a reversal of roles. Rather he appeared to extend the range of the human itself: from most formidable in life to most base and abject in death. The corpse that Tony spoke of—as a foul becoming whose olfactory potency outpaced all other forms of carnal rot—at once complicated any overwhelming division from the animal realm and yet intensified the exemplarity of the human type.

But, then again, what could be more exceptional than that superlative capacity to cope; to transform oneself according to the demands of new and toxic surroundings, so that by traversing them and letting them traverse you, they became less forbidding? Even if there were nothing singularly human in that ability, even if.

Such thoughts would engage me in the months to come as I pondered how the human concept, which in one instance teamed together with violent acts to impose a sense of law, could in another be displaced onto historical narrations but under wholly different cover. I pondered as well whether the act of personal narration, when it relied too firmly on an assumed unity of the narrating subject across time, would not fail to account for the ways that events of violence and shifts in political regimes fractured the self more than they gave it coherence. Making sense of the boom demanded both conceptual and narrative stability that had to be creatively enacted before they could ever be put to representational tasks.

What impressed me more immediately about Tony's story, however, was hearing it only a day after meeting him for the first time: when in answer to my hail for a cab he had pulled his car out of the flow of late-morning traffic on Avenida del Ejército and come to a stop right before me. Now in his living room, as I stripped away the plastic wrapper from another cassette, placed it near the recorder, and took a drink from my glass, I wondered if these events were really past for Tony or if rather the mere fact that we were in Lima, and far from the Huallaga, offered sufficient distance to talk about them. How else, I asked myself, could he speak so freely and generously to someone he barely knew? In the Huallaga I was familiar with, people clung far too tightly to their personal histories for this to happen so soon and in so straightforward a fashion. Distance was decisive in this case, though more from place than time.

For even if the boom had now passed, in the Upper Huallaga one still lived under the constant stress of having every action observed and every word overheard in the strange ways that the agrarian, small-town, everyone-knows-everyone-else world melded with the secrecy and paranoia that permeated overlapping networks of drug traders, state intelligence, and Sendero. The visceral gravity and force of such persistent scrutiny—visceral because it can and will get under your skin, disrupt digestion, disturb dreams—come with living in the Huallaga. But Lima, because of its sheer immensity and anonymity, diluted and dissipated the vitality of such fears and from far away made them seem no more than frail, weightless abstractions.

taxis and little trucks

Tony had spotted me outside the state orphanage, which sat at the southerly edge of the depressed middle-class neighborhood of Magdalena del Mar, the same neighborhood where I rented a small apartment. It was a dark and chilly day for early April. A thick imposing mat of graying clouds covered the sky and descended to envelope the street in a light fog. From where I stood, bundled up in sweater and scarf as if winter had already arrived, I could see the mist billowing over the orphanage walls in hazy translucent puffs. The air was wet and pungent with the sea and trace elements of urine, feces, and rust it had swooped up from Magdalena's blighted shores as it crossed the coastal road and scaled the cliffs of tawny rock and earth up to where people lived.

"Where to?" Tony asked, rolling down the passenger window of a white Japanese compact. He cleared off the front seat as I got in, and we headed south.

"Coming down hard today," Tony said, motioning to droplets beading up his windshield. Precipitation in the city rarely approached a steady shower, and what many *limeños* would call "rain" was a thick mist bordering on drizzle. I offered that the cold weather had come too soon, and Tony laughed. "Yeah, you're right, but only over here. In Chorrillos where I live it still feels like summer."

In shorts, a V-neck T-shirt, and old sneakers over bare feet, he dressed as if he meant it. Somewhere in his mid-thirties, Tony was less tall than stocky and had dark, wavy hair that together with his smile gave him a certain boyish air. He didn't look the part of a full-time *taxista*, cruising the streets for as many hours as physical energy or gas in the tank would allow. The jumble of cell phone parts, telephone wires, and brochures he had pitched onto the floorboards in back to make room for me suggested he had other things going on. Like many in Lima, Tony put the family car to work whenever he had to drive across town, picking up anyone who happened to be going his way, and in so doing mitigate, at least, the cost of gas.

The gray, foggy pallor of Magdalena fell behind as we moved into the affluent San Isidro district, where the path became greener as tree branches and shrubs popped through red brick walls of residences spaced by restaurants, small retail stores, and offices. Here traffic stepped up, and we didn't say anything more. Tony just kept his eyes to the road, left hand guiding the wheel, right planted on his thigh and leaving only to shift gears, which he did with the playful resolve of someone who likes to drive. Soon he picked up the conversation again. Tony wanted to know where I was from and what I was doing in Lima. I told him I studied history and was currently trying to learn whatever I could about the Marginal Highway, or at least the portion of it that ran through the Upper Huallaga Valley.

Tony, pondering what I had said or simply having sized me up to his satisfaction, didn't respond, and when we reached the intersection of Avenida Arequipa and Angamos, he brought the car to a stop before a raucous wall of traffic. Anticipating a long wait, he turned the ignition key off to conserve gas and together we watched distractedly as the conductors of small buses and vans fought each other for position, rushing riders off and on, before being whisked away themselves—to the left toward downtown Lima or to the right toward the commercial center of Miraflores. Minutes later as the light changed to green, Tony engaged the engine, and as he waited for the way to clear, he turned to me and said, "I know that road. Used to take it all the time, my brothers and me."

I barely mustered an inquisitive "Yeah?" as I grasped the unlikelihood of this stroke of luck, but that was enough for Tony, who took it from there as he accelerated through the intersection. He told me how he had grown up in the highlands of Huánuco and while still a teenager had become a merchant truck driver. It was the family trade, after all. His father had spent much of his life in a Ford F350 traveling the winding road from Huánuco City to Tingo María, selling staple foodstuffs, hardware, and whatever else he could to the roadside store owners who lived in between. When construction on the Marginal Highway began in the mid-1960s, the new settler communities of the Upper Huallaga Valley became his preferred destination. There was lots of work for anyone with a set of wheels and sufficient will to make the trek.

Tony got his turn in the late 1970s, and over the next ten to twelve years he made weekly runs between his hometown and the Huallaga. It was a fascinating time, he said, because he loved to drive and because on that road you never knew what was going to happen. You had to be good at what you did and that was part of the thrill. Things happened, things that most people wouldn't believe, even if you told them.

Tony admitted he missed what he called "that life," which he put behind him when his family moved to Lima in the early 1990s. His gig these days was "telecommunications," and recently he and his brothers had started their own cell phone company. Tony offered to sign me up right then and there, but I declined, explaining I wasn't staying long enough to make it worth his while. If Tony was disappointed, he didn't show it, and I took that as a cue to suggest we meet up again to talk some more about his truck driver days. He agreed without hesitation, and when he stopped to let me off he handed me a card and said, "You can come by my house. Just give me a call."

Twenty-four hours later I was sitting across from Tony in his home as he told me how, when his two older brothers were old enough to drive, his father bought a second truck, a Chevrolet, so they could help out with the business. Tony followed them a few years later, first with his father at his side, and then alone. The final destination was often Uchiza, and because his father considered Tony the best driver, he entrusted him with the Ford. Both trucks would depart Huánuco on Monday to make stops along the way throughout the week and then head home by week's end. The following Monday they'd be stocked up and ready to go at it again.

In those early years the valley teamed with life the likes of which Tony had never seen before. From the main towns to the villages that lined the highway, people lived what seemed a permanent vacation. Yet no place, Tony said, compared with the excitement and effervescence of Uchiza. "In the main plaza there were so many people, walking here and there. You could hear music. The whole world drinking, the whole world passing by in their fancy cars, four-by-four pickups, tremendous motorbikes. The bars were full, and the girls . . . *pucha, ¡qué increíble!*" The parties that happened almost every night were so wild, so volatile, he said, they could as easily end in hugs as in a hail of gunfire.

Tony swore he never got to enjoy the festivities up close, feeling obliged to sleep in the truck and keep an eye on his merchandise. This may have been true, and while I didn't press him on the point, I couldn't help thinking how common it was for those who caught something of the boom to later claim they had been passive spectators. More often than not in the stories it was others who took a direct hand in events. While it was no secret that during the boom the Upper Huallaga acquired national renown as a center of decadence and debauchery, in Peru the stigma infusing the notion of *vicio* (vice or addiction) is as intense as it is pervasive. Little wonder people preferred to tread carefully around anything that might implicate them and cause them to lose face. Tony, I suspected, saw no advantage in elaborating right there in his house or in giving details that could very well come back to haunt him, if only in the form of mischievous needling from a relative or recriminations from his wife, who he surely sensed was nearby.

The commercial movement of Uchiza, Tony said, was extraordinary. Big trucks pulled in from Lima, Pucallpa, or Huancayo and unloaded their wares: be it tennis shoes, women's cologne, or blue jeans. On a good day they would sell everything on the spot. Tocache . . . same story. Chickens would arrive by the truckload. Tony said it was amazing to behold, how the people wanted poultry so much they would line up to buy them right off the truck. And then he would watch how they headed back home, bird in hand, to make their *caldo de gallina* (Peruvian chicken soup), which he insisted was the best hangover remedy around.

Money abounded. Tony said there was no mistaking that cocaine was what made everything move at a frenetic pace. Coca was everywhere you looked, from the fields that covered the hills visible from the town center to the peasants going to and fro with their *fardos* (bales) of green leaf. When the planes weren't coming in to take the product out, however, everything came to a stop: for the owners of general stores, boutiques, bars, and brothels; for the butchers and the hairstylists; as much as for the drug traders and all those who labored to help them make, protect, and transport their goods. That everything came to a stop was, for Tony, evidence enough that cocaine was the engine that made things move in the Huallaga. Coca was everything, and all of it went to the *pozo* (stomping pit) and from there to the *patrón* and then on to the light planes that ferried it up and away to Colombia, the place where all the dollars came from. The Huallaga no longer produced anything else, and so at the end of his weekly runs Tony headed home to Huánuco with little or nothing to haul back in the bed of his truck.

Such was the opulence of the towns, where people would later tell anecdotes of highland peasants who got rich off the boom. They would tell how, in those days, even the most destitute, Quechua-speaking farmer carried a wad of dollars in his pocket. Those stories pivoted on not so subtle anxieties over the indigenous poor getting rich, which obscured a far broader tendency: the wealth of the boom accumulated in the mestizo-dominated towns without spreading evenly enough to the Huallaga countryside or the closest highland communities to rid them of the poverty endemic to much of rural Peru.

Tony, a mestizo himself, claimed that in the countryside he saw "people so poor they were yellow, yellow and gaunt because of the worms, because of the water they drank. Parasites, lots of them." His contact with the families of impoverished farmers and farm workers who resided near the road was what he liked most about his trips. The sound of what Tony called his "little truck" was well known, and when he took it down into the valley, he would honk the horn and young children would come up from the ravines where their mothers were washing clothes, and they would stand in the middle of the road until he came to a stop. Tony always traveled with a bag of candy to give sweets to all the kids, and then he would say, "Hey, when I come back through bring me some plantains, a little yuca, and I'll buy them from you."

Sure enough, on his return there the women and children were, waiting for Tony with his plantains and lots of yuca. They would say, "Don't pay us. Give us some rice, beans, sugar." And so Tony would leave them their rice, their beans, their sugar. Sometimes he would even take them used clothes he'd picked up in Huánuco. Other times when they told him someone was sick, he would deliver medicine. "I liked how they would run up to the truck. I liked how all the kids would come running up from the ravines, kids of all sizes, bringing me my yuca and plantains, peppers, limes, papaya."

wear

The irregular distribution of cocaine profits together with the perceived vices of the boomtowns and their profligate ways were thrown into critical relief by the Maoist interpretive frame of the Shining Path. Here on the territorial outback of Peruvian law, here where frontier commodity capitalism was in full bloom, Sendero had no trouble recognizing in crystalline form its own imperative to wage a protracted "People's War" from country to city, even if the so-called "urban zones" upon which it set its regional sights were but gritty farm towns with populations that seldom surpassed ten thousand. Implicitly assuming the role of boom-time policeman and administrator of new law, Sendero would wager its strength on disciplining the coca/cocaine trade and its social excesses along this rural-to-town vector.[1]

Tony, however, didn't speak about such things. At least not in those terms. Like every trucker, he knew his route, and he knew the highway. Every week going up and down the road he would have a grasp on what was up ahead. Before each bend, he already knew when a hole was coming, and he knew how he would veer to get around it. That's not to say the trip was a cinch, because for all the talk of the jungle being a beautiful place, Tony said, he and his brothers endured days in the heat and mosquitoes, and more than a few nights caught in the muck.

Most of the problems came with the rain. Water would leak into the back of the container and put his cargo at risk. Once it poured down so hard that the packets of noodles he was shipping fused together, and *pucha*, he said, "it was utter disaster." But the problems didn't stop there. When the rain came down days on end, as it frequently did during the rainy season, there were places where the surface of the road became a precarious trough of mud, and drivers could spend days at a time stranded on the highway. One truck might be lucky enough to get through, but the next one was sure to get waylaid, causing traffic to back up in both directions and tempers to flair.

All that got worse, much worse, after Sendero began blowing up the bridges and digging up the asphalt sections of the highway. Then the trip took even longer, and where bridges had been felled there was often no choice but to go right through the water, taking the chance that the current would drag your vehicle downstream.

When the government stopped sending road repair crews (either out of neglect or because the crews got fired on by Sendero when they tried), truckers had to do what fixing they could on their own. They would pull rocks out of the way, shovel muck, or do whatever was necessary to dig a path through and get their rigs to firmer ground. "It was that way every week I made the trip back then," Tony explained. "It got to the point that the drivers ended up fighting among themselves for the road. Everyone wanted to get by, to pass everyone else, and when someone got stuck, they'd trade insults."

They'd yell: "If you don't know how to pass, why do you jump in there?"

And they'd curse: *¡Huevón!* and bang their fists on the door of the stranded vehicle as they pushed by.

Deciding on the best place to cross a bridgeless stream was largely guesswork. That moment when you committed yourself and everything you were carrying to the capricious movements of the current was nothing less than maddening. One trip when Tony was traveling with his brother, they had the Ford loaded down with almost three and a half tons of cargo as Tony started across. He entered just right of center, going slowly and feeling his way so as not to come up against a large rock or drop into some unseen hole. All of a sudden a Volvo truck, nearly twice the size of his, came up from behind and cut in onto the right so fast and with such force that it pushed Tony and his small truck into the middle of the stream. Because it was so big, the Volvo had no problem rolling right on through and down the road, its driver not even bothering to glance back to see that Tony's truck was getting dragged away by the current. Tony yelled instructions to a tractor that was right behind them. "Run ahead! Run ahead! I'm tipping over." The tractor heard his plea, and as it trudged forward to the other side Tony's brother jumped into the water to attach a cable that pulled them to dry ground. It was a close call, because finding someone willing to help you out on the highway was at best a chance affair.

Pendencia was one of the hardest spots. If it rained hard, the stream would swell up so you couldn't do much more than pull to the side of the road and wait through the night for the water level to drop. You might make up for lost time by tracking back to the Central Highway and heading out to Aguaytía, make a few sales there, and then be back at Pendencia by dawn, to try your luck again.

You suffered a lot, Tony said. There was the constant wear and tear on your rig, the holes and rocks that busted the suspension, the sand that leaked into the engine the times you crossed when the river was too high. And then there was the constant jumping out and going at it with the pick and shovel to try and dig yourself out of the mud. It was a constant push forward, pull back, tighten the cable, and watch it cut your hand.

bridges and curves

Tony had clients up and down the Marginal Highway, so it was only natural that he become friends with those with whom he did steady business. He learned soon enough that it was better not to grow too attached, as they might not be there the next time around. Things were mercurial in the Huallaga: people were always coming and going, appearing and disappearing without notice of any kind. There were times when Tony might see a store or a filling station well stocked and making good sales, only to find it boarded up or abandoned on his way back. A business could vanish from one day to the next: maybe the money ran out, maybe the owners fled, or maybe "the terrorists" as he called them demanded a tax that no one wanted to pay. It was always like that.

You'd ask: "What happened?"
People would say: "They killed him."
You'd ask: "What happened?"
They'd say: "He left because they were going to kill him."
You'd ask: "What happened to your wife?"
He'd say: "Oh, she got a death threat."
And that's the way it was.

Tony told me about a customer who lived a little beyond the village of Sitully and an hour before the turnoff for the town of Uchiza. He couldn't remember the name of the place, but the village's school was visible from the road, and

I suspected it was the hamlet of Yanajanca. The teacher of that school had a little store that Tony helped stock with the goods he brought down each week from Huánuco.

"We called him *el Cholo*,"[2] Tony said, "because of his patriotism." The teacher was from Ayacucho and extremely devoted to his Peruvian flag and national symbols. Every morning he would raise the flag and make all his students sing the national anthem. "And that was his undoing," Tony explained, because everyone knew Sendero had prohibited the display of national symbols, the teaching of civics courses, or the participation in patriotic activities of any kind. "The teacher received a warning that he'd better heed the rules," Tony recounted, "but bullheaded man that he was he didn't pay attention and continued on with the flag and the anthem."

One day an armed group claiming to be Sendero showed up and called him out in front of his students. They said, "This guy doesn't listen to the Party. He just keeps at it."

Three days later Tony drove up with his truck and found the man's wife looking pale and distraught. "I asked her, 'Señora, what happened, what's come over you?' 'They've killed my husband,' she replied and then broke down in sobs." Tony said he felt obliged to comfort her as best he could: "Okay, Señora, calm down. What can you do now? It's done. This has happened because your husband was so stubborn."

Tony shook his head for a brief second, took another sip from his glass and cleared his throat. Then he said what a shame it was that his friend had thrown his life away like that. Because "if he hadn't raised that flag . . ." Tony let his voice trail off but it soon returned to sum up his point: "In those days, that's the way it was. You just had to keep your cool. We weren't so disturbed by such things. They happened all the time. Then again we rarely witnessed it ourselves but only heard about it later: that they had killed so-and-so, that they killed him over there, that they broke him, for this reason or that."

Simply hearing about events of violence was to be at a distance from them. Merely hearing about them also taught one how to keep that distance in place, but only at the risk of recognizing and thus getting snared in the murky force fields that emanated from the violence and circulated as so many tacit rules.

There were two lives of the highway. At least two: one for those who traveled it and who depended so completely on the state of the surface; another for those who lived on either side—those "stationary" people who for better or worse had no

choice but to confront directly the political demands of place. As for Tony, so
many things happened along the Marginal Highway that could not concern
him. The main thing was to get to where he was going, to get there fast. In his
head he held tight to his destination as the inexorable goal of his immediate
future. On that everything depended.

Because of his intimate knowledge of the road, Tony was keenly aware of
those places where he had to be most careful. Not just the streams or where
either the runoff or Sendero had destroyed the integrity of the road, but along
the desolate stretches where he could drive half an hour without seeing a single soul. Highway robbery was not the problem it would become in the post-
boom, when "necessity," as Tony put it, turned so pressing. The section that
made him most nervous was north of Madre Mía, where his teacher friend
had been killed and where there were plenty of tight curves that forced him to
slow his truck to a crawl, where it was easy for the guerrilla to appear out of
nowhere and make him stop.

Admittedly, of all the years he traveled the Marginal Highway, Tony never
once had any problems with Sendero. At most they asked him to make a
small monetary contribution or share some of his cargo. Even so, the human
corpses Tony would regularly see strewn about the road were potent reminders of what they were capable of.

Mutilated and almost always with signs on top or lying close by that specified the crime committed, the bodies had a habit of coalescing around certain
spots on his route. There was Pacae. There was the curve just past Fundo San
Luis, nine kilometers north of Aucayacu. And there was the Honoris bridge
at Pucayacu, where Tony once came upon what was left of a police patrol that
had been ambushed only a half hour before.

They were places of heightened surveillance where you wouldn't want to
stop. They were places that became infused with the Party's presence and
might—what could well be called the atmosphere of its law. Stop and take a
closer look? You knew better.

Bridges and curves.

No place compared, however, with a village just north of Nuevo Progreso
known as Río Uchiza. Tony guessed the year was 1987, but he couldn't be sure.
All he remembered was driving through the village and crossing the bridge
over the river that gave the place its name, when he saw a cluster of corpses
lined up in the middle of the road.

Only someone who had lived in the Huallaga would be aware that Río

Uchiza was a hamlet quite separate from the town of Uchiza, which for its part was one of the region's oldest settlements that had emerged as a nationally renowned center of the raw cocaine trade during the boom. Río Uchiza, the village, was a quite different place. Virtually unknown outside the valley, it had been founded in the late 1960s by homesteaders from the northern department of Piura. In the late 1990s, I would know the village as one of many points on the Marginal Highway where the army manned a checkpoint with a base in clear view of the road. A decade earlier, however, Sendero had been in charge, and its Popular Guerrilla Army (Ejército Guerrillero Popular, or EGP) regularly used the village as a place to take prisoners for trial and summary execution. On account of this, Río Uchiza acquired a fearsome reputation for those who lived in the towns of Uchiza or Nuevo Progreso. The village was a place of death and the bodies that appeared there underscored that fact. Located strategically on the Marginal Highway between the main cocaine markets of the mid- to late 1980s—Uchiza and Tocache to the north; Nuevo Progreso and Paraíso to the south—Río Uchiza was an opportune place for Sendero to make a show of its force.

"There must have been seven or eight," Tony recalled. "Each with their little sign. Face down, hands tied, and you could see they were starting to bloat." The stench of death was already unbearable, and because of the heat and a light breeze that was blowing, Tony said he could smell it from over fifty meters away. Yet what caused the greatest impression on Tony was that the corpses had been left there to rot and no one in the village dared to do anything about them.

And over the next three weeks, each time Tony came through he saw them there in progressive states of decomposition. The first time, he was approaching from the south. He had clients in Río Uchiza and stopped to see if there was anything they wanted. His customers never let on much about the goings on of the village, but the smell was so bad and pervasive, it was hard to act as if nothing had happened. One shopkeeper confided her frustration, halfheartedly calling the situation "outrageous" and asking, if only rhetorically, how it could come to pass. The worst part, she said, was that they couldn't do anything. In truth, they couldn't, Tony assured me, because of the prohibition. They couldn't retrieve the corpses. And since no one knew who the dead were, there was no kin to go to the local Sendero leader and request permission to give the bodies a proper burial. The victims had been killed somewhere else and dumped by the bridge. The villagers had no choice but to bear with the stench.

Tony carried on his journey to the town of Uchiza and a day later when he passed the village on his return trip to Huánuco he drove past the bodies as if they weren't even there. Another week went by. When he came through again, the position of the bodies remained unchanged, forcing him, once again, to the edge of the road. By now they had turned purple and were covered in worms.

It was a calamitous sight. There they were, with their rubber boots. Those boots had become all inflated, because the bodies, they had swollen up like they were about to burst. You realize there comes a moment when the body does explode. The body swells up and it explodes. Either that or the skin peels away, like when you burn yourself with scalding water. I know this, because I passed by.

On his next trip out from Huánuco, Tony's teenage sisters, Pilar and Milagros, tagged along. School was between sessions, and they were bored and wanted to join him. Tony tried to dissuade them, saying the trip wasn't all that enjoyable, but they wouldn't believe him and insisted so much he finally gave in. The journey was uneventful until Río Uchiza, and when they saw the bodies, his sisters started to cry. They knew the Huallaga was a violent place. They had seen the newspaper headlines. They had heard the talk. Then again, Sendero was no stranger to Huánuco city, where revolutionary graffiti appeared almost everywhere. Attacks on the police, assassinations of politicians and labor activists, and electrical outages were commonplace. Still, they had no idea that in the Huallaga the situation was so awful. And though Tony and his brothers spent so much time on the Marginal Highway, when they came home they never talked about their travels or what they dealt with on a daily basis.

It was this silence in part that fueled the sisters' outrage. Milagros said to Tony, "what if one day you leave and never come back. You'll end up just like them," referring to the bodies. Tony tried to brush off her concern, insisting that he had grown so accustomed to seeing these things that it no longer fazed him. Even so, Tony admitted to me that the scene was pretty appalling. Baked by the sun the bodies had become waxy masses of fat wrapped in a shriveled skin.

Tony and his sisters covered their mouths as they passed by, to keep the stench at bay, but they could not help staring at the corpses and their continued transformation.

"It's just human curiosity, no?" blurted out Charo, taking sudden steps toward the couch until she was right behind her husband. "No matter how ugly, you want to keep looking. As you drive by, you just keep looking until the very last moment. No matter if the person is dead or not."

I didn't know whether Charo was just referring to traffic accidents she had seen, or if she had spent time in the Huallaga, or if she had heard and mulled over this story many times before. Perhaps she just wanted to offer a defense for morbid inquisitiveness, for the voyeur in us all. And that was fine and well where narration was concerned. But I had trouble believing that in the actual moment, when Tony, Pilar, and Milagros found themselves confronted by the corpses, that what held their gazes boiled down to simple curiosity. Their eyes might have latched onto the dead bodies, but what kept them there could not be separated from the fact that they felt themselves addressed through the rotting flesh by a most menacing force.

Tony was not surprised by his wife's abrupt entrance—as if he knew all along she were close by—and he nodded in support before going on to finish his story. He said that on his next trip out, Pilar and Milagros decided not to accompany him, and so he went alone. When he stopped in Río Uchiza, he found the bodies still in the middle of the road but now they had been covered with sand, which had the effect of reducing the smell considerably. In the village he was told that the remains had already taken on a deformed and plastic appearance when an army dump truck showed up and poured earth on them. That was the last trip in which Tony saw the bodies, because a week after that a bulldozer arrived and pushed them down underneath the bridge and into the river. Or at least that's what Tony heard.

mute earth

"Dump truck burials" became, if not routine, then common in the final years of the 1980s, according to the drivers of cargo trucks and passenger vans I spoke with in Uchiza and Tocache. They were a makeshift remedy for an extraordinary situation on the Marginal Highway where the proliferation of the dead combined with a prohibition on their recovery. Back then, bodies would appear every week or two, especially along the twenty-five-kilometer stretch between the village of Sitully and the town of Nuevo Progreso as well as in the vicinity of Río Uchiza. As much as the drivers wanted to stop, to identify if not retrieve the bodies, they said they felt prevailing conditions had turned so hostile that even the tropical landscape conspired against their good intentions.

"What is the jungle like?" one driver asked aloud, before offering his own response: "It's dense, and because it's dense, *they* could also be there. So if you stopped and got out to take a look, for your curiosity they could well let you stay there to keep the other bodies company. That's how it was."

That's how "it" was, which is to say the situation and its rules. Bodies would appear, begin to rot, and eventually a dump truck or maybe even a front-loader dispatched from Tocache would come along and cover them up with sand or earth. No police inspection, no legal *levantamiento*, no prayer. At a minimum, the act of sending out an earthmoving machine was a gesture, however feeble, toward reclaiming the highway.

The drivers said you could still see some of those mounds of earth when you drove past, and I believe I have seen them too, tan piles of stony dirt at the edge of the road. The drivers insisted "everyone" in the 1980s knew bodies were buried there, yet when repairs were later made to the highway, no one had much, if anything, to say about them. Nothing to say when heavy machinery came in to scrape, compress, and reconstitute the jungle road top into a rounded arc: a smooth surface that makes the journey so much easier and less stressful, that is, until the next torrential rains. Nothing to say about the bodies buried on the side of the road or who they might once have been. Nothing to say as the seasonal repairs went about grounding them into the mere material of road. "Everyone" knew they were there. And then no one knew, or they just acted as if it no longer mattered . . . if it ever had.

Darick, a close friend who lives in Tocache, explained to me once that during the boom years people in town gradually lost what he called "that superstitious fear of death." It is fear, he said, that one sees in other parts of Peru, where a human corpse is almost always treated with respect. In the rest of the country, he said, a lifeless human body produces alarm, indignation, and even sorrow for those who come into contact with it. The person who encounters it contracts an obligation to sympathize with the pain of the next of kin. When Tocache became a center of the cocaine trade however, encounters with the dead gradually ceased to provoke compassion of any kind. Darick phrased it like this:

> In other places people see a dead body and they cross themselves, but here it's not like that. They approach, they look carefully—it doesn't matter if there is blood—they'll look for distinguishing marks perhaps to see if it is a missing relative. They'll look . . . but there isn't any emotional feeling any more.

That feeling died. And not only did it die, it's worse, because people here will say, with regard to the circumstances of death, that "there must have been a reason."[a] That's the justification they give. It may have been a crime of passion. It may have been vengeance. Or it may have been mistaken identity. There have been cases where the wrong person was killed simply because he looked like someone else and that's the end of it. . . . . The excuse given is it must have happened for some reason[b] or that the victim must have done something[c]. . . . That's the explanation. How should I put it, it's like the affirmation they give to the deed itself.[d]

Darick was not from Tocache originally but from the Lower Huallaga city of Tarapoto, some three hundred kilometers to the north. But when he had barely turned twenty Darick landed a well-paying job as the manager of a major Peruvian soft-drink distributor in Tocache, a position for which he had no training. Such fortune was a symptom of the era. On account of the rising violence, the company had difficulty keeping its operations in Tocache staffed. Darick's predecessor had skipped town after a close scrape with death, and no one with administrative experience was willing to go and take his place. Young and eager for adventure, Darick signed up and soon he found himself in charge of company sales throughout the region.

It was Darick who first told me about the episode at Río Uchiza, about the bodies that villagers refused to remove for fear of their lives. And until I met Tony in Lima, thanks to our happenstance encounter, I had never found anyone who could confirm what Darick had seen. In the late 1990s it was hard to determine with precision what had happened during that earlier time.

Violent events like those at Río Uchiza had taken their toll on most people who still lived in the Huallaga. Darick said the long-term effects of the violence were palpable in Tocache, where he lived, especially the change of disposition that came over townspeople during the boom and that persisted long after it was gone. Yet I was especially struck by the status he claimed townspeople accorded to the act of killing itself, as if the event of giving death were not only final but that it contained in a very self-sufficient sense its own justification or grounds. Darick chose a curious word to describe the attitude townspeople developed toward the human corpse. He called it an *aval*—rendered above as "affirmation," though the semantic valences and resonances of the word

---

[a] *por algo habrá sido;* [b] *por algo será;* [c] *algo habrá hecho;* [d] *el aval que le dan al acto*

are more complex and extended. *Aval* suggests guarantee, protection, surety. It can connote a quality of firmness (*firmeza*), but also a signature (*firma*) function that avows—and thereby confers greater stability to—a statement, proposition, or claim. An *aval* is a guarantor's signature, such as that required for official documents or commercial transactions, as well as any spoken or written pledge.

In the local, social landscapes of the Huallaga boom years, binding agreements tended to be word of mouth. Along with *garantía* (guarantee), the word *aval* was commonly used to describe what townspeople or villagers gave when they vouched for someone who was new to the area and ran the risk of raising the suspicions of drug traders or the Shining Path. An *aval* was given to "recommend" someone, so that his or her life would be spared. Such vouching always involved a personal stake, because putting in a good word for someone else required putting oneself at risk. What ultimately guaranteed the life of another was always your own.

However, Darick's use of *aval* pointed to a related but fundamentally dissimilar situation. Acting as the guarantor for a person's life, where you put yourself at risk, was hardly of the same order as a casual vouching for someone under less ominous circumstances. Moreover, Darick spoke to a collective tendency during the boom to endorse the act of killing in a way that effectively authorized what happened simply because it had come to pass. By virtue of a "generosity" toward the event that took life, the violence that pervaded the boom time received affirmation. That affirmation found expression in part through a broad insensitivity toward human life in the abstract; that is, the life of others as distant, separate, and nonidentical to one's own particular existence and sympathies. It was the seeming absence of value of human life (for its own sake) that manifested with the appearance of every new corpse.

The widespread transformation in disposition Darick spoke of entailed a tacit support for the violent act itself and placed whatever blame there might be for the death on the extinguished life of the corpse itself. Instead of outrage, instead of any questioning of what might have happened, a swift judgment determined that the victim must have done *something* to deserve such a horrible end.

The phrase *por algo* ("for something" or "for some reason") set the death within a cycle of exchange and lent the act itself a presumed if unspecified sense. It *must* have happened for a purpose, even if the ultimate or real causes remained forever ambiguous. A substitution was invoked: "for some reason" implied "(something) for some reason"—with parentheses serving here to designate the ambiguity or uncertainty of the cause, motive, or reason behind the killing. The *aval* was granted to that bracketed-off unknown as well as to the overall transaction. It conferred an unquestioning acceptance and trust of whatever had transpired. *Por algo* assumed the violence was not capricious but happened for a logical reason and in response to something. As an a priori formula, the circle of exchange was closed before the act and regardless of "the facts." There was nothing to weigh or interpret. Above all, there was nothing to be done.

In this way, the appearance of a dead body marked the end of speculation for something that happened somewhere else, perhaps, because it was too unnerving to draw it close, too dangerous to get involved. By the time the corpse appeared, the dispute was resolved. There was nothing left to do or be concerned about.

After all, there were plenty of ways to die: through the "private" justice of the cocaine trade or through Sendero's "people's trials"; in the course of an anti-narcotics sweep by the police or during an army counterinsurgency operation; or even for other, less explicit causes. Conditions during the boom time almost never offered a chance of discovering what had really transpired or who in the end was responsible. Between the perils that infused the Huallaga as a place and the impossibility of verifying events with a good degree of certainty, to say *por algo,* that it must have been for some reason, became as ready an interpretation as any. Yet it was an explanation in form only. *Por algo* stood in the stead of an explanation or rather indicated the place of its absence so as to express a readiness to accept that the victim had brought misfortune upon him or herself.

Thus, as wild-card categories go, *por algo* folded neatly into a situation where the best bet (namely, the bet for survival) was not to make a fuss. For as much as "public" zones of transit were saturated with the immediate proximity of death, for as much as the reiterative presence of the corpse shaped and charged space, the superlative level of violence did not halt movement through the valley. There were means of making one's way. Everyone fashioned as best they could their own "moral" or rule of thumb for securing safe passage.

A seasoned veteran of the cocaine trade summed it up for me once: "If you keep to the good road, you'll be okay." Ten years before I met her, she had been a teenager who had gone to Uchiza bent on fulfilling a dream. She wanted, in her words, to be a *mujer de narco*—the sweetheart of a successful drug trader. That was her original goal, and over the ensuing decade she realized her dream several times over and through it picked up enough trade knowledge to become a cocaine entrepreneur in her own right. Not that she landed a fortune, but she did well enough to stay in the game.

"What does it mean to keep to the good road?" she asked, and immediately answered: "That if I see something, I keep quiet. If I see someone getting robbed, if someone is getting killed, I simply move on. Better put, I don't get mixed up in other people's problems."

Her moral was "mind your own," and as a guide for safe passage it was not so different from the take of the *colectivo*, truck, and van drivers who said, in regard to the bodies on the road, that they "knew" absolutely what they could and could not do. Dead bodies were but signs, signs in the valley landscape from which those who traversed it, drivers and passengers alike, would infer their own rules. Those rules were good and useful only as long as they served to get travelers and themselves to where they were heading without too much mishap along the way.

corpses in time

Perhaps, as Darick claimed, there came a point when a dead body no longer aroused feelings of respect, superstitious fear, or even compassion. However improbable it might seem that a corpse could ever cease to draw a "human(e)" reaction absolutely—that is, for all who came in contact with it—Darick nonetheless remarked on a widely held perception. And even if in some cases the victims of violent death were rendered incapable of provoking sympathy, human remains, for all that, never stopped being appropriated as a sign ridden through by multiple registers of time.

Corpses became signs, in one respect, through their proliferation. During the boom the visible abundance of dead bodies served as an index of actual political conditions. The recognition of a prevailing state of affairs suggested which rules were in play and how they would shape the contours of what was possible. In the boom's aftermath, that same proliferation—this time as an image of a *former* present—would be called upon to denote a radical difference between historical eras.

When directly encountered, however, corpses could point simultaneously to an immediate past and to an impending future and, in so doing, connect contiguous befores and afters that cohered in an individual lived present. In the specific context of the boom, a static, disfigured body often lay positioned along a well-traveled path. For many who came upon it, that corpse indicated the act of killing, the lingering proximity of the killers, and the real chance that they might reappear any minute to kill again.

Along that same vector the steady course of decomposition marked a progressive distance from the act that delivered death and as such mediated—though without necessarily diminishing in the short term—the intensity of corpse encounters. These, at their most extreme, could tear at the lived moment and color the immediate future with deep foreboding, though hardly for everyone or in the same way. The force of encounter fluctuated not only in proportion to the elapsed time of rot (or distance from the killing event) but in line with the circumstances, stations, and stakes of those who beheld them. As such, the intensities that flowed through a corpse were not distributed equally. For travelers, the freshness of the kill raised their own awareness of situational vulnerability differently than for those who lived close by. This was especially the case in locales and times where the strength of Sendero made the prohibition on removing, touching, and even overtly expressing remorse for the dead on display nearly uncontestable. People who resided near where the bodies were laid often had no other option, barring flight, than to bear with the stench of decay. For them, corpses put on spectacle spoke to a ruling structure, and to their own place within it, in ways far more onerous than for those who merely passed through.

As for soldiers and senderistas, policemen and *sicarios,* as well as the direct kin of the dead, the temporal registers of corpses found other inflections still. For all, rotting bodies became a durable feature of the Huallaga landscape. Yet it was those claiming to have never been involved in the killing, to have never belonged to any armed group, who later would wonder aloud about the loss of sympathy for the dead. It was they, those who professed to have been no more than bystanders, watching what happened but incapable of actively opposing it, that Sendero and the Peruvian army would treat as political communities in the making. For those "spectator publics"—made possible by the boom itself and distributed along a town and country divide—there were at least three ways corpses moved into the setting of the Huallaga Valley:

Though organic decay—as each dead body followed its own cycle of rot, as variable and dependent on the interface of a species' biological constitution, an individual corporeal resilience, and the physical atmospheric factors of the place. As each body on its own biometeorological time, often sped along by the animal life that fed upon it, turned into mute material of river and road.

Through the contraction of habit—as corpses by means of their repetition founded a specific historical present where certain "living" rules of thumb acquired force: for those who regularly crossed the Huallaga River, transited the Marginal Highway, or lived nearby—the many ways in which they, each and alone in their solitude, grew accustomed to the presence of rotting bodies. Taken together, such encounters created a mode of habit that in drawing upon corpses as an observed series of recurring empirical elements would establish a rigorous, causal connection between them. That connection had profound temporal effects: it engendered an expectation that what was repeating would continue to do so. In other words, the habit of coming across lifeless human bodies crafted an arrow of time that stretched from a contiguous past toward an anticipated future and served to orient the lived present.[3]

A corpse was not a repeating element like any other, rather one that had direct bearing on the possibility and conditions of political community. The magnitude of its recurrence made the boom appear to be an extraordinarily dangerous era, but it was at the level of affect that one could grow used to the violence or even feel "turned" through a puzzling alteration of interior disposition. It was also on the plane of affect that practitioners of lawmaking violence could shape subjective horizons of expectation by explicitly indicating the everyday bounds of the social.

People sensed that the spread of corpses touched them, but it did so in ways they could not precisely represent or explain. For while habit had effects that were palpable, it acted by means that were prior or exterior to consciousness. The connections produced through the observed repetition of corpses operated in the mind as so many minor events of law, which opened tracts of time intimating what could and could not be done.

Through contemplative distance—as a sign of "the times" and as a means for making sense of what was happening during or even long after the fact; less in the empirical thickness of encounter than from a more consciously thinking place of remove that reflected on present conditions or crafted representations of the past.

— Consider Darick, who in post-boom Tocache discovered the vestiges or legacy of cocaine's violence in local attitudes toward the dead.

— Consider Tony in his living room in Lima, so far from the boom in space and time, who called upon rotting corpses to define an era.

— Consider Marusha, too, visiting her hometown as a passenger taking in the scenery; while not immune to habit contracted outside consciousness, she would nevertheless contemplate "the situation" from the variable stream of dead bodies that served to measure the direction of those times.

In sum, the effects produced by the display of human remains traveled across several temporal registers. The layering of those registers as well as the resonances produced between them accounted in large part for the enduring force of the corpse as a Huallaga boom image. Whether as proliferating; immobile and numbing; or simply rotting into mute, anonymous nature; those images conveyed through stories owed much of their vitality to practitioners of the political who asserted new law through the repetition of lifeless human bodies.

compassion

The processes by which events of violence generated associations in thought and altered internal dispositions were tightly woven together. Their effects spanned a spectrum that was broader than the domain of representations. Thus it was impossible to trace them through their intricate flows. Accounting, simply accounting, for what happened was no facile matter.

Radical shifts in social value, however, were less elusive, and people never failed to mention them when recalling the boom. Everyone talked about how easy making money became while, at the same time, the very life needed to amass it was rendered a trifle. Perhaps a perceptible depreciation in the value of human life tends to accompany frontier commodity rushes, be they for gold, oil, emeralds, or rubber. The boundless wealth imagined to be there for the taking sits juxtaposed with the specter of interlopers coming in to dilute the spoils. The downward slide in respect for human life comes with the mad scramble for riches; yet it intensifies all the more where the production and trade of the sought-after commodity converges with armed ideological conflict.

In the Huallaga the idea that the cocaine boom attracted too many people, among them those of criminal and abject traits, was widespread. And when that notion found a point of resonance with the Shining Path's message of revolutionary change, it thickened severalfold. Sendero claimed to wage war for the purpose of ushering in a new society. It was a society that would be built through the heroic sacrifices of many Peruvians, whom the Party would form into committed militants through their separation from what it considered the corruption and vice that plagued life under the old "reactionary state." Violence was the primary tool in this process of selection, and the Shining Path conceived of that violence as having a purifying force that revealed but also substantiated the revolutionary character of its armed struggle. In the towns of the Huallaga, the Party had little trouble finding ready examples and personifications of social ills. They were often the same ones townspeople complained had arrived with the boom and which Sendero vowed to remove through what it called a *limpieza social* (social cleansing).[4] That for Sendero the forms of life it proscribed deserved no consideration, no recognition as "human," was expressed through killing, topped off with the handwritten signs calling the victims, among other things, "miserable dogs."

People spoke as if all innocence withdrew from things human. Or rather, as if innocence was what one left behind upon entering the boom. For during those years, if there was innocence, it belonged only to those foreign to human affairs and perhaps to them alone. People lamented this and invariably pointed to how, back then, corpses no longer produced much thought. That is, unless something occurred to force the situation into greater relief. There were stories to that regard, such as one from the late 1980s as told to me by a friend:

> On one opportunity I was traveling in a car returning from Tingo María. We had already passed a bunch. I don't remember how many. It was as if we didn't care about them or about their lives. But as we got near Río Frío [a small village about five minutes before Aucayacu], we came across a little dog that had been run over by another vehicle, apparently no more than a moment before. And what surprised me was the reaction of some of the people who were riding in the car with me. Their reaction was one of anguish. "Poor little dog," they said, "who was the bastard who ran you over?" They were angry. Indignant. I didn't give it much thought at the time, but later when I got back home, I remembered their reaction. It made me question what life was about here, where the life of a little animal was far more worthy of compassion, of sorrow, than that of a human being.

cruelty

Throughout the decade of the 1980s Marusha pursued her studies in Huánuco. The progress she made toward the law degree was incremental. In the political turbulence of those years, public universities became active theaters of protest, agitation, and recruitment among the different factions of the Left, constituing a separate front in struggles, sometimes armed, against the state. The university in Húanuco was no exception. Everything there was politics, and there were few realms of activity that were not construed as political at their core. Strikes and stoppages came in rapid succession. Sometimes they were called by teachers, sometimes by students, and sometimes imposed on all by the Shining Path. Rare were semesters when classes fininshed on schedule, that is, if they fininshed at all. Frequent interruptions created their own opportunities. In Marusha's case it made it easier for her to get away whenever she liked, to visit her family a few hours off in Aucayacu and in so doing to keep tabs on that other world.

Throughout the 1980s there was a consistent morbid feature of Marusha's trips back home. Once she got past Tingo María, she knew they would be there lining the way: hands tied back, heads split open. The stream of the dead had long since become a normal and expected part of her trip. But as the decade came to a close and a new one started, Marusha noticed that the bodies were becoming less constant. They didn't vanish altogether, but they didn't appear in the same number or frequency as they had before.

"How odd," Marusha thought to herself on one occasion as she gazed at the road. "It's diminishing."

Marusha once commented to me that she had grown so accustomed to the presence of dead bodies along her route home that when they were no longer around, it surprised her (in her words: *me pareció extraño*) and so much so that she practically "longed" to see them again (*extrañaba ver muertos*). Their absence was a notable shift in the ongoing state of affairs, one that left her somewhere between astonsished and nostalgic.[5]

There was one trip she remembered especially well. The year was 1991. As usual she arrived in Tingo María, but this time even before changing cars, she found herself thinking about those bodies, wondering why in her most recent visits there had been so few, wondering what could possibly be going on. The war with the Shining Path was not in any sense over. The Party's strength did not appear to be waning. The Huallaga remained Sendero country. And so, on the way to Aucayacu when she did not see a single corpse on the road, Marusha could not believe it.

Arriving home, she found her mother restocking the shelves of the store. At that moment there were no customers, and so Marusha, keyed up about what she hadn't seen, couldn't help herself. It was the first thing that came out of her mouth: "Mamá, I've come in from Tingo and on the Marginal Highway there wasn't even one dead body!"

"Well . . . ," her mother said gazing at her daughter with a studied look, "that's . . . good."

"But, *mamá*," Marusha emphatically declared, "it's strange not seeing the dead!" (*¡me extraña no ver muertos!*).

The look on her mother's face became preplexed. "*Hija mia*, don't talk like that. You'll make me think you're turning into a cruel-hearted person" (*que te estás volviendo sádica*).

Marusha, feeling misunderstood, gave up trying to explain and instead moved the conversation to the latest news from the university. Yet changing topics did nothing to ease the odd sensation she could not quite nail down but that bit at her all the same. *Esa extrañeza.* That feeling. Was it simply surprise? Some kind of longing? She didn't know. But Marusha did tell me it lingered a few days more, until word came that some poor soul had gotten himself killed and that his body had shown up on the highway for all to see. By then Marusha's visit was at an end, and when she headed back to Tingo María the next morning, she made sure to keep an eye out to get a glimpse for herself.

4 cement house

two years

Judging from the exterior of the house, Marusha had come onto better times. You could see it in the cement façade, newly painted white and rising two storeys high; in the two front doors, made of sheet metal and adorned with overlapping diamond shapes; and even in the tall garage gate, cut from the same smooth metal and welded onto iron tubing, which would have offered cover for a car if Marusha could have afforded one. The signs of improved living didn't stop there. The windows of the house were framed in steel with panes of glass still intact, while a second-floor balcony looked northeast to the village of Yacusisa and the scrubby hills that lay beyond.

Situated just off the main plaza, Marusha's new home couldn't have been more central, not that her previous residence was out of the way. Her former home sat on the "good end" of Jirón Huaraz: two long blocks away from a string of cheap bars that lined both sides as you moved toward the Huallaga River and which gave the street much of its local fame. What had been Marusha's home since she was a young girl was relatively far from the cantina scene but within respectable proximity to Avenida Lima, which stretched from the Marginal Highway down to the Aucayacu River and came as close as any street to being the main strip in town.

The house on Jirón Huaraz was a small, one-storey, mud-walled structure with wooden doors, dirt floors, and a corrugated steel roof. It had been home to Marusha's family ever since her mother, Herminia, had brought Marusha and Nico from Monzón. As many families still do, Herminia opened a small bodega in the part of the house that faced the street and used

157

the remaining couple of rooms in back as a space for her and her two young children to live.

Of Marusha's childhood home I only came to know the store, or more specifically the front room with its sallow wooden tables and benches set against walls, where customers would go to eat or drink but also where the family received visitors. It was at one of those tables that Marusha introduced me to Mariela on my first visit to Aucayacu.

The house on Jirón Huaraz had two entrances that led into the sitting area and through which flowed the sounds and smells of the street. On the rear wall of the front room a large opening or window had been cut for a counter. Herminia tended shop from the other side, rarely moving from her stool since most everything was within easy reach: the stacks of powdered milk on wooden shelves, stored above the cooking oil and beneath rolls of toilet paper; the Kolynos toothpaste next to the Hamilton cigarettes and Sublime chocolate bars, stored inside a Plexiglass case that rested on the counter. The point being that by the time I made Marusha's acquaintance, little distinguished her mother's bodega, or any of the bodegas in Aucayacu, from those outside the Huallaga Valley. Long gone were the days when Marusha's mother stocked the shelves with canned imported cheeses and fish fillets, or when the most prized liquor, Chivas Regal, sold for forty bucks a pop.

"Back then forty dollars wasn't even money for most people." Those were *other times*, Marusha explained, when the bars on Jirón Huaraz stayed open round the clock and there was never a day when the waft of stale beer didn't roll in off the street.

Other times, to be sure. Because when I came to know her mother's store, there was at best a dusty bottle of cheap wine perched high on a shelf waiting for an occasion.

I visited Marusha's former home a handful of times the year I met her. "A warm smile set in a full, round face, with dark eyes and hair, and a sincerity so welcome and unexpected." Those are words from the journal I kept on that trip. But what I remember most is how everything about Marusha exuded vibrancy and strength, even though she got around on a pair of metal crutches on account of the polio that had afflicted her when she was very young.

At the time Marusha was taking on lots of clients, as demand for legal advice was high. Many people needed to regularize their legal situation vis-à-vis the Peruvian state, though I suspect that getting paid for her services was another matter altogether. With the local economy in a nosedive, everyone was hurting, Marusha and her family included. Her fledgling law practice did, however, create other opportunities. It enabled her to keep close tabs on the ongoing political landscape, both in and outside of town, and she regularly sent reports to human rights organizations in Lima.

During the span of the several months that I was in Peru that year, 1995, I made three trips to Marusha's town. The first was for almost two weeks; the other two lasted less than a day. The extreme social and political tensions of the moment, given the Champa-Cristal conflict and the ongoing war for the countryside, took a heavy toll on the people of the region, and because of it my presence could easily become a liability for anyone I depended on while I was there. Though I stayed in contact with both Marusha and Mariela, nearly two years went by before they told me it was fine to visit again.

Two years was a long time in the Huallaga, and much had changed around town in the lapse between my first trip and my return in 1997. Drug planes were said to no longer be leaving the valley. The Champa and Cristal gangs had fled town, and no one had come to take their place. Padre Orlando had been recalled to Lima, definitively. Padre Saúl was still around, though he too would leave before the year was out. The army had left, for a time, to go defend the northern border with Ecuador. While they were away, Sendero raided the town one August afternoon and held it for several hours. The attack made national news, but its impact locally was promptly overshadowed the following day when President Fujimori himself made a surprise visit and gave a speech before the main plaza, overflowing with astonished town dwellers. He promised to bring the soldiers back. And come back they did, to reoccupy the base they had left behind—much to the vocal relief of many Aucayacu residents.

Yet none of those events touched Marusha and her family nearly as much as the passing away, in early 1996, of Herminia, who succumbed to a long bout with a chronic nervous illness. Upon her mother's death, Marusha became the head of the household: for three siblings (Nico, Bianca, Caro) still finishing up their studies, a stepfather (Magno) with only sporadic employment, and a grandmother—whom everyone called simply "Abuela"—in poor health well beyond a working age. It fell to Marusha not only because she was the eldest child but because she was often the only one bringing in any income at all.

The decision to move came a year later. Marusha explained to me that upon obtaining her law license she required a place large enough for both the family and an office where she could receive her clients. The death of Herminia never figured in her reasoning as I heard it, and it was a silence that asked to be respected.

Still, I often wondered if the justification she gave for the move—as a question of merely needing more space—was said out of modesty. Marusha was not unaware of the significance of the change from a small adobe dwelling to an imposing cement house. Especially in this town, where not unlike many places throughout Peru, if your home was constructed with *material noble*, that is, if you had managed to deliver yourself unto concrete, cinderblocks, or brick—which was to say, from a dirt floor that turned to mud each time the roof sprung a leak or from the wood planks that would warp and split over time until they let in drafts of cold wet air whenever it rained—well . . . that was something to admire. It was more: you had arrived.

Perhaps no different than anywhere that people have seen their luck go decidedly sour, in post-boom Huallaga anything that suggested the abrupt stirrings of economic promise was noticed. From one day to the next you got a house, replaced a roof, bought a car. "Now how did they do that?" went the talk. The answer—said in listless resignation or with a lingering hope of elbowing in on the action—was almost always the same: ¡Habrá llegado plata! (Money must have arrived!)

Though political conditions in Aucayacu had dramatically transformed by 1997, many townspeople were still reeling from the reverberations of coca's demise. In contrast to their economic woes, Marusha's situation had visibly improved. Not only did her law practice appear to be doing a brisk business, she had also been elected to the municipal council and was gradually becoming known about town as the local representative of "human rights," a term people used as if it signified a monolithic institution or force that acted from one centralized headquarters in Lima. Most everyone had taken to referring to her simply as *la doctora,* as if she were the only professional in town, which for me was more than evidence enough to suggest her new importance. Still, for townspeople nothing spoke of Marusha's auspicious rise so convincingly and with such eloquence as her new house—a cement house adorned with expensive windows and steel doors—which made our first conversations on the benches of the old bodega seem even more distant in time.

noble materials

Palpable traces of cocaine's former prosperity were hard to find in the Huallaga. Townspeople would gripe that the boom left little of worth in its wake, that the boom invested so little in the actual place. Nothing in the way of basic infrastructure, neither running water nor paved streets, not even electricity outside the strict confines of town. Nothing that was good for present or future.

There was, however, one tangible vestige of the affluence of that earlier time. Buildings built of cement proliferated, and not only around the plazas of the main towns where they often appeared vacant and conveyed an air of underpopulation. Concrete houses, foundations, and open-air slabs were found along the Marginal Highway and scattered throughout the countryside. In fact, a good indicator of where and to what degree cocaine wealth had reached into rural areas was the material's enduring presence. Cement that at the moment it was poured had manifested very real desires, not only to express social distinction but to give form and solidity to the fleeting spirit of the boom itself.

In Peru, cement has a deep cultural association with notions of social progress, modernization, and class ascension, and its strength as a marker of status no way diminished with the boom's passing. It was also a substance from which history could be read. Prior to the arrival of the Marginal Highway, there was very little cement in the Huallaga. Buitrón in his 1948 ethnological survey found none at all south of Yurimaguas, with the exception of the town of Uchiza where a "cement well-head" and two houses with cement floors were the "wonder and envy of the population."[1] Unlike cane, wood, and mud, cement was not readily available and had to be brought in from outside by river raft or by small plane—a prohibitively expensive solution considering its weight and bulk. That changed when the road was built in the 1960s, though the use of cement did not become widespread until coca transformed the regional economy and through it the Huallaga landscape.

In Marusha's case, local perceptions that she was on an "upward" movement were not without basis. To go from a small family store—when there were two or three like it on every block—to having the only lawyer's office in town was no small turn. At the same time, such impressions were not all they were made out to be. Marusha's law practice brought in very little money, as the majority of her clients were poor and among those hardest hit by the downfall of the cocaine economy. Nor had she built or even bought the house her family now occupied. They moved into it already standing and then only on a temporary basis. She didn't even pay rent but lived there on the condition that she would chip away at the property taxes, which had been neglected for so long the place was in danger of being seized by city hall. She and her family occupied the first floor, but given that the upstairs rooms never had tenants who stayed any length of time, the idea set in that the whole house *belonged* to Marusha. That assumption was somewhat forced, since the town didn't want for properties abandoned by their owners and taken over by squatters.

Under most circumstances, merely living in a house would not have been enough for it to have been considered as one's possession. In Marusha's case, however, the two-storey cement building became *la casa de la doctora* (the lawyer's house) at least in the way people talked, which in lieu of the facts functioned as truth. So much so that telling the drivers of the *motocarros* (three-wheeled taxis) that circled about town, or of the sedans that shuttled between Aucayacu and Tingo María, that you wanted to get dropped off *donde la doctora* (where the lawyer lives) was enough to make sure you got there.

This was the house where I came to stay the times I returned. Taking lodging at the parish no longer seemed necessary by 1997, since the general feeling was that inside town, at least, conditions had settled into a relative calm and going out on the streets no longer gave cause for fear. The first time I stayed at the new house, for only a few weeks, Marusha put me up in her stepfather's room. When I returned the following year for a much longer term I settled into an upstairs room that opened out onto the second-floor balcony. Where I would live in the house was an arrangement worked out between Mariela and Marusha. Mariela's role was as the representative of the owner, who lived in Lima and had left the care of his house in her hands.

As for the old place on Jirón Huaraz, I hardly heard mention of it again. It was as if that house and its store had passed away with Herminia. Never did I hear Marusha say she missed the place, and rarely did anyone from the family go back there except to retrieve a piece of stored furniture or other article overlooked in the initial move. Nor did they sell it, either, but instead found a family to stay and keep watch over the place. This was common practice during the post-boom when properties seldom fetched a reasonable price, often not even compensating for the value of the building materials. I always assumed the caretakers of the old place to be somehow related to one of Marusha's *patrocinados* (clients)—so many people I met through her were, or they had some connection to a recent legal case—but I never knew for sure.

By virtue of being so close to the main square, Marusha's new neighborhood was much more caught up in the town's official and social business. Be it the Sunday-morning flag raising, be it the weekday buzz around city hall, be it even the nightlife that concentrated there from Thursday evenings on. Sounds from the square spilled onto adjacent streets, streets that could be dreadfully still if not for the occasional burst of activity. On the dirt road that passed in front of the house, the scattered transit of people to and from the square created constant movement. And whatever happened in the plaza would quickly make its way into earshot of the new house, where sound reverberated against the cement walls, floors, and ceilings enough—before slipping out through the open roof of the back patio—to create a feeling of being somehow connected to whatever important was going on in the town center.

Directly across from the house sat a large Baptist church that, except for Sunday and an occasional weeknight, stood empty, its black entrance gates chained shut. Unlike the nightly and often clamorous prayer services of the score of Pentecostal parishes about town, this church and its congregation were so quiet, that if you didn't happen to look over there at the right hour, you'd never notice that the gates had been swung open, the lights turned on, and the rows of pews filled with people. Between the church and plaza was an empty lot with a few patches of grass, a tall mound of packed dirt, and rusty stove parts strewn about. On the other side, moving away from the plaza, was the store of a man who sold the same staple goods Marusha's mother had once stocked and who was always willing to make conversation with anyone who had the time.

The cement house itself was large and austere and in good condition, as buildings went in Aucayacu, and the absence of a sign painted on the outside wall was about the only thing that distinguished its exterior from the better commercial establishments in the town. Marusha never got around to posting a sign for her practice, perhaps because it would have been redundant in a place where everyone already knew where she lived and what she did. More likely, she didn't bother because she never knew how long they would be sticking around.

The place had been designed with some thought toward security. The only access was from the street, through one of the two front doors, or the garage that sat on the far left. And there was no easy way to climb onto the second floor or the roof from any of the adjoining properties, at least not without having to make inhuman leaps and, after that, to negotiate a thin precipice topped with broken bottles or a well-placed coil of razor wire. Only the rooms facing the street had windows. Opaque panes of glass hindered unwanted glances, and the window frames on the ground floor opened just enough to allow air to circulate freely.

Facing the house from the street, the left front door, which was to the immediate right of the garage, opened onto the waiting area of Marusha's office. Inside, the walls were lined with long benches, and a typewriter rested upon a small table in the middle of the floor. It was there that Marusha's secretary received the clients of the day and prepared legal documents. To her back a thin wooden partition separated the waiting room from the study. A doorway had been cut on the far left side of this partition, and above it a taped paper sign read "Consultations 10 sols" (approximately three dollars). Beyond this doorway Marusha's study was small—just enough room for her large desk, a couple of white plastic chairs for her *patrocinados* to sit, and a glossy, wood-stained cabinet with shelves and glass doors where she stored law books and case briefs. On the wall behind her desk several framed pieces of paper hung at eye level, among them a law school diploma and a certificate Marusha had received for participating in a municipal training program in the United States: two weeks, six cities, all expenses paid by USAID, the foreign aid office of the U.S. government. Against the wall opposite these emblems of professional stature, a new computer of dated technology sat atop a small table, where it promised efficiency but delivered mostly trouble. Technicians made regular visits to resolve the glitches that would arise, but all too frequently the problems overwhelmed their expertise and the machine would get boxed up and sent off to Tingo María, back to the store where Marusha had bought it.

If through the left front door passed the clients of Marusha's practice, it was through the front door on the right, which opened onto a large sitting room, that the domestic space of the house began. Marusha had furnished the room with a bright burgundy upholstered sofa and two matching chairs. It was here that her family welcomed the occasional visit of friends or relatives, yet most of the time the furniture sat unused, except at night when Magno would sit at the sofa and persist with an old, beat-up television set that only he seemed to have patience for—switching between the only two channels that half worked, and jiggling the dial every few minutes to coax the picture into a more discernible fuzz. Sometimes Abuela would pass the morning or afternoon on one of the upholstered chairs, waiting, waiting, like she so often did, for Marusha, always for Marusha, to come home or to get finished with whatever she was working on in the office. In the back of the room there was a long dining room table, never used to eat on except for holidays or other important celebrations. On it accumulated whatever notebooks, poster board, or papers Carito was using for her latest assignments at the teachers college.

At the back left corner of the sitting room a curtained entryway led to Marusha's study, while a swinging wooden door accessed a hallway that opened onto the rest of the bottom floor. On the left side of this corridor were two bedrooms: in the first slept Marusha, Abuela, and Caro; in the second, Magno. At the entrance to Magno's room, the right wall of the hallway dropped away into a large, open area that contained a well and a washbasin. This small patio was enclosed by two cinderblock walls that extended up to the top of the second floor. No one could look in from the outside, and from within there was no looking out except up onto open sky. From this rear corner of the house, there were few indications that Marusha and her family had neighbors, save the intermittent noises that filtered in, of animals being tended to next door, or save the young girl who would appear once a day with a bucket to carry away slop for her hogs. Abuela presided meticulously over this operation—it was an important part of the day's events—as she did over everything that had to do with the kitchen that lay in front of the courtyard, nestled to the right of the hallway and behind the sitting room.

The kitchen was Abuela's territory even if her sight had deteriorated so much that she could no longer see well enough to get her seasonings right or even to fry a plantain without burning it. Still she refused to admit she had lost any of her culinary command and just about made life impossible for anyone else who tried their hand at it—be that Carito or any one of the several *muchachas* Marusha had at one time or another hired to take over the chores. Abuela only needed a few days to run off the help.

pushes

As you moved back through the house there were many signs that the construction of the place had never been finished. The basic shell was there, but throughout details small and large betrayed that there had once been hopes for something more. Whereas cement flooring on the first level had a smooth, finished surface, the upstairs floors were irregular and coarse. Most of the walls and ceilings were unpainted, and the electrical wiring was a patchwork. A few rooms had switches and plugs nicely set into the walls and covered with plastic lids. In others, electrical boxes were wired but dead, requiring extension cords to be drawn from adjacent rooms. Elsewhere the boxes were empty and accumulated insect debris.

Single-bulb sockets provided most of the lighting: one per room, generally in the center of the ceiling. Some places—like the long corridor that ran behind Magno's room and connected the patio with the garage and the second floor, had no light at all. Passage along this hall would have been completely blind, if not for a few rays of early-morning sun that slipped in from the open patio on one end, and the faint emanations of an incandescent bulb underneath the stairs on the other, above a small cramped space that had been set aside for a toilet.

The house had plumbing but there was no hookup, and water was hauled from the well and dumped into one or two plastic buckets, the large ten-gallon cylinders that you see all over the Huallaga, dingy white from use, with the faded yellow and green lettering of Palmas del Espino, a palm oil factory near Uchiza. Because there was nowhere on the first floor specially built for taking a bath, the hallway behind Magno's room was refunctioned for that purpose, being close to the well as it was and because there was a wooden door that could be closed to shut it off from the patio. It worked alright as along as you didn't mind bathing in the dark and as long as no one from upstairs or entering through the garage walked in on you on their way to the well or the front part of the house. A broom was kept there for sweeping the soapy water out of the hall after you were done bathing, and down into the drain at the edge of the patio floor. When the weather was nice, most of the family preferred to bathe in the river, though that option was less feasible for Marusha, because of her crutches, or for Abuela, on account of her frailty.

Aucayacu seemed too important a town—officially the third-largest population center of the department of Huánuco—for its people to depend on wells and untreated local streams for its water. There had been talk for years that a potable water system was in the works, but a history of delays and missed opportunities made the project a notorious boondoggle. When I visited the town in 1997, the streets were all torn up with workmen busy laying plastic tubing and the townspeople were high on the idea that they would finally be getting their water. They told me it was worth trudging through the mud that filled the streets making them all but impassable to cars whenever it rained. And it rained a lot those two months I was there. A year later I came back to find that the long trenches had been filled, the streets cleared, but there was still no running water. Word had it that the company contracted to do the job—an outfit everyone remembered by the initials RAF—had skipped town without finishing, without paying rent on the spaces they'd used to store their heavy machinery, without paying the workers. The situation was a mess, and all the more so because RAF was rumored to have collected most of its fees up front from the municipality. The lack of financial accountability was only one of the things about the matter that seemed strange, not to mention that no inquiry with any teeth to it could ever seem to get under way. "Money must have changed hands," was all Marusha would say.

All the same, when it came to basic utilities, people in Aucayacu considered themselves luckier than most. Residential telephone service had recently been introduced, and Aucayacu, they would point out, had electricity round the clock, unlike the towns to the north that made due with at most five hours dispensed in evening rations. One of those towns, Uchiza, was starved for electrical energy but had running water, which might have seemed the better end of a bad situation. Well water in Aucayacu was of dubious quality. Most everyone drank it, but many never boiled it, with some expressing a robust pride in their preference for what they called *agua cruda* (raw water), insisting that "uncooked" water had a far better taste. Others with weaker stomachs, meanwhile, learned to have great respect for its virulence and a few claimed that merely bathing with it could cause lesions to break out on the skin.

Early settlers of Aucayacu say that the ground around what is today the main plaza was originally an *aguajal,* or marshland. They tell how many truckloads of earth and rock were needed to dry it up. At their best reckoning, the wells dug for the houses that sprung up around what had become the town center necessarily drew from the same swampy yellow water that formerly seeped at the surface. When the municipal water project was finally completed several years later, fresh spring water was piped in from a distant hill; this fact alone seemed to confirm all doubts about the wholesomeness of the stuff drawn from below.

At the end of the hallway and turning left past the makeshift half bath was a small, dark, triangular cavity formed by the slope of the stairs that stayed crammed with things that didn't invite exploration: bags of cement or sand, scraps of cardboard and wood, coils of wire and a large barrel turned upside down. Rats nested in this dark space under the stairs. Quiet by day, they would come out once everyone had gone to bed to scurry across the patio and into the kitchen, where they would ruffle through the drawers of a tall wooden cupboard, nose around the hotplate for food scraps, and jump onto the large sacks of rice or corn that sat on the floor next to the table. When the rodents got out of hand Magno would lay out poisoned bait, which usually quieted them down for a time.

Building supplies were stored not only underneath the stairs, but scattered throughout the house, in Magno's bedroom downstairs and in the unoccupied rooms of the second floor. Living side by side with construction materials contributed to the feeling that the place was still unfinished. This was hardly strange, but rather indicative of a more common, even "national" approach to urban housing in Peru, where so few can qualify for a loan, much less afford to buy a home outright. A house is something you put away for. You put away to buy the plot of land and later the materials. It's a piecemeal thing, bag by bag, cinderblock by cinderblock. The house you must have comes in a series of pushes, and whoever gets as far as pouring a foundation and raising four walls sets aside a space for leftover supplies: a receded corner, an unfinished room in the back, along the wall of an interior walkway or up on the roof underneath a temporary shelter. There the materials wait and accumulate until there is time and money enough for another push. In the meantime you live around and trip over them and their promise.

Only that here, in this house, which many thought belonged to Marusha, the bags of cement, the steel reinforcement rods, and the wire coils were props in someone else's dreams: the man who left for Lima and placed this property in Mariela's care. With him went all intentions of making further improvements. Sure, Marusha and Magno would get enthused at times about fixing things up, installing a water tank on the roof, let's say, so as to have running water. But their ideas would quickly run aground on the fact that it just didn't make much economic sense to put what little money they had into a place that wasn't theirs. So the building materials sat there and became so much stuff.

The garage was kept spare. There was Magno's rusty bicycle, leaned up against a wall near the garage gate, tires half inflated and pedals long ago stripped of their rubber. Across from it, several plastic sacks packed with trash waited for the cowbell rattle of the town's open-bed garbage truck. Farm animals would show up too: a couple of hens, maybe a turkey, now and then a piglet tethered and frightened—all gifts or payment in kind to Marusha for her legal services.

Moving up the staircase, the steps were as coarse as the unfinished floors they led to. Though they were mostly even, one of the steps, just below the second floor, was so deceptively out of tune with the rest that if you weren't careful it could send you tumbling. What made the climb more precarious was that there was no place to grab onto for balance. Whether the absence of a rail was by design or just another task whose time hadn't come around, I never knew. Little wonder Marusha refused to go upstairs and so never saw for herself what was on the second floor or on the roof that lay another flight up. Those of us who used the stairs regularly made a habit of hugging close to the wall on the way up and down, above all at night, or at the very least of letting a finger skim along the coarse surface of the wall so as to measure the distance from the edge.

The second floor contained a wide hallway—the largest open space in the house—surrounded by nine small rooms. Three were clumped against the back wall between the top of the stairs and a bathroom at the opposite corner. The remaining six followed the hall toward the street, evenly distributed on either side. Two of them were empty and used to absorb the building materials and junk from the triangular hold downstairs. The others served as bedrooms, at one time or another, and had hollow, plywood doors with numbers painted and circled in blue. The room numbers indicated that once there had been plans or an attempt to turn the second floor into a boarding house.

The anomaly of the upstairs was the bathroom, which had a pristine air about it that contrasted with the barrenness and unfinished character of the rest of the house interiors. New porcelain fixtures adorned the sink and shower, and tiles of alternating sky and marine blue covered the shower stall, walls, and floors. No other space had received such attention or expenditure, and yet without running water the bath was functionally worthless. Hauling water from the well and then up the stairs was a long and tiresome exercise. No one bothered.

On the opposite end of the floor, a large translucent door opened onto the shallow balcony that ran the full length of the façade of the house and that overlooked the dirt street below: enough space to stand and rest your body against the metal railing, too tight to accommodate a chair.

The room where I lived was one of two with windows that looked onto the balcony. In many ways this room seemed the pick of the place. Above the traffic of the first floor, the room was quiet, private, and took in the most light of any. It was also the only bedroom where the concrete walls had been plastered and painted. However, because the full blast of the afternoon sun bore down on its northwestern wall, the room was unbearable from three until the late evening. The heat was enough to make one question the wisdom of using cement for housing and to wonder if the purported "nobility" of the hardened substance was not merely standing in for abstract concepts of modernization and development—as if all that was needed to get a little progress was to pour some concrete. But whenever I put these doubts to people I knew in town, they almost always gave me a no-nonsense reply, one that cut right through my simple critique of cement's irrational prestige and was incisive because it was grounded in recent personal experience: "Concrete blocks the FAL." Unlike mud, or wood, or even brick, concrete was impermeable to heavy caliber munitions, and in the Huallaga that made its utility as building matter beyond reproach.

The other room that provided access to the balcony was across the main hall from where I stayed. It had a door that was unnumbered and visibly more sturdy than the rest. The room remained sealed most of the time but would be opened up once a month when the owner's sister arrived in town, always accompanied by a small boy I took to be her son. Doña Loreta was a middle-aged farmer who kept mostly to herself. She lived off a parcel of land near Pacae, which she left only when she needed supplies. Whenever Doña Loreta was in town, the door to her room would be ajar, revealing an interior filled with cardboard boxes stacked up to the ceiling. No one knew what was in those boxes, other than the housewares Doña Loreta would occasionally produce: pots and pans, plastic tubs, eating utensils, a small stove, whatever she needed to prepare food for her son on the coarse floor of the hall. Sometimes, if it had been an especially hot day, she would drag out a little bed she'd make up for the two of them, so as to take advantage of the cool air that poured in off the balcony after dark. Typically they would stay the night and be gone before sunup, always leaving the door to the room locked tight.

With the exception of Doña Loreta's brief visits, I had the upstairs to myself for the months I lived there in 1998 and 1999. From time to time Magno would stake out one of the rooms between the stairs and bath, or else the one next to mine, but in only a few days or a week at most he would return downstairs to the bedroom the family recognized as his. Magno's restlessness went largely without comment, though Marusha suspected the upstairs held special attraction for him because of the independent access through the garage, which left open the possibility of receiving his *gorda*, or stout lady friend, without the rest of the house knowing. Occasionally other relatives of the owner would show up in town and take a room on the second floor. But the owner himself, I'll call him Gregorio, never came back to Aucayacu while I was there. Mariela had told me that he couldn't on his life, not yet, and perhaps never.

gregorio

Long before I ever associated him with his cement house, I heard something of Gregorio's story from Mariela. He was the subject of our first conversation the night we met in the front room of Marusha's mother's store. Marusha had arranged the meeting, because she said Mariela had direct knowledge of a man who had turned himself over to the army and was later processed as an *arrepentido*, a "repenter."

Mariela and I fell into an immediate confidence from that first night forward. I'm sure it helped that I was staying with the priests, as she was a longtime and active member of the local Catholic lay ministry. It helped too that she had known Marusha and her mother going way back. Yet there was something more, a fundamental trust, a chemistry of some kind that lay the groundwork for an enduring friendship.

Mariela was a natural storyteller, and that night she recounted to me an extract from the life of Gregorio—a migrant from the central highlands who as a teenager in the early 1970s had arrived in Aucayacu, attracted by the promise of free land in the pre-boom Huallaga. She told how a decade later he had fallen in with Sendero, like all farmers who grew coca in the *banda*, the name given to the expanses that lay on the other side of the river. The recruitment of rural communities into the Party had not been instantaneous; still, Mariela condensed the process into one emblematic episode. She explained how one day the guerrilla showed up, called everyone away to assembly and instructed the farmers to compose letters declaring their obedience to the Party. Gregorio didn't know how to read or write, so he dictated to one of his farmhands, who jotted his words down on a piece of notebook paper. These *cartas de sujeción* (letters of subordination), as they were called, could be elaborate testimonials of life experience and conviction, but in Mariela's telling, Gregorio's letter got straight to the point of the exercise:

Yo me entrego al Partido de corazón	I surrender wholeheartedly to the Party
Me olvido de mi familia	I forget my family
Me olvido de mis padres	I forget my parents
Me olvido de todo	I forget everything
Yo doy mi vida por el Partido	I give my life over to the Party

At the bottom of the page the farmhand wrote Gregorio's real name, just like all the other growers did on theirs. Nor did they have much choice. They knew what would happen if they refused: have their land taken away and given to someone else. So, short of throwing their livelihoods away, most went along.

As soon as the letters were collected, Mariela explained, the Party handed out tasks. Gregorio was told to prepare food whenever the *fuerza principal,* or elite guerrilla column, came through the area. And because he owned a small boat, equipped with an outboard motor, the Party called on him to do errands: to go to town to buy medicine, or to taxi groups of combatants on short *comisiones* (assignments) down the Huallaga. Beyond these chores, the Party charged Gregorio twenty percent of his coca harvest and kept close watch on his movements. "He couldn't leave the area when he wanted," Mariela told me. "He had to ask permission and give them his exact dates and all that. They monitored everything."

The time was the mid- to late 1980s, when Sendero had undisputed control of the countryside and maintained an active presence in town. But as long as Gregorio turned over his quota and obeyed the Party's law, he got along fine. His land, all seven acres of it, produced. Gregorio even had the foresight to plant citrus groves, plantains, and yuca. But it was coca and coca alone that let him get ahead. Enough so, I would learn, to build the cement house in Aucayacu that, combined with his dugout, afforded an ease of movement between town and country that would have been the envy of almost anyone. A rich peasant in Sendero's eyes, at the very least Gregorio had a good routine.

That good life changed one day in 1991, when the Peruvian army made a surprise raid on the *banda.* Caught unaware and unable to hold their ground, the senderistas took off for the distant hills, leaving everything and everyone else behind. Shortly thereafter the names from the Party's letters of subordination appeared in the Lima dailies and on television. Gregorio and the other coca farmers were all identified as members of Sendero, but the telling detail that their participation had not been free of coercion got lost in the excitement of the story. Now a wanted man, Gregorio could no longer leave the *banda* for Aucayacu without fear of being detained, or worse. And it didn't help either that a new army captain had arrived in town with novel methods that were causing a stir. Unlike those before him, this captain had come to the Huallaga less intent on getting rich than on taking Sendero apart, or so went his acclaim. Gregorio covered himself for a time by changing his name, buying forged papers, and even clearing a patch of land to grow coca on the right bank of the Huallaga River, a site that was relatively far from where the letters had been confiscated. Above all, he tried to lie low. If it was absolutely necessary to go to town, he would slip in when soldiers were not patrolling the entrances.

Living like that, a couple of years went by. The fearsome army captain left. Others came and went, and soon the talk was about repentance. Mothers and siblings of known senderistas were picked up by soldiers and taken to the army base. Radio waves carried their pleas, urging their sons and daughters to turn themselves in, in exchange for the freedom of their families. It was a powerful ploy, and detentions led to more detentions.

Gregorio knew it was only a matter of time, and so he decided he would flee the Huallaga for the city of Huánuco. He confided as much to Mariela, and since they were old friends he asked her to help him slip unseen onto a *colectivo* bound for Tingo María. Mariela, however, insisted the idea was too risky. "You'll never get past all the checkpoints," she said. "And if you do, then what? You're still wanted. You can't be on the run forever. It's better to face the problem. Turn yourself in, but not alone. We'll get the church to act as your go-between."

Because that was the danger: if you showed up by yourself at the gates of the base, there was no guarantee of what would happen next. The army had to be made to understand that someone was watching. Someone in a position to press the case *if need be.* Someone who knew you were turning yourself in and under what precise terms. Otherwise, there would be nothing to prevent them from mishandling you until they got what they wanted and then tossing your body somewhere out of the way to rot, as had been done so many times before.

Gregorio conceded the point, and a few days later two nuns from the parish arranged the rendezvous. Soldiers arrived at the agreed-upon spot and took Gregorio away as if under arrest, in order to camouflage the fact—to the eyes and ears of Sendero—that he was giving himself up by his own volition.

Gregorio languished inside the cinderblock walls of the Project compound for a month, bunked up with thirty other *arrepentidos*, all down on their luck and exposed to the elements and the not so random jabs of rifle butts from young recruits ever anxious to pass on their pain. The army commander told Gregorio that the only way to secure his transfer was if he provided the names of forty senderistas. A few times soldiers led him with a hood over his head around town. They stopped traffic on the Marginal Highway. They had him board buses. They told him to finger anyone he recognized. Recognize Gregorio did, but he wasn't about to let on. After all, they were all like him, farmers or farmhands, those who had gone along under pressure or to protect their interests, their living, their dreams—so as to stay in with coca and the prosperity only coca could promise. These people weren't the ones who had organized the thing, *los verdaderos*, the ringleaders. To finger *them* Gregorio would have had to go to the *banda* and discover where they were hiding, but even then it would have been all but impossible to come up with the forty names the commander demanded.

Mariela kept alert to his situation and often went to take him food at the base. She could see him growing ever more desperate by the day, and seeing that the army wasn't keen on letting him go, she went to the courthouse in Tingo María to file for his repentance. In Aucayacu there was no place that would receive the paperwork. It was early 1994, when anything approximating the rule of procedural law was still a long fifty kilometers away. What lay in between was only Sendero justice, police interdiction, and the army's decrees.

A special district attorney had been appointed in Tingo María to attend to hundreds of cases of *arrepentidos*, the majority of them peasant farmers like Gregorio, with whom the government had little quarrel or interest other than getting them fingerprinted, processed, and permanently separated from Sendero. With a little effort Mariela managed to have Gregorio moved to the Los Laureles army base and into the jurisdiction of the civilian courts.

In Tingo María Gregorio found himself in a much bigger pond. The pool of *arrepentidos* at the base alone was near 150, and many more crowded the local courts. A young lieutenant took Gregorio aside, listened to his story, and treated him so well that when I later met Gregorio, he had only kind words to say about him. In no time the paperwork got pushed through and Gregorio was free to go. There being no heading back to Aucayacu, he moved his family to Lima and gave Mariela the keys to his house.

The cement house was just about all Gregorio had to show for his years in the Huallaga. Everything he'd saved from the boom had been put into its construction. While it was a foregone conclusion that because of Sendero's continued presence there would be no recovering his farm or *chacra*, there was still hope regarding the house. But he couldn't use it as long as it was unsafe for him to return, and because the post-boom economy was so depressed, the house literally had no value on the local market.

Mariela did her best to rent out the place. She worried that Gregorio was out of his element in Lima, that he was having a hard time getting by on what little he earned helping a cousin sell clothes at a kiosk in downtown Lima. But finding someone willing to rent the whole house was almost impossible. Sure, there were people who would take a single room—teachers from out of town or itinerant loggers who had arrived to take advantage of the lull in coca to cut down hardwood forests in the *banda*—but collecting was never easy. Mariela quickly got fed up with running after the tenants to get them to pay, and eventually decided to offer the first floor to Marusha. She knew her friend was looking for larger quarters and that Marusha could be counted on to pay the back taxes that were accumulating on the place.

Marusha had never met the man who came to be her absentee landlord and did not know the details of his personal history and situation. That much I gathered from the polite and at times uncomfortable distance with which she referred to him—perhaps because of the power she felt he exercised as the owner of the house her family would have loved to have had as their own. Perhaps, too, because all dealings with him went through Mariela, who despite her desire to do right by all involved had difficulty in keeping the communication free of mistrust and bad feeling.

I knew enough about Gregorio to realize he had been lucky to have escaped the legal limbo that had weighed over him and made him so vulnerable. To have gotten to Lima—where he was no longer caught between antagonistic foes, their respective regimes of law, and threats of brute force—was a good and necessary thing in itself. Yet at his age and with nothing to call upon from his life's work, Gregorio was not going to thrive in Lima, at least not working for a retail stand operator in the Mercado Central. I can only imagine his disappointment.

A month after Mariela told me Gregorio's story, I went to visit him in Lima. Mariela had given me a letter in which she explained it was safe to talk with me about his experiences as an *arrepentido*, not to worry. At that time I did not yet know his house in Aucayacu as I would later come to know it, nor did I know about the life he had left behind in the Huallaga. What Gregorio made clear to me during our first conversation was that under no uncertain terms could he ever go back. He was scared to try, he said, because Sendero, "they keep their word and that is what is so frightening about them: they never forget."

Gregorio had gotten away with his life and won a chance to start over. And over time his economic situation stabilized enough for him to open a hardware business in an outlying district of Lima. His good fortune, however, was one denied to many others. There was no scarcity of stories in the Huallaga about *arrepentidos* who had come to far worse ends. They were the ones who had been deeply entangled with Sendero but were without influential friendships, without lucky breaks, or perhaps more important, without the sense of timing to know when to get far enough away or when not to return. For those who stuck around, it was a gamble as to how best to take cover. Some found a precarious safe haven by serving as scouts in the lowest rungs of the army or even by returning to the guerrilla, though one wonders under what awkward or exacting terms. Others, unable or unwilling to be so assimilated, bided their time in fear, equally unsure of what the next day would bring. For them, the only places that afforded minimum shelter were the larger towns where Sendero didn't feel confident to roam at will.

marusha

What was evident to anyone who lived during the boom years was that roots were fragile and easily ripped up. That situation of vulnerability continued well into the post-boom. During the course of my research I had several friends and acquaintances who fled, were killed, or simply disappeared. And while I didn't always understand when close friends would forget or else choose not to tell me when something bad happened to someone I knew, in time I ceased to be surprised. There was so much suffering that most preferred not to talk about it. If it touched them personally, they might mention it, but they would seldom elaborate. Marusha once drew my attention to this, saying that people had seen so many awful things happen to others that they tried to keep their own problems to themselves. Her explanation conveyed a different tone than that offered by those who would claim people in the Huallaga had become inured to the sorrows of others. She gestured less to a numbing than to a reticence. Silence as a tacit mode of respect.

Yet there were few who wore so plainly their share of personal suffering as Marusha herself. She who had lost the use of her legs in early childhood to a wholly preventable disease and had ever since been forced to live with so much metal. Heavy stainless steel braces ran from her hips all the way down her legs, where they strapped into a pair of black leather shoes. The air of outmoded technology was unmistakable. Aluminum crutches accompanied her whenever she stood or walked—cupping her upper arms as her hands seized padded grips in a propped-up, shoulders-forward posture that was hers alone. The crutches were there for all to see, but Marusha was sensitive about the braces and did her best to keep their presence hidden. Whenever she went out, whether for a meeting in town or to attend to one of her cases at the provincial or departmental tribunals, she always dressed in dark slacks with a matching double-breasted coat on top of a delicate light-colored blouse. This regular outfit of hers, while noticeably formal for the Huallaga, served well the purpose of concealing the contours of the flat steel rods that twisted around and fastened at the lower part of her back. In no way unflattering, the suit tended rather to accentuate the dignified carriage that was so much a part of her personality. The tradeoff came in having to unduly bear the Huallaga heat, though when Marusha was at ease with her company she often took the coat off and let it hang on the back of a chair.

I often thought that in her work with clients as well as in local politics, Marusha's physical impairment accorded her a moral authority denied most others and made her in the eyes of many a natural defender of the downtrodden. Her disability certainly went a long way toward, if not disarming her detractors then, forcing them to be more judicious in their attacks, for which there was much opportunity. Marusha was constantly butting heads with some of the most powerful people in town. Among them were the local police chiefs and army base commanders, with whom she'd had her share of run-ins. The score of those clashes tilted decidedly in her favor. More than one uniformed officer had been transferred out of town well before his tour of service was up on account of a complaint she had filed. This gave the police and army cause to respect if not fear her.

Bad feelings could also fester around her legal cases when things went her client's way or even when they didn't. But far more intractable and bothersome were her political adversaries on the council. When Marusha withdrew from local politics at the end of her only term, those who were formerly the opposition took control of the municipal government. They continued to view her with suspicion because it was no secret that she was a popular figure in town, and every time elections came around, her name circulated as a possible mayoral challenger. Her former opponents, apparently not wanting to take any chances, never failed to send subtle provocations her way.

Sometimes these were direct, as when two journalists attached to the new municipal regime tried to implicate her with some alleged misstep during her time in office. But given the chance to respond, Marusha more than held her own. Less easy to defend against were the cutting rumors that circulated from time to time. From experience, Marusha was mindful of how reputations could be harmed with hearsay skillfully crafted to do as much damage as possible. Though rumors appeared as if without author, few regarded them as baseless, and great effort could go into guessing their source. All the same, rumors were one of those day-by-day, mundane perils of living in Aucayacu. And if in the end there was nothing one could do but be patient and hope that the slow turn of events would ultimately show their real truth, the anonymous messages never stopped being a distraction. They couldn't, because people were terribly willing to give credence to something they'd heard but for which they had no evidence, and because of the strength with which questionable information could take hold of the local imagination.

I remember one December tenth when the local radio carried declarations made by then-Archbishop of Ayacucho Juan Luis Cipriani. A Fujimori loyalist, member of the Opus Dei, and notorious for his staunch endorsements of the Peruvian armed forces, the archbishop was approached by the press and asked if he would like to congratulate the country's human rights advocates on the occasion of International Human Rights Day. In his characteristically acerbic style, Cipriani said he would be glad to congratulate them as soon as they stopped earning "million-dollar salaries" and got serious about defending "the *real* human rights."

It didn't take long for the Archbishop's remarks to resonate in Aucayacu. Barely two days had gone by when Marusha told me that clients had already come forward to share the latest "discovery" that was circulating about town: "Oh that explains why the *doctora* does that human rights work, so she can earn a fat wage—and in dollars, no less!" So went the talk. I had no doubt that Cipriani's comments spread through town in part because they gave wings to already existing suspicions about Marusha's propitious rise and her connection to human rights advocacy.

Still, she found the claims exasperating. Her interest in human rights was based on deeply held convictions that had developed since she was a teenager, when the boom went into full swing and the Shining Path began to make its presence known. That interest later became concrete when as a law student she helped found a legal services organization in Huánuco that provided assistance to internal refugees. The people she worked on behalf of were mostly poor farmers and farmhands, coca growers who had fled the violence of the Upper Huallaga for the relative security of the highland city. Now back in Aucayacu, Marusha had enough trouble simply getting reimbursed for costs incurred for her efforts to report on local conditions to the national organizations, much less receive a salary, and a hefty one at that. Then again, she couldn't ignore the insinuations, because, as recent local history clearly bore out, rumors of misconduct potentially conveyed a threat of serious harm or worse from Sendero. As such, being the target of rumors was enough to make anyone nervous, and that alone made them extremely valuable as weapons.

In personal disputes I've seen people insinuate friendship with a Sendero leader as a way to strike fear in their rivals. And wherever Sendero has been active, there have always been those tempted to appropriate its name to settle a score or extort some kind of advantage. Not that this ever happened to Marusha, but the potential was there and she felt it.

Of course, Marusha also had to be wary of the real, unimpersonated Sendero during the two years she was on the town council and afterwards in her increasingly public role as a human rights advocate. The danger from Sendero was not so much in town, but rather on the road between Aucayacu and Tingo María, where the chance of running into the guerrilla was more likely. In 1998 and 1999 Sendero frequently stopped traffic during the day along the Marginal Highway, to paint their slogans on cars and trucks, distribute flyers trying to explain their reasons for going on with their armed struggle, and to ask for voluntary contributions. They would also kill anyone who appeared on the list of names they carried. It was a well-rehearsed routine, and they were usually long gone before the police or army showed up, much to the relief of the people delayed on their journeys and of everyone else involved. On most stretches of the road, there was little place to run for cover, and nothing could be worse than to be caught in the firefight that would inevitably ensue should the soldiers and Sendero meet face to face.

As a close friend, one would be hard pressed to find anyone more understanding, compassionate, or patient than Marusha. She was also strong willed when it came to anything she considered improper or inappropriate. Everyone in the house knew the wrath of her justice, but they also knew her poise. Marusha was not one to get stoked without due cause, yet she knew how to dress down someone she found abusive or dishonest or unwilling to recognize fault. Because what was not immediately evident about Marusha, if you didn't know her well, was that under her calm, cordial manner there was a reserve of fire. When provoked, Marusha held her ground with frightful skill and precision, and I imagine she has sent more than one foe reeling, overwhelmed by the intensity of her fight.

At home she possessed a manner that I can only think to describe as matronly, maybe because I always saw her overseeing family affairs. Whenever there were problems to solve, it was to Marusha that everyone turned for advice. And while she ran things in consultation, there was never any doubt that the ultimate decision rested with her. No one wanted to be on her bad side.

In her mid-thirties, Marusha was a handsome woman, and that was something that usually went unnoticed when she engaged in her work or in her role as house matriarch. Neither tall nor short in stature, Marusha had lovely features in the olive-toned complexion that Peruvians call *trigueño*. She had never married, and if she had romantic admirers or interests she never said so. Nico once told me that Marusha knew her disability made her an undesirable choice for most local men, and so early on she decided to devote herself to her education and profession. What he neglected to mention was that, growing up, his sister had been a very attractive girl, something borne out by an old glossy snapshot she kept in a drawer of her office desk. In it a much younger Marusha appeared with five of her female classmates, all dressed in matching uniforms and sitting in a grassy area of what presumably was the school courtyard. She must have been sixteen at the time, and yet even then she kept her wavy, dark hair cut to the shoulder as she would in the years to come. Only someone who knew her would appreciate how she carefully positioned herself at an angle in a way that allowed her to smile at the camera while still keeping her legs, and the braces she considered ugly, tucked behind the backs of the others and out of sight.

Marusha explained that the other girls in the photograph were her best friends in school, the group she always hung out with, and that the picture was taken around the time of their graduation. Yet what was most striking to me was that she was by far the prettiest of her companions and had probably been one of the most charming young women in her class.

If Marusha deliberately avoided amorous relationships or even internalized as fact that she would never have a partner, as Nico suggested, I don't know. What I can say is that she held very different, even contradictory attitudes when it came to the love interests of her siblings. In what concerned her brother, whose romantic liaisons were not few or infrequent, she largely looked away, at most expressing a fretful chiding that he take care to not bring home unneeded problems. She knew well enough that it would have been impossible to control him anyhow, and so chose instead to plead to his better judgment. But Marusha could be far more stringent, if not severe, with her younger sisters. The threat to withdraw financial support for their education if they didn't mind was more than once held over their heads. Marusha kept the eighteen-year-old Caro on a very close watch, making her ask permission when she wanted to go out at night and then requiring an account the next morning of where she had been and what she had done. Caro resented this and was often evasive and misleading when it came to reporting in. She was aware that Marusha would ply her sources around town to learn what her youngest sister was up to and what company she kept, and when versions didn't match up Carito was in deep shit. It was a site of periodic if not constant struggle, and I often wondered if it were this same zeal on Marusha's part that kept Bianca from coming home from the university. Bianca had a boyfriend there a couple of years running, and the situation bothered Marusha so much she couldn't bear mention of his name.

While Marusha's unequal expectations may in part have had to do with age—Nico was already in his mid-twenties, five and seven years older than his younger sisters—still, it was hard to escape the conclusion that what played out so clearly along lines of gender was patently unfair. Marusha no doubt feared for her sisters' futures, having seen the formal education of so many women truncated by sudden motherhood. It was also hard to ignore how young women were often treated with little or no dignity by men their age and older, or even that the local opinion where sex was concerned was much more generous and sympathetic to men. Still, Marusha's differential treatment tended to reinforce, instead of interrupt, the greater privilege and freedom men enjoyed regarding sex. Yet Bianca and Caro never seemed to hold their older sister's severity against her. In the end, they were devoted to her, and neither of them could bear a falling out for long.

shirley

Toward the second half of 1998 Marusha began to have health problems that lay her low for several days at a time. Her doctor in Tingo María diagnosed a liver ailment and put her on a strict diet with medication to take whenever her symptoms flared up. Prohibited were pork, fried foods, soft drinks, and bread of any kind, which eliminated much of what restaurants had to offer in Aucayacu and anywhere else from there to Lima. Boiled foods and vegetable broth were all she could eat. On her long trips to the capital she would sometimes go fifteen or twenty hours without food due to her difficulty in getting around, due to lack of time, and, because she didn't know

Lima well, due to the problems she had in locating places that could attend to her dietary needs.

Those trips were hard. She would always travel by night, so as not to waste money on hotel accommodations, taking the red-eye bus from Tingo María and arriving in Lima at eight A.M. Then on little or no sleep she would spend the day attending to cases at the tribunals or having meetings with human rights organizations. Sometimes she would catch the evening bus back to Tingo María that same day. Sometimes she would stay longer. No matter what, Marusha would return to Aucayacu exhausted if not sick, and often she'd come home only to crash in bed.

In the midst of these hardships Marusha hired a young woman, Shirley, to work as a *muchacha*, helping Caro out with the domestic chores and to look after Abuela. Shirley was another acquaintance Marusha had made by way of her law practice. Twenty-two years old and mother to a baby girl, Shirley was waiting on her daughter's father, Ronal, to get out of jail and share the burden of raising their child. When Shirley came to work at the house, Ronal had already served six months in the Huánuco prison, ever since he had been picked up by the Peruvian anti-narcotics police along with much of the Cristal gang in Pucallpa. Marusha had given Ronal's family some legal advice during the court proceedings. That was apparently how she met Shirley, who continued to visit her in her office, to follow the progress of his case and, I suspect, to move along the legal papers that would ensure that he would be compelled to provide financial support for their daughter Vanessa once he was released from prison.

Shirley was a character. Small set but outspoken, with "a no one is going to push me around" air to her, she knew how to negotiate her way with Abuela far better than any of the *muchachas* who had preceded her. Shirley was not one to scare easily and liked to mark her boundaries. Still, never once did I hear Abuela get angry with her or protest about how she did things. It was almost as if the two of them had an understanding. As for Caro, Shirley hadn't been working at the house a week before they became good friends, and it wasn't uncommon to walk into the kitchen and find them whispering in low voices about some secret or another. With Magno and Nico and sometimes with me, Shirley tended to be freewheeling and mischievously cavalier. She especially liked to speak in mocking innuendo, usually around some supposed rumor she had heard but always with an aim at getting a rise out of one of us. It was a playful side she tended to hide from Marusha, with whom she was always serious and deferential, rarely failing to address her as *Doctora*.

The special respect Shirley accorded Marusha was more than just a nod to her authority or a mere expression of appreciation for having given her employment. It seemed to stem from the relationship of professional confidentiality they shared around Ronal's case, in the details of which Shirley had an obvious stake. The flow of secrets was largely one sided, and I suspect there were many things about Shirley that only Marusha was privileged to know. Yet more was involved than the protection of personal information. Because of Marusha's profession and her position, there was much that she could do for a young, poor, and for all purposes single mother like Shirley. So it was not surprising that somewhere along the way, Shirley had asked Marusha to be her daughter's baptismal godmother. While it was unclear to me if the baptism ever ended up taking place, I know that Marusha accepted. She felt a genuine sense of solidarity with Shirley's predicament. All the same, it is important to note that in rural Peru such requests to assume a role in the future care and education of a young child are hard to refuse, even if one tries to carefully negotiate beforehand the exact terms of the social binding and modes of unequal exchange that they often seek to establish. For Shirley, Marusha's acceptance was a point of great satisfaction. It signaled initial success in transforming their professional relationship into one of informal kinship, with hopes for a durability and continuous reciprocity independent of Ronal's eventual legal fate.

Over the six or seven months that we coincided at Marusha's house, Shirley and I developed at best a guarded familiarity. Not that she was tight lipped. She loved to talk about things going on around town, or about what I was doing or who I was talking with in Aucayacu. However, she generally deferred telling anything about herself that didn't have to do with her own maternal responsibilities for her baby girl, who was about a year and a half old at the time. The exception to this was Ronal, who was never far from conversation, even if she rarely referred to him by name. Shirley made a habit of musing aloud about when he would be getting out of jail, an eventuality that marked off the horizon of her immediate existence and hopes during the months that I got to know her. Judging by the frequency with which she would mention him, Shirley seemed to derive a certain pride from the fact that Ronal had been a bodyguard (the word she used was *seguridad*) for Cristal.

Less sympathetic townsfolk would have considered Vanessa's father a *sicario* (killer or hired gunman), which as a term packed a lot more sting for people in Aucayacu. Most remembered Cristal as much for his drug addiction and bloodthirsty swagger as for the gun battles that his men waged on the streets, keeping people locked up in their homes and scared for days at a time. For all that, Shirley relished in Cristal's negative celebrity and would frequently drop his name into conversation whenever Marusha wasn't around.

Such semblance of lethal depravity had been built up around Cristal and his gang by the way townspeople spoke of them, that I was surprised at what I saw the first and only time Shirley handed me a snapshot of Ronal. Instead of a burly, thickset man—the physical type conjured up for me by someone who specialized in providing "security"—with the thuglike demeanor fitting of Cristal's gunmen, here was a short, skinny teenager. He was standing on the shore of a jungle creek, dressed in military fatigues and army boots, his chest bare and wearing a black headband with the yellow letters COMANDO written across his forehead, like any sixteen- or seventeen-year-old army recruit freshly pressed into service. In a pose somewhere between stand-up-straight serious-ness and playful innocence, Ronal leaned forward onto a rocket-propelled gre-nade launcher, which he held propped up on end, and smirked at the camera.

As best as I could figure, the photograph had been taken sometime around 1992, that is, about five or six years before I saw it. Shirley had told me she and Ronal were about the same age, and if so, he would have been of draft age right about then. While he didn't have the build to fit the part Shirley claimed for him, at least as I had imagined it, the fact that Ronal had been in the army gave me a thread to stitch together some provisional understanding. Soldiering was a marketable trade in the Huallaga, as military weapons training was highly prized. Ronal had been well placed for future employ as a *sicario*.

Whatever stories were attached for Shirley to the photograph of Ronal, she didn't volunteer them. She didn't say if the picture had been taken before or after they first met or even how far back their relationship went. And while I would later wonder how Ronal had wound up with Cristal and his gang in the first place—whether because of some family connection or, also likely, on the personal recommendation of a military superior—in that moment, picture in hand, I didn't think to ask. I was too struck by his youthful and boyish air, which didn't square with the serious, grown-up notions that Shir-ley often used to describe him. Here was not Ronal the bodyguard or the fa-ther, it seemed to me, but rather an early image of Shirley's love, perhaps her first, captured when their future together must have looked so much more promising than what it had become, before the unfolding of unlucky events had retrospectively transformed earnest hopes into wishful thinking.

Everything I came to know about Shirley and her world was revealed to me like that: in fleeting gestures picked up here and there and pieced together with what she told me and what she left unsaid. Shirley always spoke in disconnected fragments that I labored to connect. Knowing I was keen to hear stories about the area, she might make passing reference to something she had done or seen, though never with anything approaching completeness. Above all, she liked to let on that she knew more than she was willing to tell. The rest was all inference and hunch. Whatever I learned or think I learned about her, I had to distill from the handful of story bits she chose to share. Mostly I learned how tough life could be for a young woman growing up in the Huallaga.

There was the time she accompanied her uncle and his daughter to a village north of Tocache, called Sión. Originally a Franciscan mission, Sión emerged in the late 1980s as a buzzing outpost of the cocaine trade. Shirley was only twelve at that time and her cousin just a year older. She told me how the three of them arrived in the village at dusk under a hail of rain that had kicked up right as the long canoe they'd boarded back in Tocache pulled in to dock. Running for cover, they took a room in the first place Shirley's uncle could find, a musky boarding house with no electricity just up from the boat landing. There they spent the night. At first light, Shirley woke to discover her uncle had already gone out. Finding themselves alone, and curious about a place they didn't know, Shirley and her cousin decided to take a look around.

With its muddy roads and small wood-slat houses, Sión seemed to be a village like any other, except for the local men who, as soon as the cousins got to what appeared to be the main street, started to approach. The men came forward one at a time and seemingly at random, each one wanting to know the same thing: *¿Llegó carne fresca?* (Did fresh meat arrive?). The first time it happened the girls looked at each other puzzled and, not knowing what to say, walked on. The second time, Shirley's cousin paused long enough to blurt back, "Why are you asking us? Go ask the butcher!" But it happened again, and then again, until someone explained it to them, or maybe they just figured it out on their own, that the men were talking about prostitutes. They were tired of the ones already in town and anxious for new arrivals. "We had gotten up their hopes up," chuckled Shirley, which was how she ended her story, without explaining what business her uncle had in Sión, how long they had stayed, or what they did to avoid the men.

There was also an episode that happened several years later in Aucayacu. Shirley was living with Ronal at the time in a house near the port, along with the rest of the Cristal gang. One day word came that the anti-narcotics police was about to make a raid on the town. That news sent all the men running off to a hideout they had on the other side of the Aucayacu River, while the women stayed behind to deal with a small cache of weapons that would have been far too heavy to lug along. Shirley and the other women hurriedly threw everything—the pistols, the submachine guns, the ammunition, lots of ammunition—into two large sacks. Unable to find a secure place inside the house, they lowered the bags down into a cement well in the back patio, before slipping away to catch up with the rest of the gang. Neighbors would later tell Shirley that right after they left, the police pulled up in front of the house, broke down the door, and finding no one home turned the place upside down. They even poked around the backyard but didn't uncover anything and eventually left empty-handed.

Several days went by before Shirley, Ronal, and the others dared return to the house. When they did, they immediately went out back and dredged the sacks out of the water, only to discover the weapons and ammunition had already begun to rust. Since it had been the women's idea to throw everything into the well, the cleanup fell to them, just as it would have, I suspect, in any case. Getting the corrosion off those guns was no easy task, Shirley said, though the bullets were what took the longest. She remembered scrubbing them individually with a coarse rag and after that setting them out under the sun. It took a whole week before they dried out completely.

If Shirley told these stories to impress me, she genuinely seemed to derive satisfaction from the memories of belonging to the extended family of the Cristal gang. It gave her a sense of community perhaps, but also a feeling of being close to something important. Shirley told me that before Ronal landed in jail, she would always accompany Cristal's señora whenever she went out. As Shirley told it, she belonged to an inner circle of "mafia wives," with all the status that conferred, which at minimum was rank enough to look down on the other women in town, especially those they believed had eyes for their men. Shirley explained the predicament of the wife or steady girlfriend of a *narco* like this:

When a man gets involved in the mafia, before long he becomes a womanizer. No exceptions. Mafia men will always fool around. It's just part of the mafia way of life. However, every *narco* has a señora, and don't forget: there's a big difference between a señora and an *amante* [mistress]. The señora is *la firme* [the steady, stable one], and it's up to the señora to show the *amante* who is who: that you are the señora and that she is nothing but a mistress! [*Una mera amante!*]

Because the *narco always* comes back to his señora [Shirley affirmed this as if voicing an unassailable truth], and she *always* accepts him back. The señora always knows what he's up to, but she also knows he will be back, and the mistress, well, she just can't say that. She's only there for a moment of fun, nothing else.

Shirley continued on at the house until the end of the year. She then moved to Lima where through a friend she took a job as a live-in maid at the stately residence of a police colonel in the affluent suburb of Monterrico. When Ronal got out of jail, he followed her to Lima. Together with Vanessa the three of them moved to the populous district of Comas where some of Ronal's relatives had a small place. By that point Shirley had quit her job with the colonel and had found employment at a ladies' garment booth in Mesa Redonda, a sprawling commercial center in downtown Lima. Ronal and Shirley split up a few months later. She stayed on at the garment stand until late December 2001, when a flash fire tore through Mesa Redonda, quickly destroying an area of about twelve city blocks. Three hundred people died in the blaze and over seven hundred shops were reduced to ruins.

At the time of the fire Shirley was at home with Vanessa. It was her day off. Even so, she couldn't help thinking it had been a close call. The last time I spoke with her, several more years had elapsed. She was working in a kitchen that prepared chicken soup for the merchants and employees of the now rebuilt Mesa Redonda. Shirley sounded tired as she explained how she worked seven days a week and, despite putting in so many hours, never earned enough to save for her daughter's future. She made no effort to hide her sense of desperation or her desire to find something better.

Life had not been kind to Shirley. Pushed along by disasters, she had gone from one condition of feeling stuck to another. Hers was but one of many strands that had passed through Gregorio's house.

As for Marusha and her family, they would move on as well. First only a block over to the house of an aunt who had abandoned Aucayacu years before. There for a time Marusha continued her practice, that is, until death threats ultimately convinced her to leave town for good.

Leaving the Huallaga meant Marusha had no choice but to pursue her advocacy work from a place more distant but also more secure.

5 esparza

The event subsists in language, but it happens to things.

Deleuze, *The Logic of Sense*

It's like they say, he did a necessary good, I mean, a necessary evil.

***El chasero* "Gato"**

1

I want to plumb the apparent unity of a name. A name that came up again and again in local renderings of the violence and generalized lawlessness that once made the Upper Huallaga Valley a fearsome place. A name that in Aucayacu people couldn't stop saying, and eventually I too couldn't stop asking about. The one said to have come to set the Shining Path back on its heels. The one said to have turned the tide.

I want to draw attention no less to a certain naïve surprise, on my part though certainly not on mine alone, that the one known for the greatest cruelty, for the most superlative violence could also be credited with breaking the pall of fear that hung over the town, with ushering in a semblance of security, and with instilling a fresh respect for the state and its law—a "trust," townspeople say, unlike they had felt in a long time.

I cannot tell you the truth of what really happened. Certainty about what took place in the Huallaga of the 1980s and early 1990s is hard to come by. Facts are near impossible to confirm. Less because so much time has passed as because it was another time altogether. In the new era, of post-boom and post–uncivil war, the people most directly and intimately involved *back then* were long gone—they were dead; or else in their *new lives*, they preferred not to speak about the role they might have once played. So privileging the life of the uncertain over fact, this chapter examines something of the story and local fame—the hearsay, if you will, from the latter half of the 1990s—of an army captain and giver of law that most knew only as "Esparza."

From this story I wish to ask: How could "good things" come from actions so grim? Against what singular background could they ever acquire positive relief, much less seem necessary, after all?

2

Of Esparza the man very little was known for sure. Not his true identity. Not where he came from. Certainly not where he went in the ensuing years. I heard it said he grew up in the Chorrillos district of Lima, that he spoke with a decidedly *limeño* accent. Though there was also talk he'd been raised in the Huallaga, near the town of Uchiza. It was there, the rumor went, that still a young man he had witnessed the murder of his family at the hands of Sendero. This harrowing event was supposed to clarify the things Esparza would later do, the person he would become; because when it came to Esparza there was always a need to huddle together some kind of explanation.

Most who met or knew him agreed he was of thin build and, at around five-foot-ten, well above average stature. Some said he was of fair complexion, others dark, though all insisted he was handsome and charismatic and had the look of *buena gente* (good folk). People remembered him dressed in military field uniform of olive fatigue shorts, black T-shirt, and combat boots. They'd tell you he liked to wear dark glasses and that he kept a pistol holstered on his right hip. Some remembered him having a little motorbike with thick, stubby tires and how, lanky guy that he was, it looked like a toy whenever he rode it about town.

Of Esparza's tour of duty there was no public record. And while it comes as no surprise that the armed forces did not share vital information about its people in the "emergency zones," the role Esparza played in the army's campaign in the Upper Huallaga was all but ignored in accounts of political violence in Peru.[1] Whatever the reasons for the oversight, outside of this very circumscribed area of the Huallaga Valley, for many years little to nothing was known about Esparza's time there, and only rarely did something of his story percolate beyond local lore.[2]

Some said he arrived as early as 1989. Others were adamant he stayed on for a couple of years. But as best as I was able to ascertain—from multiple interviews and conversations I had with people in and around town—Esparza served as Aucayacu base commander for only seven months: December 1991 until late July 1992. To my knowledge no news or information about his tenure there appeared in the regional or national press at the time. Nevertheless, a Lima news magazine did publish a short article in March 1993 that detailed accusations made against him earlier that year, while stationed in the nearby city of Tingo María.[3] The story involved the kidnapping, near Aucayacu in January 1993, of an ex-soldier whose lifeless, mutilated body was later found floating in the Huallaga River. Eyewitnesses who remembered Esparza from his days as base commander linked him to the crime. Still, beyond a cryptic allusion to his local notoriety, the article made no specific mention of the incidents that took place in town during the period Esparza was there, the magnitude of which would have made what happened to the former soldier appear minor in comparison.

Possibly more significant, however, was the photograph that accompanied the article, significant because virtually no photographs taken of officers stationed in the Huallaga during the worst years of the violence survived to the present day. In it, an army officer was shown standing beside several townspeople during a public ceremony. A caption underneath read "Capitán EP Carlos Esparza in Aucayacu," suggesting that the image dated from the time he was in charge of the base. The officer depicted fit the overall description I had of him amazingly well, and yet because only a grainy profile of the face was visible, when I showed the image to people who had known him, they could not all agree it was him.

The ambiguity surrounding Esparza's identity was not hard to fathom. More than a dozen base commanders had rotated through town since the army first set up shop there nearly two decades earlier. For many years those officers never used insignia of rank. They also surrounded themselves with tight-knit "working groups" of lieutenants, sergeants, and technicians with whom they were easily confused.[4] Add that base commanders never went by their real identities but donned "warrior names" instead, and it becomes apparent that the difficulties of keeping them straight came less by accident than design.

Not unlike Sendero militants and leaders, Peruvian military officials went by code names in the theater of war to shield themselves and their families from reprisals. The threat was real, as insurgents targeted off-duty military and police officers for assassination, even to the extreme of bombing their personal residences.[5] For the military, however, pseudonyms were no less useful in the parallel theater of procedural law, for the purpose of limiting present and future attempts to establish institutional responsibility for atrocities and corruption. Moreover, pseudonyms could ostensibly be shared with, passed on to, or traded among different officers as a means of further masking their activities.

So many faces, so many names, and yet so little to hang memory upon. In Aucayacu there was a "Pantera" (Panther) and a "Lince" (Lynx), a "Fantasma" (Ghost) and a "Lobo" (Wolf), and many more than most can now recall at any one time. And while I never met anyone who could tell me, off the top of their head, more than a few of these pseudonyms, Esparza was always among those that came to mind. Even if they could remember only one. Some would tell you that his complete name was "Carlos Esparza Salinas," which was apparently how he signed army memoranda while stationed in town. And while Esparza's code name assumed a *proper* form—unlike other noms de guerre that unambiguously announced their invented nature as wild animals, spirits, or Hollywood movie characters—no one assumed for a second that his was any less made up.[6]

All recalled Esparza. He was the most famous, or infamous, depending on who you talked to. And it was that very ambivalence from which his name seemed to accrue some of its power. All remembered him and all associated him with a critical shift. As if more than a man, Esparza were an event, an event that embodied an almost unforgettable affect of command.

3

The farm people were used to seeing death, but they said they had never seen anything like this. For years they thought little of coming across a corpse tossed on the side of the trail, along the highway, or floating face down in a stream. It was the way the drug traders resolved their disputes, how they established hierarchy among themselves, how they obtained and preserved market share. It was also how the Shining Path made examples of villagers who couldn't follow orders or didn't want to toe the Party line. But to find those sacks pitched into the Huallaga River, sacks filled with heads and legs and arms lopped by a chainsaw, *that* was something else.

In those days, which were still the height of the cocaine boom, drug traders would constantly crisscross the river in small dugouts. Over to the farms to buy the kilos, which they packed into large nylon sacks known as *costales* before heading back to town to sell to the *patrón*. The Huallaga is a treacherous river, and because of it from time to time these dugouts would flip over, sending sacks of cocaine paste—and whatever other valuables the traders had with them—swiftly downstream. The farm people knew about this, and so whenever they went to the river to bathe they would always dive down, especially in the summer months when the water turned crystal clear. They'd go underwater and look around, and when they came across a sack, they'd say: "Maybe this is the fortune." And so they'd call for help, they'd pull it to shore, but when they opened it up they were unprepared for what awaited them.

It was like they got hit hard by the punch line of an excessively morbid joke. A punch line that effected an extreme reversal of expectation, sending tremors across the land. Because when those sacks started appearing, they said, many farmers just packed up and fled.

4

Only from a perspective that takes a collective to be shifting and shapeless, a collective ripe for being given form, could such an event come to pass.

Only from the perspective of a very specialized labor, one that stands as if outside and selects by imposing an inescapable choice, could forging new law for all be conceived.

This choice that literally cuts across a collective as a whole, leaving no gray: "It's us or them," says the advice it imparts. "Choose well. The world is not so complicated after all. The most concrete truths in life are simple, brutally simple."

This is the realm of "the political," which appears "as if by fate" to clear the social field of petty strife. The political that founds "a people" out of what was once haphazard collective, and in so doing, fashions new time.

Such was the "work" of Esparza.

5

You are what they call a *chasero,* a guy who peddles *chas,* or sulfuric acid, but also kerosene and potassium permanganate to the farmers who use them to convert harvests of leaves into blocks of cocaine paste for later sale to the local *firmas.* It's the early 1990s, and you live in town where your family has a house. You also have a piece of land fifteen minutes out of town that you cleared yourself. You don't go there much anymore on account of the guy with the farm next to yours. He is a Sendero leader who doesn't much take to you and is always looking for some pretext or other to confiscate your land—for the Party, I mean for himself. Everyone in town knows you, knows where you live, knows your brothers and sisters, your mother and father. They know your name but call you Gato, or Leche, or Negro, or whatever your *chapa* (tag, nickname) is, and when they see you out and about town on your big Honda XL 185, the same bike that takes you on your weekly trips out to your clients' farms, they notice.

One night you're at a party and you see Esparza. He's alone at the bar and working on two beers. He's only been in town a couple of weeks now, but he is already your *pata*, your buddy. That is, you know him well enough to say hi, to kid around, because in your line of business you must stay on good terms with whoever is in charge at the base.

¿Y compadre? he calls over to you. *¿Y mi capitán?* you reply, hoping to keep it short and move quickly on your way. But he invites you to join him. He pours you a glass. You can't refuse and so you pick up the glass, smiling as if that was what you wanted all along. And when you swallow that first sip of beer, he says in a voice for all to hear:

"Compadre . . . you may be a *droguero* [druggie], a *chasero*. What of it? But if you're a *terruco* [terrorist], then *cuello* [neck]." As Esparza says this, he draws a finger across his throat.

"Hey listen, Señor Capitán," you whisper back, shaking your head. "I don't get mixed up with those things. I'm fine with my democracy."

"Very well," he says, raising his voice to a shout. "That's the way I like you, compadre, you don't go near anything that has to do with politics."

"No, no," you say, raising your voice, but not as loud as his, "I don't know the first thing about it."

6

More than a man, and yet even today his name covers and condenses what was a complex state of affairs. For while the political violence, which engulfed Peru throughout the 1980s and into the 1990s, spread unevenly across varied geographic and social landscapes, it manifested through singular events whose significance and weight often revealed themselves in extremely local settings and to relatively small groups of people. The mere fact that these incidents *happened* did not guarantee their impact would ever become legible beyond the specific locales where they occurred, or even beyond those most intimately touched. This is only to say that the violent manifestations of war were as plural as their spheres of reception were constrained.

In and around Aucayacu, Esparza was not one event among many but was said to have ushered in a new epoch all its own. As if a hinge in time, the arrival or rupture that carried this name came to denote a turn in fates and fortunes. Much like the capture of Shining Path leader Abimael Guzmán—in Lima on

September 12, 1992—would acquire national significance as a mortal blow to Sendero's revolutionary aspirations,[7] Esparza's "coming" would inaugurate a palpable turnaround in the townspeople's everyday experience of the war.

Curiously enough, this change of political fates was attributed to Esparza even though other evidence suggested the circumstances that set this transformation into motion not only exceeded the short period he was actually stationed in town, but reflected the efforts of more than one man. As an army officer Esparza was part of an institutional hierarchy. He acted on the basis of orders received and within a strategy that was not of his own design. There can be little doubt he executed an institutional will, and even to the degree that will was multiple, ambiguous, or even contradictory, it preceded him and continued long after he was gone.[8]

And yet to hear people talk, there was something about him, at the very least an exceptional style of command,[9] that broke with or, from a more nuanced perspective, *complicated* the institutional mold of the army that people had grown accustomed to. There was something about him and the ways he acted that was so unexpected, so open, and yet so severe that people came to realize that times had changed and would now follow a wholly different itinerary. A new temporal pathway, a new "civic" schedule or calendar, would thereafter organize the townspeople—their attitudes, actions, even some of their most common modes of address—thereby announcing that the law once imposed by Sendero was no more.

Esparza, as event, proclaimed a change in political conditions just as his very name contained a command to return to the state. For if Esparza was associated with an uncompromising severity, this ruthlessness, which some understood as a "rigor" of purpose, signaled to people that the authority of the state—and not merely its violence—had returned. It signaled that the force of state law writ large, shriveled and fallen away before the overlapping paths of the cocaine boom and the Shining Path's "People's War," was now charging up again. This quality or image of rectitude was above all what fascinated the townspeople, and this same fascination was what later came to color if not dominate the stories told about him. *Memory* of Esparza, if that is what we can call all this talk, was inseparable from the memory he "created" and inseparable from the ways memories of him continued to labor upon the future. By carrying forward the traces of prohibitions set down during the four years during which the army turned the tables on Sendero, a new civic spirit was crafted—a memory that impressed upon the townspeople their need for the state. During these years new lines of cause and effect were established that let the people draw their own conclusions about what they "did" and "did not" want.

This is the period that was condensed into the figure of Esparza's "coming." Time was compressed, no less than law, for Esparza's message was simple and unmistakable: "*This* is what happens."[10] From this message, the townspeople would infer a set of basic rules that put them on the right side of fate. They would pick up a few *¡no quiero!*—a handful of inner *illuminations* specifying what they did not want to do.

And even so, as a name Esparza acquired a different valence or sense, depending on which side of the town/country divide one fell. Within Aucayacu, it was never hard to find people who would express admiration for Esparza and were sympathetic to the "work" he did. In the countryside, however, the story was different, and it was hard to find a redeeming word about him. Appraisals had a strictly negative value and direction. Esparza was a butcher, a sadist, perhaps even a *mantequero*.[11]

A farmer and coca grower who lived several kilometers north of town told me once that Esparza was *un Pinochet*, drawing in this way upon the name of the former Chilean dictator to emphasize the enormity of the captain's crimes. For this farmer, Esparza, as a manifestation of extraordinary evil, belonged to a line of genocidal despotic types so notorious for their ability to kill without mercy that their proper names could turn into common nouns. The name Esparza in its stead would become part of the local vernacular, used to describe any military or police officer who killed with a passion unrestrained by moral or ethical limit: *Él es "un Esparza"* (He's "an Esparza") they would say, or with greater emphasis still, *Él es todo "un Esparza"* (He's a complete "Esparza"). The difference being that in the countryside, and for those who lived there, Esparza was just and only that: the one who killed without bounds. Whereas in the town, he was that . . . and he was so much more.

7

Townspeople would talk as if, with Esparza, there was no uncertainty. That you knew where he stood and that he demanded the same of you. That unlike the police, he couldn't have cared less about the cocaine trade or its traders. That he didn't bother himself with collecting the kickbacks the army always culled from the local operators. True, it was under Esparza's watch that drug planes first started landing and taking off from the Marginal Highway just inside city limits. And sure, the base got its share of every shipment that flew out of town. It was the way things worked. But the drug traders would tell you that Esparza's game was another.

He only cared about one thing: whose side you were on. Standing in between, or with nobody at all, was no longer a choice. You had to declare yourself for one side or the other. You had to commit. It was your life. It was the bag.

For Esparza came to town not only to deal with Sendero, it seems, but to make a people. A people the state could call its own.

How does one *make* "a people"?

I can only tell you what they said Esparza did. He painted the plaza white, for one, and then every Sunday made the townspeople gather there to watch the flag go up the pole, sing the national anthem, and perform the part of loyal citizens.

Esparza restored the symbolic center of town, and that was no small thing. Few in Aucayacu had gone to see the flag raised or marched in a civic parade ever since the Shining Path made it clear it would not tolerate demonstrations of fidelity or reverence for what it called the reactionary state. Not since the early 1980s. Eons ago. Seven years at least.

In Peru, as in so many places, flag-raising ceremonies and school parade competitions are the mainstay of patriotic expression. Before the advent of Sendero they used to happen two or three times a year, on or around the main national and local holidays. Throughout the 1980s, however, almost no civic ceremonies took place in this Huallaga town; the ones that did occur were at best muted affairs in the main plaza attended by the thinning ranks of officials that had not been scared off by Sendero threats. The mayor, when there was a mayor, might show up along with the justice of the peace. Most of the time, though, it was only the army and police. Sometimes the situation was so tense that the ceremonies were not held in the plaza at all but safely within the fortified confines of the Project, that large, open-air compound with tall cinderblock walls to which the army and police and a pared-down contingent of state bureaucratic offices had withdrawn. Everyone else would stay far away or skip town altogether.

The 1980s were a time when Sendero had succeeded in separating most of those who lived in the Huallaga from the state, be it the state in symbol or embodied by its living representatives. In Aucayacu, as in other towns, merely being seen talking with someone from the army or police could be your death sentence. The fear of being accused of being a *soplón* not only caused people to keep their distance but saturated and patterned even the most casual of interactions—such was the unrelenting weight of what Sendero called its "thousand eyes," its "thousand ears." There was perhaps no surer way of getting onto Sendero's blacklist than to publicly embrace symbols deemed national or patriotic. Anyone would tell you that the Party made examples of those who contravened its decrees. They would tell you that the mayor of Aucayacu himself was gunned down in 1989, one day after he had publicly kissed the flag during a June 7 Flag Day ceremony.

With Esparza all of that changed . . . if we are to believe the stories. Every Sunday morning the townspeople converged on the main plaza. All the stores had to close. No one could stay home. No one could miss the raising of the flag. Esparza called on town notables to escort the national colors of red and white, and then he made the rest of the town—not just school kids, but everyone—march behind.[12] Never before had the ceremonies been so frequent. Never before had everyone participated. Never before had homage to national symbols been so intense. Flag raisings and parades became not the occasional acts they had once been but a weekly civic obligation,[13] which was nothing less than the compulsion to declare, for all to see, what side you were on.

Perhaps there never would have been an emphasis on a "return" of patriotic expression had Sendero not been such a stickler for national symbols, and had it not placed such onerous prohibitions on them in the first place. Perhaps. But in bringing them back, Esparza—which is to say the army—had a plan.

By putting the townspeople on display he could gather them into a mass. He could force them into a collective disobedient of Sendero rule. He could demonstrate in a mechanical and yet provocative way which side the people were on. Putting them on display, he could send a simple message to Sendero and also advise the townspeople of their own domination.

Everyone would march, and when they filed by, Esparza's hooded informers would be there to pick out the suspects that soldiers would cart off to the base. People feared those *soplones*. They were Esparza's eyes and ears. They helped him sharpen the force and focus of the violent means at his disposal. With them, it is said, he pruned back, one by one, the branches of Sendero's suffocating scrutiny.

Every Sunday morning people would march about the plaza. No one dared stay home. While any night of the week, bags might appear downstream. Because in those days, parades and the saw were a package.[14]

8

The townspeople marveled most at Esparza's confidence. They were used to army officers who stayed secluded in the base and exercised extreme caution in their movements outside the Project compound, officers who never went anywhere without a large retinue of soldiers and bodyguards. It was a time when fear reigned but when danger pressed most firmly of all on those in uniform and on anyone who got too close to them.

But Esparza acted as if none of that mattered, with a flair that won the approval of many. When the army left town to make forays into the country-side, Esparza was always there at the front of the pack, ready to face death or whatever else came his way. But what impressed people more was how he would tarry alone in broad daylight, on foot, on bike, on that tiny motorcycle of his. How outside town he would motor up and down the Marginal Highway in military uniform, all by himself and with nothing more than his sidearm for protection. How he would turn off onto trails that took him into the thick of Sendero territory. *Medio loco* (half crazy) they insisted he was, playing on euphemism to say it was more than a little crazy, back then, to throw all cau-tion to the wind, to so brazenly test fate.

Yet few places conveyed the mystique of Sendero's dominion like the shores of the Huallaga River just opposite the town. Up until the mid-1990s none of the townspeople could venture there without first getting the Party's permission. Esparza, however, was determined to show he wasn't scared to go, even there. So one morning, they said, he went to the port and took a dugout to the other side. Not content to just stand there on the beach, he walked up and down the shore. "Here I am! Here I am!" he shouted at the top of his lungs. "Kill me! Kill me!" He shouted for all to hear: for the townspeople who looked on from the port more than a little amazed, just as much as for all the senderistas real or imagined hiding in the bush and not so far from where Esparza paced.

If anything, Esparza had a keen understanding of the wonders a little theater could work, and everything he did seemed to be with an eye toward maximizing his performative effect. He wanted to be seen and wanted everyone to see above all that he was not scared of anything or of anyone. And he wanted them to feel no less that the dangers they heeded and were compelled to steer around even in their most everyday of routines—*somehow*—did not apply to him. Doing the stuff that nobody did, nobody in their right mind, that is, it wasn't long before rumors spread that Esparza was a little larger than life. It wasn't long before a certain invincible air accrued to his persona as a man with no limits.

Esparza seemed to be everywhere, always about, and if you lived in town, you were struck by his inimitable effusiveness. Gregarious, so easy to talk to, never stressed out by his duties, but always asking how you, your friends, and your family were faring. You'd see him on the street, he'd call out to you; he'd come over, shake your hand, strike up conversation.

And if you were that shopkeeper who happened to be sweeping the sidewalk out in front of her store, early one morning when Esparza strolled by with his men, you would have heard him say to you: "*Hola* Señora. How did you sleep? Now you can go to bed at night without fear. Now you can take your kids to play in the park. Don't be afraid. I am here to protect you."

And if you were that shopkeeper, you would remember how, even as your hands clamped down tight on the broomstick, you were a little startled when a grin, you knew not from where, took over your nervous face.

To hear it told, no base commander had ever been so neighborly and so sure of himself, none had tried so vigorously to break the distance that had hardened between state and town folk ever since Sendero had arrived in the Huallaga. And yet Esparza cut through that distance as if that cold detachment had been a figment of people's imagination. Like everything he did, he made it seem easy, even natural.

People were drawn to him and, not surprisingly, he made his share of friends. Of those he befriended, some maintained he never asked them for help, he never mixed them up with his work. For as much as they dreaded that that moment would come—when he would draw upon their acquaintance to ask for a name or two—much to their surprise, he never did. They wondered: how a man so affable, so affirming, and yet so unselfish—how could he not be a good guy? And if here was where the claims on Esparza's nobleness of character corroded the limits of credulity, those same friends insisted they never doubted he was agreeable and bighearted only so long as events never implicated them with the guerrilla.

Problem was, staying clear of Sendero often did not hinge on personal choice. The Party had a way of seeking you out and then there was not much you could do, short of making a major life change. If the Party called on you, you were "it." This was, of course, a more intractable condition for those who resided in rural areas where Sendero called all the shots, than for those in the towns who had a better chance of sidestepping Party advances.

9

Well into the post-boom there persisted the notion that Esparza never killed anyone who didn't somehow deserve it. You would hear it in town. That he did his detective work well and kept his sights fixed on those who *truly* belonged to Sendero. Others would go as far as to say that Esparza was so skilled, so good at what he did, he almost never made a mistake. A welder and machinist who considered Esparza a close and trustworthy friend said that the captain, in a rare commentary on his nighttime labors at the base, confided to him once: "Out of a hundred, maybe I'll make a mistake with one."

And that's something people would say repeatedly about Esparza: that his aim was true. It was an assertion that conveniently paralleled how the government of Alberto Fujimori described its overall approach to the internal war.[15] Esparza *mató a los verdaderos*, they claimed, that he killed the true believers.[16] This was a good measure of the trust he imbued: the truth and efficacy of his line of fire. No longer did the army kill indiscriminately. It picked out the real enemy in its midst with an accuracy that townspeople found novel, novel enough to turn a blind eye when it seemed like a good idea.

Esparza was also unique from his predecessors in another important respect. Many if not most base commanders had been willing to make deals, to trade a little money for the safe and timely release of a prisoner. Esparza, however, always towed the strictest of lines: never to be bought and forever implacable with the foe. It was as if he had come with one and only one goal in mind: to destroy Sendero, and nothing would stop him. An arrow so straight it sobered. The welder who knew him said he was convinced Esparza had been sent on a special mission to rescue the town. It was as if Esparza had been sent "to win the peace."

And so, when the wives and mothers and sisters of men who had been detained in town or, more often, during one of the army's raids into the countryside—when those women came to the Project compound with whatever money they had managed to scrape together, when they pleaded with him, Esparza would send them away, unmoved.

"Do you have children, Señora?" he might ask. "Well, spend that money on your kids, because your husband (or your son or your brother), you are never going to see him again."

Some, like Lucio, the town tax collector, never could quite square the affable nature of the captain he knew with the things that went on at the base. Years later he would wonder if Esparza didn't have a dual personality:

> By day we knew him to be a very friendly, charismatic, approachable in every way possible. He greeted everyone—*hola, hola, hola*—from the poorest of the poor to the richest of the rich. He spoke to everyone, and then there was that

sense of humor of his that made people open up to him. But many didn't know—how should I call it?—that other part, that other face of his personality. To judge from his manner you never could have imagined. It never would have crossed your mind. Of course, later it became known, but even then nobody knew for sure.

10

Nobody knew for sure, but they knew.

Carlos and Doris, municipal worker and primary teacher, husband and wife, they told me about it one of the many afternoons I visited with them at their home, inside the Project compound, where they had lived for years.

"Now, over there," Carlos said, motioning with a quick nod, "coming from that building you would hear the *ta-ta-ta*, whenever the chainsaw came on. We could hear it, that *te-te-te* . . . couldn't we Doris?"

"From over *there*," Doris agreed, "we could hear the screams . . . but they'd put on . . ."

"Their big sound equipment," Carlos said, completing the thought, "and at full volume, too."

"They'd put music on," Doris added, "but, still, the others . . . they'd do their "*Aaaay . . .*"

"And it was horrible," conceded Carlos, "but you know what? In a way I liked Esparza, because to be blunt: Before, this town belonged to no one, and he came to impose order."

"But the problem," Doris said, "wasn't really Sendero. In those days, you know what the problem was? The whole world did whatever they wanted, and then they blamed it on Sendero."

"Yeah," said Carlos. "They'd kill someone. They'd take the money and then, they'd leave the hammer and sickle behind."

11

The Esparza event gathered relief against a background of unbearable chaos. People would tell you: "Before he arrived, this town wasn't even a town, more like the wild west. Everyone did what they wanted and because of it, everyone else suffered." They would speak of the lawlessness that bore down like an intense atmospheric pressure, a heavy, anxious air of immediate peril. Esparza's "coming" followed from this image of no law, of life plagued by senseless violence. In this way, the Esparza event linked up with a figure of no man's land. Through it, Esparza not only became intelligible, but gained a structure and a justification. No man's land foretold him and his labors, just as it carved out a space for his arrival. Everything happened as if Esparza came to answer the town's desire to abandon what had turned into an excruciating state of affairs.

While people might describe the lawless air that took hold of town in ambiguous terms, they had less difficulty locating some of its "causes" or principal agents. Above all, there was the arbitrary use of force by those who wielded it. Doris and Carlos underscored this, emphasizing the problem of impersonation by those who committed crimes under the guise of the Shining Path. But townspeople would also point to the extreme corruption and treachery of the police who, they insisted, regularly passed information along to Sendero. Why else in those days, they would ask, did those who came forward to report on guerrilla activity end up dead on the streets of the town?[17] The police were in cahoots with Sendero, they insisted, whether infiltrated or simply cowered into submission. Some would say they did it for their own protection, as a way of staving off attack. Others didn't bother with explanations but found in the pervasiveness of such rumors immediate proof of what they considered the police's reprehensible and "uncivic" character. Either way, the police became a blockage to an adequate if not cordial communication between people and state, when not an active source of disorder.

Yet nothing conjured the figure of no man's land for townspeople more intensely than the Urbana, which ran roughshod over Aucayacu in the years prior to Esparza's arrival. "La Urbana" was local Huallaga vernacular for the Shining Path cells that appeared in the towns north of Tingo María sometime around the mid-1980s.[18] The Urbana was a continuing vector of Sendero violence that issued from the rural areas where the Party conserved its principal base of support.[19] It was formed to carry out espionage on the movements of the police and army, to collect war taxes from shopkeepers and drug traders, and to make selective attacks on enemy targets. Though intended to operate clandestinely wherever the state still maintained an armed presence, the Urbanas quickly acquired such dominance that they moved about openly and even came to exercise a de facto form of rule. Killing was by no small means responsible for this, and soon dead bodies began appearing all over town, dumped on street corners with signs tossed on top: "This is how snitches die"; "This is how dogs of the old state die." Then there was the strength the

Urbanas owed to their proximity to the cocaine trade, which in those years was concentrated in the towns. Close access to the trade allowed them to establish a high degree of control over local *firmas*, and thanks to the wealth they skimmed off, the Urbanas came to operate with a great deal of autonomy vis-à-vis the Party hierarchy located in the countryside. Within the Huallaga Shining Path, the Urbana emerged as a counterpower of sorts, when not a rebellious faction. However, in no place did it act with the brash abandon and in ways so contrary to the Party's rigid moral ethos as in Aucayacu.[20]

Nothing defined the Aucayacu Urbana so much as the extreme youth of its members—most were in their late teens—and the swagger with which they wore their identification with the Party. People remembered them as weak on revolutionary commitment though strong on the advantages Party membership afforded: a way to get money, a way to eat and dress well, a way to be "somebody." They gained a reputation for being abusive and cavalier,[21] quick to enforce Sendero rules but lax when it came to following them themselves. Above all, and with a cruelty perhaps only teenagers could mete out, they knew how to take advantage of the terror they bred. They kept a blacklist of undesirables whom they slated for elimination. The fear of that list went a long way in gaining the compliance of the townspeople. If there was something a store had that they wanted, they went in and demanded it. If they wanted to go someplace, they commandeered cars and motorcycles. And when cash was low, they collected contributions "for the Party." Their feeling of entitlement, people would tell you, even extended to the young women of town, whom they would pick up at gunpoint if need be. Those who protested—that she already had a boyfriend or simply wished to be left alone—risked being killed and having it said later they had consorted with a policeman or an army spy. "The list" was always being updated to suit individual members of the Urbana.

The Urbana's hair-trigger readiness to kill combined with the complete lack of stability in the distinctions of friend and foe roiled the public space of town. While Sendero was known foremost for how it killed, people were used to there being some compelling reason attached to its violence—whether as *limpieza social* (social cleansing)[22] of those deemed to be asocial, or as the necessary elimination of opponents of the revolution (state sympathizers or collaborators). It was not essential that people agree with the Party's reasons. Yet it was indispensable that the Party *have* its reasons, be they what they were. The violence of the Urbana, however, followed no apparent logic, other than sheer cruelty or personal gain.

"The Urbana put down whomever they pleased, whether they were a target or not." This was the gist of the townspeople's complaint—that the Urbana dissolved all sense of law. That in enforcing Sendero rule, at times on little more than a whim, their violence lost all direction while hovering ever present. Coming out of nowhere, striking without warning, and yet leaving nothing behind out of which to fashion navigational rules of thumb, rules that would be durable enough to carry over from one situation to the next. The recklessness of Urbana violence frustrated, it would seem, the townspeople's ability to draw out basic norms for keeping misfortune, when not death, at bay. The excruciating experience of this frustration, where living, simply living, seemed near impossible, is what townspeople pointed to when they spoke of no man's land.

12

Esparza put a stop to Aucayacu's days as no man's land. At least that is what townspeople said, because it was he who brought the Urbana's reign to an end. They were as if inseparable—Esparza and the Urbana—and so much so that one can rarely be mentioned without the other coming in close behind. Yet question a little further, cross-check versions, and the picture grew complicated, disparities appeared. Most blatantly—and once again—time frames didn't quite match up. The Urbana's hold on Aucayacu lasted at best four years, until 1989 when the army began its counteroffensive against Sendero. Never again would the Urbana roam about Aucayacu at will or strike the same terror.

The Urbana's decline began when the army did a house-by-house search of the town, looking for subversive materials, weapons, and suspects. During the search, it was said, soldiers rounded up all the men they found, young and old, and took them back to the base. The officer in charge at the time was "Fantasma" (Ghost), though most people recalled the search and the detentions it produced more clearly than the man who ordered them. Members of the Urbana would continue to fall in the coming two years, especially as Sendero tried to reconstitute its urban guerrilla. However, the Urbana had already taken a mortal hit during and immediately following the army's initial sweep through the town, that is, long before Esparza ever became base commander.

Lucio the tax collector swore that it was during Fantasma's time at the base that prisoners accused of belonging to the Urbana were stuffed inside large sacks and then taken up in a helicopter. As the craft made passes over the town, the sacks were dumped out one by one, sending the supposed Urbana members to their deaths. It was a message to the townspeople, Lucio said. And yet, as dramatic a gesture as tossing prisoners—bound and still breathing—from a lethal elevation must have been, I never met anyone, besides Lucio, who actually remembered that particular event. During the course of its counterinsurgency war, the army regularly carried suspects away in helicopters only to return back to base with their cargo holds empty. There are many stories of how prisoners were bumped off or forced to jump from terrifying heights down into the oblivion of the jungle abyss. Less talked about was how the army bagged its victims before taking them to a place of final disposal. But as many would tell you in Aucayacu, sacks and bodies . . . well, that's Esparza—with the proviso of course that Esparza and his group rarely bagged their victims alive, but only after mutilating or chopping them up with that signature chainsaw.

The reasons why Esparza, and only Esparza, literally captured the local imagination were not wholly transparent, but he did. Perhaps his "method" of killing conjured for townspeople a superlatively horrible end. Perhaps it evoked a uniquely potent terror that made a more lasting impression than the many other violent acts that permeated those years. Then again, the use of chainsaws to torture and kill during the war was not necessarily restricted to Esparza, even if it became associated with his, more than anyone else's, name. Some townspeople might simply have appreciated what they perceived as his efficiency, while others admired what they called his *habilidad*, indicating innate skill, cleverness, and artistry all wrapped into one.

Regardless, Esparza, it seems clear to me, established a new threshold in the violence, and a symptom of this is the way he appeared to transform his violence into authority. Not that I claim to understand it, I don't. But what I am sure of is that the new threshold did not depend on the lethal quality of Esparza's violence alone. There were others before him and after who were just as ready and willing to kill. A teacher and school administrator who worked for years as an educator in and around Aucayacu—I'll call him Wilmer—told me once that Fantasma was far more dangerous than Esparza. It's true, he said, that Fantasma started the "extermination" of the Urbana, but he went against the townspeople in general, doing a poor job of distinguishing between friend and foe. "With this señor even us [teachers] were at risk," but, he said, there were so many complaints that it wasn't long before Fantasma got his marching orders. As for the Urbana, Wilmer explained, what Fantasma started Esparza came along and finished. He did so selectively, however, without random bloodletting. This "refinement" in Wilmer's opinion went a long way toward forging a degree of trust, if not winning the tacit approval of the town. If it is true that by the time Esparza showed up, Aucayacu's Urbana was at most a shadow of its former prowess, he got the credit even so.

If he did in fact finish off what remained of the Urbana—to the degree the urban guerrilla still had any operational capacity left and was not just a scattering of former members, disbanded and set adrift—Esparza's time at the base marked a more fundamental transformation: a shift in movement, momentum, and direction of the conflict itself. Esparza arrived at a particular historical moment: when the war with Sendero no longer would be fought in town but increasingly carried out in the rural villages and farms where it would continue for many years to come, largely out of sight of the people of Aucayacu. Esparza would designate, then, the moment when the front lines of the war swung definitively out of town and into the countryside.[23] With the Urbana no more, and the Huallaga towns finally under army control, Sendero would from then on be a "rural problem," a problem almost exclusively of and for the farm people. Esparza could be said to mark or denote a turn in the direction of the times; or better, his name became attached to this shift in the course of the war as well as the new political and legal conditions it ushered in.

It was rare to hear townspeople say Esparza acted indiscriminately, and yet this was exactly what you heard from those who lived on farms outside of Aucayacu. In the countryside Esparza was known not for the precision of his aim but for the callousness, brutality, and heartlessness with which he killed. There, no one would tell you he only targeted *los verdaderos*, a term that gained smooth contours only from a safe distance. No, they'd tell you what he did to their brother, sister, husband, son, aunt, cousin. They would tell you how they found the body, or rather a piece or two mixed with parts of so many other bodies, how they had to search and search for the right pieces of sawed-off flesh and bone, in desperate attempts to bring them back together again, if only for a decent burial. They might tell you that they never could find the head.

And yet this could go some lengths to account for the respect Esparza enjoyed among some townspeople, that is, among those with few if any ties to the countryside. Beginning with and following Esparza's stint at the base, the army, for the most part, spared "the town"—I mean, those families that did not straddle the urban-rural divide and so lost few loved ones in the coming carnage.

The army spared the town and precisely at a moment when, nationally, the Upper Huallaga was widely perceived to be a Sendero stronghold. In the national press and even in the writings of the most perceptive political analysts, rarely was a distinction drawn between the Huallaga of the towns and the Huallaga of the countryside.[24] The army made the distinction, no doubt because it knew it needed allies and could not wage a successful war in the region without them; the army chose the towns, and the towns threw their lot in with the army. Their privilege at not having been taken wholesale as "terrorists"—precisely at the time when those residing in rural areas were to receive the full force of the army's fury—no doubt made for a powerful bond. So it is possible to see in Esparza's prestige something of a compensation, a certain gratitude felt among the towns for being located outside the free-fire zone that the countryside was to become, a quiet sigh of relief for getting the chance to ally themselves with the army and through that alliance to return to the fold of the nation "once again."

None of these "advantages" could be far from the legitimacy townspeople conferred to Esparza's deeds, which, in a manner of speaking, put time on their side.

13

The townspeople, they would say, knew nothing about the chainsaw or the bags tossed in the river . . .

And then, if pressed, they might say it was necessary. "Because things just couldn't go on like that"—they'd mean with the Urbana doing whatever it liked. They might even compress an explanation into the saying, as I heard them do on more than one occasion: *Que no hay mal que dure cien años,* suggesting that there is no bad situation, however appalling, that will not succumb to the passing of time. They would say this, it seemed, as a way of tying off discussion on a forceful note: as if to suggest that something *had* to happen, that a major turn in events was unavoidable, in any case. And then, they might go on to say that Esparza or what he did was "the only way of putting an end to *it.*" This "it" was, for some, Sendero, or the broad nondescript phenomenon of "terrorism." For others, "it" referred rather to the various abuses, extortions, and killings committed in Sendero's name but that transcended the organized actions of the Party. What people seemed to admire about Esparza was the way he combated not simply Sendero, but a Sendero perceived to have devolved into utter unruliness, violence without motive. This unruliness was expressed above all by those who misused their positions of power in the Party, or those who appropriated the terror exuded by the very notion of the Party in order to prey upon the townspeople for personal profit. Esparza's prestige—to hear him talked about as a celebrated figure—drew in part upon the idea that he was a force against social corruption—social corruption construed as an ever-latent human temptation to take advantage of contingent circumstances in order to do whatever the hell one wants.

The fascination with Esparza, thus, was not wholly different than that which Sendero had inspired only a decade earlier.

In the retrospective accounts of many townspeople, however, Sendero's original popular appeal as a corrective force to social injustice was lost. Instead, unbounded chaos gathered into Sendero, where it was rendered indistinct from the Party as political-military organization and revolutionary dream. Sendero *in hindsight* became so much senseless violence and destruction. This was perhaps to some degree a surface effect of the "promise," that memory for the future engendered through Esparza's "civilizing" labor, but only if we are to take "his work" seriously. For by order of that promise, what was and forever would be Sendero had to be deprived of all ground.

And yet, as much as a decade had passed, times had changed. And despite the fact that the Sendero experience still belonged to the recent past, the appeal of *anyone* who would come to lay down a rule with unwavering severity seemed undiminished. Some called it *rigor* and said that deep down that's what "the people" really wanted. As best as I can understand, through such "rigor" life was thought to be given a clear direction, and when times appeared altogether out of sorts, any direction whatsoever could appear preferable to no direction at all. It was there, in the townspeople's rendition of events, that the violence Esparza wrought acquired purpose and resolve.

Perhaps the more fundamental question, however, is how violence comes to acquire sense at all? By which I do not mean some kind of transparent meaning, but more precisely a heading and momentum. For it is possible to speculate that what the townspeople found intolerable was not violence per se, certainly not Esparza's violence, but violence with no clear course. Nietzsche once suggested that what people find unbecoming, if not unbearable, is not suffering in itself but *senseless* suffering.[25] Nietzsche is relevant here because it is as if Esparza—not the man but as *event*—gave violence a sense, that is to say a *direction*, against which navigating the streets of town, the everyday lives of townspeople, turned more predictable and tolerable. For them, under

Esparza, life and the violence that permeated it got simpler. While increasing what could be called the volume of violence, he honed down the spectrum of chaos, specifying more surely what made a friend and what an enemy. To hear it told, he laid down clear vectors of cause and effect, an equation demonstrating what happens: "Do this. Get that." And gradually, as his violence started to have and make more sense, the townspeople began to feel they could find their way. This is what I understand by the statement that Esparza was the one who pacified the town.

Thanks to Esparza, townspeople would tell you, life got appreciably better, enough so for them to find justification for his methods. As Lucio the tax collector put it, "There were all these problems, and many believe it was necessary what Esparza did. Yes, necessary, indispensable, because if he hadn't corrected them, Sendero would never have died. To the contrary, it would have continued and gotten stronger too, all over the Huallaga."

Some said that what Esparza did was just about "the only way," and by that they meant a semblance of peace could not have been fashioned without recourse to extreme—and extremely unpleasant—measures. A steady, firm hand was needed to set things right. Some would point to his work ethic and the knack he had for his trade. Esparza "knew how to work" (*sabía trabajar*). Esparza "worked well" (*trabajó bien*). Then they would lament he didn't stay longer.

Wilmer suggested that people liked what he called the "seeds" Esparza had sowed, above all the way he called on everyone to come on Sundays for the parade and the flag. Wilmer said they wished Esparza would come back, that rigor—again that word—was what the people felt they needed. Wilmer didn't make explicit on what exactly that rigor was predicated, but in sharing a knowing kind of silence, he and I both seemed to understand. The "art" of Esparza's ways, his violence but also something ineffable in his character, was integral to his "power of convocation."

Lucio, for his part, explained to me that because of what Esparza did, those who were unwilling to quit Sendero packed up and left while the rest of the population came to grips with the error of their ways and began "to correct themselves." For me, this self-rectification on the part of the populace (a populace continually winnowed down, selected, and crafted) gestured toward the memory that Esparza made. It was a memory seared and chopped into the body of "the enemy," though not for the enemy so much as for "the friend," for the collective shaped into "a people."

This is to say that the "seeds" Esparza implanted, a kind of memory for the future, were nothing more than a small set of internalized prohibitions, a few implicit affirmations of *¡no quiero!* instilled in those who remained to speak and act the part of "the people." At the time, no one dared spell them out; everyone knew and assimilated them as best they could, repeating to themselves and maybe only to themselves:

> *No quiero:* I don't want to say *compañero* (the word is *terrorista!*).
> *No quiero:* I don't want anything to do with "politics."
> *No quiero:* I don't want to miss the parade.

14

Here's how it goes:

> Someone else's flesh and bones receive the work.
> You get the memory. It's *your* memory.
> They get the affect of terror.
> You, the affect of command.

15

So much contained in a name. Esparza was the end of the Urbana. The return of parades and patriotic fervor. He was the chainsaw and the relation or ensemble of *costal* and human corpse–reduced-to-pieces. He was screams from the base at night and the shift in the war front from town to country. He was a relaxed walk to the town market without even once looking over your shoulder. He was the señora who knew she could now sleep well at night or let her children play in the park. Just as he was the nervous grin that took over her face. This is to say Esparza was more than anyone could quite get a handle on, which might well be why the stories about him went on and on.

16

Mystery surrounded the circumstances of how Esparza, the man, left Aucayacu. Most agreed that he was transferred out at the start of the national Fiestas Patrias festivities in 1992, though his departure was interpreted as owing neither to a scheduled rotation nor to his own personal request. Esparza, townspeople said, had taken a lead role in the festival preparations, having invested a lot of time and effort coordinating with the schools and city hall. It was the first time since the early 1980s that Independence Week, the most important of all Peruvian patriotic celebrations, was going to take place in Aucayacu. Esparza was keen on making a splash.

Some said he was recalled as early as July twentieth, though others said it was July twenty-seventh, one day before the big parade. They recounted how he was in the midst of directing the final dress rehearsal when a special detachment arrived from Tingo María and took him away. Urgency was such that the captain wasn't even allowed to go back to the base to gather his things, and this only added weight to the idea that Esparza had been relieved of his command.

There were at least a couple of rumors as to why he got orders to leave. One was that his superiors had received reports of the atrocious killings he had perpetrated, suggesting Esparza's labor had not been authorized from the get-go, or that it had gotten out of hand. This version, however, did not preclude the possibility that what concerned the army leadership was that Esparza's notoriety was in danger of spilling beyond the restricted local sphere of Aucayacu; therefore, it was deemed prudent to move him to another assignment, to relocate such a valuable "asset." There was also a rumor that Esparza got pulled on account of two *costales* of drug payoff money that had either been discovered or had somehow gone missing. Whether the captain's error was receiving payoffs or failing to pass them along to superiors was unclear.

Less uncertain was where he went immediately after Aucayacu. Several Project employees, who on the morning of July twenty-eighth had traveled to Tingo María for the main day of the Independence celebrations, saw Esparza marching in the parade. Other sources suggested that the Los Laureles base in Tingo María became, for the following year at least, his new home.

After that Esparza's trail went cold, though new information, vague and authorless, would continue to turn up now and again. In 1998 when I first began my most extended stint of field research in Aucayacu, several friends, Marusha and Magno among them, told me they had heard Esparza had been promoted to Major after his assignment in Aucayacu, but they were also under the impression that he was embroiled in legal problems. A few suggested he was rotting away in jail: *Pobre Esparza*, they would say, in a way that conveyed their disappointment and compassion for his plight. As if Esparza had somehow been misunderstood, or that he was "too good" for the army high command, politicians, and judges who conspired against him.

For a long time that's where things stood as I continued to the visit the Upper Huallaga. In January 2005, and then again in July of the next year, I

heard Esparza was still on active duty and that by now he had surely been promoted to colonel or even general. Though Mariela recalled someone telling
her he had been held for a time in the Lurigancho Prison of Lima, no one else
mentioned anything about his earlier legal problems or what became of them.
Nor had anyone learned his real name. All they could tell me was there were
"people who knew such things," and I had no doubt there were.

17

As it would happen, two months later in September of 2006, Esparza's legal
identity was finally confirmed. Through the superb investigative work of journalist María Elena Hidalgo, Esparza was tracked down to a military base in
Cusco. *La República* ran the story on its front page two days in a row and then
followed up with additional reporting in the ensuing weeks.[26] The newspaper
not only published his legal name, it included photographs that enabled the
kin of several of Esparza's victims to present eyewitness testimony to a local
prosecutor in Aucayacu, who promptly opened a judicial inquiry.

Altogether it was a remarkable turn of circumstances, even if the revelations did not have their intended effect of bringing Esparza to legal justice.
The army recalled the former captain to Lima, where he disappeared once
again inside the military. Meanwhile, the proceedings against him went nowhere. What did change was that for the first time Esparza's actions, if only
those of his nighttime persona, reached a national audience. The newspaper
exposé detailed atrocities with due emphasis placed on his chainsaw and on
the kin of some of his victims. This left little room for considering the parades
much less the sentiments, now unspoken or simply well guarded, of those
townspeople who still felt affection for Esparza and many more who had been
deeply touched by his affect of command.

6 flag

It was nine A.M. sharp when Caro banged on my door. "Richard! Marusha says there's a red flag in the port. Don't you want to take a photograph? She says you'd better hurry, before the army gets there, before they pull it down." Being Sunday I had hoped to sleep in, but since little in Aucayacu could quite compete with the sudden appearance of a Sendero flag, I jumped out of bed. Pulling on the jeans I had left bunched on the floor, I grabbed my camera from underneath the bedside table, stowed it in my knapsack, and headed downstairs. Somewhere in between laziness and wanting to make haste, I decided to take the motorbike, which I rolled out of the garage and onto the street. It took a few kicks to get the engine going, but soon I was motoring away from the Plaza de Armas along Marusha's street. At the corner where Jirón Tingo María crosses Jirón Huánuco, I hung a left in the direction of the port, still unsure of what I was going to find.

Jirón Huánuco looked as quiet as it did on any Sunday morning. The rolling steel doors of most storefronts were up, signaling that shops were open for business and waiting for customers, yet the only people out and about were young children. A few scattered groups of grade-schoolers—boys and girls neatly dressed in blue/gray-and-white uniforms—walked on sidewalks in twos and threes toward the plaza for the ten A.M. flag-raising ceremony. A block away, two small boys stood in the middle of the street taking turns at kicking a dirt-caked, underinflated rubber ball against the side of a house. They paused as I drove by and then went back to their play. Save for a car that passed me going the opposite way, there was no traffic at all.

Looking at the street on that day, it was hard to believe that Jirón Huánuco only ten years before had been a bustling commercial drag with several three- and four-floor hotels, abundant shops and boutiques, hardware stores, and motorcycle outlets. There had even been a large movie house. Most of those businesses, sprung up with the arrival of cocaine, had long since closed or been scaled back so that the businesses that now took their place operated out of commercial spaces several times larger than their meager sales warranted. The main hotels along Huánuco, like the Tumi or the Monte Carlo, had managed to weather the bust better than most. They did not turn a profit but limped along enough to ward off being shut down or transformed into something else. Not so with the Cine Américas, the movie theater that was once a favorite hangout for the young *traqueteros*. Its front entrance and ticket booth were boarded up. In contrast to the buildings of many defunct businesses that could at the very least serve as makeshift living quarters for the transient, few uses could be found for this windowless two-storey structure with its slanted bottom floor and bolted-down rows of theater seats. Had this been a large provincial town or a commercial strip in a lower-middle class neighborhood of Lima, the Américas would have been converted into a Pentecostal or Evangelical church. But of the dozen and a half such *templos* in and around Aucayacu, none could have filled the movie house even to half capacity. Though eventually that would cease to be the case, for now the *cine* slouched immovable, a depressing vestige of an earlier, more auspicious time.

Jirón Huánuco dead-ended into Malecón Huallaga, a narrow, breezy riverfront road running north-south along the far western edge of town. Starting at its southernmost tip, the Malecón overlooked the Huallaga River from a bluff a hundred feet above the shore. It was one of the few places high enough in Aucayacu to take in the town's surroundings. The view that extended from there across the river and out onto a low range of rolling tropical mountains was exquisite when the sun shined hard and towering white clouds were strewn across the blue sky. Surely it was from there that Sendero flags once could be seen adorning the hilltops as people said they did in the days when the guerrilla presence was still strong. However, as the road meandered northward in its gradual descent toward the port, the river rose up and the separate presence of a distant landscape slowly disappeared. During the rainy season the lowest point on the Malecón road stopped just shy of the water's edge. But in the dry months of May to October the river receded and a long patch of parched earth pushed up to buffer between the end of the Malecón line and the lapping, brown translucent waves of the Huallaga.

I'd been told that the port was the commercial hub of Aucayacu during the cocaine heyday. Situated on a thin elbow of land bordering the point where the shallow Aucayacu River emptied into the larger and more vigorous Huallaga, the port was the entryway for people and goods from the communities on the other side of the river as well as from up- and downstream—for coca farmers and their farmhands who came into town to buy supplies, and for the *traqueteros* who regularly crossed over to buy their kilos at a better price than could be had in town. To capture the wealth of the cocaine trade, stores and bars popped up and clustered around the port, and from there spread up the riverfront along Malecón and in toward town along the several streets that broke off from it, Jirón Huánuco in particular. It could even be said that together the port, the Malecón, and Jirón Huánuco formed the pole around which the town's economic affluence gravitated. From there all eyes turned toward the other side of the river, toward the fields on whose productivity everyone's prosperity ultimately depended.

Yet unlike Jirón Huánuco, the port showed far fewer, if any, recognizable traces of the times of boom. There were no large structures to speak of, no boarded-up businesses. And to see the intermittent and unhurried transit of canoes from one side of the river to the other, ferrying determined but visibly impoverished farmers to the town market with a hen or pig tied and ready for sale or back to the *chacra* with a sack of supplies thrown over one shoulder, it was hard to believe that the port could ever have been so thriving.

In boom as well as in bust, however, the port was something more than the border or entryway between town and country. It marked a decisive political divide. Ever since the early 1980s, to cross over to the *banda* was to cross into Sendero territory. While the Maoist guerrilla had operated and maintained contacts in Aucayacu town itself for nearly twenty years, with varying degrees of secrecy, it was on the other side of the Huallaga River that the Shining Path came to consolidate what might be called its form of rule. In fact, it was in the *banda* that Sendero installed one of its original Huallaga bases. There it had organized villages into "people's committees" and appointed authorities who, as late as the mid-1990s, still regulated land tenure, taxed agricultural production and trade, and even imposed the puritanical mores for which Sendero was so well known.

While army incursions eventually disrupted the Sendero local governing structures, the land across the river remained the unquestioned territorial center of Maoist power. As such, the *banda* exuded fear that from time to time pressed deep into the heart of town. The mere act of looking out at the other bank of the Huallaga—not to mention crossing the river itself—was much more conflicted than it might at first seem. The lingering threat of Sendero, fused as if seamlessly with the *banda* itself, was so strong that it tended to overpower the rural landscape's striking natural beauty when set beside the gritty, run-down face of town.

As I turned right from Jirón Huánuco onto the Malecón I could already see that I was too late. A block down the road a military truck painted in National Police dark green sat parked facing the port, obstructing the way. I slowly coasted toward the truck, which was an open-air troop hauler, until a cop stepped into my path and with a casual upward turn of his left palm signaled me to stop. He was in a uniform of solid dark-green fatigues tucked into military boots, a black T-shirt with the round red-and-white PNP emblem of the National Police over his heart, as well as a visor cap that matched his trousers and the color of the truck behind him. An imposing type, he was too tall and muscular to be from around here, I thought, as I came to a gradual halt.

Por aquí no hay pase (This way is closed), he said, resting his right arm on the barrel of a beat-up assault rifle that hung loosely from his shoulder.

I insisted, claiming that I had to visit a friend in the port.

No . . . hay . . . pase, he said again, separating his words far apart this time as if I hadn't understood him. Then he looked at me somewhat quizzically: "What are you, he asked, a tourist?" reaching for the category for light-skinned foreigner most available to him. "Where are you from? What do are you *doing* here?"

"I live here," I said, brushing off his questions if only to give him some of my own. "What's going on? Why won't you let me through?"

Here he appeared to become apprehensive and looked away without answering, perhaps to motion to one of his buddies to come help him out. Yet upon seeing no one was paying attention, he turned back around and in terse, almost stammering phrases said: "You can't go through . . . it's dangerous . . . there could be a bomb."

I didn't insist further but didn't go away either, deciding to stick around a little while to see what would happen. For his part, he didn't seem to mind as long as I didn't try to press any further ahead.

In this lull I looked beyond him and toward the port. I could see two of his cohorts with their rifles strapped to their backs, nozzles pointed up in the air, heading down toward the boat landing. The port was at a standstill, which was unusual even for a Sunday morning. No dugouts were coming or leaving, and no loading or unloading was being done. Besides the police, the only people I could see were on the right-hand edge of the Malecón, along a row of dwellings that sat opposite the river and at a far remove from the shore. There were six or seven in all, looking on with what seemed a silent indifference at what the police were up to. Women mostly, they were standing in doorways, some with small children in their arms. A young girl, maybe eight or nine years old, busied herself sweeping off the cement stoop of a store, her back to the police. Perched above her inside a large wooden window frame, a lanky teenage boy bit intently on a finger. Every few seconds he would glance toward the river, where I could now see the object of everyone's attention.

It wasn't *in* the port, as Caro had told me, but planted onto a long tract of dry silt and rock: a sandbar island that appeared in the middle of the Huallaga River whenever the water ran low.

For a flag it was hardly glorious, just a thin, rustic fabric, dyed red with a small yellow hammer and sickle bled into its center. Thin as a bedsheet but smaller, it was hung not high on a pole, but tied taut between two large bamboo stakes and strung low to the ground. Swelled by the river breeze, the scarlet cloth shimmered as it bulged out toward the riverbank.

Because of *this*, I thought to myself, the police send out a patrol to cordon off the port? True enough, it was conspicuous. You could not miss a dark-red screen set against the ashen gravel of a river bar. And that there could be a bomb attached to it was not far-fetched at all. Local lore had it that Sendero liked to booby-trap its flags. But even rigged to explode, this small, flimsy-looking thing was surely too far away to pose a danger to anyone standing on the shore.

While I was in the midst of these thoughts, one of the two cops who had been walking toward the dock turned around and rushed over to the people who were standing in front of their houses. "What are you staring at?" he snapped. "Go inside, go inside!" he said, taking his gun and fanning it vigorously before them. He treated them as if they were a crowd that had gathered too close to the scene of a crime. Yet there was something excessively nervous and aggressive in his voice and motions before people who were not interfering but merely looking on from homes and hangouts at a distance from which they couldn't possibly get in the police's, much less harm's, way.

Perhaps the police feared that people's eyes would commingle with the Maoist flag, that something dangerous would happen if they did. Yet, since the police were not about to rush out to the island half-cocked and tear the flag down, on account of the bomb, if there really was a bomb, they denied the spectacle the only other way they knew how: they stopped everyone from looking on.

Sensing the agitation of the police, I knew I wouldn't be getting any closer for a better view. I also knew it wouldn't pay to press the point. Besides, if I had come to take a photograph, the Sendero flag was too far away to get a decent picture, which they wouldn't have allowed anyway.

So I turned the motorcycle around and headed back to Marusha's house.

Along the way I thought about that red flag and wondered about its residual force. The year was 1998, and so this was not the Sendero of old. Not the Sendero that only ten years before had looked poised to win its revolution. Whether it was in fact ever strong enough to topple the Peruvian state militarily was beside the point. More important, the perception that Sendero was rapidly getting to where it *could* was, back then, very much on the minds of many Peruvians. In the late 1980s Sendero as a political-military movement appeared to be on an ascending arc and in a position to make a wager on Peru's future. The Party seemed to have a tight grip on times to come. That is to say, the idea of Sendero ruling the country someday soon was not all that far-fetched, and much of the Party's earlier force was predicated upon that hold on the near future: on the credibility of its claim that victory was imminent.

But ten years hence Sendero's former arc of progress had been decisively truncated—ever since the arrest of its central leadership, ever since the defection of many midlevel militants, ever since the Party's military structures and most of its front organizations had been disrupted or destroyed. In the previous ten years Sendero had been reduced from a national movement to a few fragmented pockets of regional activity, largely unable to communicate with one another and therefore unable to coordinate their actions. Under such limitations, what lingering force could its flag still have?

Was it only in places like the Huallaga—here where the Party still retained an ability to alter the local political climate—that the red flag could be considered dangerous? Was it only here that a red piece of cloth could tense the police? Or was the police's stress, anxiety, and rigidity before this symbol not only out of step with the times but unwittingly imbuing it with more power than it really had?

While Sendero had suffered many defeats in the Huallaga, the war continued, though rarely through any kind of direct confrontation. Instead, the opposing sides had settled willy-nilly into a situation of uneasy avoidance and near misses, where enemies met less face to face than battled over the display of each others' signs. Much of the ongoing war had come to little more than this: to the day-in, day-out control of surfaces that came into public view—a state of affairs in which the Peruvian state now had the upper hand.

As I pulled up in front of Marusha's house and parked the bike on the curb, I could hear the war chants of soldiers as they trotted along Jirón Grau and into the plaza, where they would join up with the National Police and the schools. It must be getting close to ten, I thought, as I went through the garage and up to my room. I tossed my knapsack down on the mattress and pulled out a spiral notebook to make a quick sketch of what I had seen in the port. When I had about finished, the crackling sounds of the Peruvian national anthem, playing over an old loud speaker in the plaza, began to come through my bedroom window. I quickly changed clothes and went downstairs.

In the kitchen I found Shirley tending the stove. "Marusha?" I asked.

"Gone to the plaza. Says the army's called a meeting about the *ronda*, in city hall after the ceremony, that you should go," Shirley said. "But first have some breakfast." So I sat down to the meal she put on the table, of fried fish, white rolls, and instant coffee. She poured herself a cup too, before sitting down across from me and asking what I had seen in the port.

After listening to the gist of what I had to tell, Shirley summed up the situation as a matter of fact: "They want to come in. It's the *ronda*, they're mad about the *ronda*. And right now, they're just on the other side of the river, in the *banda*. At least that's what the people say, that they're waiting for a chance, waiting to see if the soldiers drop their guard." Shirley was usually up on the latest news from the port. She lived a couple of blocks from it and often brought word of what her neighbors, who she always called *la gente* (the people), had to report. The families that had homes near and around the dock, because of their physical proximity to the other side, were generally considered a source of information about Sendero's movements and intentions. For some, however, these residents were also of suspect loyalty. This was especially true among the police and the military and even among those who lived closer to the main plaza, which was after all the symbolic center of town.

Rumors that the army wanted the villages in the *banda* to form civil defense patrols, or *rondas campesinas* (peasant squads) as they were popularly known, had been all over Aucayacu in recent weeks. I had first heard about it from Marusha, who told me that the army was talking about imposing the patrols, regardless of whether the communities wanted them.

For most people the mere notion of a *ronda* was strange and unsettling. Unlike other parts of Peru—the southern and central highlands in particular—where peasant patrols had played an important if not decisive role in precipitating Sendero's defeat during the late 1980s, *rondas* in the Huallaga had enjoyed neither widespread distribution nor popular support.[1] Only near Tingo María and outside the town of Uchiza had there been at most a handful of them, and then only under the active direction and control of the army. Whereas the armed forces had elsewhere played a support role for civil patrols, at times more extensively than at others, in the Huallaga the *rondas* were entities wholly generated by the army and subject to its directives. But neither their mere novelty nor the army's heavy hand in their operation were what made bringing *rondas* to Aucayacu so strange, even at such a late date: 1998. It was, rather, that the countryside of Aucayacu had and continued to be a major Sendero bastion ever since the early 1980s—a bastion so deep and enduring that the very idea of a *ronda* taking root there was close to imponderable.

Marusha for her part was outraged at the army. Compelling the communities to create *rondas* was tantamount to forcing them into direct confrontation with Sendero. She said she was going to send a report about the matter to her human rights contacts in Lima to see if they could apply pressure from there. However, now that village leaders had been invited to what the army had billed as a "coordinating meeting" to address "the convenience" of forming the patrols, what had until then been only rumors had taken on the solidity of fact.

The only other thing Shirley had to say about the *ronda* was that this morning's meeting was sure to be contentious. "They're not going to take it sitting down," she said of the villagers, shaking her head. And with that I got up to go, but not before promising to fill her in later on the details of what I had seen.

the decision

Taking leave of Shirley I went outside and walked to the main square. The flag ceremony in front of city hall had disbanded, and vehicles were beginning to circulate again along the adjoining streets. As I moved through the plaza toward the far southern side where three flagpoles faced the municipal building,

I could feel the intense heat of the morning sun bearing down from overhead. Unlike the port, the air around the square was still, and the flags, recently hoisted high, hung down loosely upon their poles: the red and white colors of Peru; the white flag of Aucayacu with its green, red, and yellow coat of arms; and the also-white *bandera de la paz* (peace flag) with a lone gray dove.

Crossing the street toward city hall I could see that most people had gone home. The National Police had returned to their barracks and the soldiers too—except for six or seven who remained posted at the principal entrances to the plaza. That these had not withdrawn was a sure sign that the captain, who was otherwise nowhere to be seen, had not gone with the bulk of his troops back to the base. Whoever else lingered on at the plaza had found shade and something to drink at one of two kiosks that stood in front of the large barren lot next to city hall and which doubled as a fairgrounds whenever a circus came to town.

As I approached city hall a familiar voice called me over. There was Lucio Cano, sharing a table and a large bottle of beer with two municipal police officers at one of the kiosks. In contrast to his companions, who sat sprawled there in their short-sleeve, light-blue uniform shirts unbuttoned halfway to the waist, black nightsticks dangling from their hips, and faces still dripping in sweat, Lucio was enjoying a day off. His faded T-shirt, bathing trunks, and plastic flip-flops suggested he hadn't attended the ceremony but had come over immediately afterwards to have a drink with his buddies as they cooled off from their weekly duty as Sunday flag bearers.

Lucio lived around the corner at a narrow two-storey brick house where he operated one of the only two or three video rental places in town. His main employ, however, was with the *Municipio* (city hall), where he had worked for years as the town tax collector. Lucio invited me to join them at the table, but I begged off, saying I was looking for the *rondas* meeting. "You're ten minutes late," he said, and with a quick tilt of his head motioned over toward the tall opaque metal gate of the municipal garage. "Not sure they're letting anyone in," he said, and pulled out a chair for me to sit down. But I said I was inclined to try my luck all the same and, backing away, promised to drop by his house later.

Walking over to the gate I found it locked. When I rapped on the metal with the back of my hand, a small shoulder-high window slid back to reveal the face of a teenage soldier. "Yeah?" he asked with evident impatience. I mentioned the meeting, that I wanted in. He tried to send me away with an almost-mechanical "Once the gate is closed, no one comes in"—as if passing on to me the order, word for word, as he himself had received it. When I tried to argue the point, he held me off with a firm "Wait," then pulled the little window shut and went off to consult a superior. As the minutes passed a small group of people started to gather behind me. Five or six farmers, men and women, plus a cameraman from one of the local television stations. All wanted in.

When the soldier didn't reappear, I knocked on the metal again. This time the little window didn't open to report the outcome of deliberations, but to my surprise the latch on the other side creaked back and the gate opened to a crack. This tepid go-ahead was as good as any, and we all slipped in.

Inside there were forty to fifty people standing to the far left along a row of empty parking spaces, the only area sheltered by tin roofing of an otherwise open-air garage. The captain, flanked by one of his officers and a young recruit, was speaking to the people who had bunched into a compact arc in front of him. The audience was made up of rural villagers in the main and a couple of local radio journalists, but I could also see Marusha leaning on her aluminum crutches close to the front row of people. She was the only municipal official in attendance and like everyone else stood there in silence, listening to the captain. Several more soldiers, apparently unconcerned with what was going on, hung back along the perimeter of the garage.

It struck me as strange that the meeting had been convened in the garage and not on the second floor of the municipal building where community gatherings were normally held, where there were chairs and tables and even a blackboard to facilitate discussion. This choice of locale, together with the fact that the meeting had been called with little advance notice, contributed to the makeshift, impromptu feel of a proceeding already infused with unease about what the army had in store.

For rural villagers, much more so than for townspeople, encounters with the military fueled feelings of deep ambivalence. Recent for them were recollections of a war waged around, over, and through them. Experience taught that the army's entreaties for collaboration were above all a referendum on one's allegiances, and no matter how inoffensively phrased, such requests always enfolded some kind of implicit threat that made it hard to refuse them outright. Then again, obliging the villagers to organize civil defense patrols in what was one of the few remaining areas of Sendero power was a provocation threatening to disturb a tenuous peace that in the previous couple of years had allowed them to go about their lives.

Not wanting to draw attention to myself, I found a place to stand close to the back of the crowd. The captain, midway through his opening words, halted every few seconds to glance at a lone sheet of white typing paper that bore long creases from having been stored in his pocket, but which now he held out in his left hand. From the loud and belligerent tone of his voice it was apparent that the meeting was going badly. He spoke of the recent upswing in what he called terrorist activity and how this had made it "necessary" for the communities to shoulder the responsibility of organizing patrols. He talked as though the decision had already been made, that this gathering, here and now, was convened only to inform the farmers of what they would do. He talked as though everything were an indivisible stream of cause and effect down to the most basic relationship of all, that it was he who imparted the orders and everyone else who obeyed.

I had never met the captain before and until now had only seen him at a distance. He was new to town, having been rotated in only a few weeks before. Marusha, along with the rest of the town council, had already had some initial contact with him. She had since advised me that it was best to stay as far away from him as possible. "Uncouth," "unreasonable," and "unpredictable" were the words she chose to describe him, adding that it had been a long time since the army had sent anyone so inept to take charge of the base. While she was not an admirer of the military and its authoritarian ways, when it came to the individual commanders who came through Aucayacu, she was never predisposed against them. If they acted correctly, Marusha had no problem in saying so. There was a certain rigor to her fairness that seemed almost generous and that was, in retrospect, quite remarkable considering all she knew about what the army was capable of. I took her appraisals of character to be sound, guiding myself by them many times.

While army officers in the emergency zones regularly concealed their real names, this particular captain was so new that his nom de guerre had yet to get around. In appearance he was heavyset with a large paunch that protruded over the top of his belt. There was something else too: a tight and sunken, almost wooden quality about his face. The gaze of his eyes did not come out to meet you but lay in wait instead, impassive, a predatory fish camouflaged among the rocks, motionless. Yet whatever mystery was contained by the deep void of his expression, partially hidden by the visor of an olive-green uniform-issue cap, was cancelled out by the aggressive tone of his words, which together with a complete absence of social tact betrayed his inability to see those gathered before him as anything other than a troop at his command.

The harshness of his initial remarks and their absence of all nuance drew stares and more silence. And so he raised his voice a notch, almost to the point of yelling, "If you want peace you must help finish the work of pacification. Or else . . ." And here he seemed to lose his train of thought for a split second as a bright, small light on top of a video camera went on—it was the cameraman who had come in when I did. "Or else . . ." he said again, now visibly uncomfortable and fumbling his words, "things will go back to the way . . . the way they were before! . . . And you don't want that! . . . Or do you?!"

As he paused for a second, an older, gray-haired woman in the front row took a step forward and began to speak. "*Estimado* Señor Capitán," she said in slow, gingerly polite words. "Why create problems? As things are, at least we're getting by. If we agree to form *la ronda* as you say, then the violence really will come back." A low murmur spread through the crowd, and a middle-aged man in the back, young for his years, followed her lead. "Señor Capitán!" he said in what was a boyish, almost smart-aleck tone. "We are farmers. We work the land. We should fight the terrorists you say. But what do we know about fighting? We are not soldiers. If terrorism is coming back, as you say, then why doesn't the army, which has the weapons, which has the soldiers, want to do its job?"

This drew scattered laughter to which the Captain seemed oblivious. Dialogue, at least as he practiced it, was getting him nowhere, even against such simple arguments, and so he cut to the chase and called on volunteers to come forward and sign up.

Seeing where the meeting was headed, the army coercing people into enrolling even over their objections, now Marusha herself spoke up, turning to address not the Captain but the villagers. Hers were words of counsel: she said they should keep in mind the implications of what the army was asking them to do. That according to the law, which regulated the formation of civil defense patrols, the communities themselves had to come to their own decision. The army, she said, was not permitted to force the patrols on anyone. "Today the army has suggested that the villages in the *banda* create civil defense patrols. This is a suggestion. Now it's up to you, the communities, to think it over and figure out if that is something you want."

No sooner had she finished, hands started going up en masse as more people sought a chance to speak out. One after another gave reasons why they were against the patrols. No one spoke in their favor and, like Marusha, they addressed their opinions to the group as a whole and no longer to the captain, who seemed increasingly pushed to the side and ignored. What was supposed to be a meeting to coordinate a timeline for establishing the patrols suddenly had become a community speak-out on the folly of their formation, with the lone dissenting voice looking on, powerless to shape the direction of the meeting he had called.

Seven or eight farmers in all aired their thoughts before the crowd began to break up and shuffle toward the gate. Some stopped to speak with Marusha on their way out. The journalists also lined up to get a word from her on tape, before heading over to the captain, who was still trying to get the attention of those who had turned their backs on him. He called out to them to come back in three weeks to finalize plans for starting the patrols, but no one paid him any mind.

With Marusha momentarily detained, I decided not to wait around but instead went outside to find Lucio. By now he had finished with his beer and returned home. Downstairs his store was open, and as I walked in a young woman tending shop arose from the table where she was seated over a textbook. Careening her neck upwards into the stairwell, she shouted *¡Don Lucio! ¡Te llaman!* While I waited, I glanced over the rows of dusty video covers displayed on the walls: a familiar stock of gringo martial arts, horror, and combat films. I scanned them for a new arrival or for anything that might have escaped notice on a previous visit. Lucio had a friend who from time to time would send him a box of whatever titles were selling well at Polvos Azules, Lima's well-known flea market. They were pirated Hollywood hits in the main, but there was always an outside chance that something novel would wend its way into Lucio's display. After discovering nothing new, I leaned up against a doorway and waited. The girl had returned to her book opened to a page of equations, which she copied down into a tablet of lined newsprint. As I silently took notice of her impeccable handwriting, she looked up and said, "He'll be right with you."

A few minutes later, Lucio came down the stairs, the rubber soles of his flip-flops smacking the concrete steps as he entered the room. Seeing me, he smiled and jumped into his usual insistence that I take a seat, as he opened the top of the large white storage freezer and grabbed two translucent cups of ruby red gelatin. He handed one over to me before pulling up a stool.

lucio

Lucio was from the industrial fishing town of Chimbote, where as a young boy he had hung around the docks back in the days when Banchero Rosi commanded the local fleet of trawlers. Lucio never said much about those early years. The life he liked to recount began later, when he left home for good, the day he and a friend from his barrio, just out of high school and anxious for adventure, caught a ride aboard a cargo truck headed to the *selva*. They paid their passage working as the driver's helpers, loading and unloading or whatever else they were asked to do. But it wasn't long before Lucio realized they were carrying some unusual freight: several hundred liters of sulfuric acid hidden in a tank at the bottom of the truck. "What need could there be for cleaning sewage pipes or plumbing in the jungle?" Lucio would say, reliving the play of his own thoughts during that trip and underscoring his boyhood naiveté and ignorance of what other ends such a strange cargo might be good for. "And why the need for secrecy?" he'd ask rhetorically. "First we had to cover up the tank with a shipment of sugar and on top of that another of produce." But the whys of hauling acid to the jungle were as much a mystery to him as where they were actually headed. For Lucio, from the coastal lowlands, the *selva* meant Chanchamayo in the lush high forests of central Peru, if not the tropical flatlands around Pucallpa in the relatively distant east. He had never heard of a place called Aucayacu, much less knew that there and in the other towns immediately north of Tingo María raw cocaine had recently become the mainstay of life.

"No, we all arrived innocent of such things . . . back then," he told me. Innocent, and amazed too, to encounter a town so crowded with people from all parts of the country, to discover "so many beautiful women" and to see, circulating freely on the street, those small dingy white balls that came to be known as *la bruta*. The year was 1978.

In Aucayacu it wasn't difficult for Lucio to feel at home because, and this was yet another surprise, he found himself surrounded by so many *norteños*—fellow northerners from Trujillo, Chiclayo, Cajamarca, and Piura; there were chimbotanos from his hometown, too, even from his own barrio of Miraflores Alto. And it was thanks to this *norteño* connection that Lucio quickly made a place for himself. His gig at the *Municipio* came only a few days after he arrived in Aucayacu, on account of the chiclayanos who controlled the roster of administrative positions. Despite his young age, a simple conversation with the head accountant was all Lucio needed to come away as the town tax collector. And soon thereafter, when he became enamored of the daughter of a local carpenter, Lucio had plenty of reason not to think about ever going back to Chimbote.

While his first try at marriage quickly soured—Lucio said his low civil servant wage couldn't keep pace with his wife's boom-era tastes—being the tax collector suited him from the get-go. He wasn't stuck at a desk all day but could go pay visits on the local merchants or whoever else owned property at a time when no one seemed to mind giving up a little of their earnings to local government.

Lucio was in his element out on the streets, greeting people right and left, and through the *Municipio* he came to know just about everyone in town. He learned to discern and appreciate who was important, who was not, those who had money and those who were keen to land their first fortune or recoup a fortune or two already lost. Once he confided to me that the good relations and contacts accrued over the years had positioned him well to broker his share of lucrative business deals, bringing together people desperate to sell to other people—Lucio just happened to know—who had a little extra cash on hand. And though he had a keen eye for the at-times subtle markers of social fortune, Lucio was careful not to show it. He prided himself on his seamless congeniality and the respect with which he treated all others, regardless of condition or station. This was something he would bring to my attention more than once, citing it as a reason why people about town held him in such high esteem. To enjoy general favor was no small claim in a town where, by the time I came to know it, there was no shortage of bad blood to go around. But that the assertion was made by the man responsible for collecting debts for the Municipio, no less at a moment when everyone was scraping to just get by, tempered somewhat its weight.

On the day of the *ronda* meeting I had known Lucio only for a few months, ever since the night of the teachers college *cachimbo* or freshman ball that was held at a local dance hall back in early May. On that night, a man walked up, set down four large bottles of Cerveza Pilsen on the floor in front of me and greeted me as the old friend I was not. At least not yet. The man's face was only vaguely familiar to me at the time, and if we had previously met, it had been only in passing. He would later tell me that it was Marusha who had first introduced us, though I never placed the moment of our original acquaintance. What I do remember well is how that night I found myself unable to recall Lucio's name, all the while nagged by the thought that maybe I should know it and yet feeling too chagrined to come out and say so. Instead I chose a more tentative or timid path of waiting to see if by chance his name would come up on its own, or that he might even help me out with a "remember me? I'm Lucio." But no, as far as Lucio was concerned, we had known each other for years. This was all the more evident when his wife Berta with a couple of her sisters and their husbands crowded around soon after the beers got slapped down on the floor, and Lucio, all excited, started introducing me to them as his good friend. At that point I just played along.

Berta, Lucio's second wife, was a *cachimba* herself, having started classes at the teachers college that same year, which explained why Lucio was there that night. As for me, a visiting instructor at the institute, I had been encouraged to attend the so-called *fiesta de gala* by the assistant director and to help out with the predance ceremony. I had looked forward to going to the party, thinking it might a good chance to hang out with my new students as well as to catch up with several of the teachers I had already met.

The *cachimbo* ball was the highlight of the freshman week activities, which among other events included a "grand haircut" auction, a chicken cookout, and a beauty pageant. There was a long wait that night before the party got under way. First the "*cachimbo* couples" had to be presented, a promenade of sorts by the freshmen students with their dates, and then the new *Miss* Cachimbo had to be announced. My contribution to this, which I was informed about halfway into what became an hour-and-a-half ceremonial, was to pin a sparkly white leaf in the chiffon hairdos of the two señoritas who came in first and second runner-ups, right before the assistant director crowned the winner.

No sooner had the lucky woman received her rhinestone tiara that evening, Lucio appeared out of nowhere to boldly plop down the bottles of Pilsen. I say boldly because the noblesse of Lucio's gesture pretty much ensured that I could not stay with him for ten or fifteen minutes and then politely excuse myself to slip off to where my students and the other teachers were standing. No. First those four beers had to be finished, and then I had to correspond in kind with another four, after which he or one of his in-laws would put down two more bottles, if not three, and so on and so on. Lucio's move essentially stranded me there for a good part of the evening, and drinking far more than I would have wanted. Because in Aucayacu, as in other small Peruvian towns where everyone knew everyone else, the rule at festive events, like large wedding receptions or *quinceañeras*[a] was that as soon as the formalities were out of the way and the band started to play, you formed your own group or joined one in the making. There you stayed put: true to it for the rest of the night,

---

[a] traditional fifteenth-birthday celebrations for girls in Latin America

true to it and to the pool of beer that you—if you were one of the men—
helped replenish.

Parties, dances, celebrations of any kind in Aucayacu as elsewhere in the
Huallaga were an implicit referendum on the measly state of things; that is,
they underscored their own poverty in relation to times past. During the
boom festivities were held at any and all times. Drug traders, eager to display
their largesse, would fly in topline musical acts and entertainers from all over
the country to play at private parties or local area celebrations. When the coca
wealth dried up, the big acts stopped coming and local bands were the only
ones people could afford. But besides the origin and occasionally poor quality
of the performers, little reflected the diminished stature of post-boom celebrations as much as beer and beer-drinking habits.

Drinking in the mestizo areas of the *selva* followed the standard ritual seen
throughout Peru. That ritual was not strictly male as much as male dominated, and the same patterns obtained whether between two drinking buddies
or among groups of much larger size. At dances and parties the beer would
usually be set right on the floor, and the group would hover near, often in a
semicircle, as a large bottle went around followed by a short glass tumbler.
Whoever initiated the cycle would fill the glass, pass the bottle on to the next
person, address him or sometimes her with a *¡salud!* and then down the contents. Whatever excess amount remained in the glass would be emptied onto
the ground with a quick flick of the wrist. The glass would then be passed on
to the person holding the bottle. This basic routine would repeat itself again
and again until beer, money, or the will to drink ran out.

The cocaine boom brought its own variant of this ritual that was predict-
ably more lavish and spectacular. The bottles set on the floor to initiate the
round became a crate, and the groups that came to form around each one
would establish rivalries with those close by over who would outdo whom.
One crate would become two, three, and more as a column would rise up at
the center of each group. Beer would soon begin to spill over the floor, because
in those years consumption was less about actually drinking as showing who
could spend and waste the most. Pilsen and Cristal from Lima were then as
now the favorite brands. Sometimes a crate of San Juan, a cheaper beer from
Pucallpa, would be brought in, too. This the drug traders used less for drinking than for washing out the glass. In those games whoever managed to raise
the highest stack of empty bottles was *el Más Más*, which was a way of saying
he was, well, something else.

After that night at the Institute's fiesta de gala, my students criticized me for having "preferred," as they put it, to spend most of the dance "over there with Cano." It was a reproach I was hard pressed to defend myself against, even if they knew well that four beers was no small gesture. Not in these times of scarcity, when people not only counted but deeply felt each coin they dished out. Lucio had spent at least twenty sols on those bottles of beer, more than a local day's wage. But what struck me most was how the lavishness of his "move" contained, if not a touch of aggression, then at least a not so gentle forcing. One bottle was sufficient to engage me. Two was generous. Four seemed almost calculated to draw me into an extended obligation, one I could not pull out of without sending him a strong rebuff. Did he know this? I somehow think he did. The question was what did Lucio want?

Because ever since that night at the dance when he pushed his way in to the then very small world of my early fieldwork—which had so far revolved solely around my teaching and the networks of friends and acquaintances that formed separate if overlapping constellations around Marusha and Mariela— Lucio always wanted to know when I was going to drop in on him. Whenever we ran into each other on the street—and it was Lucio's way to drive up as if out of nowhere on his baby-blue scooter—he'd insist on treating me to a coke or a juice or something to eat, and then, if there were time, we'd start talking. He'd begin to tell me stories, sometimes about himself, sometimes about others, and soon he was promising to take me around, introduce me to someone I just had to meet. "Come by later. Come by my house later," he'd insist, as he got back on his scooter and rushed off to deliver a bill.

I didn't seek out Lucio out as a friend. Nor did anyone intercede to bring us together with the kind of recommendation that a stranger to Aucayacu usually needed to break the hard edges of suspicion. No. He picked me: with a determination that caught me off guard and with an insistence that our acquaintance would be more than fleeting. Those first four beers and so many smaller overtures after that seemed, in retrospect, to be Lucio's way of saying as directly as he could: "Listen, you *need* to know me."

For a month, maybe two, I didn't follow up on his offers, but after hearing them enough times I began to go see him. At first I'd go in the evening after a long day of work under no other pretense than to rent a video. But eventually his store would become, if not a haunt, then one of the places I'd drop in on any time I was over on his side of the plaza. Whenever he could, Lucio would engage me in long conversation, and he appeared to take sincere interest in my fascination with local history. Or perhaps it was only that my fascinations were also his: the drug trade, Sendero, the first *colonos* (settlers), and those who had helped build the Marginal. No matter the topic, even and especially those that most people tended to shy away from, Lucio could tell me something or take me to someone who did. Much of what I came to know about that other, earlier Aucayacu—the one of the boom years—I learned thanks to Lucio. Sometimes these were factual details: the name and location of the brothel where Sendero used to assemble the town's wealthy merchants and make a pitch for contributions, or the secluded points outside town where the Peruvian Investigations Police (Policía de Investigaciones del Perú, or PIP), in the days before Sendero arrived, would negotiate the release of those they arrested for drug running. He even once shared his own character analysis of the feared Capitán Esparza, whom he'd had the "benefit" of knowing. Over time Lucio would become one of my more dependable friends and one of those special people without whose generosity, patience, and careful insight my fieldwork would have been all but impossible.

The morning of the *ronda* meeting our relationship was only then beginning to become close, and we had yet to pay a visit on any of the people Lucio had promised to take me to see. I remember how we sat that day, in card-table chairs a bit removed from the entrance of his store and talking just above a whisper, since it never hurt to be extra careful. I gave him the general outline of what I'd seen in the meeting, of the captain's hostile attitude and of how little it had served him. Lucio listened on with a steady nod, before echoing the exact sentiments of those I'd heard expressed by the farmers that morning. He said the farm people, after having served Sendero at incredible cost to themselves, were now living a period of relative peace. To actively do the bidding of the army now, he explained—and what better way than to form a *ronda*—would only place themselves at odds with the Party. The last thing they wanted was to upset the balance.

"Sure, Sendero's not what it used to be," Lucio said, "but the army spends nights safe behind the walls of the base out there by the Grifo Santa Catalina. Meanwhile, these folks, they've gotta go back over there," he gestured with a flick of his left wrist in the direction of the Huallaga River, "to the other side to sleep. When they need help, the army is going to be too far away," he said shaking his head before declaring finally: *eso de la ronda es bien bravo* (the *ronda* is bad news). What Lucio did not mention, but we both understood, was that up to that point the inroads the army had made into the countryside had been limited to recruiting individual informers and forcing group participation of villagers in public displays of allegiance, the likes of flag raisings and parades on major civic holidays. Forming a *ronda* required much greater commitment and risk on the part of villagers.

Somewhere in the midst of our conversation, four high school guys walked into the store. They were a "set" in their untucked floral polyester short-sleeve shirts and bunched-up trousers worn over beat-up tennies, all with dark baseball caps pulled down close to their eyes. They hovered over the video selection for a few minutes before whistling over to Lucio. "I'll be right back," he said to me. Whereupon he got up and escorted them to one of the viewing rooms in back before coming out front again and pushing a recent Van Damme cassette into a tape deck.

When Lucio sat back down, the conversation shifted. He wanted to know why Marusha wasn't planning to run for office again, and that got us onto the topic of the upcoming mayoral elections and how the two "opposition" council members had gotten their campaigns off to an early and powerful start, trailing the candidacy of one Dr. Aimar Villanova. Although the municipal elections were less than six weeks away, the Villanova group had made a big jump on the other candidates. The rest of the field was only then beginning to open headquarters and put up advertising around town. But there were few surfaces left that were not already covered with the Villanova party name and party colors, which had been posted since early July. They could even be seen plastered outside town along the Marginal as far north as Madre Mía and all the way to Tulumayo in the south. The crowning touch of the Villanova publicity blitz was a big portrait of the candidate himself, painted above the entrance to his campaign office, which was just a stone's throw from Marusha's house. It greeted all traffic passing through the Plaza de Armas en route to the Mercado Central.

While well known to most townspeople, the name Aimar Villanova was new to me. He had not lived in Aucayacu for several years, though I soon learned he had grown up there. I also learned that in the early 1990s he had been *gobernador*, or the local representative of the Ministry of the Interior. After his stint as governor, Villanova left Aucayacu for reasons, to me at least, unexplained. While away he had studied for and earned a law degree, which was how he came by his professional title of "Doctor." Now he was back in town amid talk that important construction industry interests in Pucallpa were bankrolling his run to take city hall. True or not, most everyone realized that in "Dr. Villanova" they had a major player, buoyed perhaps by outside money, who was already beginning to make a big splash. All that I knew for sure was that since his reappearance, Aucayacu was no longer a one-lawyer town.

As for the group Marusha had run with to get elected to city hall, this time around most of them had gone separate ways. The current mayor was running for reelection as the candidate of Vamos Vecino, the latest "independent" party founded by President Fujimori and funded with monies from the state coffers in Lima. Abel Fonseca, the lieutenant mayor and son of a first-generation settler-become–wealthy rancher, had decided to make his own solo run for the top office, recruiting Marusha's brother Nico to be his campaign manager. Marusha, meanwhile, after having decided early on to bow out, limited her involvement to being a quiet consultant to Abel.

In all there were six parties vying for election, though the three running under the colors of national organizations—APRA,[a] Acción Popular, and Vamos Vecino[b]—were not thought to have much of a chance. Through the month of August many people I spoke with told me that the contest would soon settle into a two-man race pitting Fonseca against Villanova, with Fonseca perhaps gaining the upper hand down the stretch. That was the reigning consensus until a group of Evangelicals threw a strong slate of candidates together just before the filing deadline. Fonseca's people, fearing that the Evangelical ticket would splinter their own base of support and tip the balance in Villanova's favor, cried foul, but to little avail.

Such was the state of things going into September of 1998.

dates and forecasts

As we talked municipal politics, Lucio weighed in with the view that all bets had shifted to Villanova, saying, in between plastic spoonfuls of jello, something that I'd heard a few times already: Abel was a nice guy but didn't want the prize as bad as Aimar. Beyond this Lucio didn't express a preference. In his twenty years in the employ of the Municipio he had seen many come and go, and it didn't behoove him to openly take sides. He was going to have to live with whoever won, regardless.

---

[a] Alianza Popular Revolucionaria Americana, or Partido Aprista
[b] literally, "Let's Go Neighbor"

Then I brought up Sendero and the red flag that I'd seen that morning as a way of asking him what he thought their intentions were vis-à-vis the elections. For a second Lucio was silent. He stroked his chin a few times with his left thumb as if mulling over a reply, before saying simply: "That's something we'd all like to know."

Even if Lucio didn't hazard an answer, the question was very much in the air. Sendero had been all but absent since the last week of July, when a small group of armed guerrillas briefly seized the hamlet of Angashyacu, ten minutes south of town, and blew up three nearby high-tension electrical pylons. The attacks occurred at the beginning of Fiestas Patrias (national independence celebrations) and as such were not unexpected. During the week of celebrations, locals said *los tucos* could be relied on to "make an appearance," lest everyone forget that they were around and "still capable of mischief." The raid on Angashyacu was, however, the first time Sendero had made its opposition to the upcoming October 11 elections public knowledge: both in a meeting with villagers and through slogans painted outside of an elementary school clearly visible from the highway. In the days immediately following the incident, electricity was rationed in town, and the army dispatched soldiers to comb the countryside. Little more was heard from Sendero.

Save for a few rumors that the guerrilla was gathering at various points outside town, the only other hints of its presence came on July 28, Independence Day itself. First a red flag was said to have been found at daybreak, tied to the suspension bridge over the Aucayacu River (no one I talked to had actually seen it). Later, scattered gunshots were heard in the hills outside town. After that everything quieted down.

In early May, shortly after I arrived to teach at the Institute and to begin my long-term fieldwork, I had been told that during the previous year Sendero had staged a resurgence. I was to be extra careful about traveling outside town, especially as any of the more notorious dates drew near. It was a warning I had grown used to hearing and was already a little tired of heeding. For as much as I wanted to take in something of the countryside and actually see so many places I knew of in name only, there never seemed to be a good time. The political situation in those first few months was always said to be too delicate, too unstable. The uncertainty, townspeople said, had to do with a cluster of potentially dangerous days. These days belonged to two separate but competing political calendars.

I had arrived on the heels of May Day, an important leftist holiday. Two weeks later was the anniversary of the start of Sendero's armed struggle (May 17), which in the Huallaga was often believed to be Abimael Guzman's birthday. Then came Peruvian Flag Day (June 7), and soon after Sendero's "Heroism Day" (June 19), commemorating the 1986 prison uprising and massacre. Those anniversaries were followed by the regional San Juan celebrations (June 24) and finally by national independence week, or Fiestas Patrias, which closed out the month of July. On or around any one of these key dates, guerrilla actions became more likely, and in anticipation, the army and police would mobilize by setting up temporary checkpoints at any of the various points of entry into town and by sending out extra patrols. The atmosphere around town would grow edgy as people advised sticking close to home.

About the heightened tension friends would say, "It's the time of the year," and in a way they were right. So many dangerous dates, and in such rapid succession, tended to blur with one another until becoming a continuous three-month block. A season in itself. People took such moments in stride; they had been there so many times before. The whispers of red flag sightings, the strange faces seen loitering about town, the word-of-mouth reports of unusual "movements" in the countryside. Sheer repetition gave those months of heightened alert a certain routinelike character. People paid extra attention, but they knew how not to overreact and went about with what they had to do, because in those days, which is to say the late 1990s, most of the incidents of political violence happened well away from town.

By early August, with the main civic holidays over, conditions usually calmed down somewhat, or so I'd been advised. The passing of the period of inclement political weather just so happened to coincide with the start of the school intersession vacation. This was a time when Aucayacu would empty out. Some parents took their children on trips to visit relatives in other parts of the country. Many families that had land nearby and no money to travel on withdrew to farms for the duration of the break. For two to three weeks the town came to a virtual standstill.

I took advantage of the August lull to go to Lima, where I needed to push along the ongoing paperwork for my visa at Migraciones (Immigration). I left Aucayacu looking forward to returning in September, with the relaxing of political tensions it promised and a chance to see something of the Huallaga beyond the immediate confines of the larger towns and the Marginal Highway itself.

When I returned during the last week of August and found the electoral campaign in full swing, I heard much speculation about how serious Sendero was going to be about its boycott. Now with the appearance of the red flag in the port that morning and the turmoil stirred by the army's calls for a *ronda*, I wondered if my friends' urgings for "prudence"—which they were quick to impress upon me—would start up again, or worse, that they might succeed in convincing me to put off indefinitely any plans for getting to know the rural communities that surrounded the town.

To my relief Lucio didn't share such dire forecasts and said he'd be more than willing to accompany me. I just had to tell him where I wanted to go. His eagerness was encouraging but at the same time it caught me a little off guard. I didn't know whether he was putting on a brave front or being foolish, or if he just had a much better sense of what was going on. Lucio, it seemed, did not ascribe to the same rule of thumb that I had acquired from others about where one could safely go, just as he did not appear to recognize the same political topography, the different shades and grades of danger, that I believed I had already gotten a handle on.

The common sense I had assimilated suggested that it was one thing to visit the visibly populated larger villages that sat directly on the Marginal, such as Anda, Pueblo Nuevo, Pucayacu, or Madre Mía, which were accustomed to regular communication with the other towns of the Huallaga and not far from one of many army posts spread out on the valley's main road. Most of these I had visited at one time or another. However, it was another thing altogether to enter the dozens of communities and hamlets that sat at a remove from the more public space of the highway, along small trails that snaked up into the hills or even more so on the other side of the Huallaga River. Going to any of these required special arrangements.

While it was generally considered safe to travel on the Marginal Highway during daylight hours, certain places alongside the road itself repelled closer inspection. These were tiny, desolate communities located far from army checkpoints. They often had no more than a few houses, a bodega or maybe two, sometimes a schoolhouse. From the road they might appear unpopulated and yet around them could gather a prohibitive atmosphere that made them large and imposing.

For Lucio, however, no place seemed to be absolutely off limits. I didn't know if it was mere bluster, but he led me to understand that his extensive connections opened many doors. He indicated that he'd ask around just to make sure Sendero wasn't planning anything, but that as long as there was someone he knew in the place I wanted to go, there wouldn't be a problem. The only mitigating consideration was his work schedule. Any time he had available, he'd be more than happy to be my guide.

As I pressed toward hashing out an arrangement, Lucio resisted my attempts to set up anything firm, preferring to leave it an open invitation. "Here it does no good to make plans," he said. "Look me up on the day you want to do it." I told him to expect me in a couple of days, after I'd finished my teaching for the week. With that, Berta called for him to come up for lunch, and I headed back home.

social meteorology

It was Wednesday afternoon before I was able to meet up with Lucio again. In between I had tried to do my own checking around about "the situation" outside town, as I was not completely convinced by his optimistic assessments. The night before I'd had dinner at Pablo's house, a friend who lived in the Project. Pablo was a middle-aged, straight-talking agronomist who kept close tabs on the movements of Sendero through the farmers he worked with. Conditions in the countryside were hardly static and could change every few weeks or even days, depending on the intermittent push and pull of the army and the guerrilla. But that night Pablo was quite explicit about where it was unsafe to go, and, in a tone that grew suddenly solemn as if to draw attention to the wisdom he was about to impart, he said: "Right now there are four places *just best avoided.*" These places, he said, were Primavera and Bambú in the *banda,* and Alto Pacae and Pampa Hermosa on the road to Tingo María. "Best avoided," he repeated for emphasis, as in you might *just best leave alone* a poisonous snake or a hornets' nest.

I knew from previous conversations that when Pablo singled out any such "no-go" spots it meant that the guerrilla or *fuerza local* was currently hiding out in those places. The local militias of Sendero rarely stayed in one place but roamed about in small groups, moving from one outlying village to the next. There was a handful of communities, however, that the guerrilla tended to favor over others, a fact that had earned them renown for being Sendero havens. They were places where no matter how often the army went in to flush them out, Sendero invariably returned. Primavera, Bambú, Alto Pacae, and Pampa Hermosa were said to be such places. Names I had heard mentioned again and again and in ways that suggested, if only obliquely, a sinister remoteness. Their distance was appreciable in political more than geographical terms. It was said that no stranger could go there without being approached by someone who would demand in menacing tones to know, not merely the purpose of the visit, but the name of the person who could substantiate what the visitor had to say. Such on-the-spot interrogations were considered a tell-tale sign of Sendero's presence and could only be the portent of more unpleasant things to come. That was not to imply that such places could never be visited. It just had to be the right moment, under the right circumstances, and above all in the right company. Otherwise, these villages remained impossibly far away.

Pablo had more than once told me that the fear about running into the Sendero militia was that they were so unpredictable. If you happened upon a group commanded by someone with *formación política* (political instruction) or as he put it, "a leader you could talk with," you were lucky. I had often heard it said that a Sendero leader willing to engage in dialogue was one capable of listening to reason. But as Pablo was quick to have me know—echoing what Mariela had told me many times—you could never be sure about who you would encounter. These days, he said, Sendero was made up of so many teenagers with little if any political training. They could kill you before thinking about checking first with someone higher up. "And with someone like that, there is no talking at all."

After dinner at Pablo's I went home to find Marusha sitting at the typewriter in her office. As late evenings were one of few times she was alone and had a moment free, I pulled up a chair and queried her about any problems outside of town she might have gotten wind of. Marusha hadn't heard of any specific incidents but said she could tell me that in the *banda,* at least, the vibe was tense and it was definitely not a good time for unannounced visits. To my surprise this news had come to her not by word of mouth, as it normally did, but firsthand. Early that morning she and Lieutenant Mayor Abel Fonseca, accompanied only by a couple of journalists, had quietly gone over to the other side of the river to meet with villagers in the hamlet of San José de Pucate. It was an unusual trip, certainly off the track of Marusha's routine movements, which rarely veered far from town or the Marginal Highway en route to Tingo María, Huánuco, or Lima. It was also unusual for being the first trip Marusha or Abel had made to the *banda* as municipal officials.

For reasons of security more than etiquette, consultations between village representatives and municipal officials—both of whom had cause to fear

Sendero's persecution—regularly took place in Aucayacu town, almost never in the countryside. But in this case village leaders told Marusha they wanted their communities to have a chance to express their views about the civil patrols in a forum unencumbered by the presence of soldiers. She and Abel agreed to go only after having received assurances that the Sendero militias were not close by.

"It all happened so fast," she said, as if feeling a need to explain to me why she hadn't extended an invitation. "We didn't tell anyone so that the army wouldn't find out and either try to stop us or, worse, insist on tagging along."

Marusha had already typed a couple of pages into an official report about the army's intentions to impose a *ronda*. At first light, she said, she would depart for Lima where she planned to deliver her report personally to the human rights organizations. I didn't press her for more details. She already looked tired and was in for a long night.

cotomonillo

I spent most of the early part of Wednesday writing upstairs in my room with the radio on in the background. Marusha had left town at dawn, and when I went downstairs, I found Caro in front of the stove preparing lunch. Abuela was sitting at the table before a pile of green peas she methodically separated from their pods before dropping them into a metal bowl. Caro explained that Shirley hadn't come to work that morning; she'd gone to Huánuco to visit Ronal in prison.

I went back upstairs a few minutes later and was surprised to hear Marusha's voice on the radio. It was a short interview recorded the day before, following her trip to the *banda*. In between the reporter's questions Marusha said she had gone with the lieutenant mayor to learn what the communities thought about the proposal to form *rondas,* and now that they had heard their opinions, she would leave for Lima, where she intended to inform the Peruvian legislature that *la gente* were unanimous in their rejection of the patrols. Abel Fonseca, who so far had had nothing to say about the *rondas* one way or another, was also interviewed and gave tepid support to Marusha, saying he didn't think it was right to force the communities against their will, though he didn't go as far as offering to do anything about it. I imagined he was leery of confronting the army, with the election still up for grabs. He knew that the military was not used to being challenged by the municipality with which, under the terms of the state of emergency still in force, it shared power only

ostensibly. There were few if any precedents of the town council directly de-
fying the army's wishes, and Marusha's strong words sounded to me then as
if she were already anticipating the end of her council days, when she could
concentrate on being a human rights advocate.

By early afternoon I was ready to look up Lucio, though it took me a couple of
tries to track down him down. A young woman sitting in a wire rocker out in
front of his house, a different woman from Sunday, told me that he had not yet
gotten off from work but that they expected him any time. I returned half an
hour later, but she simply shook her head.

Another thirty minutes went by and another shake of the head; it would
soon be too late to do anything that day. So I decided to look for Lucio around
the corner at his work.

Entering from the plaza into the large white cement building of the Municipio, a clerical worker pointed me a few doors down the main hall to where
a small metal sign, that traced out the word "RENTAS" (revenues) was raised
just above eye level. Inside the office I could see Lucio sitting at a gray metal
desk, which except for a single black binder he leisurely perused, was otherwise bare. There was no furniture to speak of, besides the desk—cleared of
all mementos or family photographs—and four narrow shelves on the wall,
occupied by a handful of document boxes with much room to spare. No rug
softened the floor, nor was there anything on the walls; not a calendar or a
poster, just a cement void that dragged in every noise from the street through
a small, barred window perched high behind Lucio's desk. Instead of the lived-
in air of an ever-accumulating clutter, there was only a hollowness suggesting
how little time Lucio actually spent there.

I rapped lightly on the door frame. Lucio looked up, smiled, and quickly
urged me to take a seat. "Something to drink?" he said, not waiting for a reply.
He went over to the back window and called out: "Pssst! Estrellita! Bring over
two cokes . . . and don't forget the straws!" Only then did I realize that the
window opened right onto his house and video store. This was a convenient
setup. Lucio could keep an eye on his store even while at the office. Yet it was
a strangely one-way flow, where he had the woman in the wire rocker on call
while at the office, yet she couldn't or didn't care to let him know when someone came looking for him at the store.

"Where should we go?" Lucio asked handing me over a soda before sitting
back down at his desk. "Wherever you've heard it's alright to go," I said. After

thinking on it for a second, Lucio suggested we go to the *banda*. I was a little surprised by this and shared Marusha's words of caution against going there. Lucio mulled this over for a second without looking all that convinced. "Even Primavera?" he asked. "Why don't we go there?" Remembering Pablo's warning, I countered that Primavera was supposed to be one of the worst places of all. Besides, I told him, it was already getting late, and once we crossed the river, we'd have to worry about getting stuck on the other side if we ran into some kind of delay.

This second line of argument seemed to hold more weight for Lucio, though he conceded that he hadn't really checked on the situation across the river: "Okay, so we'll leave the *banda* for another day. Today let's go to Cotomonillo."

"Just as long as you know people there," I said.

Lucio grinned and said, "of course," and then assured me an old friend of his lived there. He'd been meaning to pay him a visit for sometime.

We agreed to meet at his house in ten minutes. Fifteen minutes after that we were crossing the suspension bridge over the Aucayacu River at the northern edge of town and heading on my motorbike down an unpaved track locally known as the road to Cotomonillo. The road was in surprisingly good condition, as if it had been recently opened or repaired, and as we traveled along its winding and at times rolling path, patches of farmland separated by barbed-wire fencing pressed in on us from both sides. The village of Cotomonillo lay to the right of the Huallaga River, a good half hour north of town and at the other end of an extended flood plain of high grasses and scattered trees that ran up to the base of a series of low hills. Though nightfall was still a good three hours off, dusk would soon begin to intrude on what was a hazy and partially overcast afternoon.

For the first kilometer or two there were many people on the road: familiar faces returning to Aucayacu after spending a day in nearby fields. Some walked or rode bicycles. Others sped past us in three-wheeled *motocarros*. Many waved to Lucio, a few to me. We ran into a mutual friend, a student at the teachers college, bicycling along with one hand on the steering wheel while holding on with the other to a bulky plastic burlap sack that he had slung over his left shoulder. Smiling profusely, he motioned for us to stop so he could shake our hands, only to apologize that he was late for class before pedaling away.

As we pushed on beyond the outskirts of town, these welcoming encounters became less frequent, and the faces we came upon quickly lost all air of familiarity. For a stretch we saw no one at all, only scattered dwellings: an occasional thatched-roof hut on stilts, of the kind rarely seen in the towns or on the main highway, interspersed with the far more common wood-plank houses and sheds.

Several kilometers down the way, we came up upon a truck parked in the middle of the road. Here four teenage boys loaded wooden crates of papayas in the back, as a fifth, perched atop one of the walls of the truck's wood-slat container, watched them work. Directly behind, a red *motocarro* loaded with passengers and large green bunches of plantains, waited for them to finish so it could get by. On the left side of the road three small children looked over this scene but then turned to stare at us as we pulled up and passed on the right, leaving truck, *motocarro*, and children far behind. Ahead there were more homesteads and more crates of papayas, stacked neatly into columns on the right of the road, awaiting their chance to be picked up.

All of this gave Lucio motive to start telling me how people from the *chacra*, whom he also called campesinos, had returned to legal agriculture: yuca and citrus fruits for family consumption or sale to the local market of Aucayacu. Plantains, bananas, papaya (year round) and rice (after the rainy season) for shipment to Lima. The big problem with legal cash crops, Lucio explained, was that the Huallaga had to vie with other regions of the Peruvian *selva* for the same urban costal markets, where fierce competition between producers tended to force prices down. Even with the continual problem of price instability, the important thing, Lucio stressed, was that the farm people were making their transition away from coca. He said this with a tinge of pride in his voice, as if he shared in their changed ways or if their actions somehow reflected on him and on his town. I didn't know whether this was a heartfelt reaction, though Lucio was clearly tapping into the emotive register of what was a widely circulated narrative. The economic state of affairs was looking up from just a couple of years ago when the cocaine boom came all unglued—that much Lucio had me know.

As we continued northward, the winding waters of the Huallaga became visible from time to time, and Lucio pointed out the scrubby hilltops that loomed beyond the opposite bank of the river. The terrain that sloped down from the crest of these hills was severely eroded, and he described them as *pelados*, as a kind of "stripped" earth. "Those used to be coca farms. Pure coca as far as you could see. Now there is nothing." The peasants bore the brunt of the bust, he went on, telling me stories I had heard so many times. How in 1994 the arroba of coca leaf soared to an incredible one hundred twenty-five dollars. The boom had returned to levels only occasionally reached in the 1980s. No one was complaining, but then everything came apart. The price fell and fell and just kept falling. A year later an arroba went for less than five dollars. Even if the peasants had wanted to sell at that price, Lucio says, there was no one around to sell to. The market had disappeared, and so the farm people became despondent. They were out of money, and since they hadn't planted anything else that year, they had nothing to eat. "Nineteen ninety-five," Lucio said, "that was the year people in the countryside went hungry." Making matters worse, it was all but impossible to get officials in Lima to see that there was even a problem. Government bureaucrats refused to believe that there could be poverty in the Huallaga Valley. "For them, we were still swimming in *narco* dollars."

Here Lucio signaled me to slow down and to hang a left on a small trail that led into a large papaya grove jutting up to the river. I headed toward a small wooden shed, cut the engine, and rolled to a stop. Lucio explained that this land belonged to the friend he had mentioned, and he called out his name. When no one appeared, Lucio suggested we get off the bike and take a look around, that perhaps we'd find him working in the grove. Except for a small clearing around the wood hut, which was surrounded by a scattering of banana tree shoots, the land was covered with papaya trees planted in even rows. Papayas had recently been harvested, and the fruit still on the trees was small and green. Here and there large papayas lay on the ground. Lucio reached down, grabbed a couple, and then tossed them back down before he found one he liked the looks of and tore it open. As we walked in the direction of the river, Lucio called out his friend's name a couple more times but then gave up. After handing me a large juicy red-orange chunk of fruit, he picked up where he had left off.

One of the peculiar influences of the boom, he said, was that the peasants stopped growing their own food. They made so much off coca it was just easier and perhaps more prestigious to go into town, eat restaurant food, and then buy whatever they needed to take back to the fields. Though the Huallaga Valley had some of the most fertile agricultural land in the country, during the boom produce that had been grown well for years in the valley was imported in from other areas of the country with a similar climate: from the high jungle of Junín or from the tropical lowlands of Pucallpa. In the Huallaga few farmers grew anything but coca. It simply was not worth their time or effort.

But when cocaine went bust, Lucio explained, intoning a well-worn refrain, people learned that there was no more future in coca. They went through a rough patch of a couple of years, he added, but now they have started to harvest again.

By now we had come to the end of the field and stood on an outcropping of earth that looked out upon the Huallaga. Here we turned to head back, and when we got on the motorcycle, Lucio said his friend might have gone into Cotomonillo. The village was another fifteen minutes up the road, and Lucio thought we should look for him there.

At a bend in the road not far from the farm, we drove by a cluster of four, maybe five dwellings. They looked completely abandoned. The windows were boarded and doors closed. Lucio let me know that we were going through Las Mercedes, which I knew to be a village outside Aucayacu, but I never had imagined it to have such an underwhelming appearance. Soon after, we reached our destination. Not much larger than Las Mercedes, Cotomonillo had a handful of wood-slat houses and a couple of roadside kiosks. Cotomonillo was also situated at a bend in the road, but unlike Las Mercedes, the places were not boarded up and people were out and about.

Lucio asked me to stop and then told me to wait as he got off the bike. In front of one of the houses, a young guy was squatting down next to a *motocarro*, tinkering with the engine. Lucio walked over and asked him something. But the man shook his head, and Lucio returned and remounted the motorcycle. "He's not here, we'll check again on the way back, but let's keep going."

About a half kilometer further the road curved toward the river before coming to an end upon a wide stony shore. A hundred meters ahead there was a large cargo truck parked at the water's edge, and we headed toward it. As I maneuvered us slowly over the rocks so as not to take a spill, we could see several men moving large planks of wood from the water to the rear of the truck.

I drove past the truck and parked us near the water's edge at a respectful distance of some fifteen or twenty feet from the men. We stood there for a minute or two looking at the other side of the river, glancing only occasionally over to the loggers. The beach lay in front of an imposing hill at a point where the river narrowed to barely a hundred feet and made a sharp turn to the left. The loggers, taking advantage of this slender pass, were using a long dugout to drag bundles of lumber across the water.

Lucio picked up some rocks and tossed several down before coming up with a small one that he sent skipping three times on the river surface. And as I looked for a stone of my own, Lucio started to fill me in about the loggers. "It's the only thing coming from the other side right now. Brazilian pine mostly, some mahogany. Notice how it looks smooth and even?" We were still a bit far away, but I could make out six men in all fishing the lumber out of the water, standing in a line along which they passed the planks of wood. As we grabbed more stones to skip, Lucio kept explaining. "They have a special instrument that they attach to their chainsaws. It makes the lumber look like it was cut in a sawmill. Before they started doing that, La Forestal (Forestry Police) confiscated their freight all the time, but this way they avoid problems."

Lucio spoke of what was at best unauthorized logging with complete naturalness and without the least charge of things illicit. In a commonsensical tone of "this is how it's done" he told me how matters were for people trying to make a living and doing whatever they had to do to get by. The question of actual legality did not seem to be an issue. What Lucio called "avoiding problems" was a question of preserving a semblance of legality, as if mastering appearances was all that was required to meet one's legal obligations. I wondered what that special instrument looked like, that according to Lucio the loggers used for preparing timber for market. I also wondered if it really existed or if Lucio was simply embellishing his facts.

If the loggers were doing anything illicit, they did not seem particularly concerned about who we were or that we had shown up all of a sudden and out of nowhere just as they were loading their goods in the truck. What was the precise degree of legality or illegality involved here? Was this wholesale contraband or merely unregulated extraction? And was there really a ruse involved in order to get the lumber past Forestry Police checkpoints?

If there was a ruse, this cosmetic change would likely be insufficient in itself to get by the police. Money must also be changing hands at every legal choke-hold point along the trade route. Because how could the Forestal not know or not be in on it? Was not the "milled-look" rather an obligatory preparation, less a means to fool La Forestal than a routine imposed by it as part of the cost of doing business, which along with monetary payments, enabled lumber to proceed to market? If this were a tacit agreement, an agreed-upon sleight of hand, it could simply be the way all wood became "legal" on its way to its buyers. At any rate, this was a preparation taken for dealing with state agents outside the Huallaga. La Forestal had not maintained any effective presence north of Tingo María since the early 1980s when it abandoned two checkpoints along the Marginal Highway because of their vulnerability to Sendero attack.

What Lucio didn't say, but I had gathered already, was that the run on the *banda*'s virgin timberlands had been partially filling the vacuum created by the collapse of the cocaine boom. Logging had emerged as the first cash commodity to replace coca—though with the substantial difference that it did not engage the adult population as a whole, only young male frontiersmen types. Unlike coca, logging was not a renewable resource in the short term, as there was no economic incentive for replanting in regions far from settlements. Clear-cutting was a one-shot deal. It came as such a flash that people in the nearest populated areas would not even know it was happening. It just was. People didn't talk about it the way they did about local agriculture, which involved so much more of the population.

From the vantage of Aucayacu town, the logging that went on in the *banda* was a quiet and mobile business. Loggers came through, took the lumber, and moved on. For a long time it was common to see trucks loaded with timber heading down the Marginal Highway toward Tingo María, but in town, with the exception of three or four carpentry shops that opened to turn the temporary abundance of timber into cheap furniture, the impact of the trade was barely visible at all.

Aucayacu merchants, however, would be sad to see the loggers—and the money they spent in stores, bars, restaurants, and hotels—go away. Rumors were already beginning to spread that the majority of the hardwoods in the *banda* within a day's walk of the Huallaga River had been cut down. The anxiety this generated, as far as I could perceive, was more about the loggers' eventual departure than out of any concern for the environmental effects of destroying the forest. As one of the few activities that was then providing employment, even if for only a few, and injecting some cash into the local economy, people lamented the physical loss of virgin woodlands about as much as they complained about the ecological cost of the cocaine boom, which was almost never. The only time concerns about the environment came up was in connection to the damage done by the aerial fumigation of coca fields and the subsequent spread of agricultural plagues. In the case of logging, the exploited land was not only distant from the cares of the town, it hovered in another political threshold altogether.

It was strange to me that despite the unease Aucayacu townspeople expressed about the *banda,* the loggers seemed to have no problems coming and going across what was a tense political border. This apparent freedom of transit had earned them a reputation for being "in tight" with Sendero. Townspeople believed there was no other explanation. Without good relations with the Party, they would not be able to go back and forth. However, being "in tight"—people well knew—was not easy, even if it was one of the inevitable costs of doing business. There were rules to be followed, and worse, there were requirements.

Regularly crossing the political threshold of the Huallaga River and in and out of Sendero areas brought demands and conditions. Sendero was in severe need of supplies of all kinds, and so their demands could be exacting. More than just the tribute they charged on payloads of timber were the requests for food, gasoline, boots, backpacks, or flashlights—a whole network of logistical support that Sendero tried to rope loggers into as the cost of being able to take away the trees. But these were also the very things the police and army would be on the lookout for, and before long anyone who went to the *banda* and back on any kind of regular basis had to find ways to deal with each group that operated there. They all wanted to know what was happening on the other bank of the river, and any perceived lack of cooperation was read as hostility or—what was worse—as evidence of being an agent for the enemy. Anyone who by trade had to traverse enemy lines got pressured on all sides. Over time that pressure would take a toll. At least logging—unlike coca—was a short-term activity. Growing coca required holding on to the land, whereas loggers went in and got out as quickly as they could. When political demands become too much they could always take their operations somewhere else. Within the narrow horizons of the lumber trade there was always more forest to fell.

Lucio and I didn't talk about any of that as we stood there on the rocky shore. After having established our presence with a few minutes of pebble skipping, Lucio strolled over to the truck and made conversation with a man who was sitting on top of a large unmilled log. A few minutes later I went over too. As I walked up, Lucio told me that this man was the owner of the truck. The other men were in his employ.

"How goes the work?" I asked him.

"Steady, steady . . . ," he replied, and then added, "This is hard wood." He thumped his fist down on the trunk for emphasis. "So hard you can't even hammer a nail into it." I nodded, feigning surprise, and he seemed pleased to have impressed me so easily.

Then Lucio asked, "How goes the situation on the other side? In Aucayacu people are saying things are kind of tense."

The truck owner answered:

Tense? No. Right now everything is pretty calm, though that would change if the army got its way and organized *la ronda*. What bad news that would be, because with the *ronda* things would be back to being like they were before. I wouldn't be able to enter the *banda*, because if I did, it would be "Come over here!" and bullet to the head. That's how it used to be. Now things are fine, I go to the other side, work all day, and no one says anything to me at all. The *ronda* would be bad news. Good thing people are saying it's not going to happen.

I was just about to ask him how anyone could be sure the army would give up on its *ronda* initiative without more of a fuss, and how he had come to such knowledge, when he abruptly got up. He then went over to join his workers— though not without first sending a quick nod in our direction as if to mark the end of our conversation.

Lucio and I stood around for a few more minutes and watched them load wood. Soon that got old and we returned to the bike, leaving them to their work.

Back in Cotomonillo Lucio looked around a second time for his friend and seemed a bit miffed that he couldn't find him or anyone else he knew. Instead we ended up taking a seat at one of the village kiosks. A woman sat behind the counter partially obscured by large clear plastic bags of brown and yellow sweet breads hanging in the front and by rows of candy and unmarked sodas displayed in a small transparent plastic case. We pulled up seats and Lucio called over to the woman: "Doña . . . two soft drinks!"

"What color?" she asked.

"Bring me a red and a black."

Taking a peek in the ice box, she said, "There's only orange."

"Okay orange, bring us two," Lucio said, "and a couple packs of crackers too."

Lucio began telling me a story about a time, many years before, when he was in Cotomonillo and had to rescue a close friend. A Sendero militia had taken the friend prisoner and was escorting him across to the *banda* to "resolve his problems," that is, almost surely to his death. But Lucio dropped the story when the woman brought over the drinks and some saltine crackers and tried to engage her in conversation instead.

"Slow sales, no Señora?"

"Too slow," she said with a sigh. "You can't make good money around here any more. Everyone's leaving."

"Yeah," Lucio responded, "but at least it's looking up from before, don't you think?" She took this as her cue to reply at length:

> Well, last year the excitement was papaya. Everyone harvested it and after a couple of decent months, the price started to fall. Now they're selling for fifty *céntimos* per crate [roughly fifteen cents for twenty kilos]. They say prices are down because it's winter in Lima, but my sister who lives there says that the papaya she buys in the market has remained steady at 1.5 *soles* a kilo [fifty cents]. With papaya the middlemen grab all the profits. They're the only ones who never lose!

Lucio then ran a few names by her but she didn't know any of them. She explained:

> We're new here ourselves. We moved here because we heard things were getting a lot better. But our oldest daughter got fed up with how slow things were going, with so few possibilities for work or for getting ahead. A couple of weeks ago she left for Lima, but when she got off the bus she was already overcome. They took her to the hospital, but by the time she got there it was too late. She was dead. Doctors said pneumonia, but I don't know. All I know is that she was fine when she left.

"Did you go to the funeral, señora?" Lucio asked.

"No, we had no money. My sister paid for the burial. I don't know when we'll have enough to go visit the grave."

A moment of uncomfortable silence followed, and when Lucio didn't say anything more, she went back to behind the counter.

Once she was out of earshot Lucio lamented our own, comparatively minor, bad luck. We didn't find his friend. Most of the people we'd run into seemed to be recent arrivals, or at least Lucio had never seen them before. And if you didn't know anyone there was nothing to do, except hang around and look suspicious.

A few minutes later we paid the woman and began the trip back to town. It was already getting dark, and so to save time we found a side road that let us cut up to the Marginal Highway. About fifteen minutes later we rode into Aucayacu, and when we reached Lucio's house, he invited me up.

Upstairs Berta was making dinner, and they both insisted I stay to eat. Knowing that I was expected for the evening meal at Marusha's house, I settled for a coffee and stayed just long enough for Lucio to tell me about the time that a red flag had appeared at daybreak in the *banda*, right across from the port, and about what happened when Captain Esparza took his soldiers over there to pull it down.

Afterword

Lucio never tired of recounting Esparza's feats, and he was not alone. Within the diminished, watchful, and expectant times of post-boom, many people expressed an unsettling fascination with the image of prowess and uncompromising rectitude that the army captain embodied in their stories. He who would come to put things right and in their rightful place. He who was *justiciero*—a man of justice—though people used the term more in the sense of a *punisher*: one who relied upon lethal force to settle a score. Sendero from its beginnings had sought to project a similarly drastic message, though along a wholly different political trajectory. With Esparza, however, the image of *justiciero* condensed into the figure of a single man, whereas with Sendero it dispersed through the shadowy, ramifying presence of the Party: always branching out and alert; a thousand eyes, a thousand ears.

Stories of radical rectitude sometimes filled the time in quiet moments set at a distance from things past and waiting for new events to gather. When those stories turned toward Esparza's exploits, they also told of those who got away. They were the handful who, through a stroke of luck, either were set free or knew how to turn the negligence of a guarding soldier into a go-for-broke dash up and over the Project's cinderblock walls into the cover of night.

Sendero had steadfast characters of its own: the dedicated revolutionaries, the true Communists, women and men who confronted the enemy without remorse or fear and even defied certain death. One woman warrior was pushed from an army helicopter flying hundreds of feet above the jungle thicket. She survived to continue the fight, or so I heard. Accounts of Sendero virtue and resilience rarely circulated in Huallaga towns, however, and if they did, then only at its margins and among the most secretive and select of company. This was because the towns were in the army's sphere, as were the villages where the military maintained active bases. In those places Sendero was out of its realm and had a far less intimate face.

The righteous confidence of *justiciero* figures seemed to be what impelled them into life-and-death situations, where they resolutely took their chances and often discovered fortune to be on their side. The hardy, relentless temperament they expressed echoed a much broader desire for justice, imagined as hard, straight lines. Such lines were often laid down with acts that claimed lives and that continued to linger through the ambience of their threat. Many people desired those lines, though not the violence that made them possible. Yet the very tension between longing and visceral misgivings that the *justiciero* produced in others might well account for its disquieting charm.

Some would insist, moreover, that the threat of that violence was required if people were to come together and work as one. A schoolteacher from a farming community on the road to Tingo María underscored that point for me once when she euphemistically remarked that "a bit of pressure" was needed for the people to come together. She explained that it used to be that villagers would not show up for community meetings unless there were some threat of consequences or reprisals. This was borne out during what she called the "era of Sendero." Villagers never failed to attend the meetings the Party called, even those held in the wee hours of the night, for fear they would be killed if they did not show. From that she deduced: "The people like to be ruled with a firm hand."[a] And I deduced, from what she went on to tell me, that she appreciated the message of rigor and rectitude, perhaps in spite of who might impose it.

Following the "bombardment years"[b] when the army was defeating Sendero forces right and left, the schoolteacher said villagers decided they must select new leaders. This had not been done in over a decade, not since Sendero had deposed the local authorities and installed Party delegates in their place. The catalyst for having elections, however, was primarily to ward off what villagers perceived to be an imminent intervention by the army. "Upon hearing the rumors that Captain Esparza was like this and like that, the people started to become more patriotic. Hearing that the army was arriving in a bad mood,[c] the

---

[a] *A la gente le gusta que le mande a rigor.*
[b] *los años del bombardeo:* between 1992 and 1994, when the armed forces conducted major operations against Sendero in the *banda.*
[c] *que el ejército va a venir a malas*

community began to organize, as a preventive measure." Along with choosing new leaders, the village organized weekly Peruvian flag-hoisting ceremonies. It also prepared its children to compete in the goose-stepping parade contests, which would soon become the focal point of area interschool rivalries.

The schoolteacher not only associated the name Esparza with a broad call to become more "civic"; revealingly, she also located that "call" at a moment in time, between late 1994 and 1995, when Esparza was no longer stationed in the Huallaga. Thus, even in the absence of the man, the name Esparza still denoted the moment of reckoning with the army and the command to return to the national fold.

One central attribute of *justiciero* figures was their ability to transform those around them. This was what I earlier described as Esparza's unforgettable "affect of command." Many were moved by him or rather by his idea, and the enduring circulation of stories about him suggested at least that much. But affect of command also referred to how Esparza as an ideal event "activated" popular imagination and sentiments for the state. Esparza—again not the man but the event that acquired ever greater life through what was said about it—converted the army's institutional will into a well-grounded common sense. Heeding and thus following the army's call would become the natural thing to do. Or as in the schoolteacher's version, villagers had the foresight to form a council and begin adhering to state rituals. They did so because it was now only reasonable to think that the army would be merciless in acting upon its threats.

Such threats animated stories. They imbued place names, significant dates, as well as material things—flags, cardboard placards, black nylon sacks, and so on—with competing perspectives. Those perspectives refracted the plural sense, which was produced by violent events and was historical in that it indexed a correlation of forces unique to the times. Forces appropriated and saturated places, words, and things by imposing interpretations upon them. That's what made the treatment of language significant. Threats required a medium of circulation so that the violent acts from which they emanated could live on. It was also through that medium that the conflict over what happened would be fought.

Deleuze wrote: "The event subsists in language, but it happens to things."[1]

Esparza *happened* to both town and country, but his incorporeal effects precipitated inconsistently and manifested different perspectives across the valley's already uneven topography. The violence that bore his name, and that of others before him, had cut hard folds, not only in time but in space—a deep territorial fissure. In the late 1990s and the years that followed, that fissure would creep ever deeper into the countryside. One sure way of tracing its extension was to follow the topographical footprint of the army's network of bases, which looked out upon lands the state claimed but did not always control.

A red flag appearing between Aucayacu town and the *banda* in August of 1998 had a palpable intensity. You could *sense* its animation—it was there— otherwise, the police would not have become so agitated. The problem was ascertaining with precision how much: how much vitality did a rustic red piece of cloth hold?

In the post-boom Huallaga, to ask what animated a Maoist flag meant to inquire into the correlation of forces that fought to impress their own per- spectives upon that flag. It was also to ask when and where. The year 1998 was a different political time for Aucayacu, Tocache, or Uchiza than it was for Huánuco City, Pucallpa, Lima, and most other places outside the valley. A perplexing uncertainty distinguished the political moment north of Tingo María, because there were no clear answers to two fundamental questions: How strong is a tattered Sendero? How willing is a resurgent Peruvian state to make its rule the only law of the land? These questions resonated again and again in concrete situations where they acquired more specific forms: Why won't a town prosecutor assert the full prerogative of Peruvian law? Why can't the army enforce the creation of a *ronda*? If we grow coca *again*, what then?

In the mid- to late 1990s the present political situation may have been in doubt but not its ultimate horizons or the overall direction of the times. There was no returning to the reckless opulence of the boom, just as Sendero had no chance of reviving its claim on power any time soon. The Huallaga's future pointed unambiguously to the increasing consolidation of state sovereignty. What was unsure was how quickly that would proceed and what would hap- pen along the way. The post-boom was thus a time of waiting.

What made the year 1998 particularly significant was that it nestled be- tween the fall of the cocaine economy and the first inklings of coca's return. For coca *would* return: not as it had been before but as a gradual collective rec- ognition that it was by no means gone. For better or worse, coca would remain a permanent feature of the Huallaga social landscape. Townspeople resisted that idea as it conflicted with their hopes for a future free from the risks of illegality. Many of them came to accept it once the rural-based *cocaleros* showed they would not give up without a fight.

Much has happened in the Upper Huallaga since I concluded the field research upon which this book is based. Nine years have gone by, and the most significant political change has been the sudden and sustained rise of *cocalero* organizations in vocal opposition to the eradication policies of the Peruvian state and their chief backer, the U.S. government.

In late 2000 Huallaga *cocaleros* initiated the first of what would become a series of mass demonstrations. The mobilizations had greatest impact through strikes and road blockades that isolated the valley from the rest of the country for days and weeks at a time. During those demonstrations, hundreds and sometimes thousands of coca farmers would congregate in towns and at vital points along the Marginal and Central Highways. Commercial establishments and open-air markets would close shop in solidarity or out of fear of retaliation. Fierce clashes often ensued with the police, leaving wounded on both sides.

Huallaga *cocaleros* quickly sought ties with coca-growers from other areas of the country with whom they shared demands that state officials halt the destruction of their crops and cease treating them as a criminal class ultimately responsible for the illicit cocaine trade. They also maintained that viable legal alternatives for coca existed in addition to the local and national markets for traditional leaf consumption. Such alternatives could be used, they affirmed, to steer their harvests away from cocaine production—if only the government would lend its support.

Nationally the *cocaleros'* protests succeeded in making their cause well known and in forcing the government into talks, though few concessions were forthcoming. State officials consistently refused to negotiate anything other than the terms under which the farmers would give up coca altogether—denying them any chance of entering into a legal market *as* "*cocaleros.*" This happened in part because the *cocalero* organizations often worked at cross-purposes and struggled to present a unified front. Differences in rhetoric, strategy, and goals cost them crucial leverage with the government.

In the coca-growing regions of the *selva alta*, sympathy and support for the farmers have been mixed yet solid enough for *cocalero* leaders and politicians sensitive to their concerns to make strong showings in area elections. Mayoralties have been won, with the most notable successes coming in 2006 when two Huallaga leaders, both of them women, were voted into higher office: one to a seat in the national legislature, the other to the Andean Parliament.

So far, electoral politics have done little to reverse the destruction of coca farms, even as presidential administrations have come and gone. The regime of Alberto Fujimori fell in November of 2000. A transitional government followed, preparing the way for a special election won by Alejandro Toledo, who took office in July of 2001. Five years later Toledo handed power over to Alan García, a former head of state who returned to the presidency for the second time in twenty years. A major aspect of state policy that remained constant during this period was the Peruvian government's unwavering support for agreements with the United States, which required the complete elimination of coca from regions where harvests went directly to the production of cocaine. Those regions comprised a majority of the zones represented by *cocalero* organizations.

Coca in the Huallaga, meanwhile, has had its ups and downs. Cultivation has sharply expanded, but government eradication teams are rarely far behind. Agricultural plagues have also taken a severe toll on the productivity of the soil. Coca plants do not flourish as they once did, and even tropical crops such as banana, papaya, and pineapple have been affected. The causes are in dispute, but many coca farmers believe that secret aerial fumigations and the deliberate dissemination of biological agents are to blame.

As armed conflict has become rarer in the Huallaga, important efforts have been made toward researching and addressing the legacies of the boom-time violence. The first and perhaps most significant step was taken when the Truth and Reconciliation Commission was established in 2001. During the next two years the Commission collected thousands of personal testimonies and conducted on-site investigations of human rights abuses in the areas of Peru most affected by the internal war. Although the Commission's focus was on the country as a whole, its televised hearings and published final report brought national and international attention to the Huallaga's largely unexamined history of political violence.

Regionally, the Truth Commission energized an incipient human rights movement. It provided training for a new generation of local advocates, many of whom served with the Commission either as volunteers or as paid staff. Since then, many have continued to promote a greater understanding and a defense of human rights principles in the Huallaga Valley, including journalists, schoolteachers, university students, health professionals, and lawyers. They have assisted regional and national human rights organizations as well as the governmental human rights ombudsman's office (Defensoría del Pueblo) in the investigation and prosecution of cases researched by the Truth Commission. The most publicized of those efforts has been a series of mass grave exhumations at the sites of army massacres as part of the inquiry phase of legal actions brought before the courts. The civilian national government, however, has been unwilling to confront the Peruvian military, and so to date no one from the army's officer ranks has been convicted for human rights offenses in the Huallaga.

Despite this impasse, the hard work of human rights advocates has received favorable press coverage as national media attention on the Huallaga has increased. Journalists who live in the valley have also benefited from improved political conditions, allowing them to work far more freely and to maintain active ties with print and broadcast media in Lima. As a consequence, the information reported on the valley is now more frequent, more precise, and more contextualized than ever before.

Since mid-2000 I have returned to the Huallaga Valley four times for stays ranging from a few days to three months. The most extensive of those periods came in 2002, when I did a small research project for the Truth and Reconciliation Commission. During that trip I traveled to the principal towns of the valley (with the sole exception of Uchiza) and to many villages in the countryside. Two years had passed since I had last been there, and the differences I noticed were palpable. The political situation, though sometimes tense on account of the continual mobilization of *cocaleros*, was surprisingly free from the threat of violence. On the highway there were far fewer checkpoints manned by the army. The countryside seemed less forbidding than in the late 1990s. I went basically wherever I wanted to go that year, and that felt strange. People expressed less reticence to talk about the war and the period of the boom, though as before they would only do so in places sheltered from the eyes and ears of others.

While in Aucayacu I worked in the locale of a new human rights office. The Upper Huallaga Human Rights Committee (Comité de Derechos Humanos del Alto Huallaga, or CODHAH) had opened its doors in late 2000, thanks in large part to Marusha's inspiration and efforts. When she later decided to leave Aucayacu, the office continued in her absence under the direction of a dedicated local journalist and a vibrant, young lawyer from the city of Huánuco. When I was in town between June and August of 2002, the human rights office had temporary closed, because its staff had been hired by the Truth Commission's regional offices in Tingo María and Huánuco. I was given the keys, and there behind closed doors I conducted many of the interviews that would form part of what I presented to the Commission.

During those three months Sendero circulated flyers that condemned the Truth Commission and predicted that its conclusions about the Party's role in the war would be biased. There were, however, no major armed incidents while I was there, but most with whom I spoke (both in the towns and in the countryside) said that while insurgents were nowhere to be seen, the Party was "around." Some insisted the insurgents had receded deep into the *banda* where they were regrouping as they bided their time.

This surprised me, since I had heard that in the last two years the Huallaga wing of the Shining Path had been staging a modest revival, taking steps to soften its rhetoric and to clarify the situations in which it would resort to lethal force. Insurgents who had come into contact with Aucayacu-area farmers explained that the Party admitted that "mistakes" had been made in the past but intended from that point on to be far more circumspect with its use of violence. Their fight was not with the farmers, but with the state, whose policies and functionaries, they claimed, were the true enemy of the people.

At that time Sendero was not militarily active in the valley. That would change in 2004, when midway through the tenure of President Toledo the leader of the Huallaga Sendero faction, Comrade Artemio, presented a challenge to the government: enter into negotiations leading to an end of the conflict or face a violent escalation. The Toledo government scoffed at Artemio's ultimatum, and two months later Sendero began a series of headline-grabbing attacks on military and police patrols.

When I returned to the valley in 2005, the cocaine trade had regained substantial ground to the north of Tocache. Friends there told me they were often frightened by a noticeable rise in homicides during highway robberies or at the hand of paid *sicarios*. Judging from a recent attack against several police helicopters, Sendero was also very much alive. It was directing its violence more and more on the anti-narcotics police, on coca eradication teams, and, as always, on anyone presumed to be an informer. With its numbers dwindling, however, the movement appeared to be less the diffuse, menacing force it had once been and more narrowly condensed into the elusive but ever more transparent figure of Artemio.

Sendero actions were most prominent in the southern end of the valley, especially around Aucayacu, though the government took steps there to keep them in check. New states of emergency were declared, and special antiterrorist units of the police arrived to track down the senderistas and their leader. Overall, the balance tilted hard in the government's favor. Each time Sendero attacked, the police or military followed with a counterattack, often resulting in the deaths or captures of insurgents as well as the release of new information on the increasingly exposed inner workings of the Party. More than ever the police and army claimed the movement was on its last legs and that soon they would nab "Comrade Artemio" himself. Their presumption was that the insurgent presence in the valley would end once the leader was gone.

The question never posed was whether the illicit cocaine economy might always attract some kind of military force to defend it against the interdictions of the state. For if by mid-decade the Huallaga seemed more assuredly than ever to have entered a period of postwar and not simply one of diminished conflict, the same three phenomena continued to form the general background of much of what happened: coca/cocaine, Sendero activity, and state responses to them both. These broad phenomena recurred, while the specific correlation of the forces expressed through them continually shifted. That correlation produced events as well as the sense people would draw upon in order to grasp how they were directly affected by what had transpired.

Coca/cocaine, the Sendero insurrection, and the Peruvian state's responses first converged during the earlier period of boom. In this book I have explored the events of that era as they were conveyed in the years that directly followed. The aftermath of cocaine's prosperity was a time when the weight of secrecy still exerted tremendous pressure on those who lived in the Huallaga. It was a time when the thought of speaking openly about conditions current and past could still have a paralyzing effect, and when the most urgent news there—not of the valley in general, but of specific locales—assumed the form of rumor and guarded messages that traveled in their own circumscribed realms, and there alone.

New aspects of boom history that I could not discern in the mid- to late 1990s were revealed to me when I returned under less strained political circumstances. Going back enabled me to grasp better what repeats in the Huallaga and what fleets away. It allowed me to appreciate even more fully the immensity and sheer complexity of the boom's history.

Nonetheless, I have tried in these pages to render my ethnographic experience of the post-boom years without subordinating it unduly to that later knowledge. My priority has been to relay the visceral atmosphere of that place and time as I encountered it *then* and as it was expressed through what people stated, gestured, and withheld.

The goal has been to grasp ways that the boom's violent history insisted in the post-boom years, while keeping in mind that recollections of the past not only are strongly affected by the knowledge of realized outcomes but necessarily reflect the orientations and pressing needs of the present. The challenge has been to relate the still-uncertain political conditions of that time while affirming the tension between what was known, what was unsure, and what refused to be revealed. That tension was the atmosphere that cropped up in states of affairs and stretched between what had already come to pass and the imminent futures that then seemed possible.

Registering that atmosphere became a central focus of this book as I examined the forms of law that hovered over and saturated the social landscape of the Huallaga: their different facets and local histories as well as the singular figurations they assumed. In the foregoing chapters I have sketched the outlines of a few of those "faces of law," but only those that made themselves ethnographically available to me: Sendero, Esparza, Marusha.

What Marusha shared with the other two would be unclear were not the ultimate claim of law to serve as a channel for achieving just ends. In that respect, all three exemplified paths to justice. Sendero, Esparza, and Marusha all stood in for that promise of law, but while offering distinct legal physiognomies that no one ever would have confused. Sendero and Esparza were *justiciero* figures that condensed the desire for plain, rigid lines. Marusha, meanwhile, represented another genre: a wise, steady hand that navigated the labyrinthine worlds of juridical consultations, documents, and proceedings. What bound the three together was the desire *others* had for justice, even though the idea that *just ends would flow from law* was a promise rarely if ever fulfilled.

Sendero, Esparza, and Marusha differed above all in their modes of practice. They also expressed divergent temporalities of law, though a strong affinity could be drawn between the actions of Sendero in the 1980s and those of the army in the early 1990s. Both had operated at those different moments of the boom from a space of *constituting* or *founding law*, where violence was the primary tool. Sendero pursued a revolutionary vector that pledged to establish a new society by demolishing the state. The army in the image of

Esparza followed a vector of restoration that ushered in a new order, if only under the banner of the nation to which it demanded all must return.

Marusha, meanwhile, performed her trade much like the local prosecutor of Aucayacu: from a field of law already constituted within which the recourse to violence was by and large foresworn. As a lawyer and human rights advocate, she used her knowledge of jurisprudence to fight against those acts of coercion committed by the Maoists and the army that were illegitimate within her realm. She worked, nonetheless, from a legal ground that had been secured through the counterinsurgency operations of the Peruvian armed forces. Thus in no small measure she owed the possibility of practicing law in the Huallaga to events that resonated in the many stories told about Esparza. Any irony or contradiction in that fact was surface deep. Whereas *constituting law* did not need to maintain a relationship of similarity to the legal regime it worked to install, Marusha and her world in no way resembled that of Esparza. They belonged to different times of law.

Deadly force has a potential to make new law. In situations of internal war this becomes brutally apparent where questions of right are settled by demonstrations of strength and when systems of legal codes and process no longer function as in times of peace. The relation of violence to law, moreover, has a critical temporal dimension in that lethal acts strongly influence perceptions of historical, and with it legal, time. In the context of insurgent-counterinsurgent warfare, the connection between time and the law-constituting power of violence manifests through disputes over how lethal outcomes will be interpreted and through the intricate ways those same realized events will shape the sense that is made of them. This is not to say that all violence seeks to create or succeeds in making law.

Organized armed groups generate their own idioms of force, which are the specific signatures through which their violence is expressed. The reiterative character of those forms is what allows for the recognition of routines through which lethal events are produced. In the Huallaga several distinct groups resorted to coercion to achieve diverse aims. Criminal bands relied on threat, theft, and murder to turn a profit. Drug traders stole from competitors and often killed them, primarily in hopes of securing more favorable conditions for producing and moving their product. The police also used force within, but also *beyond* the limits of the existing Peruvian legal code it was charged with upholding. Although none of these three employed violence with a deliberate lawmaking intention, this is not to imply that their coercive acts did not some-times reveal that inherent possibility.

By contrast, Sendero and the army purposely had sought to found new legal orders and to mold subjects obedient to them. They worked consistently and organizationally with future collectives in mind. In so doing they acti-vated the intrinsic capacity of violence to create political-legal community. Brute force put to that task is what I have called "the political." For its practi-tioners do not seek to achieve private ends or simply to dissuade certain kinds of behavior. Rather they take lawmaking as their chief purpose and employ a spectacular violence to "make a people" and to introduce a new legal era. What characterizes practitioners of the political is how they direct their rou-tines specifically toward crafting a particular kind of *ideal* event: the incor-poreal transformation of violence into law, of brute force into authority. The accumulation of lethal acts along the way is but a means to that goal.

Both the Shining Path and the army systematically used corpses to deliver messages of horrendous brutality. Mutilated human remains announced the advent of new law upon the land with rules of what could and could not be done. Such rules defined the basic terms of political belonging—that which made one a friend rather than a foe—and in turn oriented the experience of time along a specific range of possibilities.

Their violence directed attention on those killed. Nevertheless, the objec-tive was to produce effects on the living. For the dead there could be no ideal event. In the Huallaga the ones chosen as new subjects for an emerging com-munity could be those who ended up neither on the road nor on the river's shores. The incorporeal transformation of violence into law could obtain only for survivors who, as spectators, endured the killing.

Violence-events of the political always cut unevenly among the living. They founded law ex post facto and then only for those—and for those alone—who would hold that law in "esteem," internalizing its threat as rules having power over them. This was the underlying conundrum of the political: flags do not attach to the bodies of the living as easily as they do to the dead, even if the various practitioners go about as if they could.

The paradoxes of the political unfolded in the transit between sensing and sense making. They derived from the attempt to attach a coherent meaning to acts of aggression that most immediately produce loss, fragmentation, and ambiguity. For violence would only "have sense" where a good, common, or moral reason was grafted upon it, whether imagined as cleansing a society of bad seeds, as setting straight what was formerly crooked, or as punishing a specific criminal act.

When people invoked the notion of a *tierra de nadie* or no man's land, they pointed to times and places where a stable and coherent sense could not be pinned to acts of violence. *Tierra de nadie* implied a domain without law. But it was more precisely where the lawmaking potential of different groups over-lapped to such a degree that it became impossible for those caught in between to discern which rules they were to follow.

No man's land was that figurative time and place where violence piled up without acquiring a lasting good or common sense, without creating endur-ing law, and engendering only nonsensical ambiguity. There, where one law could not assure its authority beyond the next violent incident, all that mat-tered was local. That, and the ability to sense what would happen next.

In the post-boom, the names of rural locales that radiated a no-man's-land aura for many Huallaga townspeople pointed to the constellation of obstacles that prevented the region from joining the era of peace prevalent elsewhere in the country. Reaching that new era, where everything would presumably be so much easier, was held out as the only path to progress. True prosperity waited just on the other side. The condition of being out of synch with the rest of the nation grated on some people, and they spoke of the dangerous topography of the countryside as if it produced a drag not only on their personal fortunes but on local history itself.

By the time of the post-boom the Peruvian state had reaffirmed its author-ity, and the violence of Sendero had ceased to have revolutionary potential. De-prived of a credible claim upon the country's political destiny, Sendero could not be the same Sendero. Its remnants were holding on, surviving until a more favorable correlation of forces came around. In the meantime, townspeople feared Sendero's lingering power but had trouble finding anything within it on which to attach political expectation. Perhaps that was why people so often spoke of Sendero as simply "them"—a kind of exterior and menacing force. Long gone were the days when townspeople had sought out Party delegates to file complaints or to seek help in resolving problems and disputes. In the late 1990s the need for legal justice would be sought in other places. In Aucayacu it expressed itself as so many knocks on Marusha's door.

ACKNOWLEDGMENTS

The direction, content, and form this book has taken owe much to the sustained encouragement, critical interaction, and inspiration of many people. What began in 1995 with Orlando's kind invitation to travel with him to Aucayacu would not have taken root if not for the continued generosity and thoughtfulness of Marusha, Mariela, and their families. Their friendships have meant the world to me. Nico patiently taught me much about the wily contours of everyday life in the Huallaga and some exceedingly practical things along the way, such as how to ride a motorbike while softening the ill effects of the falls that inevitably came with it. Both Lucio in Aucayacu and Darick in Tocache befriended me and, thanks to their insatiable interest in the area's history, took me to meet many people in and around their towns. Without their guidance there is much I never would have learned. I am also most grateful to Marusha's landlord Gregorio for allowing me to live for a time at the house where he himself could not return and for graciously receiving me (with all my questions) at his hardware stand in Lima. Special thanks, too, to Tony, for the conversations that followed our serendipitous encounter; to Rino, for his morning radio show; and to Shirley, Carlos, and Doris, who in being yourselves were simply wonderful. I am deeply indebted to all of you and to many others (either still in the Upper Huallaga Valley or no longer there) who shared their personal experiences and stories of the boom. To all I do not specifically mention here, even in pseudonym form, I trust you know who you are and understand why.

During my initial research in Lima the Pro-Human Rights Association (Asociación Pro Derechos Humanos, or APRODEH) provided extraordinary assistance, including unlimited access to its vast news archives and crucial orientation on the political landscape under the government of President Alberto Fujimori. Charo Narvaez and the documentation center staff were exceptionally kind in facilitating my work, while Juan Mendoza offered me a place to stay on my subsequent visits to the city. He and Estela Bejar always received me as a close friend of the family, and I am most obliged for their hospitality.

Between New York and Peru, I learned much from Paul Gootenberg about the Peruvian history of cocaine: during conversations as my early research in the Huallaga was beginning to take shape, and through the essays and chapters he since has published. In 1998 generous grants from the Wenner-Gren Foundation and the Social Science Research Council enabled me to undertake long-term fieldwork, and I am most appreciative of their support. At that time the Institute of Peruvian Studies (Instituto de Estudios Peruanos, or IEP) invited me into its vibrant intellectual community, where I had many rewarding discussions with those who attended the group's conferences, among them Patricia Ames, Tito Bracamonte, Carlos Iván Degregori, Ponciano del Pino, Fanny Muñoz, Patricia Oliart, and Gonzalo Portocarrero. I thank you for your generosity and friendship.

On my frequent visits to Lima from the Huallaga, Patty Ames and Ana María Quiroz listened to nearly every story I had heard about the boom, and never failed to suggest other ways to think about them. Ana María also lent me a hand with the arduous task of transcribing my taped interviews, and then when she had had enough, introduced me to Tita Revollar. Because of their patient and careful efforts, I returned to New York in 2000 with a manageable collection of research materials. I am immensely grateful to them and to my friends José Luis Anco, Segundo Jara, José Vásquez, and Claudia Vega, of the Upper Huallaga Human Rights Committee (Comité de Derechos Humanos del Alto Huallaga), who later kept me up to date on what was happening in the region and assisted me with cross-checking versions of events whenever I asked. I wish as well to thank Bladimir Angulo, Sergio Madueño, Felipe Paucar, and Mónica Vecco, who at different moments shared their journalistic insights and expertise on the history of the Huallaga. In Tarapoto, Laly Pinedo and Roberto Lay always offered encouragement as they contributed their thoughts on the boom, while in Huánuco, during the research phase of the Peruvian Truth and Reconciliation Commission, Luis Alberto Calderón and Pilar Taboade imparted sound advice of their own.

The ideas and reflections I have developed in these pages owe no less to the many conversations and often impassioned discussions I have sustained with professors, colleagues, and friends in New York City. To Michael Taussig and Deborah Poole I cannot sufficiently convey my gratitude for their inspiration and steadfast support, each in their own unique ways. Mick's seminars at Columbia University on state magic, sacrilege, and secrecy drew my attention to the paradoxical relation between force and law and later had a formative and lasting influence upon my approach to ethnography. Most of all Mick taught me to be ever more demanding of my writing, as everything of importance would find there its ultimate expression. Debbie followed my research from its inception, always pointing out perspectives I had not considered. My studies have benefited enormously from her ongoing work on law and the Peruvian state, while her sage, timely advice has gotten me through more scrapes than I can recall.

Neni Panourgia offered excellent and sustained counsel at a moment when my disparate writings had yet to acquire a cohesive shape. She, together with Nadia Abu El-Haj and Elizabeth Povinelli, later provided crucial insights and commentary on what became developed drafts. Beth assisted me, in particular, with tightening the overall conceptual frame of the text. I thank all of you for the clarity, enthusiasm, and attention with which you engaged my work and the many ways you showed me how to make it better. I also wish to thank Claudio Lomnitz for his thoughtful comments.

Olga González, Katie Kilroy-Marac, Juan Obarrio, and Todd Ramón Ochoa also offered meticulous commentary on significant portions of the initial manuscript. Olga fielded many phone calls during the early stages when I often encountered impasses. Todd Ramón did the same and made a wonderful suggestion on how to refashion my translation of a Huallaga refrain that later became the title of this book. I often rehearsed ideas in conversations with friends and colleagues, among them, Jaime Borja Gómez, Narges Erami, Daniela Gandolfo, Jacquelyn Grey, Amira Mittermaier, Lenio Myrivili, Valeria Procupez, Kate Ramsey, Lisa Stefanoff, Shahla Talebi, and Drew Walker, as well as with Ulla Berg, Lourdes Blanco, Adriana Garriga López, Greta Goetz, Jennifer Kramer, Alejandra Leal, Caroline McLoughlin, Nick Moustakas, Isaías Rojas Pérez, Karina Rosenborg, Karis Wold, and Gabriela Zamorano. Though even this list is not anywhere near complete, the constructive criticisms, camaraderie, and affirmations you and others offered have meant a great deal to me.

A postdoctoral fellowship in the Program in Agrarian Studies at Yale University in 2006–7 allowed me to make critical revisions to the final text. I wish to convey my profound appreciation to Jim Scott and to Kay Mansfield for the vibrant community they made possible that year, and for the generous spirit with which they welcomed me. I thank Jim as well for the interest he took in my work, just as I am indebted to Valentine Cadieux, Seth Curley, Harold Forsythe, Liza Grandía, Mike McGovern, Susan O'Donovan, Erika Olbricht, Christophe Robert, Beltrán Roca Martínez, Jenny Smith, Finn Stepputat, John Varty, Gavin Whitelaw, and other participants of the Agrarian Studies seminar, who also read or listened to one or more of these chapters and gave their impressions. I extend thanks, too, to Enrique Mayer for being exceedingly generous with his time and critiques and to Abigail Dumes and Ryan Sayre for inviting me to present my work in Yale's Department of Anthropology. Throughout that year Christophe Robert and Finn Stepputat were ever spirited in challenging me to push my ideas harder. Later Christophe and Finn each gave invaluable suggestions toward correcting deficiencies in the final manuscript.

The patient encouragement and expertise of my editors at Stanford University Press, Jennifer Helé, Emily Smith, Joa Suorez, and Kate Wahl, have deftly guided this book through the process of publication. I want to thank them. I also wish to thank the two anonymous reviewers who read the manuscript—one of whom, Orin Starn, later broke anonymity and allowed me the opportunity of discussing his written remarks with him directly. The wonderfully detailed comments from both reviewers provided a strong template for undertaking the final revisions. Mary Carman Barbosa, for her part, applied her fabulous skills as a copy editor to smooth out the kinks still lingering in the text, and I am deeply grateful. For whatever flaws remain, I assume full responsibility.

The community of Fordham University at Lincoln Center has been very supportive as the book goes to press. I want to express appreciation in particular to my students and also to Hugo Benavides, Ayala Fader, Heather Gautney, Allan Gilbert, Jason Greif, Stuart Rockefeller, Clara Rodriguez, Orlando Rodriguez, Candy Sturm, and Cynthia Vich.

Diario La República kindly granted permission to reprint its coverage of the May 28, 1998, shooting in Pacae, and I wish to give special thanks to Ernesto Carrasco Benites and Luis Poma, who kindly expedited the process. My gratitude also extends to José Luis Bardales and David Jara of *El Matutino* of Aucayacu. David went to extra lengths to track down the article I needed amid the files of the now-defunct paper, while José Luis kindly provided the authorization for its inclusion here.

As this research has slowly acquired concrete form, my parents and my sister have been amazingly supportive. Jane Kernaghan read every page of the manuscript—at least twice—fixing what I would let her fix of my errant punctuation and rambling sentences. I am extremely indebted to her for her time and efforts. My most special thanks, however, go to Angela Mesía Ruiz for accompanying me day by day during the last eight years and giving me so much more to anticipate.

NOTES

Introduction

1. The Communist Party of Peru—Shining Path (Partido Comunista del Perú—Sendero Luminoso, or PCP–SL) is one of several Maoist parties within the kaleidoscope that has formed the radical Peruvian left since the 1960s. Throughout this book the terms "Shining Path," "Sendero Luminoso," "Sendero," and "the Party" are used interchangeably to designate the armed group that in 1980 initiated an insurrection with the goal of overthrowing the Peruvian state. Relatively unknown at the time, Sendero Luminoso became notorious for the ruthlessness and utilitarianism of its tactics, no less than for the broad definition the movement applied to what constituted an enemy of "the revolution." Sendero appeared to be cast from a wholly different mold than other leftist insurgencies in Latin America. Its fierce hostility extended not merely to state officials or to those it considered state sympathizers, but to popular organizations on the political left as well as to peasant and farming communities that resisted joining its armed struggle.

The literature on the Shining Path as a movement and the history of its insurrection is extensive. See especially Carlos Iván Degregori, *El surgimiento de Sendero Luminoso: Ayacucho, 1969–1979* (Lima: Instituto de Estudios Peruanos, 1990); Gustavo Gorriti Ellenbogen, *Sendero: Historia de la guerra milenaria en el Perú* (Lima: Editorial Apoyo, 1990); David Scott Palmer, ed., *The Shining Path of Peru* (New York: St. Martin's Press, 1994); Deborah Poole and Gerardo Rénique, *Peru: Time of Fear* (London: Latin American Bureau, 1992); and Steve J. Stern, ed., *Shining and Other Paths: War and Society in Peru, 1980–1995* (Durham, NC: Duke University Press, 1998).

A detailed but concise countrywide overview of the organizational history and structure of the Shining Path can be found in Comisión de la Verdad y Reconciliación (CVR), *Informe final*, Tomo 2 (Lima: Universidad Nacional Mayor de San Marcos, Pontificia Universidad Católica del Perú, 2004), 24–98.

For a discussion of the Shining Path's place within the broader spectrum of Peruvian Maoism, see Iván Hinojosa, "On Poor Relations and the Nouveau Riche: Shining Path and the Radical Peruvian Left," in Stern, *Shining and Other Paths*, 60–83.

2. Reinhart Koselleck, "'Space of Experience' and 'Horizon of Expectation'; Two Historical Categories," in *Futures Past: On the Semantics of Historical Time* (New York: Columbia University Press, 2004), 255–75.

3. Notably, *Nietzsche and Philosophy* (New York: Columbia University Press, 1983); *The Logic of Sense* (New York: Columbia University Press, 1990); and *Difference and Repetition* (New York: Columbia University Press, 1994).

4. David Hume alluded to this nonrepresentational and temporally structuring aspect of memory when he claimed that the primary work of memory is less to retain simple ideas or images than their "order and position." *A Treatise of Human Nature* (New York: Oxford University Press, 1978), 9, 85. Expanding on this insight, Gilles Deleuze asserted that in Hume's philosophy memory reproduces not the past but "different structures of the given"—which is to say it reflects and manifests a habitual orientation toward the demands of the present. What recollections convey, Deleuze suggested, is less the past itself than "the old present"—that which is represented in a particular moment as what precedes it. *Empiricism and Subjectivity* (New York: Columbia University Press, 1991), 94. For the past is something other than the recollections that seek to represent it or the habitual turning toward the needs of the present through which it manifests. The past is "not only that which has been, but also that which determines, acts, prompts, and carries a certain weight." Ibid., 95.

5. In 2002 and subsequent to this study, the departmental level of political division in Peru was officially redesignated "region." Huánuco and San Martín, thus, are now legally considered "regions" even though in common parlance they are frequently still referred to as "departments."

6. The Marginal Highway was renamed the Fernando Belaúnde Terry Highway in 2002 in honor of the former Peruvian president who is widely considered responsible for its construction.

7. Most notably, the Tingo María-Pucallpa segment of the Central Highway in the 1930s. For discussions of settlement policies of that era, see Magdaleno Chiro C., *Tingo María: Ensayo Monográfico* (Lima: Librería e Imprenta El Competidor, 1943), 6–12; Wolfram U. Drewes, *The Economic Development of the Western Montaña of Central Peru as Related to Transportation: A Comparison of Four Areas of Settlement* (Lima: Peruvian Times, 1958), 22.

Unlike earlier jungle road projects, which followed latitudinal itineraries linking the Peruvian coastal and highland regions with the tropical lowlands, the Marginal Highway was designed to hug the eastern edge of the Andes along a longitudinal course and to create an integrated road system with east-west "penetration" highways.

8. Presidents Manuel Prado y Ugarteche (1956–1962) and Fernando Belaúnde Terry (1963–1968).

9. Although the Franciscans succeeded in founding missions on both sides of the Huallaga River, among groups described as Panatahuas, Chucos, Tulumayos, Chunatahuas, Tinganeses, Quidquidcanas, Tepquis, Payansos, Cholones, and Hibitas, not all of these peoples were receptive to the Franciscans' presence or doctrine. Incursions by Shipibo Indians forced the missionaries to abandon their settlements in 1704. Half a century later they returned, however, to begin their religious enterprise anew— this time solely with the Cholones and Hibitas in Sión, north of present-day Tocache. While the Franciscans failed to establish a lasting presence, the chronicles they left documented one catastrophic consequence of their intervention: the spread of mortal disease. Epidemics of smallpox and measles accompanied the priests wherever they went, ravaging the very peoples whose souls they sought for religious conversion. See Bernardino Izaguirre, *Historia de las misiones Franciscanas*, vols. 1 and 2 (Lima: Provincia Misionera de San Francisco Solano del Perú, Convento de los PP. Descalzos, 2001–2004).

Nonetheless, illness alone did not reduce the valley's indigenous population. Some communities survived into the late nineteenth century, according to the accounts of European and American explorers and travelers who plied the waters of the Huallaga in the decades following Peru's independence from Spain. See Eduard Poeppig, *Viaje al Perú y al Río Amazonas 1827–1832* (Iquitos, Perú: CETA, 2003), 278–86; also William Lewis Herndon, *Exploration of the Valley of the Amazon* (New York: McGraw-Hill, 1952), 83.

10. In 1948 a University of Chicago–trained anthropologist, Aníbal Buitrón, conducted a short ethnological study of the Huallaga as part of a research expedition funded by UNESCO and the Peruvian government to examine the practicality of settlement in the valley. Although the survey team stayed close to the river, Buitrón surmised there were no culturally distinct Amazonian groups left inhabiting the valley. He further speculated that the Huallaga's original Amazonian groups had either assimilated or fled the advance of jungle colonists. Aníbal Buitrón, *Ethnological Survey of the Valley of the Rio Huallaga, Peru* (Paris: UNESCO, 1948), 15.

11. Although people used "cosmopolitanism" as a catchall notion, the phenomenon it referred to had specific proportions and patterns. Studies of government settlement programs conducted in the 1970s concluded that roughly half of the population of the Upper Huallaga had migrated from highland areas adjacent to the valley: the sierras of Huánuco, San Martín, La Libertad, and Ancash. A quarter to a third had come from the Central and Lower Huallaga basin and Saposoa. The rest were either originally from the Upper Huallaga or had migrated from Lima, Piura, and Arequipa. The rural population tended to be farmers and seasonal migrants from neighboring highlands, whereas the administrative and professional classes found in the towns were far more

likely to have migrated from more distant locations, principally cities. See Volker Jül-ich, *Colonización como complemento de la reforma agraria en la selva peruana: El valle del Huallaga Central* (Santiago de Chile: Instituto Latinoamericano de Investigaciones Sociales, 1974), 69; also Carlos E. Aramburú, "Problemas del desarrollo rural y la colo-nización de la amazonía peruana," *Debates en sociología (Lima)* 6 (1981): 65.

12. INEI (Instituto Nacional de Estadística e Informática), *Censo Nacional de Po-blación y Vivienda 1993* (Lima: INEI, 1993).

13. Multisite construction of the Marginal Highway began in different areas of the *selva alta*, in 1964, during the first administration of President Fernando Belaúnde Terry. State settlement programs during that period, however, were focused exclu-sively on the Upper Huallaga Valley. Following Belaúnde's ouster in 1968, construction of the Marginal Highway continued, as did the state support for settlement, though reconceived as part of the military's sweeping agrarian reform program. As elsewhere in the country, large landholdings in the Upper Huallaga were expropriated and orga-nized as agricultural cooperatives.

14. The reasons for failure varied. The lack of agricultural experience on the part of new settlers, low crop yields, and problems in obtaining credit all contributed. At-trition, however, disproportionately affected those *colonos* (settlers) who had been recruited by settlement officials; they became disillusioned when promises of aid or assistance went unfulfilled. So-called "spontaneous" migrants who had followed bud-ding networks of family and friends and never relied on state support were far more likely to stay. See Aramburú, "Problemas del desarrollo rural," 53; Jülich, *Colonización como complemento de la reforma agraria,* 156.

15. According to Plowman's detailed botanical descriptions, there are four cul-tivated varieties of coca stemming from two South American species of the genus *Erythroxylum.* They are: *Erythroxylum coca* var. *coca; E. coca* var. *ipadu; E. novogran-atense* var. *novagranatense;* and *E. novogranatense* var. *truxillense.* The first, *E. coca* var. *coca,* so-called "Bolivian" or "Huánuco" coca, is the principal commercial source of coca leaves and cocaine in Peru and Bolivia. Of the four, it has the greatest geo-graphic distribution, spanning the eastern tropical edge of the Andes from southern Ecuador through Peru and Bolivia to northern Argentina. Plowman speculated that *E. coca* var. *coca* originated in the Huallaga Valley before its eventual domestication in pre-Colombian times and expansion to other areas of the *selva alta.* He asserted, moreover, that *E. coca* var. *coca* was in all likelihood one of first plants to be farmed in the *selva alta,* contributing to the growth of agriculture in that ecological region. See Timothy Plowman, "The Ethnobotany of Coca," *Advances in Economic Botany* 12 (1984): 62–111.

16. The ethnological literature on the uses of coca in Peru that predate the emer-gence of the cocaine market, and that have continued alongside it ever since, is exten-sive and addresses a variety of separate themes.

On the crucial but often overlooked differences between the roles coca plays in the cultural practices of highland Andes rural communities as opposed to the international trade in illicit cocaine, see Enrique Mayer, "Coca as Commodity: Local Use and Global Abuse," in *The Articulated Peasant* (Boulder: Westview Press, 2002), 173–203; and Juan Ossio et al., "Cosmovisión andina y uso de la coca," in *La Coca . . . tradición, rito, identidad* (Mexico: Instituto Indigenista Interamericano, 1989), 231–307.

Regarding the ritual use and everyday consumption of coca as a cultural marker of Andean indigeneity, see Catherine Allen, *The Hold Life Has* (Washington, DC: Smithsonian Institution Press, 1988); Ossio et. al, "Cosmovisión andina," 231–307; also Mayer, "Coca as Commodity," 173–203.

On coca as a means of economic exchange in Huánuco peasant communities of the late 1960s and early 1970s, see Roderick E. Burchard, "Coca y trueque de alimentos," in *Reciprocidad e intercambio en los Andes Peruanos,* ed. Giorgio Alberti and Enrique Mayer (Lima: IEP, 1974), 209–51. On the economic role of coca in highland Huánuco in the 1980s during the cocaine boom, see Edmundo Morales, *Cocaine: White Gold Rush in Peru* (Tucson: University of Arizona Press, 1989).

17. Until the mid-twentieth century, raw cocaine was produced and traded legally in Peru. A small industry had in fact cropped up in the central sierra (Pozuzo and Huánuco) during the latter half of the 1800s, where it thrived thanks to the overseas and principally European demand for medical-use cocaine. In the 1920s the United States began exerting diplomatic pressure on Peru to ban production and sale. Yet it was not until the late 1940s, during the military dictatorship of Manuel Odría, that cocaine was first criminalized in Peru's penal code in accordance with the protocols established under a United Nation's narcotics prohibition regime.

On the transformation of Peruvian cocaine from a legal to an illicit commodity, see the extensive and insightful research of historian Paul Gootenberg, especially, *Between Coca and Cocaine: A Century or More of U.S.-Peruvian Drug Paradoxes 1860–1980* (Washington, DC: Woodrow Wilson International Center for Scholars, 2001); but also, "Reluctance or Resistance? Constructing Cocaine (Prohibitions) in Peru, 1910–50," in *Cocaine: Global Histories* (New York: Routledge, 1999).

In the post-boom Huallaga, some still remembered when, in the 1950s and before, backwoods artisans known as *pichicateros* produced small amounts of raw cocaine called "*pichicata,*" which was carried by foot and mule trail over to buyers in the sierra and the coast. *Pichicatero* and *pichicata* were names from an earlier era when contraband cocaine networks were still small and piecemeal. The terms had largely fallen out of use by the 1990s, in favor of *pasta básica* or the more generic *droga.*

18. For discussions of the nexus of coca and agrarian settlement in Colombia during the 1970s and 1980s, see Alfredo Molano, *Selva adentro: Una historia oral de la colonización del Guaviare* (Bogotá: El Áncora Editores, 1987); Alfredo Molano, *Aguas arriba: Entre la coca y el oro* (Bogotá: El Áncora Editores, 1990); and Jaime Eduardo

Jaramillo et al., *Colonización, coca y guerrilla* (Bogotá: Alianza Editorial Colombiana, 1989). For Bolivia of the same period, see Harry Sanabria, *The Coca Boom and Rural Social Change in Bolivia* (Ann Arbor: University of Michigan Press, 1993); and Jaime Malamud-Goti, *Smoke and Mirrors* (Boulder, CO: Westview Press, 1992).

19. The production of cocaine is a multistage process that chemically extracts cocaine alkaloids from dried coca leaves, removes impurities, and converts the alkaloids into a water-soluble hydrochloride form. Approximately one hundred kilos of dried leaf are required to produce between one and two kilos of hydrochloride. Methods and terminologies of illicit processing techniques varied during the Huallaga boom. For a detailed description of illicit processing in the Andean region of the period, see U.S. Drug Enforcement Administration, Office of Intelligence, *Coca Cultivation and Cocaine Processing: An Overview* (Washington, DC: U.S. Dept. of Justice, 1991); for raw cocaine processing in the Huallaga Valley in particular, see Morales, *Cocaine*, 1989.

20. Of course, where the narcotics trade was involved few things were transparent. The evidential nature of state statistical measurements was highly dubious because the overtly political context of their construction made them anything but neutral. An analysis of the polemical nature of anti-narcotics statistics exceeds my objectives here, though it is important to note that the production of such figures, if of ambiguous truth value, conferred upon the Upper Huallaga a certain bureaucratic "visibility." The United States in particular would draw upon CIA satellite images of the area to estimate changes in numbers of hectares under coca cultivation, while relying on Peruvian police figures (detailing seizures of coca and cocaine paste, arrests, destruction of drug laboratories and air strips, and so on) to advocate domestically and abroad for an interventionist anti-narcotics policy at the "source" of cocaine production. While these kinds of numerical representations offered a woefully feeble index of the boom's social complexity and potency, they did allow each government in its own way to portray the valley as it saw fit: here as a chronic source of internal instability; there as a major front line in an endless international "war" on drugs.

For excellent discussions of the Upper Huallaga's place in the U.S. anti-narcotics strategy of the 1980s and early 1990s, see Jo Ann Kawell, "Going to the Source," *NACLA, Report on the Americas* 22, no. 6 (1989): 3–22; and Deborah Poole and Gerardo Rénique, "Coca Capitalism and the New World Order," *Peru: Time of Fear* (London: Latin American Bureau, 1992), 167–202. For an important Peruvian perspective on how illicit cocaine has shaped Peru's relationship with the United States in the twentieth century, see Julio Cotler, *Drogas y política en el Perú: La conexión norteamericana* (Lima: Instituto de Estudios Peruanos, 1999).

21. Following the rise of the Shining Path, another leftist insurgent group, the Movimiento Revolucionario Túpac Amaru (MRTA), began its own armed actions against the Peruvian state. Besides its organizational ties with labor unions and university students in Lima and other major cities, the MRTA had a strong rural base of support

in the department of San Martín. This base extended from the Lower Huallaga and Mayo river basins around Tarapoto toward the Central Huallaga (Picota, Bellavista, and Juanjui). In the mid-1980s armed groups of the MRTA attempted to move into the Upper Huallaga in hopes of gaining leverage over the drug trade. Clashes with the Shining Path ensued for control of the town of Tocache and resulted in an MRTA retreat. Those early confrontations effectively determined a territorial repartition of the Huallaga, with the town of Juanjui marking the border. The Shining Path's area of influence extended from Tingo María to just south of Juanjui, while the MRTA operated from Juanjui to the north. The MRTA would have a short-lived access to the cocaine trade in the late 1980s and early 1990s as coca cultivation spread from the Upper Huallaga into the Central and Lower Huallaga. That ended by 1993 when army counterinsurgency operations effectively destroyed the MRTA's armed wing.

22. In Peru a *narco* is someone who makes his or her living by financing and directing the production, transportation, or wholesale trade of raw and refined cocaine. Throughout the book, *narcos* are also referred to as drug traders.

23. This is not to imply that Tingo María scarcely felt the repercussions of the times. To the contrary, the war and the boom each flowed in their own ways over and through the city. Since the mid-1970s, Tingo María had been a major center of legal commerce where people who earned their money in the drug trade would go to buy expensive items, such as new cars and motorcycles. The Shining Path also maintained a secret network of armed cadre and Party informers in the city. However, due to the strong presence of the armed institutions of the Peruvian state, neither the drug trade nor Shining Path operated in the open as they would at different moments elsewhere in the Upper Huallaga.

24. Alberto Fujimori, president of Peru from 1990 to 2000, headed a secretive and authoritarian regime responsible for significant violations of human rights. The son of Japanese immigrants, affectionately known as "el Chino" (the Chinaman), Fujimori enjoyed considerable popular support thanks to his government's military and police successes against leftist insurgents (Shining Path and the MRTA) as well as to the drastic reduction of economic instability, which had been inherited from the previous presidential administration of Alan García. In 2000 Fujimori fled to Japan when his supporters lost control of Congress after a failed bid to rig national elections. He remained in Japan for five years, eluding extradition until he was arrested during a trip to Chile and returned to Lima to stand trial on charges of corruption and human rights offenses.

25. Since the mid-1990s, Sendero in the Huallaga has functioned autonomously from the other main armed faction of the Party, which operates in the *selva alta* region of the Rio Apurímac and Rio Ene Valley. While the Huallaga wing has at least in rhetoric favored reaching a negotiated solution to the internal war through peace talks with the government, the faction in the Rio Apurímac and Rio Ene Valley has expressed no desire to abandon the armed struggle.

26. By demanding that all who lived in the countryside conform to Party rules and express support for its objectives, the Shining Path was able to bind the rural population to the land and to regulate the trade in coca/cocaine while, at the same time, raising and maintaining an army for its clashes with the Peruvian state. See Comisión de la Verdad y Reconciliación (CVR), "El PCP-SL durante el auge de la hoja de coca en el Alto Huallaga," in *Informe Final*, Tomo 5 (Lima: Universidad Nacional Mayor de San Marcos, Pontificia Universidad Católica del Perú, 2004), 186–208.

27. While I do not closely follow his categories here, this discussion would not be possible without the acute and groundbreaking insights of Walter Benjamin, as laid out in his 1921 "Critique of Violence," in *Walter Benjamin Selected Works*, vol. 1, ed. Marcus Bullock and Michael W. Jennings (Cambridge, MA: Belknap Press, 1996), 236–52. For contemporary interpretations of Benjamin's essay, see Jacques Derrida, "Force of Law," *Cardozo Law Review* 11, no. 5–6 (1990): 919–1047; Giorgio Agamben, *Homo Sacer* (Stanford, CA: Stanford University Press, 1998); and also Stathis Gourgouris, "Enlightenment and Paranomia," in *Does Literature Think?* (Stanford, CA: Stanford University Press, 2003), 49–89.

28. For the sake of my schema, "violence makes law" could be called the "might is right" proposition, often associated with (though not necessarily espoused by) Thucydides, Machiavelli, and Hobbes; whereas "law excludes violence" could be described as the "liberal proposition," in which conduct deemed violent ostensibly disqualifies one from participating in political community.

29. For one prominent explication of how coercion exercised in the name of law is sequentially structured as a rightful (and necessary) response to transgressions figured as logically "prior," see Hegel's *Philosophy of Right* (New York: Oxford University Press, 1967), 66–67.

30. Maurice Hauriou, *Principios de derecho público y constitucional* (Madrid: Reus, 1950), 19–26.

31. This is one of Benjamin's crucial assertions in his "Critique of Violence."

32. Carl Schmitt noted that in the context of war or revolution all concepts used to grasp political questions turn polemical and become "incomprehensible if one does not know exactly who is to be affected, combated, refuted, or negated by such a term." Severed from their specific historical context, such terms "turn into empty and ghost-like abstractions." See *The Concept of the Political* (Chicago: University of Chicago Press, 1996), 30–31.

33. Ibid. "The political" in Schmitt's theorization involves a situation of sufficient intensity in which the "real possibility of physical killing" hangs over a society and in which the question of who is a friend and who an enemy becomes a defining factor of everyday life. Ibid., 33. Schmitt asserted that the political cannot be grasped apart from a concrete historical situation in which those antagonisms have reached an extreme point. I interpret this to mean that gauging the atmosphere of that intensity

can only be done in close proximity to events. "Friend" and "enemy" for Schmitt were strictly public categories that manifest where two collective groups face off in conflict. One can always attempt to sustain a bond of personal friendship with one's "public enemy," though perhaps only at great risk. Ibid., 28.

34. Hume, *A Treatise of Human Nature*, 406.

35. Occurring at a moment when the boom had tapered off in the Upper Huallaga, the return of an invigorated cocaine economy to Aucayacu was largely unexpected. Heightened interdiction by the DEA and Peruvian police in the late 1980s combined with Sendero's attempts to fix prices had displaced the trade north into the lower Huallaga River and Mayo River basins as well as east toward Aguaytía, San Alejandro, and Pichis-Palcazu.

Chapter 1

1. *Doctor/Doctora* is a respectful mode of address reserved not only for physicians, but for lawyers, such as Marusha, or for anyone holding an advanced degree.

2. *La terrucada*: an adaptation of *terruco*, itself a colloquial rendering of *terrorista* (terrorist). *La terrucada* is vernacular for the Shining Path as a general activity, movement, or way of life.

3. The *nuevo sol*, or "new sun," is the Peruvian national currency, valued at approximately thirty U.S. cents during the period of this study.

4. See Introduction, note 24.

5. Technical aspects of Sendero terminology seldom took to everyday speech in the Huallaga. The semiclandestine Sendero militias of the towns became known simply as "La Urbana" because people tended to distinguish town and country in terms of "zones"—*la zona urbana* (urban zone) and *la zona rural* (rural zone). The Urbanas corresponded in the Maoist organizational framework of Sendero to *comités populares paralelos* (parallel people's committees) because they operated in locales where the army and police had headquarters or bases. They were considered "parallel" forms of local government because they existed, if clandestinely, alongside the armed institutions of the state. By contrast, in remote rural areas where the state had no institutional presence whatsoever, Sendero called its most basic units of local government *comités populares abiertos* (open people's committees)—"open" because they operated freely in what were considered liberated zones. Sendero's rule in the Upper Huallaga countryside was overt during much of the 1980s and early 1990s; with the exception of a short few months in 1987 in Tocache and Nuevo Progreso, Sendero never openly governed the towns of the Upper Huallaga.

6. As much as Sendero privileged violence as a central means of political praxis, Sendero militants and combatants were inculcated with a strict moral code. In their encounters with sectors of the population with whom Sendero wished to cultivate support, combatants were taught to be respectful. There was a refrain common in

the Party: "Don't steal from the people *(la masa)* so much as a needle or thread, and return whatever you borrow." Combatants were told not to use coarse language, not to sexually harass or commit adultery, and never to kill without cause. This moral code paralleled a broader message of moral correctness that militants sought to impose on the communities they came into contact with. However, the Aucayacu Urbana members were later said to be anathema to the ideals of Sendero militancy; townspeople remembered them for their decadence and complete lack of discipline, calling them *relajados* (shirkers).

7. Laments about coca being a "bad road" appeared to echo and thus register the rhetorical force of anti-narcotics discourses in Peru, which have had their own particular twentieth-century histories and very real effects. Those effects have included public support for militarized interdiction in coca-growing regions as well as public tolerance for ecologically devastating fumigation campaigns, conducted with no independent oversight as to their short- or long-term effects on health or the environment. Anti-narcotics discourses have also had an important international dimension to the degree that Peru has received financing and technical support from the United States, Europe, and the United Nations not solely for directly combating the illicit trade but for shaping public opinion. They are, however, not univocal. Some variants have expressed a "modernizing" assimilationist slant that effaces the difference between coca and cocaine, thus implicitly, if not overtly, denying legitimacy to indigenous cultural, social, and economic uses of coca. Others have championed coca as a symbol of Andean cultural identity while demonizing its "illegitimate" diversion to the international cocaine trade. In this respect, anti-narcotics discourses have drawn upon and reworked debates over coca's virtues and vices as they affect the governance of Andean subjects. The genealogy of these debates can be traced to the Spanish colonization of the Americas. For a historical survey of the major arguments as they pertained to Peru from the colonial period to the 1960s, see Joseph A. Gagliano, *Coca Prohibition in Peru* (Tucson: University of Arizona Press, 1994).

8. Much of Deleuze's *The Logic of Sense* and part of *Difference and Repetition* were dedicated to fleshing out the obscure workings of what might be called sense-producing machines.

9. Gilles Deleuze, The *Logic of Sense* (New York: Columbia University Press, 1990), 5, 24.

10. Ibid., 21–22.

11. Regarding the difficulties involved in explaining sense, Deleuze observed: "It is not surprising that it should be easier to say what sense is not than to say what it is. In effect, we can never formulate simultaneously both a proposition and its sense; we can never say what is the sense of what we say." Nietzsche, *Difference and Repetition* (New York: Columbia University Press, 1994), 155.

12. Deleuze, *Logic of Sense*, 56.

13. On the judicial figure of *pentimento* (repentance) in Italy, see Marco Jacquemet, *Credibility in Court* (New York: Cambridge University Press, 1996); also David Moss, "The Gift of Repentance: A Maussian Perspective on Twenty Years of Pentimento in Italy," *European Journal of Sociology* 42, no. 2 (2001): 297–331.

14. Between 1992 when the repentance program became law and late 1994 when it expired, the Peruvian government released monthly and weekly statistics of the number of militants who renounced membership in the Shining Path and MRTA. Government figures indicated that the majority of so-called *arrepentidos* (repenters) were from the Sendero-dominant Upper Huallaga Valley.

15. In the realm of counterinsurgency, the military and the police alike made much of there being only one true flag: the Peruvian red and white national colors. Insurgent banners were mere *trapos*—lowly, old, and beat-up pieces of cloth good for no more than cleaning dirt and filth.

16. *Diario La República,* July 18, 1994.

17. One notable exception was a timely piece of reporting by journalist Cecilia Valenzuela that made the cover of the Lima weekly *Caretas* in 1994, the previous year. The article told how suspected Sendero members or collaborators who turned themselves in to the Aucayacu army base, seeking the protections promised by the law, were told they would not be handed over to the judicial branch in Tingo María until they gave their interrogators a minimum of forty names. Forty names was the price demanded in exchange for safe passage from the "anything goes" realm of martial rule to the procedural guarantees of civil legal justice. Cecilia Valenzuela, "La cuota de los cuarenta," *Caretas* (March 10, 1994): 29.

18. Most notoriously, Operation Cuchara (1992) and later Operation Aries (1993–94) spared not even women or children. See Comisión de la Verdad y Reconciliación (CVR), *"La estrategia de pacificación en la margen izquierda del río Huallaga,"* in *Informe Final,* Tomo 5 (Lima: Universidad Nacional Mayor de San Marcos, Pontificia Universidad Católica del Perú, 2004), 259–81. On Operation Aries, see also Coordinadora Nacional de Derechos Humanos (CNDH), *Los sucesos en el Alto Huallaga* (Lima: Coordinadora Nacional de Derechos Humanos, 1994).

19. Peru had three principal and largely autonomous law enforcement branches— the Guardia Civil (GC), the Guardia Republicana (GR), and the Policía de Investigaciones del Perú (PIP)—until they were administratively restructured and brought under the umbrella of the Policía Nacional del Perú (PNP), or National Police, in 1988.

The jurisdiction of the Guardia Civil comprised urban centers and rural towns, where it was responsible for preventing crime and preserving public order, including traffic control. In times of war, however, or when a state of emergency or siege was declared, those functions would customarily become the prerogative of the armed forces, with the Guardia Civil operating at its discretion. Several special operations units belonged to the Guardia Civil, including the UMOPAR and the Sinchis, a

paramilitary counterinsurgent battalion that was formed in the mid-1960s and received training from U.S. Army Green Berets.

The Guardia Republicana (GR), for its part, was responsible for protecting state
and governmental offices and for providing security both in the penitentiary system
and along the national borders.

The PIP, meanwhile, was the branch that investigated crimes and supported the
judicial system in building criminal cases. The PIP also provided personal security for
public officials. As such, it had no strict territorial jurisdiction.

20. Ministry surveyors, engineers, and agronomists organized the cadastral division of plots and oversaw their allocation to homesteaders. On paper, if nowhere else,
the frontier colonization program gave the settlement of the valley an appearance of
order. In the years that followed, the Ministry of Agriculture would provide technical
assistance and loans to farmers and ranchers.

21. The first Huallaga *cocalero* movement emerged around 1979 in response to the
harassment of the PIP and the first large-scale coca eradication operations (Verde
Mar I and II, or Green Sea I and II) carried out by the Sinchis' counterinsurgent
battalion of the Civil Guard. Within two years the Shining Path had arrived and
gradually had begun to assert itself as the only group that could represent the farmers politically.

22. For a concise discussion of the resurgence of *cocalero* organizations in Peru, see
Hugo Cabieses, "Peru: the Cocalero Struggles and Good Governance," *Transnational
Institute Drugs and Conflict Debate Paper* 10 (April 2004): 16–26; on anti-narcotics policy as it affected coca cultivation and *cocaleros* in the years immediately following the
Fujimori government, see Isaías Rojas, "The Push for Zero Coca: Democratic Transi-
tion and Counter-narcotics Policy in Peru," *Drug War Monitor*, Washington Office on
Latin America (WOLA), Washington, DC, February 2003; also, on the degree to which
cocalero organizations form a social movement, see Anahí Durand Guevara, "El movimiento cocalero y su (in)existencia en el Perú: Itinerario de desencuentros en el río
Apurímac," *Bulletin de l'Institut Francais d'Etudes Andines* (2005: 34, 1): 103–26.

Chapter 2

1. One patent indication that distinct sovereignties clashed in the Upper Huallaga
Valley was the coexistence of different political calendars (those of the Peruvian state
and the Maoist Shining Path) as well as the lengths to which each force would go to
coerce the population into recognizing its own organization of time and commemo-
ration. Such efforts rarely went uncontested by the other side, and that was why significant dates on both sides brought with them a heightened probability of violence.

2. In Peruvian vernacular *piña* (literally, "pineapple") connotes "rotten luck" or
a state of being jinxed. Here the driver expressed disappointment or disgust, and as
such the phrase can be rendered: "Rats . . . rats, why did we have to be the first?"

3. Here given in its plural form, *tuco* is a regional diminutive of *terruco*, itself slang for *terrorista* (terrorist).

4. As the local representative of the Ministerio Público, or Public Prosecutor's Office, the *fiscal* was responsible for initiating legal proceedings when a crime had been committed. His function was to defend the legal order, as it addressed both the interests of society and the rights of citizens. In sum, it was up to the *fiscal* to facilitate if not ensure the administration of legal justice.

5. Peruvian penal law specified that a *levantamiento de cadáver* (literally, the "lifting up" of the cadaver) be performed by a *fiscal* (state prosecutor) in all cases of suspicious death. See article 239 of the *Penal Code Procedures Manual* (Trujillo, Peru: Editora Normas Legales, 1999). This is part of a broader propriety claim that the Peruvian state has established over the human body and any of its parts after death. For one clear expression of this claim, see article 2 of law no. 23415 regulating organ transplants: "Al ocurrir la muerte, los restos mortales de la persona humana se convierten en objeto de derecho, se conservan y respetan de acuerdo a ley" (Upon death, human mortal remains become the object of law. They must be preserved and respected according to the law). "Normas Legales," *Revista de Legislación y Jurisprudencia* 41, Tomo 115 (Tercer Bimestre, Mayo–Junio, 1982): 239.

6. The prosecutor had used an inflected version of the saying that brought the nominal form *la vida* up front and let it resonate with the pronominal *la* and verbal form *vivir* that followed. This not only had the effect of accentuating the emphasis on the word *vida*, it gave the spoken phrase an undeniable meter and even grace.

7. Elias Canetti, *Crowds and Power*, trans. Carol Stewart (New York: Farrar Straus Giroux, 1984), 303–33.

8. Elias Canetti and Theodor Adorno, "Elias Canetti: Discussion with Theodor W. Adorno," *Thesis Eleven* 45 (1996): 14–15.

9. Gilles Deleuze and Félix Guattari, "November 20, 1923: Postulates of Linguistics," in *A Thousand Plateaus: Capitalism and Schizophrenia*, trans. Brian Massumi (Minneapolis: University of Minnesota Press, 1987), 79.

Pieces of advice as well as public advisories are not so far removed from commands and orders and the death sentences they contain. Perhaps they are no more than "veiled" or second-generation threats in that they not only enclose but are a means for delivering them.

10. John Locke, *Second Treatise of Government*, ed. Richard Cox (Arlington Heights, IL: Harlan Davidson, 1982), 73. Locke's "doctrine" on this point was quite broad: permanent dwelling or living within the territorial confines of a commonwealth was not necessary to demonstrate tacit recognition of the sovereign authority; taking temporary lodging or "barely travelling freely on the highway" would also suffice. Rousseau later echoed this principle, anchoring it more firmly to the notion of domicile: "When the state is instituted, residency implies consent; to inhabit the

territory is to submit to the sovereign authority." Jean-Jacques Rousseau, "On Social Contract," in *Rousseau's Political Writings*, trans. Julia Conaway Bondanella (New York: Norton, 1988), 151.

11. Like Operation Cuchara two years earlier, Operation Aries targeted villages on the left bank of the Huallaga River between the villages of Venenillo and Magdalena. See Chapter 1, note 18.

12. According to Deleuze and Guattari, "order-words" travel in hearsay and often go unrecognized. Ultimately, they argue, the purpose of language is not to instill belief but to "compel obedience": "We see this in police or government announcements, which often have little plausibility or truthfulness, but say very clearly what should be observed and retained. The indifference to any kind of credibility exhibited by these announcements often verges on provocation. This is proof that the issue lies elsewhere. Let people say . . . : that is all language demands." Deleuze and Guattari, *A Thousand Plateaus: Capitalism and Schizophrenia*, 76.

13. Notably in Hobbes but also Locke and Kant. For an insightful analysis of the relationship between "states of nature" and liberalism as regards the Peruvian Andes, and specifically on the particular ways in which the "law and its extrajudicial shadow" reinforce one another to (re)found the legitimacy of state power, see Deborah Poole, "Between Threat and Guarantee: Justice and Community in the Margins of the Peruvian State," in *Anthropology in the Margins of the State*, ed. Veena Das and Deborah Poole (Santa Fe, NM: School of American Research Press, 2004), 35–66.

14. Carl Schmitt, *The Nomos of the Earth in the International Law of the Jus Publicum Europeaeum*, trans. G. L. Ulmen (New York: Telos Press, 2003), 93–100, 293–94. For an important contemporary, if particular, reading of several crucial passages of *Der Nomos* as well as Schmitt's thinking generally, see Giorgio Agamben, *Homo Sacer* (Stanford, CA: Stanford University Press, 1998), 15–38.

15. For a concise analysis of the legal framework for states of exception in Peru from the 1930s until the mid-1980s, see Diego García-Sayán, "Perú: Estados de excepción y su régimen jurídico," in *Estados de emergencia en la región andina*, ed. Diego García-Sayán (Lima: Comisión Andina de Juristas, 1987), 93–125.

16. An indication that the law is understood ostensibly to still be in force during a period of legal exception can be discerned in the organic law of the Ministerio Público (article 8). This law expressly stipulates that the activities and therefore authority of the Public Prosecutor's Office are not interrupted, except with respect to those rights and guarantees declared to be in abeyance and—revealingly—as long as its functionaries do not in any way obstruct the activities of the armed forces. Peru, "Ley Orgánica del Ministerio Público," in *Código Penal* (Lima: Editora Jurídica Griley, 2005), 738.

17. "Judicial punishment (*poena forensis*) is entirely distinct from natural punishment (*poena naturalis*). In natural punishment, vice punishes itself, and this fact is not

taken into consideration by the legislator." Kant, *The Metaphysical Elements of Justice: Part I of The Metaphysics of Morals*, trans. John Judd (Indianapolis, IN: Bobbs-Merrill, 1965), 100.

18. Although a thorough social history of the Shining Path in the Huallaga has yet to be written, insightful perspectives and analyses can be found in the following: Comisión de la Verdad y Reconciliación (CVR), "El PCP-SL durante el auge de la hoja de coca en el Alto Huallaga," *Informe final*, Tomo 5 (Lima: Universidad Nacional Mayor de San Marcos, Pontificia Universidad Católica del Perú, 2004), 186–208; José Gonzales Manrique, "Sendero Luminoso en el valle de la coca," in *Coca, cocaína y narcotráfico: Laberinto en los Andes,* ed. Diego García Sayán (Lima: Comisión Andina de Juristas, 1989), 207–22; Felipe Páucar Mariluz, *La guerra oculta en el Huallaga, Monzón y Aguaytía* (Tingo María, Peru: Centro de Estudios y Promoción para el Desarrollo Agroindustrial, CEDAI, 2006).

19. Early in the following year (1999), Rino's show was cancelled after he was picked up by a group of *sicarios* at gunpoint. They took him out of town to a place where they said they had orders to kill him. Instead they let him off with a warning. He subsequently left town and resettled in Tingo María, where he worked for a time as a correspondent for a Lima-based newspaper.

20. The small eight-to-ten–page weekly had a limited circulation in town in 1998, making a several-month run before eventually folding.

21. *El Matutino*, May 30, 1998 (my translation).

22. *Diario La República,* May 30, 1998 (my translation).

23. Months later, when searching news reports that had been published on the Pacae shooting, I discovered that Reuters had covered the incident with Spanish- and English-language versions posted the day following the shooting: "Sendero Luminoso mata a cinco personas en la selva peruana," *Reuters Noticias Latinoamericanas,* May 28, 1998; and "Shining Path kills five villagers in Peru jungle," *Reuters News*, May 28, 1998.

Reuters reported there had been two simultaneous attacks by separate Sendero columns on "two jungle villages" (Pacae and Cachicoto) and that these resulted in the deaths of five villagers. The father of the two brothers killed in Pacae gave the following description of what had happened: "They accused my sons of being 'snitches' and collaborating with the army and police . . . Everybody objected and screamed that they were community leaders who worked hard for the village. But they killed them all the same." In the Spanish-language version Reuters added that in both places Sendero stopped traffic on the roads and made the passengers get out and join the villagers for "indoctrination." The English-language report included the following remark: "Such attacks on remote villages form part of a traditional Shining Path strategy aimed at scaring peasants into keeping silent on the rebels' movements, according to political analysts."

Chapter 3

1. *Limpieza social* (social cleansing) was the term Sendero used to designate the practice of ridding the communities it wished to organize politically of those it considered criminal, asocial, or sympathetic to the state. Sendero generally initiated the process with written death threats, which if unheeded were followed by executions. Forced exile and killing thus became convenient means for winnowing communities of anyone deemed inassimilable to the Sendero project of armed struggle. On the notion of *limpieza* in the context of paramilitary violence in Colombia, see Michael Taussig, *Law in a Lawless Land* (New York: New Press), 2003.

2. *Cholo/chola* refers to a person of indigenous heritage who appropriates the outward cultural forms of national Spanish-dominant society. It frequently conveys, as in this context, disparaging overtones, though it may also be used as a term of endearment.

3. This Humean reading of causation is guided by Deleuze's discussion of what he called "passive synthesis" in *Difference and Repetition* (New York: Columbia University Press, 1994), 70–85. As a phenomenon of perceived physical repetition, passive synthesis names a time-generative process. Recurring particulars are retained in the mind where they are contracted together to form the dimension of an immediate past. From this same perceived recurrence, however, a general condition is drawn off and projected as the immediate future. This general condition is a set of "living rules" for the future, based in the anticipation that "it"—the situation of repetition—will continue. Crucially, and directly relevant for my argument above, Deleuze insisted passive synthesis is *pre*representational: it happens as if it were *prior* to conscious thought. The connections traced by a perceived repetition happen not by but *in* the mind, in its condition of passive receptivity. Through this receptive state, habits are contracted *before* they are recognized or recalled. The mode of time they inaugurate is sensed or felt before "it" can be interpreted or reflected upon. If passive synthesis can be considered a "memory," then it is involuntary and not directly available to consciousness. As such, it is opposed to what Deleuze called "active synthesis," which operates at the level of representation, recognition, and voluntary (conscious) memory.

4. See note 1, this chapter. Social categories Sendero classified as deviant included cocaine paste users (*fumones*); thieves and other common criminals; transgender male-to-female individuals (*travestis*); women suspected of consorting with either the police (*tomberas*) or the army (*moroqueras*); drug couriers who swindled coca farmers; and adulterers (*sacavuelteros*). The most flexible category within the Sendero system of criminalized types was the informer/enemy collaborator (*soplón*), which could be applied to anyone on the spur of the moment and as need or convenience dictated.

5. The polysemous verb *extrañar* (adjectival form: *extraño/a*) connotes the action of "surprise," "estrangement," "alienation," but also "longing." Thus it was well suited

for describing the range and confusion of Marusha's emotive responses regarding the disappearance of bodies from the road.

Chapter 4

1. Aníbal Buitrón, *Ethnological Survey of the Valley of the Rio Huallaga, Peru* (Paris: UNESCO, 1948), 18.

Chapter 5

1. Until recently one of the few exceptions had been the Peruvian Truth and Reconciliation Commission (Comisión de la Verdad y Reconciliación, or CVR). See CVR, *Informe final* (Lima: Universidad Nacional Mayor de San Marcos, Pontificia Universidad Católica del Perú, 2004). The Northeastern Regional Office of the CVR collected dozens of testimonies that attributed human rights violations to Esparza and those under his command. However, the Commission's *Informe Final* contained only four brief mentions of Captain Esparza. See Tomo 7, 273–74, 299, 301. In all four, the name "Esparza" appeared in italics, indicating that it was presumed to be a pseudonym. The first citation identified him as the Aucayacu base commander in March 1992 but did not specifically implicate him in human rights abuses. The remaining citations referred to events that happened at the Los Laureles army base (BCS 313) in Tingo María, apparently subsequent to Esparza's transfer from Aucayacu. For these, no specific dates were given. Two involved disappearances, and one was a case of torture. The victim of torture identified Esparza as being in charge of all prisoners at the Los Laureles base. Ibid., 301.

2. This chapter focuses on how Esparza was discussed and described in and around Aucayacu during the years of immediate post-boom: a time when knowledge of his actions had yet to circulate publicly outside of the Huallaga. National attention was finally directed to the Esparza event in September 2006, when the Lima news daily *La República* published an outstanding series of articles on Esparza's activities in Aucayacu. Since my concern is with the power of the Esparza figure in Aucayacu of the late 1990s, I do not address here how the *La República* exposé may have later affected the townspeople's opinion of him.

3. Cecilia Valenzuela, "Falla fatal: Crimen en Aucayacu," *Caretas* 1253 (March 18, 1993): 76–78. The victim, the magazine explained, was abducted near Aucayacu on January 23, 1993, by a group of men in plain clothes. Eyewitnesses saw Esparza behind the wheel of the car in which the men made their getaway. The family of the victim filed legal charges in Tingo María, demanding his immediate release. A police officer advised them to desist for their own safety, because against Esparza nothing could be done. Seven days later they found the body floating in the Huallaga River, arms tied behind the back, tongue cut out, eyes destroyed, and with three bullet wounds to the head. The *Caretas* article intimated that Esparza worked in military intelligence

following his transfer to the Los Laureles Base in Tingo María, from where he continued to conduct operations in the Aucayacu area.

4. According to an employee of the Proyecto Especial del Alto Huallaga (PEAH), during the captain's tenure in Aucayacu, Esparza had a team of at least three active-duty servicemen. There was Lieutenant "Israel," remembered as being tall, thin, and dark. Some called him *el demonio de Esparza* (Esparza's demon) because he was the one believed to have done Esparza's dirty work, while others insisted that he merely took turns with the captain. There was "Felipe el Dulce," originally from Cajamarca, who went AWOL because he couldn't stomach the killing. There was also an official who went by the pseudonym "Jaufino," about whom little else was known. Of the informers who worked closely with Esparza's group, the PEAH employee mentioned "Rayo," "Rambo," and "Lucifer": all three were young men from the Aucayacu area who had completed their mandatory service with the army before joining Esparza's team. There was also a former senderista known as "Araña" (Spider), who left the area after finishing his work with Esparza; later he returned to Aucayacu and was killed. The *Caretas* article (March 18, 1993) cited above also referred to one "Guiño" as a close collaborator of Esparza. Ibid., 76.

Some townspeople claimed that Esparza belonged to an elite commando group assigned to hunt down and eliminate members and collaborators of Sendero Luminoso. If true, then Esparza's appointment as Aucayacu base commander was almost certainly only one of several roles he played in the Army's counterinsurgency campaign in the Huallaga Valley and adjacent regions. This might account for the incongruencies in the dates of his presence in Aucayacu.

It is interesting to note that several testimonies gathered by the CVR's Northeastern Regional Office accused a Captain "Espartaco" of having committed multiple cases of abduction, torture, and disappearance while stationed at the base of Aguaytía in the department of Ucayali. Moreover, on a trip I made to Tingo María in January 2005, a local journalist told me that when Esparza was stationed at Los Laureles (1993) people first referred to him as "Espartaco," though soon enough he became known as Esparza. His reputation as a very dangerous person preceded him and circulated in Tingo María in the form of vague rumors that most journalists decided were better not to follow to their source.

5. See, for example, the destruction of a San Borja district Lima residence of the then-military chief of the Frente Huallaga, General Manuel Varela Gamarra: *La República, El Comercio,* and other major Lima papers, July 30, 1996; also "Domínguez Voló," *Caretas* (August 1, 1996).

6. The use of military pseudonyms would become a matter of renewed national intrigue, if not controversy, many years later. During the 2006 presidential elections, one of the leading candidates, former army officer Ollanta Humala, was accused of human rights violations. The allegations involved events between 1992 and 1993 while

Humala was stationed in Madre Mía, a small village north of Aucayacu, where he had operated under the nom de guerre Capitán "Carlos." Journalists who arrived in Madre Mía from Lima to cover the story soon learned, however, that not one "Capitán Carlos" but three had operated in the Upper Huallaga. Among the three, of course, was none other than Capitán Carlos Esparza, no matter that locally emphasis had never been placed on his first name, only on the last.

With all eyes on Humala and his electoral prospects, little was made of Esparza at the time. The Lima-based reporters did not convey, and perhaps did not adequately grasp, that Humala's notoriety in the Huallaga paled next to that of Esparza. Humala had been but one of the many army officers who rotated through the valley without making much of a show. Though the revelations of his alleged abuses did have a major impact on the 2006 presidential race, they did not prevent Humala from forcing a runoff, which he eventually lost.

7. Social distance was such during the internal war that for communities far from the capital—remote towns, villages, and settlements—such critical or "epoch-making" events, those perceived as shaping and radically altering the direction of the conflict, assumed multiple forms and guises. In some places what people attributed as a major turning point might have been a bludgeoning army offensive. It might have been the sudden flight or even defection of a powerful Sendero *comisario* (commissar). Or it might have been a showdown between a peasant defense patrol and other peasants accused of collaborating with the guerrilla. In other words, there was not one unitary history of the violence, no single version that could stand in as truly representative for all.

8. The very shift in state of affairs to which people referred happened not as one great event but in a series of minor occurrences over a period of no more than four years. In the latter half of the 1980s the Shining Path was at the height of its dominance over Aucayacu, and much of the Upper Huallaga Valley seemed firmly under its sway. But by 1992 the Party had been definitively pushed out of Aucayacu and other valley towns such as Nuevo Progreso, Tocache, and Uchiza. Though certainly not defeated, for the first time Sendero appeared vulnerable in the Huallaga.

9. The army rotated commanders in and out of the bases in the Huallaga on a regular basis. A typical tour of duty could last anywhere from six months to a year. The people who lived in towns and villages where bases were located therefore became quite familiar with the military officers in charge and paid keen attention to their personalities, attitudes, and actions toward the local population. They noticed for one thing that the ruling styles of the base commanders could be radically different from one to the next and that the conditions for getting along with the army could change with every new rotation. Esparza's position was notable in the sense that he was talked about as if he were somehow dissimilar to all of the other army commanders, exceptional in almost every respect. At the same time he was credited with laying down most effectively the institutional will of the army.

10. Doing one's civic duty meant, in its most basic expression, doing whatever was necessary to keep that atrocious "this" at bay.

11. *Manteca* is Spanish for grease, fat, or lard. *Mantequero* refers to the fat-extracting evil henchman of Andean folklore and legend, known as the *pishtaco* or *naqak*. There is an extensive scholarly literature on the *pishtaco*. See Efraín Morote Best, "El Degollador (naqak)," *Tradición: Revista Peruana de Cultura* 2 (1952): 67–91; Anthony Oliver-Smith, "The Pishtaco: Institutionalized Fear in Highland Peru," *Journal of American Folklore* 82, no. 326 (October–December 1969): 363–68; Juan Ansión, *Desde el rincón de los muertos* (Lima: GREDES, 1987), 173–79; Michael Taussig, "Indian Fat," *Shamanism, Colonialism, and the Wild Man: A Study in Terror and Healing* (Chicago: University of Chicago Press, 1987), 221–43.

12. I have heard that the first times the army forced townspeople to participate in the ceremonies were unnerving experiences. No one was sure how Sendero would react. A hotel owner told me he had been so frightened when, one Sunday, Esparza made him carry the flag and march around the square, that as soon as it was over he caught the next car to Tingo María. But once there, feeling not yet far enough away, he bought a bus ticket to his hometown of Trujillo on the north coast of Peru, where he took a long vacation.

13. For people in and around Aucayacu the return of parades and national civic spirit was inseparable from Esparza. Many claimed it happened because of him. Their assertions notwithstanding, weekly flag-raising ceremonies and parades were a widespread occurrence throughout Peru, beginning in the early 1990s. Together with the renovation of municipal plazas, they served to reaffirm the symbolic centers of cities and towns. They also coincided with the waning of political violence and the state's increasing strategic advantage in the internal war. For more on how the Peruvian state used civic and school parades in the Upper Huallaga Valley, see my "Fidelidad o el viento en una pierna bien alzada," *Debates en Sociología* (Lima) 25 (2000): 49–62.

14. As compelling an image as it was, there was no reason to suspect that Esparza's use of chainsaws was an exception within the army. A former army special forces commando I met in early 2000 explained that not only was the quartering of suspected senderista leaders common in the Huallaga region, the use of chainsaws on enemy prisoners comprised part of the training he received in counterinsurgency techniques. In commando courses he took in the highlands, he and his classmates practiced their hand at the chainsaw on dogs provided by the army. Subsequently, when sent for additional training to Tingo María and to the lower Huallaga city of Tarapoto, they practiced on "suspected terrorists." He claimed they had no choice: "Everyone had to do it."

After his training, the former soldier said he served at bases in Aucayacu, Ramal de Aspuzana, Madre Mía, and Tocache. He claimed that in the early 1990s the army gave commandos like himself "complete freedom to work." The stress of serving in the Huallaga was intense; so great, he said, that all the soldiers used drugs. Otherwise, "you couldn't keep your sanity."

Testimonies collected in 2002 by the CVR's Northeastern Regional Office documented the army's use of chainsaws to torment, torture, and execute suspected insurgent leaders and collaborators. While chainsaw torture received only sporadic national coverage, the degree to which distinct forms of terror circulated in tightly circumscribed, local circuits without obtaining social recognition in a wider field should not be underestimated.

15. President Fujimori often touted his government's counterinsurgency strategy for its emphasis on the collection of intelligence. This, he claimed, allowed for a more focused pursuit of insurgent leaders while avoiding widespread human rights violations, such as those that had characterized the previous two presidential administrations of Fernando Belaúnde Terry and Alan García. The disregard for civilian casualties had been a prevalent feature of the internal war in the highlands since the early 1980s. General Luis Cisneros Vizquerra, minister of defense under Belaúnde, famously remarked that for the government's counterinsurgency strategy to have any success against Sendero in the southern department of Ayacucho, state forces would have to kill sixty people in order to eliminate at best three senderistas. See Poole and Rénique, *Peru: Time of Fear*, 6. While Fujimori's administration transformed the government's approach to the war, human rights abuses by no means ceased. His government did, however, go to greater lengths than his predecessors to restrict the public visibility of such abuses.

As regards Esparza's alleged "selective aim," in the town of Aucayacu there was possibly some truth to that claim. In the Huallaga countryside, nevertheless, the army applied the same old "3 out of 60" rule well into the mid-1990s.

16. What these types of claims elided altogether were the thorny difficulties that plagued accurately assessing the degree and quality of such belonging—difficulties that stemmed from the Shining Path's use of coercion as a means of political and military recruitment and from the Party's control over access to land in the countryside.

As early as 1983 and well into the late 1990s, anyone who farmed the land outside Aucayacu inevitably came into contact with the Party. Furthermore, because of the way Sendero organized the rural population and incorporated it actively into its armed struggle, anyone present in the area was in at least an indirect sense "supporting" the Party.

This pattern led to the tendency on the part of townspeople to equate farm people with Sendero. The army did the same and often took the further step of assessing guilt or innocence along pure geographic lines. (See the earlier discussion of residency as indicating consent to be ruled by the sovereign authority in the "violence through language" section of Chapter Two.)

In their defense, rural settlers would point out the coerced character of their participation, making a distinction between those, like themselves, who were *los obligados* (those who were compelled) and *los fanáticos* (those who actually liked the Sendero life). Guilt in their calculus hinged on the degree of one's agreement with Party rule. Of course, determining a person's degree of conviction, especially when someone's life was in play, was not only hard to figure, it could easily change over time.

17. Another explanation of course, one that would clear the police of blame, was that Sendero had well-placed spies who reported on the movements in and out of the police headquarters.

18. See Chapter 1, note 5. The area of deployment of the Urbana comprised the main towns of the Huallaga and the smaller villages along the Marginal Highway. The basic function that the Urbana performed for the Party was as an intelligence and surveillance service: an early-warning system in case of army or police operations in the countryside. But it also provided logistical support, collecting monetary and in-services collaborations from drug traders and prosperous merchants. When necessary, it commandeered transportation or confiscated supplies needed by the guerrilla. In Aucayacu the Urbana appeared sometime in 1985, roughly a year after the army established its first base in town. Analogous groups formed in Uchiza and Tocache were autonomous and operated independently from their counterparts in Aucayacu.

19. In line with this vector, the most significant Sendero military actions were always direct assaults on the towns. State violence, in contrast, moved from city and town—where the army and police kept bases and headquarters—toward the countryside.

20. See Chapter 1, note 6.

21. The Urbana's reputation as terrible militants was shared not only by Aucayacu townspeople. Both a former leader of a Sendero guerrilla column and a former Party delegate from a village on the left bank of the Huallaga River expressed similar assessments to me of the Urbana.

22. See Chapter 3, note 1. The Urbanas introduced the process of social cleansing, already underway in rural areas since the early 1980s, to the towns. For Sendero, Huallaga towns figured as places from whence state power, corruption, and social vice emanated. As the economic centers of the cocaine trade and where the sumptuous expenditures of the boom were most evident, Huallaga towns were tempting targets for Sendero not only as sites for extending its moralizing proclivities but also for collecting the funds it needed to finance its operations.

23. 1992 was the year the army began to conduct large-scale scorched-earth operations on the left bank of the Huallaga River.

24. See for example, the otherwise excellent investigative essay on the cocaine trade and insurgent violence in the Huallaga Valley of the late 1980s: Raúl González, "Recuperar el Huallaga: Una estrategia posible," *Quehacer* 58 (Abril/Mayo 1989): 14–19.

25. Friedrich Nietzsche, "Second Essay: Guilt, Bad Conscience, and Related Matters," section 7, *On the Genealogy of Morality* (New York: Cambridge University Press, 1994), 48.

26. See María Elena Hidalgo, "Testigos reconocen a militar que mató a pobladores en Aucayacu," *La República*, September 10, 2006; "Yo soy el capitán Carlos Esparza," *La República*, September 11, 2006; "Testigo ubica tumba clandestina de víctimas del 'Capitán Carlos,'" *La República*, September 24, 2006; "Que 'Esparza' venga a Aucayacu y que nos diga en la cara que no mató a nadie," *La República*, September 26, 2006.

Chapter 6

1. Unlike other parts of the country, in the areas around Aucayacu there was no precedent for *rondas*—*either* as an autonomous mechanism of local community-based law enforcement, such as pastoral communities of the northern departments of Piura and Cajamarca had long relied on to defend against the violence of cattle rustlers, *or* as a militarized peasant response to the violence of the Shining Path, known as *comités de autodefensa* (self-defense committees), which were formed at the initiative and in close liaison with the Peruvian army. In the late 1980s *comités de autodefensa* played a pivotal role in the eventual reversal of Shining Path influence in the rural communities of Ayacucho, Apurímac, Huancavelica, and Junín. In the national media the successes of the *rondas* became one of the great moral narratives of the defeat of the Shining Path and was often pointed to as evidence of a heroic impulse within the rural peasantry, who defended their communities against Maoist invaders and, in so doing, demonstrated to the nation their patriotic stripes. When it came to the Upper Huallaga, however, there were no national-hero narratives based on *rondas,* nor did *rondas* play a major role in determining the course of the conflict.

On peasant patrols in northern Peru, see Orin Starn, *Nightwatch: The Making of a Movement in the Peruvian Andes* (Durham, NC: Duke University Press, 1999); also Ludwig Huber, *"Después de dios y la vírgen está la ronda": Las rondas campesinas de Piura* (Lima: Instituto de Estudios Peruanos, Instituto Francés de Estudios Andino, 1995). Regarding *comités de autodefensa* in central and southern Peru, see Carlos Iván Degregori, José Coronel, Ponciano del Pino, and Orin Starn, *Las rondas campesinas y la derrota de Sendero Luminoso* (Lima: IEP Ediciones, 1996).

Afterword

1. Gilles Deleuze, *The Logic of Sense* (New York: Columbia University Press, 1990), 24.

WORKS CITED

Agamben, Giorgio. *Homo Sacer.* Translated by Daniel Heller-Roazen. Stanford, California: Stanford University Press, 1998.

Allen, Catherine. *The Hold Life Has.* Washington, DC: Smithsonian Institution Press, 1988.

Ansión, Juan. *Desde el rincón de los muertos.* Lima: GREDES, 1987.

Aramburú, Carlos. "Problemas del desarrollo rural y la colonización de la amazonía peruana." *Debates en Sociología* 6, Lima (1981): 41–70.

Benjamin, Walter. "Critique of Violence." In *Walter Benjamin Selected Writings.* Vol. 1, 1913–1926, edited by Marcus Bullock and Michael W. Jennings. Cambridge, MA: Belknap Press, 1996.

Buitrón, Aníbal. *Ethnological Survey of the Valley of the Rio Huallaga, Peru.* Paris: UNESCO, 1948.

Burchard, Roderick E. "Coca y trueque de alimentos." In *Reciprocidad e intercambio en los Andes Peruanos.* Edited by Giorgio Alberti and Enrique Mayer. Lima: Instituto de Estudios Peruanos, 1974.

Cabieses, Hugo. "Peru: The Cocalero Struggles and Good Governance." *Transnational Institute Drugs and Conflict Debate Paper* 10 (April 2004): 16–26.

Canetti, Elias. *Crowds and Power.* Translated by Carol Stewart. New York: Farrar Straus Giroux, 1984.

Canetti, Elias, and Theodor W. Adorno. "Elias Canetti: Discussion with Theodor W. Adorno." *Thesis Eleven* 45 (1996): 14–15.

Comisión de la Verdad y Reconciliación (CVR). "El PCP-SL durante el auge de la hoja de coca en el Alto Huallaga." In *Informe Final,* Tomo 5. Lima: Universidad Nacional Mayor de San Marcos, Pontificia Universidad Católica del Perú, 2004.

Comisión de la Verdad y Reconciliación (CVR). *Informe final,* Tomo 2 (Perú, 1980–

2000). Lima: Universidad Nacional Mayor de San Marcos, Pontificia Universidad Católica del Perú, 2004.

Comisión de la Verdad y Reconciliación (CVR), "La estrategia de pacificación en la margen izquierda del río Huallaga." In *Informe Final*, Tomo 5. Lima: Universidad Nacional Mayor de San Marcos, Pontificia Universidad Católica del Perú, 2004.

Coordinadora Nacional de Derechos Humanos (CNDH). *Los sucesos del Alto Huallaga.* Lima: Coordinadora Nacional de Derechos Humanos, 1994.

Cotler, Julio. *Drogas y política en el Perú: La conexión norteamericana.* Lima: Instituto de Estudios Peruanos, 1999.

Degregori, Carlos Iván. *El surgimiento de Sendero Luminoso: Ayacucho, 1969–1979.* Lima: Instituto de Estudios Peruanos, 1990.

Degregori, Carlos Iván, José Coronel, Ponciano del Pino, and Orin Starn. *Las rondas campesinas y la derrota de Sendero Luminoso.* Lima: Instituto de Estudios Peruanos, 1996.

Deleuze, Gilles. *Difference and Repetition.* Translated by Paul Patton. New York: Columbia University Press, 1994.

———. *Empiricism and Subjectivity: An Essay on Hume's Theory of Human Nature.* Translated by Constantin Boundas. New York: Columbia. University Press, 1991.

———. *The Logic of Sense.* Translated by Mark Lester with Charles Stivale., Ed. Constantin V. Boundas. New York: Columbia. University Press, 1990.

———. *Nietzsche and Philosophy.* Translated by Hugh Tomlinson. New York: Columbia University Press, 1983.

Deleuze, Gilles, and Félix Guattari. *A Thousand Plateaus: Capitalism and Schizophrenia.* Translated by Brian Massumi. Minneapolis: University of Minnesota Press, 1987.

Derrida, Jacques. "Force of Law." *Cardozo Law Review* 11, no. 5–6 (1990): 919–1047.

"Domínguez Voló," *Caretas,* August 1, 1996.

Drewes, Wolfram U. *The Economic Development of the Western Montaña of Central Peru as Related to Transportation: A Comparison of Four Areas of Settlement.* Lima: Peruvian Times, 1958.

Durand Guevara, Anahí. "El movimiento cocalero y su (in)existencia en el Perú: Itinerario de desencuentros en el río Apurímac." *Bulletin de l'Institut Francais d'Etudes Andines* 34, 1 (2005): 103–26.

Gagliano, Joseph A. *Coca Prohibition in Peru.* Tucson: University of Arizona Press, 1994.

García-Sayán, Diego. "Perú: Estados de excepción y su régimen jurídico." In *Estados de emergencia en la región andina.* Edited by Diego García-Sayán. Lima: Comisión Andina de Juristas, 1987: 93–125.

Gonzales Manrique, José. "Sendero Luminoso en el valle de la coca." In *Coca, cocaína y narcotráfico: Laberinto en los Andes.* Edited by Diego García Sayán. Lima: Comisión Andina de Juristas, 1989.

González, Raúl. "Recuperar el Huallaga: Una estrategia posible." *Quehacer* 58 (Abril-Mayo 1989): 14–19.

Gootenberg, Paul. *Between Coca and Cocaine: A Century or More of U.S.-Peruvian Drug Paradoxes 1860–1980.* Washington, DC: Woodrow Wilson International Center for Scholars, 2001.

———. "Reluctance or Resistance? Constructing Cocaine (Prohibitions) in Peru, 1910–50." In *Cocaine: Global Histories.* New York: Routledge, 1999.

Gorriti Ellenbogen, Gustavo. *Sendero: Historia de la guerra milenaria en el Perú.* Lima: Editorial Apoyo, 1990.

Gourgouris, Stathis. *Does Literature Think?* Stanford: Stanford University Press, 2003.

Hauriou, Maurice. *Principios de derecho público y constitucional* [Principes de droit public]. Spanish translation by Carlos Ruiz del Castillo. 2nd ed. Madrid: Reus, 1950.

Hegel, G.W.F. *Philosophy of Right.* Translated by T. M. Knox. New York: Oxford University Press, 1967.

Herndon, William Lewis. *Exploration of the Valley of the Amazon.* Introduction and edited by Hamilton Basso. New York: McGraw-Hill, 1952.

Hidalgo, María Elena. "Que 'Esparza' venga a Aucayacu y que nos diga en la cara que no mató a nadie." *La República,* September 26, 2006.

———. "Testigos reconocen a militar que mató a pobladores en Aucayacu." *La República,* September 10, 2006.

———. "Testigo ubica tumba clandestina de víctimas del 'Capitán Carlos.'" *La República,* September 24, 2006.

———. "Yo soy el capitán Carlos Esparza." *La República,* September 11, 2006.

Hinojosa, Iván. "On Poor Relations and the Nouveau Riche: Shining Path and the Radical Peruvian Left." In *Shining and Other Paths: War and Society in Peru, 1980–1995.* Edited by Steve J. Stern. Durham, NY: Duke University Press, 1998.

Huber, Ludwig. *"Después de dios y la vírgen está la ronda": Las rondas campesinas de Piura.* Lima: Instituto de Estudios Peruanos, Instituto Francés de Estudios Andino, 1995.

Hume, David. *A Treatise of Human Nature.* Edited by L. A. Selby-Bigge. New York: Oxford University Press, 1978.

INEI (Instituto Nacional de Estadística e Informática). *Censo Nacional de Población y Vivienda 1993.* Lima: INEI, 1993.

Izaguirre, Bernardino. *Historia de las misiones Franciscanas y narración de los progresos de la geografía en el Oriente del Perú: : Relatos originales y producciones en lenguas indígenas de varios misioneros,* vols. 1 and 2. Lima: Provincia Misionera de San Francisco Solano del Perú, Convento de los PP. Descalzos, 2001–2004.

Jacquemet, Marco. *Credibility in Court.* New York: Cambridge University Press, 1996.

Jaramillo, Jaime Eduardo et al. *Colonización, coca y guerrilla*. Bogotá: Alianza Editorial Colombiana, 1989.

Jülich, Volker. *Colonización como complemento de la reforma agraria en la selva peruana: El valle del Huallaga Central*. Santiago de Chile: Instituto Latinoamericano de Investigaciones Sociales, 1974.

Kant, Immanuel. *The Metaphysical Elements of Justice: Part I of The Metaphysics of Morals*. Translated by John Judd. Indianapolis, IN: Bobbs-Merrill, 1965.

Kawell, Jo Ann. "Going to the Source." *NACLA, Report on the Americas* 22, no. 6 (1989): 3–22.

Kernaghan, Richard. "Fidelidad o el viento en una pierna bien alzada." *Debates en sociología* (Lima) 25 (2000): 49–62.

Koselleck, Reinhart. *Futures Past: On the Semantics of Historical Time*. New York: Columbia University Press, 2004.

Locke, John. *Second Treatise of Government*. Edited by Richard Cox. Arlington Heights, IL: Harlan Davidson, 1982.

Chira C., Magdaleno. *Tingo María: Ensayo Monográfico*. Lima: Librería e Imprenta El Competidor, 1943.

Malamud-Goti, Jaime. *Smoke and Mirrors*. Boulder, CO: Westview Press, 1992.

Mayer, Enrique. "Coca as Commodity: Local Use and Global Abuse." In *The Articulated Peasant: Household Economies in the Andes*. Boulder, CO: Westview Press, 2002.

Morales, Edmundo. *Cocaine: White Gold Rush in Peru*. Tucson: University of Arizona Press, 1989.

Molano, Alfredo. *Aguas arriba: Entre la coca y el oro*. Bogotá: El Áncora Editores, 1990.

———. *Selva adentro: Una historia oral de la colonización del Guaviare*. Bogotá: El Áncora Editores, 1987.

Morote Best, Efraín. "El Degollador (naqak)." In *Tradición: Revista Peruana de Cultura* 2 (1952): 67–91.

Moss, David. "The Gift of Repentance: A Maussian Perspective on Twenty Years of Pentimento in Italy." *European Journal of Sociology* 42, no. 2 (May 2001): 297–331.

Nietzsche, Friedrich. *On the Genealogy of Morality*. Translated by Carol Diethe. Edited by Keith Ansell-Pearson. New York: Cambridge University Press, 1994.

"Normas Legales," *Revista de Legislación y Jurisprudencia* 41, Tomo 115, Tercer Bimestre, Mayo–Junio, Trujillo, Peru, 1982.

Oliver-Smith, Anthony. "The Pishtaco: Institutionalized Fear in Highland Peru." *Journal of American Folklore* 82, no. 326 (October–December, 1969): 363–68.

Ossio, Juan et al. "Cosmovisión andina y uso de la coca." In *La Coca . . . tradición, rito, identidad*. Mexico: Instituto Indigenista Interamericano, 1989.

Palmer, David Scott, ed. *The Shining Path of Peru*. New York: St. Martin's Press, 1994.

Paucar Mariluz, Felipe A. *La guerra oculta en el Huallaga, Monzón y Aguaytía*. Tingo

María, Peru: Centro de Estudios y Promoción para el Desarrollo Agroindustrial, CEDAI, 2006.

Peru. *Código Penal.* Trujillo, Peru: Editora Normas Legales, 1999.

———. "Ley Orgánica del Ministerio Público." In *Código Penal.* Lima: Editora Jurídica Griley, 2005.

Plowman, Timothy. "The Ethnobotany of Coca." *Advances in Economic Botany* 12 (1984): 62–111.

Poeppig, Eduard. *Viaje al Perú y al Río Amazonas 1827–1832.* Translated by Federico Schwab. Iquitos, Perú: CETA, 2003.

Poole, Deborah. "Between Threat and Guarantee: Justice and Community in the Margins of the Peruvian State." In *Anthropology in the Margins of the State.* Edited by Veena Das and Deborah Poole. Santa Fe, NM: School of American Research Press, 2004.

Poole, Deborah, and Gerardo Rénique. *Peru: Time of Fear.* London: Latin American Bureau, 1992.

Rojas, Isaías. "The Push for Zero Coca: Democratic Transition and Counter-narcotics Policy in Peru." *Drug War Monitor,* Washington Office on Latin America (WOLA), February 2003.

Rousseau, Jean-Jacques. "On Social Contract." In *Rousseau's Political Writings.* Translated by Julia Conaway Bondanella. New York: Norton, 1988.

Sanabria, Harry. *The Coca Boom and Rural Social Change in Bolivia.* Ann Arbor: University of Michigan Press, 1993.

Schmitt, Carl. *The Concept of the Political.* Translated by George Schwab. Chicago: University Of Chicago Press, 1996.

———. *The Nomos of the Earth in the International Law of the Jus Publicum Europeaeum.* Translated by G. L. Ulmen. New York: Telos Press, 2003.

"Sendero Luminoso mata a cinco personas en la selva peruana." *Reuters Noticias Latinoamericanas,* May 28, 1998.

"Shining Path kills five villagers in Peru jungle." Reuters News, May 28, 1998.

Starn, Orin. *Nightwatch: The Making of a Movement in the Peruvian Andes.* Durham, NC: Duke University Press, 1999.

Stern, Steve J., ed. *Shining and Other Paths: War and Society in Peru, 1980–1995.* Durham, NC: Duke University Press, 1998.

Taussig, Michael. "Indian Fat." *Shamanism, Colonialism, and the Wild Man: A Study in Terror and Healing.* Chicago: University of Chicago Press, 1987.

———. *Law in a Lawless Land.* New York: New Press, 2003.

U.S. Drug Enforcement Administration, Office of Intelligence. *Coca Cultivation and Cocaine Processing: An Overview.* Washington, DC: U.S. Dept. of Justice, 1991.

Valenzuela, Cecilia. "Falla Fatal: Crimen en Aucayacu." *Caretas,* March 18, 1993, 76–78.

———. "La Cuota de los Cuarenta." *Caretas,* March 10, 1994, 29.

INDEX

Velasco Alvarado, Juan, 8, 10
La vida, hay que saberla vivir, 87–92, 94–95,
    98–102
village-level political representation, 105,
    109–11, 285n23
violence
    atmosphere and, 5–6, 17, 19, 26, 216, 252. *See
        also* threat
    causal vectors of, 19–20
    commands and, 90–92, 253
    constitution of no man's land and, 20
    events of, 4–5, 52, 93, 102–3, 114, 122, 130, 133,
        141, 147–49, 153, 208, 262
    illicit economies and, 19, 123, 261
    incorporeal transformation of, 205, 262
    internal disposition and, shifts of 131,
        147–48, 152–53

insurgent. *See* Sendero Luminoso
justification, structures of, 147–150. *See also*
    aval; La vida, hay que saberla vivir;
    por algo
law and, 16–20, 123, 152, 260–63, 278n28
narration and, 4, 133, 253
of the political, 123, 152, 153, 260–62
relation to threat, 17
repetition of, 20, 93, 128, 130, 146–47, 152–53
sense and, 6, 18, 94, 128, 201–2, 208–9,
    261–63
as signature, 114, 261
state. See Peruvian state
time and, crafting sense of, 2, 19–20, 29,
    67–68, 94, 104, 123, 133, 152, 192, 206, 208,
    254, 261–62